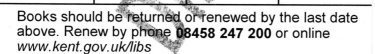

FINGS AIN'T WOT THEY USED T'BE:

THE LIONEL BART STORY

FINGS AIN'T WOT THEY USED T'BE:

THE LIONEL BART STORY

DAVID &
CAROLINE
STAFFORD

OMNIBUS PRESS

London / New York / Paris / Sydney / Copenhagen / Berlin / Madrid / Tokyo

Copyright © 2011 Omnibus Press
(A Division of Music Sales Limited)

Cover designed by Mike Bell
Picture research by Jacqui Black

ISBN: 978.1.84938.661.6
Order No: OP53823

Exclusive Distributors
Music Sales Limited,
14/15 Berners Street,
London, W1T 3LJ.

Music Sales Corporation,
257 Park Avenue South,
New York, NY 10010, USA.

Macmillan Distribution Services,
56 Parkwest Drive
Derrimut, Vic 3030,
Australia.

Printed in the EU

A catalogue record for this book is available from the British Library.

Visit Omnibus Press on the web at www.omnibuspress.com

To Clementine, Connie and Georgia.

Introduction

H E wrote some of the best, most popular, most enduring songs of the past 60 years. He had a breathtaking theatrical imagination. He was as complex, flawed and damaged as a proper human being should be. His story is extraordinary, and, from a narrative point of view, near perfect – with three acts, a journey, a climax, a crisis, a catharsis and a calming denouement. These seemed like good reasons for writing a biography.

A cheerful economics lecturer we got chatting to at the British Newspaper Library told us that his uncle used to be Lionel Bart's postman. He regaled us with a labyrinthine tale about a parcel. A hotel receptionist in Cornwall told us she had once been a contestant in a beauty contest judged by Lionel Bart. She was unplaced. Marty Wilde's chiropodist did Lionel's feet as well, and when he'd finished the feet he would take Lionel's musical dictation. Most London taxi drivers over the age of, say, 50, number themselves among Lionel's closest friends.

After a bit you begin to suspect that everybody in the world has a Lionel story. The problem for the biographer is not one of finding material but of avoiding it. That and sifting the fragments that could be loosely based on fact from the rubble of hearsay and rumour and exaggeration.

Lionel himself, of course, was a major source of inaccuracies about the life and times of Lionel Bart. He'd invent and embroider stories to favour journalists with good copy, to big up his latest project, to take the piss, because he couldn't be arsed with the pedantic tedium of reality, but mostly because the lie – his lies, anyway – were usually neater, funnier and more satisfying.

When the anecdotes lie so thick, it's also difficult for anybody to keep clear the notion that the guy you're talking about was a major figure in the history of music and theatre. So while there have been works of academic criticism written about, for instance, Stephen Sondheim, Lionel's mastery of internal rhyme and bold use of tritones are always pushed into the background by the racy anecdotes and one-liners. It's partly the result of Lionel's inability to stay po-faced about his life and work for more than a couple of sentences (or, to put it another way, it's Stephen Sondheim's fault for not hanging out with Keith Moon).

Lionel loved vulgarity. His earliest efforts at lyric-making were in the playground. He'd invent mucky words for the latest pop songs in exchange for a turn on roller skates. It was a skill he prized throughout his life. Vulgarity is a precious, life-affirming commodity, but it rarely wins honorary professorships or the Prix Goncourt.

If you can tear your gaze away from the gags and vulgarity, though, you quickly realise they're shielding a formidable clutch of achievements. The magnificence of *Oliver!* is generally acknowledged, but there is little recognition of Lionel's pioneering role in, say, the creation of the British rock and pop industry that went on to dominate the world: his continuing contribution to that industry as pal, mentor, financier and host to The Beatles, the Stones and their managers; his pre-Beatles conquest of America; his pre-David Bailey, pre-Terry Stamp, pre-Michael Caine, pre-John Lennon invention of what a working-class hero should do, wear and think; or even the blessed wonder of his hats. The sheer range of his work astonishes, too. We have encountered people who simply refuse to believe that he worked extensively in political and experimental theatre, that he wrote 'From Russia With Love' – words and music – or that he was once in a position to demand official Universal Studios headed notepaper for a teddy bear named Spencer Tracy.

Another difficulty is the sneer. You come across it all the time. A lot of people ever-so-slightly sneer when they speak of Lionel, as if extending an invitation to share an awareness that there was something not quite right about him. If asked to be more specific they'll mist over and maybe say, "Didn't he steal most of his best tunes?" – a common calumny that is no more justified when applied to Lionel than it is about any other composer – possibly less so. Or they'll hint at a generalised sort of naffness, the way one might about, say, Jeremy Clarkson or Gyles Brandreth.

Maybe it's aftershock. Lionel's career, from first hit to first majestic flop, lasted about nine years. His success in the charts and onstage was unprecedented. His spectacular fall, with *Twang!!* the musical with more exclamation marks than tickets sold, made headline news for weeks, and reduced his reputation to brickdust. The usual story, oversimplified and inaccurate, was that this precipitated his slide onto bankruptcy and alcoholism. Are the ripples resulting from that cataclysmic fall still settling, perhaps, causing wobbles in the folk memory? "Lionel Bart . . . wasn't he the bloke who . . . did something . . . sort of bad . . . or silly?"

The main text addresses itself to the snobbery Lionel attracted as a working-class Jew with no formal musical education. That provoked a lot of vile sneering at the time. And he was also the victim of his own big mouth. His barrow-boy habit of shooting his mouth off as publicly as possible made, for many, the urge to see him cut down to size irresistible. There was a narrative imperative, too. After years of reporting triumph after triumph, editors became desperate for a new angle on the Bart story. Falling on his arse fit the bill to a tee.

But the sneer's probably mostly related to the vexed question of cool. When Lionel was making hits with Tommy Steele, Cliff Richard and Anthony Newley in the late Fifties, it was desperately uncool to be British. Even now critics single out 'Move It', the song that Ian "Sammy" Samwell wrote for Cliff Richard, as the first 'proper' British rock'n'roll record on the grounds that it sounded most like the American product. Lionel's songs – 'Do You Mind?', 'Rock With The Caveman', 'Living Doll' and the rest – carried the evocative aroma of the chip-shop. In later years Ray Davies, Ian Dury, Pulp and Blur were revered for being so resoundingly British, but back in 1957 it was the antithesis of cool.

And by 1964, when British pop was the coolest pop in the world, Lionel had become the toast of musical theatre in the West End and on Broadway, which was, of course, uncool. He was also, at 34, old enough to be a Beatle's uncle.

Britpop when he should have been Yank, showbiz when he should have been pop, riding the crest when he should have been up-and-coming, 37 when he should have been 17, ahead of the pack when he wanted to run with them, Jagger and Richards could have written 'Out Of Time' just for Lionel.

The people who really knew Lionel, his close friends and colleagues, slag him off something terrible. They tell tales of his monstrous egotism, his infuriating obsessions and his white-faced rages. But then they smile indulgently and talk of his generosity, his vulnerability, his charm. He had the magic power to make people love him unconditionally.

We started the research for this book wondering whether the sneer could be justified. We never met him, but still he worked that magic.

Caroline and David Stafford, July 2011

One

"We lived in a one-up one-down in Ellen Street . . . we 15 kids slept in three beds, head to feet."

Radio Times, August 15, 1974.

"I was the youngest of 12, three died in infancy."

Daily Mail, January 13, 1978.

"He tells me he was the 11th child in a family of 11 brothers and sisters."

Sunday Express, December 17, 1972.

"I was the youngest of eight children, four boys and four girls."

Sunday Dispatch, July 3, 1960.

"I was the youngest of a family of seven."

Daily Mail, January 31, 1995.

MORRIS and Yetta Begleiter had six living children at the start of 1930: Stan, Fay, Harry, Sam, Debbie and Renee. The birth of Lionel, onAugust 1 at Mother Levy's Jewish Maternity Hospital on Underwood Street, brought the tally up to seven. He was indisputably the baby of the family, six years younger than Renee; an afterthought or, as he put it, "the last shake of the bag".

Dad was a tailor, with a workshop in a 'shed' at the bottom of the garden next to the outside lavatory. On a good week he'd turn out 50 ladies' coats. In the early days, at least, there weren't many good weeks.

Among the poor, there are many gradations of poverty. East End Jewish poverty was even more intricately calibrated. Harry Landis, who later worked with Lionel at Unity Theatre, can remember as a very small child having to go with his mum to the Jewish Board of Guardians in order to plead their case for a soup-kitchen token. They invented a baby sister for Harry, 'Rose', who'd been left in the care of a neighbour and made their fiction convincing enough to earn an extra dollop of stew. Compared to Harry's soup-kitchen poverty, the Begleiters, with a workshop to their name, were practically bloated capitalists. It's also likely they'd had it a bit easier in the old country than some of their neighbours.

Morris and Yetta were from Galicia, an area encompassing what is now the South East of Poland into Western Ukraine. No Eastern European country ever provided lasting security for its Jewish communities, but in Galicia, then part of the Austro-Hungarian Empire, they were certainly better off than their neighbours over the border in Imperial Russia. For one or two brief and glorious periods during the 19th century, the Galician Jews fought for and won limited emancipation, but otherwise they endured the usual humiliations and sanctions. At one time, in a bid to prevent 'them' breeding, a tax was be levied on Jewish marriage. In 1911, Jews were forbidden to sell alcohol, a move that put 15,000 innkeepers and vintners out of work. But unless a rogue Prince, tired of chasing boar, decided to go hunting in the ghetto, threats to life and limb were infrequent and, despite everything, the Jewish community provided the province with a more than representative sample of lawyers, doctors, professors, entrepreneurs – even politicians.

Family legend has it that Morris was once an officer in the Austro-Hungarian cavalry. Years later Lionel, the artist, painted a fanciful portrait of his dad in the blue and red uniform with cape and frogging.

"My father was a relic from the Austro-Hungarian Empire," he said. "I think Vienna was the centre, the hub of his universe when he was a young fellah. And I think he was in the army. He took me to see this film about Austrian waltzes, about Viennese waltzes and I remembered all the waltzes, and he was very impressed that I remembered all these waltzes."

Given the way their son's career panned out, the Ruritanian-operetta notion of the dashing young Morris Begleiter, booted and moustachioed at some country fair, admired by villagers and townspeople as he leads his Yetta, the Rabbi's daughter, in a one-two-three, one-two-three, is as tempting as it is almost certainly inaccurate.

Galicia was the arsehole of the Austrian Empire. Paved roads and railways were the stuff of dreams and a summer without cholera something to be grateful for. Every year a few thousand fled west in search of a better life. When the Great War came, the trickle turned into a flood.

In August 1914, the Russian army broke through the Austro-Hungarian defences on the northern borders of Galicia. On September 1 they marched into Lviv, the capital city. By the end of the month they'd overrun the whole province. In every town and village, the Russian soldiers harassed and stole from the Jews. In some places mini-pogroms resulted in beatings, burnings and murder. A quarter of a million decided it was time to up sticks.

The Begleiters travelled as a family: Morris and Yetta – with one baby in her arms and another on the way – and Yetta's mother. The rapture of reaching British shores was modified when Morris, as an enemy alien, was immediately seized and shipped off to an internment camp.

There were two internment camps on the Isle of Man during the First World War. Statistically it's likely that Morris was sent to the Knockaloe camp, though, once again, records are scarce: it's rumoured that mountains of official paperwork relating to the camps were tipped down mineshafts at the end of the war. One of the inmates at Knockaloe was a one-eyed former circus performer and prizefighter by the name of Joseph Hubertus Pilates, who developed a novel regime of health-giving exercises. These he foisted with evangelistic aggression on his fellow inmates, particularly the sick and the lame. As far as can be told, the inmates were not harshly treated.[1] Most finished the war in reasonable health and those who encountered Herr Pilates would have enjoyed uncommonly well-developed core-strength.

Meanwhile Yetta, heavily pregnant and unable to speak English, with an aged mother and a baby son in tow, was left to fend for herself. Somehow she found her way to Whitechapel and contacted friends from the Old Country who were able to give her a roof and the means to keep body and soul together. When Morris came home, a lightning series of pregnancies resulted in another four children being born in the six years between 1918 and 1924.

In the days when the poet T.S.Eliot held down a day job for Faber & Faber, the publishing house, he championed a memoir by Willy Goldman, a 'proletarian' writer who had been making a name for himself in *The Left Review* and *New Writing*. The memoir, *East End My Cradle*, contains a pen portrait of one of Willy's former bosses, a tailor by the name of Mr Begleiter.[2]

Willy Goldman worked for ten weeks at Begleiter's 'sweat-shop' some time in 1924. "We waded our way through domestic utensils to the work-shop. It was adjacent to the lavatory and you had presumably to know which was which by the smell." He describes the boss as a 'short, plump, fussy man', a lazy, self-important bully, who, despite having lived in the country for years, could still read no English other than the back page of *The Star*, the dockets sent to him by his customers and the names of all venereal diseases. Mr Begleiter confided to the 14-year-old Goldman that he had practised 17 variations of the sexual act. His recreations were "betting on horses, drinking brandy and taking vapour baths" and he attended synagogue only once a year on the Day of Atonement. He paid Willy just sixpence (2.5p) a week, took the view that Willy should in fact be paying him for being taught the business and responded to any argument with, "If you don't like what I say, you can kiss my arse."

Years later, Sammy Bergliter, Lionel's nephew, came across a copy of *East End, My Cradle* and showed the passage about 'Mr Begleiter' to his uncle. Lionel was initially upset. He claimed it must be about a different tailor called Begleiter who had a workshop down the bottom of his garden next to the lavatory. Eventually, though, he grudgingly acknowledged it was a biased but broadly accurate portrait of his dad.

In 1994, ITV's *The South Bank Show* made a special in which Lionel is taken to see a modern-day sweatshop, very close to where his father's would have been. He's amused by the machinists' chatting, saying his dad would have imposed absolute silence, and goes on to describe him as a ". . . slave-driver, and a terrible man." Immediately he relents. "No he was all right, my dad. My mother always thought he was after other ladies – which of course he was."

If Morris was a bully, Yetta was never his victim. By all accounts she was a "chuckling little dynamo", a heavyset woman, a fighter, loud and forthright, with more than a touch of the barrow boy in her make-up.

"My mum and dad had this love-hate thing," Lionel said. "I was like a go-between. It was 'tell him this' or 'tell her that'. I was brought up in a house were there was always shoutin' and fightin' [. . .] so it was rare that one ever got to finish a sentence. I guess that's how I got so good at one liners."[3]

Yetta was 45 when Lionel was born, Morris a few months younger. Lionel was, in every sense, the baby of the family, indulged by his mother and spoilt by his sisters. In the home his glorious self-belief was allowed to flourish unchallenged.

Out on the street was another matter. He was a skinny little runt with sticky out ears.

Those brought up in straitened circumstances adopt any one of a range of attitudes towards their childhood. Some boast about their poverty, thereby making their subsequent success all the more impressive ("There were 27 of us living in a cardboard box"). Some grow dew-eyed about family and neighbourhood ("We never had two brass farthings to rub together, but there's some sorts of happiness no amount of money can buy"). Some become bitter and angry ("Poverty is the most obscene kind of violence").

Lionel tried all of these at one time or another, depending on whether he was turning up the schmaltz talking about *Blitz!* (his 1962 show about his wartime childhood) or throwing himself on the mercy of a court. "My mother was 49 when I was born," he said at the time of his bankruptcy hearing in 1972, "by which time she had very little strength to give me the love and affection I craved. We were a very poor East End family, and not only was I deprived of love, I had no money either. So you can imagine – when I hit it really big with *Oliver!* . . ." and so on. Class act.

A fourth option, though – the appeal of which seems to have recommended itself to Lionel at an early age – is to observe one's life with the eye of a showman; to take a detached professional's interest in the quality of thrills, spills, tears and laughter the passing parade provides; to regard the whole boshed business as a glorious work of theatre. "Very colourful," he replied in a 1995 BBC interview, when asked to describe his childhood. "Very noisy, it was. My house was like a Marx Brothers movie."

The East End, or at least Lionel's bit of it, has always provided an impressive backdrop to melodrama, comic opera and broad farce. At the time of writing, the incursions of gentrifiers, with their vanilla pods and jogging strollers, have begun to add the odd splash of Farrow & Ball *Terre d'Egypte* to the bright Bangladeshi glow that's dressed the place since the Seventies. In Lionel's day, it was decorated in the blacks, greys and earth tones of the shtetl. A walk along Wentworth Street, between Middlesex Street market and Brick Lane, would take you past Zlotnick's grocers, Bardiger's the furriers, Silver's the drapers, Cohen's the mercers, Ruda's the fishmongers, Abraham's the drapers, Brilliant Harris the kosher butcher and Louis Simon the oil merchant.[4] It was an overcrowded, smelly, noisy, fidgety place: a show that never closed.

Shoreditch, Whitechapel, Bethnal Green and Mile End were the boundaries of Lionel's world. Some of it was pretty much unchanged since the days of the Great Fire. There was a proper working blacksmith's forge next to the United Synagogue. Down the road from his school was Cave's Dairy, which still kept a herd of cows around the back. Now and then the cows would be taken for a walk down Jubilee Street.

"As a kid in the East End, in streets of terraced houses, we didn't see cars," he said. "I was bought up on all the traditional kids' games – and have since recalled a lot of them in my work – and we could play in the streets very safely. Occasionally you would get a brewers' dray, with the barrels of beer and horse brasses – we used to jump on the back, until the driver's whip came over to dislodge us! There was a lot of dried-up horse manure on the streets – I really miss that smell."[5]

At Petticoat Lane market, a 15-minute walk from Ellen Street – even closer when the family moved to Brick Lane in 1936 – among the clothing and fabric stalls, and the bedding and curtain stalls, in front of the shops selling latkes, lox and herrings, you could watch escapologists and crockery-jugglers, fortune-tellers and weight-guessers. There were barrel organists, cross-dressing skirt-dancers and Wilson, Keppel and Betty clones who'd sprinkle sand on the pavement to do their soft-shoe shuffle. The barrow-boys themselves were acts, parodies of 'positive thinking', Max Millering the money out of the punters' purses. Sometimes the three kings would come down from Spitalfields: the Eel King, the Corn Cure King and Harry the Banana King. Most days you could see Prince Monolulu from St Croix in the Danish West Indies, selling his racing tips – "I gotta horse, I gotta horse" – dressed either in impeccable morning suit with spats and topper, or a kilt of sorts with embroidered weskit and tall feathered headdress. For a few shillings he'd give you a sealed envelope containing the name of a winner, whispering as he did so, "If you tell anybody the name of this horse, it will surely lose." His lamentable success record suggests that few of his punters could keep a secret.

There were stranger sights, too. An elderly, very Orthodox gentleman was often seen slinking around Lionel's neighbourhood. In his hands he carried a large sheet of brown paper, or, if brown paper was temporarily beyond his means, a simple sheet of newspaper. On hearing the approaching footsteps of a woman, or, God forbid, accidentally catching sight of one, he would cover his face with the paper and turn to the wall until she had passed by and it was safe to slink some more.

Death came into the drama early in the first act. "My grandmother only spoke Yiddish," Lionel said.[6] "When I was good she would give me a farthing and when I was bad she would pinch me and curse me. Terrible curser, she was. I remember her dying. I was only about four or five at the time – four-and-a-half, I think. She was in the only good bedroom in the house – our two up, one down house. She was under a huge feather bedspread and I was playing with my mates in her bedroom. She beckoned to me and said, 'Labi' – she always called me Labi – 'I'm dying.' So I said, 'Go on then – die.' She laughed and laughed. She opened her mouth and I could see her only remaining tooth – her pickled onion spike we used to call it. Laughed and laughed. And then she died."

For those who preferred their drama in a more conventional form, there were 30 or 40 Yiddish theatres to choose from. The Pavilion, on Whitechapel Road, and the Rivoli opposite were bigger and more sumptuously decorated than anything they had on Shaftesbury Avenue. They boasted

Hollywood stars, too. Paul Muni played the Pavilion; Edward G. Robinson the Rivoli. Food was a vital element in the theatrical experience. At the back of the Pavilion was a huge, unauthorised snack bar. If you couldn't afford to purchase, you brought a picnic. God forbid anyone should go hungry.

"My mum and dad used to take me to a place called the Yiddish Theatre [. . .] down the Commercial Road. And they played the same plots of these old Middle European stories – by Sholem Aleichem[7] I think they were. Tiny little theatre called the Grand Palais, and there were these dramas and the leading man, the young juvenile lead, was about 55 with black hair in the days before Grecian 2000 and red Cossack boots. He'd be singing this terribly dramatic song in this scene where somebody had just killed themselves or something and he'd see somebody in the audience, like Mrs Goldblum, and he'd say, 'Hello, how's the kids, all right? And your little boy still doing well at school, all right?' And then he'd go back into the scene. Yiddish people went to see these plays and they knew them. They knew the plays. And I used to make a beeline for the pit and lean over and watch the fiddlers and the drummers and be really close up to the actors so you could really see the greasepaint. I had the buzz even then."[8]

The best of times and the worst of times – certainly the best of times for spectacle and drama – came on Sunday, October 4, 1936 when Sir Oswald Mosley, founder of the British Union of Fascists, tried to march his Blackshirts through the East End. The Board of Deputies warned Jews to stay away. The Communist Party organised a rally in Trafalgar Square to lure their members away from a possible pitched battle with the fascists. Nevertheless, an estimated 300,000 people turned out to oppose the march. They came together under a slogan borrowed from the Spanish Republicans and Socialists, then fighting the fascist General Franco in Spain: "They shall not pass."

Some 10,000 police, including 4,000 on horseback, turned out to 'defend the fascist's right to march'. In Cable Street, the police charges were fought off with sticks and rocks. Women emptied chamber pots on the coppers' heads from upstairs windows and pelted them with rubbish and rotten vegetables. Eventually Mosley abandoned the march and held a meeting in Hyde Park instead. At least 100 people were injured in the Battle of Cable Street and 150 arrested; and six-year-old Lionel watched the whole show from the best seat in the house thanks to his eldest brother, Stan – called Shear because of his skill at his dad's cutting table: "Shear was very bolshie and left wing. He was my hero. He was a champion swimmer, a champion boxer and worked as a docker. He did all the things a good Yiddish boy didn't do and I loved him. I used to go round on his shoulders – I was there for the Mosley March on his shoulders at Gardeners Corner."[9]

Music was a constant. The market had barrel organs, one-man-bands, spoons and bones players, fiddlers and banjo-boys. The pubs had sing-songs. The Sally Army had tambourines. In the years between the wars, the core repertoire – a mixture of light classics, wartime favourites and music–hall novelties – was as deeply ingrained as coal dust. 'My Old Man', 'Daisy', 'Any Old Iron', 'Knees Up Mother Brown', 'Roses of Picardy', 'Pack Up Your Troubles', 'Tipperary', 'The Sabre Dance', 'The Anvil Chorus', Delibes' 'Pizzicato' from 'Sylvia', 'The Blue Danube' and a few hundred others were, give or take local variations, the common musical currency of every British city.

There was music at home, too. "My mother used to sing lullabies and there were street songs and kids nursery rhymes. And games. Of course, the radio was always on. Gracie Fields was always there."[10]

And there was Jewish music everywhere. "I used to go to the synagogue with my dad. Certainly a few times in the year. I loved the music. I loved the sound of that ram's horn on the Black Fast and Yom Kippur. It said something to me. I didn't understand what they were blathering on about in Hebrew, but I loved the music."[11] And there was another, more modern, kind of Jewish music, making a splash in theatres, music shops and on the wireless.

The Jewish immigrants in America had encountered a thousand new musical influences: jazz, ragtime, blues, Scottish reels, Irish jigs, French quadrilles. They absorbed, adapted, stole.

Irving Berlin was originally Israel Baline from a village near Mogilev in modern Belarus. Mr and Mrs Gershowitz, parents of George and Ira Gershwin, were from St Petersburg, Richard Rodgers' family had come from Russia earlier, in the 1860s. Lorenz Hart was the son of Max Hertz, from Hamburg. Henry and Fannie Kern, parents of Jerome Kern, were from Germany and Hungary. Lerner and Loewe, Yip Harburg and Harold Arlen, Sammy Kahn, Leonard Bernstein, Stephen Sondheim; it is much easier to list the pioneers of American musical theatre who were not Jewish rather than the ones who were and that can be done in two words: Cole Porter. And even he admitted the secret of writing a hit tune was to ". . . write Jewish tunes." American musical theatre was, from the outset, as Jewish as the *Shemoneh Esrei* or the salt beef sandwich.

★   ★   ★

Nobody lived more than a short walk from the nearest cinema. In the East End you'd tailor your night out according to your pocket. If you were feeling flash you'd treat yourself to the marble and deco, the mirror-lined restaurant and the throbbing Wurlitzer of the Troxy on the Commercial Road. If you were strapped for cash it was the Ideal on King Street, with its corrugated iron roof and fleas the size of rats. Either way you got to sit in the dark and were allowed glimpses of cars and suits and legs and America. Lionel's childhood coincided with Hollywood's Golden Age. In the cinema he heard those songs of Berlin and Gershwin. He took some of his most important lessons in style; he learned about glamour and spectacle; and he first encountered some of the people – Judy Garland in *The Wizard Of Oz*, Cary Grant in *Bringing Up Baby*, Noël Coward in *In Which We Serve* – who later became his friends.

Round the corner from Lionel's house was Dempsey Street mixed infants. By the time Lionel was old enough to start there, big sister Renee had moved on. He was alone, without filial protection. His saviour was cheek. He was Lionel the show-off, Lionel the smarty-pants, Lionel who could talk back in ways that made even the teachers laugh.

Classmates remember him as a clever kid. When he was six, the headmistress summoned Yetta and spoke the words that every mother longs to hear, "Your son is an artistic genius whose talent must be nurtured."

Morris and Yetta did what they could to nurture their son the genius. When he showed signs of having a decent singing voice, they decided he would become a great cantor. Their ultimate disappointment, bearing in mind the gentle croak his voice matured into, was undoubtedly Judaism's gain.

When the boy was 13, Morris conceived another ambition. "My dad wanted me to be Yehudi Mehunin, I think. So he bought me this Yehudi Menuhin violin down Petticoat Lane for one and a half pounds – 30 bob – and I was useless. He even paid for me to have lessons down the street. This old man with a floppy bow tie, must have been about 80, Professor Dworzak – he was probably only 50, but he felt like 80 to me then. And the dear man tried to teach me to play the violin. And I was quite good. I played *Ave Maria* – both versions (pause for self-effacing 'as if' chuckle) – and I played 'The Bluebells Of Scotland' and I think he then realised I couldn't handle the instrument. Yehudi Menuhin I wasn't gonna be. And he suggested I try something else and my mother was delighted. 'Cos she had these terrible migraines and she used to call it 'the wailing cat'. She threw the fiddle in the dustbin. She was delighted, my mother."[12]

His skill with lyrics was better received. In the liner notes to the original cast recording of *Maggie May*, he says: "From an early age, when I could first put one syllable words together, I used to take great delight in my prowess at getting an edge on the other street urchins around me because I was good at thinking up and singing spontaneous naughty words versions of the then current pop songs, like 'Lady In Red' and 'Sally'. Every audience for one of my shows represents, to me, an extension of that gang of kids in the East End of London. Every laugh means a free turn on someone's roller skates, and every first night is like a kerbside debut performance of a brand new naughty song. You see, I was the first in our gang to know all the rude words to 'My Old Man's A Dustman' (not Lonnie Donegan's version), 'Eskimo Nell, She Was A Lulu', 'Maggie May'."

Sadly, oral history doesn't record any of the "spontaneous naughty words versions" that Lionel invented when he was a kid, but it was a skill he liked to show off, when circumstances permitted, all his life. James McConnel, the composer who worked with Lionel in the 1980s, remembers two tiny fragments that perhaps give a taste of the great man's artistry.

To the tune of 'On The Street Where You Live': "There's a house I know / down on Golders Green / and I bet you'll never see a house with mould as green . . ."

To the tune of 'My Favourite Things': "Crabs on my rectum and sperm on my nipples / something and something like raspberry ripples / acid that sits on my prick till it stings / these are a few of my favourite things . . ."

In 1939, Hitler made sure that Act II of Lionel's childhood would raise the bar for action, spectacle and jeopardy. The synagogue on Philpot Street, with its huge, deep cellar was turned into a bomb shelter. Gas masks were issued to every child at Dempsey Street School and they were shown how to use them. Birmingham, Liverpool and Edinburgh saw the first raids, then on September 7, 1940, wave after wave of bombers with fighter support came for Lionel. And indirectly gave him his first lessons in composition and musical theory.

He was evacuated many times, but disliked the countryside so ran away back to London. "Every time I came back to London, the Blitz got worse. They called me the jinx. 'Oi, Lionel's back. Get down the shelters.'" Finally, they sent him away to Wales. He and two other kids stayed with a farm labourer and his wife. In the front parlour of their little cottage was a piano. In those days the *News Of The World* printed free sheet music, the popular song of the week. "And above the lyric and the music you'd get the tune in tonic sol-fa, which I could just about handle – *Doh, ray, me, fah, soh, lah, te, doh*[1]. And the next octave would have a little dot above the letter. The ones below the octave would have a dot below. And I learned how to write music with one finger from the *News Of The World*, and to this day that is still the way I remember tunes at the piano. I have to then decipher them and play them to people that write real music."[13]

A visit by the King and Queen to the shattered East End made a particular impression on Lionel – not because of their show of solidarity, or their bravery, or their innate dignity, but because of their colour. They were bright orange. Pathé News was filming and somebody, presumably fearing that ashen-faced royals would have a detrimental effect on morale, had had the presence of mind to slap on the Leichner 5 and 9 – the greasy foundation universally favoured by the theatrical profession. For the boy it was the revelation of a great truth about elders and betters, and the nature of the world in general. "I knew then," he remembered later, "at the age of ten, that they were all in show business."

At the start of the war, Shear, Lionel's beloved eldest brother, had volunteered for the Scottish Seaforth Highlanders. Nobody knows why. "He must have been the only Jewish cockney with a kilt. He was an amazing guy."

On leave, in 1943, he went swimming. There was an accident. He drowned.

"I remember the funeral. It was in the summer, and you know how things strike you in a comical way even though it's very sad for you? But there was a flash – an image. I was in the first floor in my mum and dad's bedroom above the street . . . above the parlour. The hearse came and they pulled out my brother Stan's coffin with the Union Jack on it. On one side of it were the pipers, the Seaforth Highland pipers. Two pipers. And on the other side there was the old yiddishe wailers, professional wailers. And the cacophony of the bagpipes and the wailing – I mean it was just very funny."

Two

"**Y**OUR son is a artistic genius whose talent must be nurtured," the headmistress had said, without specifying in which particular branch of the arts the genius lay. As it turned out, at this stage it wasn't music at all. What Lionel did best was painting and drawing.

At the age of 13, he was one of nine children from across England to win a junior scholarship to St Martin's School of Art on the Charing Cross Road in the West End of London. Nine kids whose early promise catapulted them into the world of beardie bohemians and the undraped form.

Londoners are territorial. When Tommy Steele was a kid living in Bermondsey, south of the Thames, anything north of the river seemed so remote and exotic he suspected it might be illegal for the likes of him to visit – a suspicion confirmed when, the first time he tried to make the journey north over Waterloo Bridge, he and his mates were stopped and searched by police. Similarly, for East Enders, abroad began at Bishopsgate and, like Tommy, Lionel had hard evidence that over that border lay a land of mystery and wonder. One day he and some pals were walking along the Strand when ". . . we saw two chaps who looked like Laurel and Hardy. We started whistling their theme tune and, when they turned round, it was Laurel and Hardy! They were staying at the Savoy. My friends ran off, but I was transfixed so they walked back to talk to me. They took me to the Black and White milk bar in Charing Cross Road."[14]

This was his new manor: the Charing Cross Road, where movie stars bought you milk. He was quick to adapt: "I lived almost a double life – an East End boy by night and a Soho Johnny during the day."

The Soho Johnny learned the ways of Bohemia. The East End boy joined the Victoria Boys Club on Fordham Street where he engaged in healthy pursuits. He proved to be a useful sprinter and took part in national competitions. Despite his avowed distaste for the countryside, he frequently went camping. On one expedition, "I got myself a nose-job when the tent collapsed and I was felled across my hooter." A proper nose-job to fix the beaky, busted hooter was one of his priority purchases as soon as money started coming in.

He was popular as a draughtsman – everybody in the Boys Club wanted Lionel to do their portrait – and as a songwriter. Fellow campers, now in their eighties, can still remember the campfire sessions. "I was recently talking to my friend Ruth London (her maiden name) who lived in Jubilee Street," says Phil Walker in his chatty website, *Jewish East End of London Photo Gallery and Commentary*. "Her father [. . .] was a manager at the Victoria Boys Club on Fordham Street off New Road. She told me about her father taking her to Broxbourne in Hertfordshire for the Victoria Club's weekend camps and the camp songs they would sing. These songs were written by an 18-year-old club member named Lionel Begleiter. Lionel Begleiter lived in Brick Lane. He changed his name to Lionel Bart and went on to write musical hits like *Oliver!* So now you know! "

And after the campfire sessions were over, the real fun would begin. Sex did not find Lionel, the Soho Johnny, in a Berwick Street doorway or a Beak Street dive. Sex found Lionel, the East End boy, in a bell-tent where he and a boy called Manny engaged in healthy man-on-man action and Lionel, if he hadn't known it all along, began to realise why he found it so easy to make friends with girls – although he never felt 'that way' about them – while around boys he often grew a little bit shy, or hyperactive which amounts to the same thing.

At St Martin's, the Soho Johnny encountered a whole new theatre of ideas and people. "One of the first models I had to draw from was Quentin Crisp [author of *The Naked Civil Servant* and one of the 'stately homos of England'] and he was a very good model, I mean he used to really do a good pose. And many, many years later when he became famous as the Naked Civil Servant, I said hello to him. I said, 'I'm Lionel,' and he said, 'Yes, I remember you, Lionel Begleiter.' He remembered my real name. I said, 'That's incredible, I didn't think many people knew that.' He said, 'You remember when I was a model and you were a baby at that school, you bought me a cup of coffee in the tea break, and you actually said good morning.' And he said, 'I'll never forget that because nobody had spoken to me for two and a half weeks.' At that time people were petrified of me – they'd walk across the road – they wouldn't be seen with this man with the pink hair and the nail varnish peeping through the sandals."[15]

There is a photograph of Lionel in these St Martin's days. He wears a fluffy mohair sweater. Even though the photo is black and white, you know the socks are yellow. Sartorially this puts him in the avant-garde of the avant-garde. Lionel's face in the photograph is even more striking. This is not the face of a street kid, or even a wide-boy making an impressive fist of chancing it up West. This is the face of an intellectual. Possibly even the face of a French intellectual. The photo leaves us in no doubt that Lionel had not just figured out how to do art school: he had figured out how to do it cooler and cleaner than anybody before or since.

This is not to say he was a model student. He was suspended at least three times. He found a telescope and trained it on the upstairs windows of the Phoenix Theatre, across the street from St Martin's and "created a scenario" about salacious goings on that could be viewed, charging fellow students a penny a look. The authorities got wind of it. Another time he sawed halfway through the back legs of a chair, "and this poor lady model called 'Radishes' because of – well never mind, that's another story – went arse over terrible things." The authorities got him for that, too. Another time he was suspended for drawing erotica which, Quentin Crisp in a posing pouch notwithstanding, was frowned upon.

At sixteen, he mounted his first exhibition at the college. ". . . paintings of pregnant women. I was attracted by the look in their eyes and their all-over glow."[16]

His talent, judging from work still in existence, was unmistakable. But it's a small sample. As soon as he left home, his mum had a good clear out and the collected works of Lionel Bart, including many major works in oil, became landfill. But Lionel was constitutionally unsuited to the atelier. "I gave up painting because painters work alone," he said later. "And I like a good mob working around me."

Philip Zec was a Jewish socialist graphic artist. Like Lionel, he'd won a scholarship to St Martin's at an impossibly tender age. After college he went into advertising, then, in 1939, became political cartoonist for the *Daily Mirror*. He distinguished himself during the war by pissing off both Hitler and Churchill: his portrayal of Nazis as vermin, reptiles and scum earned him a place on Hitler's black list; his critiques of wartime profiteers lining their pockets at the expense of front line troops provoked questions in the House of Commons and threats to have the paper closed down.

Zec eventually became the *Mirror's* strip-cartoon editor, a role that gave him – theoretically at least – responsibility for the paper's primary asset, Norman Pett's and Don Freeman's *Jane*, the girl who put the strip into strip-cartoon. Running since 1932, *Jane* charted the adventures of an ingénue to whom clothes simply would not stick. High winds, snagging fences, rogue aeroplanes, cow's horns, bombs, parachutes – it was as if the whole world was conspiring to get Jane down to her scanties. Even Churchill rated her as one of Britain's most formidable secret weapons and when she appeared without even her scanties it's reckoned the British forces in North Africa advanced an extra five miles.

Lionel went straight from college into Zec's studio. His time there, though short, is significant for two reasons. First, because it was the only 'proper' job that Lionel ever held and as such should be celebrated. And second because, by his own account, while he was there he in some way participated in the creation of the *Jane* strips, an experience that would have attracted as much kudos among the lads in those days as boasting you once worked as senior nipple stimulator for *Nuts* magazine would in these.

In the autumn of 1948, the job came to a bitter and brutal end when Lionel's enlistment notice thudded through the letterbox, together with four shillings (20p) advance pay, a railway warrant and instructions to report for basic training to RAF Padgate. The National Service Act committed all reasonably healthy 18-year-olds to an 18-month sentence in His Majesty's Armed Forces.

Padgate is on the outskirts of Warrington, then in Lancashire, now in Cheshire, famous for rugby league and its illustrious role in the history of wire mesh manufacture. To Soho Johnny, a Siberian labour camp would have seemed more inviting. Compared to the Army and the Navy, the RAF was generally considered the soft option, but that must have provided scant consolation when, on December 7, Lionel got on the train at King's Cross.

In accordance with the impeccable rules of narrative structure that his life so often obeyed, at this moment, when his spirits were at their lowest, he stumbled upon the best bit of luck he ever had. Sitting opposite in the train carriage was a ginger-headed East Ender who was also bound for Padgate. His name was John Gorman and he would remain a constant source of good in Lionel's life for the next 50 years. He also wrote an invaluable autobiography, *Knocking Down Ginger*,[17] which gives an unvarnished and reliable account of their friendship.

John Gorman was born within days of Lionel, only a few miles away in Stratford, London E15, opposite the Forest Gate Sick Home for 'imbeciles' and expectant mothers. With only mum, dad and one sister in the family, the Gormans' three-bedroomed house must have seemed luxury compared to Lionel's "one-up, one-down". To supplement dad's less than adequate carpenter's wages, though, at least one of the rooms was usually let out to lodgers and, when dad went off to war, mum had had to take in washing and go out cleaning to further supplement his 35 bob (£1.75) army pay.

John won a scholarship to grammar school and, in 1946, was

apprenticed to a silk-screen printer. His innate bolshiness manifested itself straight away. On the day he got his first union card, he started a campaign (which failed) to turn the workplace into a union-only closed shop.

He described Lionel, sitting on the train, as ". . . a lad of my own age, with a downcast expression, jet black wavy hair, a wide-shouldered bespoke draped suit and a tie with a broad Windsor knot." To John, the lad seemed impossibly glamorous.

At Padgate, they stuck together through the medical examination and in the queue for uniforms and paybooks with the result that they were allocated consecutive service numbers. Gorman was 2416698, Begleiter 2416699. This proved serendipitous. It meant that for the entire 18 months of their conscription, they shared billets, were posted to the same stations and worked in the same sections.

They stuck together in the barracks, too: in the intimate and intimidating company of strange men from all over the country, any or all of whom could, and probably did, nurse a range of irrational prejudices about cockneys, college boys, Jews and smart arses – all boxes that Lionel ticked with a thick black crayon. As always, he kept the bullies at bay with art – taking out his sketchpad and drawing their likenesses as they huddled around the stove.

Basic training lasted from eight to 12 weeks. Mostly it consisted of bull: obsessive-compulsive cleaning, polishing, marching, saluting and standing still, which had the effect of turning a disparate group of undisciplined 18-year-olds into a very pissed off disparate group of undisciplined 18-year-olds. Guns were cleaned and lubricated by drawing a flannel soaked in oil through their barrels. All webbing had to be treated with 'Number Three Green Blanco'. Buckles, badges and buttons were brought to a blinding shine with Brasso. Trouser creases you could cut your wrists on were created with damp brown paper and a defective iron.

John Gorman described their first parade.

"An Irish corporal by the name of Buckley stood in front of Lionel with eyes burning from beneath the black, curved and shining peak of his drill cap, the peak flattened over his eyes so that he could only see by thrusting his chin upwards in a Mussolini pose.

" 'You're a spiv. What are you?' he shrieked. Lionel remained silent as if petrified.

" 'Where do you come from?' he barked.

" 'London, corporal.'

" 'I thought so,' said Buckley. 'You are a fucking spiv, I can tell by your tie.'

"He pronounced it as 'toy' and, staring at the broad Windsor knot at Lionel's neck, he proceeded to grab hold of the thin end of the tie while at the same time he pulled downwards on the thick end, drawing the knot tighter and tighter, then sliding it upwards towards the throat, the knot shrinking to the size of a tied bootlace as Lionel's face reddened. Buckley then repeated his rhetorical question.

"'You're a fucking spiv, what are you?'

"But Lionel remained silent, a response known in the services as dumb insolence. Back in the billet the tie had to be cut from his neck."

The conscripts were woken between 5.30 and 6am. After washing and breakfast they would file out to the parade ground for an hour or so's institutionalised bullying by people with a psychopathic aversion to the Windsor knot. Field training or rifle practice would usually follow. After tea, barracks had to be cleaned and kit maintained. An on-the-spot kit inspection could descend at any time. Any mistake with the damp brown paper, the Brasso or the Number Three Green Blanco would result in a few days CB – Confined to Barracks. More serious misdemeanours were punished with pay stoppages or sessions of lavatory cleaning.

The end of basic training was marked with a passing out parade in front of the commanding officer. As the band played, every one of the conscripts would sing – in their heads, but never with their mouths . . .

> *Stand by your beds,*
> *Here comes the Air Vice Marshall,*
> *He's got lots of rings,*
> *But he only got one arsehole.*

The passing out parade was, by custom, followed with a night of heavy drinking. Remarkably for what was to follow in later life, John mentions that Lionel "was not a drinker and contrived to stretch a couple of beers throughout the session."

The next day, Lionel and John were posted to a camp in Hereford to train as clerks. They learned to file and to type. After six weeks filing and typing they were considered 'Aircraftsmen First Class' and posted to RAF Innsworth, just north of Gloucester. Here, at last, they saw an aeroplane: a Spitfire had been embedded in concrete at the gates of the camp.

The work was tedious, so Lionel, with the effrontery of Oliver, dared to ask for a different job. To everyone's amazement (except Lionel's), his wish was granted and he was put in charge of the stationery store. The duties were light, but Lionel hated being on his own, so he asked the officer in charge, a fierce little Scottish woman, if he could have an assistant.

"It was an absurd request," said John, "but Lionel always had a strong belief in his own ability to achieve anything on which he had set his mind and had a cunning but charming way of persuading people to accede to his demands. Against all probability it was agreed that he should have someone to share the work. Having won the first hand he then played his luck by specifically asking that I should be the one to join him. It was an audacious suggestion but for a reason that was never understood that tough little Scots lady agreed. Together we were ensconced in the cushiest job on the whole station."

There was an oil stove where they cooked beans and toasted bread. They did crosswords. They talked politics. John joined the Communist Party. Lionel honed the skills learned at school and the Victoria Boys Club, adapting lyrics to make scurrilous songs about the RAF. He painted.

A full-length portrait of a pasty-face colleague called Kirby was given the elegiac title 'The Pale Airman' and submitted to the Whitechapel Gallery. The gallery accepted it for exhibition. Lord Ismay, formerly Churchill's Chief Military Assistant, and Mountbatten's Chief of Staff in India, bought it for eight guineas (£8.40). This windfall, combined with an allowance from his father, whose business must have been booming, permitted Lionel, born with a pathological mistrust of chores, the luxury of paying skint colleagues to do his Brassoing, blancoing and brown-papering for him. For a few coppers more, they'd do his guard duty, too. He had it made. If the RAF had been an actual rather than a virtual prison, Lionel would have been The Baron.

Another painting brought his first brush with the censors. The CO gave him permission to brighten up the stationery hut with a mural – a circus scene showing trapeze artists in mid-flight. John Gorman spotted a potential problem.

"His painting of the man appeared as a handsome and muscular figure, who from the size of the bulge in his trunks was obviously well-endowed in the essential male attribute. The finished mural became the subject of artistic censorship when viewed by the squadron leader, a short, slight man, who may not have been so well-blessed by nature. He prudishly argued that the size of the bulge in the man's trunks was too provocative to be displayed in a building that was also used by WAAFs. The issue was settled by the squadron leader using his authority to order Lionel to reduce the size of the offending bulge."

To further while away the idle hours, John and Lionel sought and were granted permission to produce a monthly magazine, a venture that came with the added advantage of frequent passes to visit the printer in

Gloucester. On one such visit they sneaked into the cinema. David Lean's film of *Oliver Twist* was showing.

The next bit would sound made-up were it not for its source – John Gorman's memoir – being an account one learns to trust for its scrupulous reliability and disdain for histrionics. As John and Lionel walked away from the cinema, Lionel, according to John, actually said, "One day, I'm going to write a musical based on that story and it will be better than any American musical."

On his last day in the RAF, John seeded the filing cabinets with Communist propaganda for future conscripts to discover and therein find the inspiration fully to engage in the class struggle. Some of it's probably still there, mouldering alongside the foot inspection records and requisitions for Green Blanco. They held their demob party at the New Inn, Gloucester, where they managed to get just drunk enough to think that singing 'The Red Flag' outside the guardroom at three o'clock in the morning was a good idea. Meanwhile much drunker pals came up with the even better idea of chopping down the camp's main flagstaff.

It was inconceivable that Lionel and John's partnership should be dissolved when they arrived back in London. John was a fully qualified screen-printer, Lionel a fully qualified graphic designer; complementary skills that, given the right backing and marketing, could be turned into a gold mine. Lionel borrowed £50 from his sister, Renee. John borrowed the same amount from his uncle. They rented two basement rooms – a scullery and a coal cellar complete with coal – below a sweet shop in Elderfield Road, Hackney, shortened the mouthful of 'Gorman & Begleiter' to something more zippy, hung up a sign, 'G&B Art Services', and waited for the world to beat a path to their door.

"One wall had three doors in it," says Eric Williams, a designer and good friend of Lionel's until the day he died. "They had signs on the doors. One called 'Dark Room' with a bulb above it, one called 'Accounts' and one called something else: but there was nothing there. It was just three doors."

A photograph of the business partners posing next to their new sign shows them huddled in thin, shabby suits against a chill wind – economic as well as meteoroligic. The sole of Lionel's shoe has come adrift from the upper, and his sock is waving through the gap. Despite their turnout, both are trying hard to look like businessmen. Lionel is doing an 'informal but nonetheless trustworthy' smile. John has opted for something more reflective. Neither is entirely convincing. These are the faces of small boys who have made a den in the park right next to a sign saying, "Do Not Make

Dens In This Park", filled it with worms and are now waiting for their first customer to come along and pay them a penny to see the worms – a business that a few moments ago they were convinced would make them millionaires by the end of the week, but now they're not so sure.

It was October 1950. Ration-book Britain. Five years after the war's end there seemed to be little easing of shortages. The extra Christmas meat ration that year was the equivalent of half a sausage. The Paper and Board (Shortage) crisis provoked lively exchanges in the House of Commons. John's dad, the carpenter, could get hold of scrap wood to make them workbenches and all the silk-screen frames the new business needed, but poster paper and showcard were hen's teeth.

A worse problem was that their scullery and coal cellar had no phone line and the waiting list to have one installed stretched far into the future. Morris and Yetta's growing prosperity had enabled them to move from Stepney to a house in Glaserton Road, Stamford Hill, which boasted among other amenities a telephone. Using parents as an answering service, though, can have its drawbacks.

"Lionel's mother never did come to terms with the instrument. If Lionel rang in from a call box to ask if there were any messages for him, the conversation, half of which was in her middle Eastern accent, sounded like a comedy act:

" 'Hello mum, it's Lionel.'

"Holding the phone at arms length Mrs Begleiter would reply, 'Lionel's out.'

" 'Mum, it's Lionel.'

" 'He's not at home.'

" 'Listen, mum,' Lionel would speak slowly and clearly. 'This is Lionel. Are there any messages for me?'

" 'I'll tell him you called.'

"Click."

Despairing, the business partners did the best they could with the phone box on the corner of Mare Street. John would make the calls while Lionel tried to sound like a busy print works, making 'shoosh-shoosh' noises in the background, keeping one arm free to fight off the belligerent pack of medical emergencies waiting outside to use the phone.

When the first orders came in and the partners found themselves with a little cash in hand, Lionel decided that an essential item of capital expenditure – more important even than ink or paper – was a sartorial makeover. Business, like everything, is a branch of show business. Expenditure on classy costumes is never a waste. They made a withdrawal of £30 from the firm's bank account and took the bus to Dunn & Co Gentlemen's Outfitters on Kingsland Road. The makeover was superficial. Overcoats, they decided, as long as they never took them off, would hide their shabby suits, so they each acquired a long-belted Crombie. Lionel topped his off with what would ultimately become a trademark – a broad-brimmed velour hat – and the professional image was further refined with new shoes and briefcases.

"We . . . looked," John decided, "like anarchists posing as businessmen."

John eventually expanded G&B Arts, as it came to be known, into a bustling multi-million pound business, but by that time Lionel had found other interests.

Three

MOST evenings, Lionel returned to his student haunts in Soho, hanging around coffee bars, checking out the action, listening to jukeboxes. Graphic artist by day, layabout by night. It wasn't a bad life. But it wasn't exactly show business.

The International Youth Centre was a hang out for left-wing students, popular with young Jewish refugees from Nazi Europe. Its premises, in the snooty surroundings of Pont Street, Knightsbridge, housed a canteen, a bar and function rooms for dances, lectures and discussion groups. John Gold, Lionel's distant cousin, was a member who had been staging political cabarets and sketches at the Centre. He roped Lionel in to help out. There was no doubting Lionel's political credentials. Two years of exposure to John Gorman's dogged rhetoric had finally coaxed him into becoming a card-carrying Communist.

Meanwhile Lionel's sister Renee – who, coincidentally, was soon to marry John Gold's brother, Danny – had developed something of an obsession for theatre. Occasionally lacking a chaperone, she'd ask Lionel to oblige. Given Renee's passion for theatre and John Gold's passion for politics, it was inevitable that the three of them, Renee, John and Lionel, would eventually find their way to the Unity Theatre.

Unity grew out of the Worker's Theatre Movement, an organisation that during the 1930s staged street plays in support of rent strikes, anti-fascist demos, unemployment marches and the like. Its performances, as befits street theatre, were not much hampered by subtlety. The music was loud, the characterisation bold, the satire withering, the humour broad – a style that eventually became known by the Russian term 'agitprop', a conflation of 'agitational propaganda'. In 1936, agiprop theatre, with backing from the Left Book Club and the Communist Party, found a permanent home in an old Methodist Hall in Goldington Street, just up the road from St Pancras Station. The Trade Union Movement sent in carpenters and electricians to convert the hall into a working theatre, giving their labour for free, and the Unity Theatre Club was opened.

It was, from the outset, a members-only club, for the very good reason that this put it beyond the reach of the Lord Chamberlain, the official theatre censor whose powers were whimsically dictatorial and who was easily provoked by the sort of scurrilous attacks on church, state, tradition and royalty that were Unity's stock in trade. It did not, however, put it out of the reach of Communist Party apparatchiks, who often tried to exert their influence over company policy, rarely with much success.

The first ever British production of a play by Berthold Brecht was staged at Unity, as were important productions of plays by Sean O'Casey, Clifford Odets, Jean-Paul Sartre and Maxim Gorky. Paul Robeson, the African-American radical singer and actor, having wowed the coach parties in *Showboat* and the high-brows in *Othello*, turned his back on the bright lights to work at Unity's disused Methodist hall, starring (if such a word can be used about a company founded on such egalitarian lines) in *Plant In The Sun*, a play about Union activism in the USA.

"The West End is decadent," he said, "because it doesn't reflect the life and struggles of the people." Working with Unity "meant identifying myself with the working class. And it gives me a chance to say something I want to say."[18] Like all the other actors, writers, directors, designers, musicians and stagehands at Unity, Robeson gave his services for nothing and took his turn sweeping the stage.

The repertoire was usually more mixed than the litany of heavyweights would suggest. Often the more serious works were alternated with satirical revues or handcrafted musical comedies. One criticism of Unity in its declining years was that it came increasingly to rely on Old Time Music Hall shows to address mounting financial difficulties. It's easy to see how, for an organisation committed to advancing the proletarian struggle against oppression and inequality through the medium of theatre, belting out 'My Old Man Said Follow The Van And Don't Dilly Dally On The Way', might seemed a sort of failure. The audiences didn't see it that way, though. And neither, most of the time, did the performers. Music Hall was working-class theatre. The songs, bulletproof crowd-pleasers every one, and the take-no-prisoners style of presentation – familiar to anybody who'd ever ventured into a pub – had been delivered into the bloodstream with mothers' milk. Oom-pah-pah, oom-pah-pah, that's how it goes.

The Unity ideal spread. At one time there were 250 Unity Theatres dotted around the country. The Liverpool branch survives, as does the one in Cardiff, renamed the Everyman.

Unity provided British theatre, TV, comedy and music with a deep well of techniques and ideas from which they're still drawing. The 'kitchen sink' revolution of the late Fifties, the 'satire boom' of the early Sixties, docu-drama, issue-based drama, alternative comedy, even reality TV to some degree or other find their roots in Unity. It was the training ground for scores of actors and writers who've supplied us with top-rated sitcoms, cop shows and soaps over the past 50 years. Alfie Bass, Una Brandon-Jones, John Burgess, Michael Gambon, Julian Glover, Vida Hope, Bob Hoskins, David Kossoff, Harry Landis, Warren Mitchell, Bill Owen, Johnny Speight, Eric Paice, Ted Willis, Roger Woddis all started their careers at Unity. And, most pertinent for present purposes, Unity had a profound and lasting influence on the works of Lionel Bart.

"It was very important," said Lionel. "I was veering towards changing the world and things left wing were interesting to me. I was interested in the theatre as well and I thought I'd better get serious. I can't spend all of my life hanging around the jukeboxes in Soho. And I sort of switched between the two. I spent a lot of time painting scenery at this theatre and it was a theatre where things were happening. Warren Mitchell was there, Johnny Speight, Bill Owen."[19]

Jack Grossman is a documentary filmmaker, who started working at Unity at about the same time as Lionel. "You finished your day job and went to Unity. The tradition was that you turned up there and were given something to do."

"I was cast as a romantic lead in a production called *The Wages Of Eve*. John Gold was cast as the foreman and Lionel was to be my understudy. It was a 'trouble at t'mill' play directed by Una Brandon-Jones and Ann Dyson. It was always a quick turnaround at Unity and when *The Wages Of Eve* finished, a notice went up asking whether anyone could write sketches for an upcoming show."

The show, *Turn It Up*, was to be a satirical revue 'in celebration of' the Coronation of Queen Elizabeth II, and the 'new Elizabethan' age.

"Lionel and I somehow got together and we decided to kick some ideas around. He lived in Stamford Hill at the time, which I did, too, and we'd go to his house. He had this old, battered upright piano that someone had given him. He was a one-finger man and I wasn't much better and we would bang out some tunes and come up with some sketches. Alfie Bass, who was directing the revue, put some of our material into the show. *Turn It Up* ran for several months and really pulled in the audiences."

"One [of the songs]," Lionel remembered, "was about these Elizabethan spivs selling coronation mugs. Alfie Bass got me off the scene painting and got me involved in that show and ended up writing it and being in it."

The programme credits him as assistant producer, too. More importantly, it gives his name as not Begleiter, but Bart – his first proper credit with the new stage name. In later life, he liked to claim, he'd come upon the name in a flash while passing St Bartholomew's (Bart's) Hospital, but John Gorman remembers mail arriving at G&B Arts from customers, clearly confused by the firms fancy logo, addressed to 'Mr Gand and Mr Bart', which always seemed a far more likely source of inspiration to everybody except Lionel.

The opening night of *Turn It Up* was described gushingly in *Electron*, a now defunct left-wing journal: "In particular, praise must go to Lionel Bart, who, in addition to writing most of the music, also helped to produce the show. Bart must surely be one of Britain's most talented composers, and his fast, rhythmical melodies are after the style of the immortal Sullivan [of Gilbert & Sullivan].

"The one disappointment of the evening," it went on, "was that neither producer Alfie Bass nor assistant producer Lionel Bart would come forward at the end of the show to take a bow in spite of repeated calls from the audience. Modesty prevented the two men whose inventive ingenuity had done so much to make the show a success from receiving the praise they so richly deserved."

Lionel Begleiter, skint printer, former 'Bluebells Of Scotland' virtuoso aka Soho Johnny aka Aircraftsman (First Class) Begleiter 2416699 had become Lionel Bart, man of the theatre, one of Britain's most talented composers, the new Sullivan, a genius whose ability was matched only by his modesty.

The Christmas show that year (1953) was a reworking of *Cinderella*. Lionel and Jack Grossman wrote all the lyrics and music. "I would go away and agonise over writing three or four songs where Lionel would breeze in with ten or twelve," Jack remembered. "Eight of them would be rubbish but the rest . . . well."

The songs titles give something of the flavour of the piece: 'The Class Slipper', 'Be A Man John Bull Be A Man', 'What A Rotten Job', 'This Dame Is Anti-Panto', 'We've Got Our Own Kind Of Magic'. Cinderella was the daughter of an impoverished John Bull, who, in a cartoon metaphor for transatlantic relations then (and now), was married to Ermintrude, an overbearing American dominatrix.

This time Lionel was performing, too, as one of the Ugly Sisters. "He sorted out his own costume," says Jack Grossman. "He had a décolleté dress and he left it open and his hairy chest was all over the place." Lionel was blessed with the pelt of a yak. "Harry Ross [the director] nearly had a fit. He said, 'Lionel, you can't go on like that.' He made him put a bit of net over it."

Lionel's confidence grew. Though he never had much difficulty being the life and soul, he was never an in-yer-face life and soul. The voice rarely had to raise itself above a whisper. Anybody who met him is liable to launch into an impersonation of that whisper at the drop of a hat. In later years booze and fags upped the sandpaper edge a grade or two, but the essence was there back in the early Fifties – a cross between Don Corleone and Tommy Cooper, with chocolate sauce and sprinkles.

There was the public Lionel – always on – and the private Lionel. There always had to be space for the private Lionel. At Unity, where the dressing rooms were overcrowded as a matter of course, he would reserve a small corner to arrange his sticks of Ugly Sister makeup – "and woe betide," says Jack Grossman, "anybody who encroached."

He was ambitious, too. Lionel and Jack had struck up a friendship with a leading light of Unity, Bill Owen – the actor who much later became best known as Compo in *Last Of The Summer Wine*. Though his Unity work was given freely, Owen was, even then, a successful professional actor with a string of film credits to his name and a comfortable home in Brighton.

"Once when we were working up some ideas," says Jack, "we went down to see Bill Owen. On the way back Lionel said, 'Did you go to the toilet?' I said I had. 'Did you see those ornaments lined up on the shelves? They were Dresden. That's what I'm going to go for, Jack. Dresden in the toilet.'"

By now Lionel had pretty much made up his mind that his Dresden-In-The-Toilet wealth would not come from printing. He had discovered he could write tunes that people remembered and lyrics that had meaning. He had found his vocation. He was learning. Although he remained a partner at G&B Arts for another 10 years, his involvement in the business gradually waned.

He solemnly told John Gorman that he'd no longer be able to work evenings and weekends at the print shop. Twice he absented himself to travel abroad to Communist sponsored International Youth Festivals: to Bucharest in 1953 and to Poland in 1955, where he appeared in an excerpt from *Twelfth Night* playing Sir Andrew Aguecheek.

In 1954, Russian oarsmen had put many noses out of joint by scoring victories at one of the highlights in privileged England's social calendar, the Henley Royal Regatta. In the following year, for the Unity revue *Peacemeal,* Lionel riffed on the theme in a song called 'Newmarket Nightmare', which imagined a Russian horse sweeping the board at the classiest racing fixtures.

Ascot was abysmal, Derby Day was dismal
We didn't even wager this St Leger
The atmosphere of horror which
Hovers near Ceaserwitch
Must be enough to turn a minor major

If you lift a half-hearted binocular
To your bloodshot half-parted ocular
And the jockey appears to be jocular
To your eye. . .
Then you've not heard the awful disclosure
Just cake hot from the horses' enclosure
Now you've got no recourse but to close your eyes and die

Chorus: *They've entered a filly from the USSR*
A nightmare surmounted by a big red star
Her name crams the programme full you see
It's for a Lasting Peace and a People's Democracy
Wherever she races all the bookmakers swarm
She's favourite but backing her is dashed bad form.

For A Lasting Peace, For A People's Democracy was the not-very-zippy name of the official journal of the Cominform, the Communist Information Bureau, based in Belgrade. To invoke the name in such a flippant way was at best irreverent, and at worst it counted as spitting in the face of the heroic martyrs who died for the people's cause. The party apparatchiks descended.

It was the sort of petty dispute that ultimately led to filigree factionalism in British left-wing politics such that, in the fullness of time, the Communist Party of Britain would not speak to the Communist Party of *Great* Britain; neither would it have any truck with the Communist Party of Great Britain (Marxist-Leninist), and members of all three factions would march out of any disco at which elements from the International Marxist Group were rumoured to be present.

It's not hard to imagine which side Lionel was on in the 'it's irreverent' vs 'it's just a song' dispute. He never actually became disaffected with Unity. Indeed he still had important work there ahead of him. It was just that certain developments in Soho required his attention: and that's where the story takes us next.

What did Lionel learn at Unity? Everything. He learned the power of simplicity in composition and theatrical effect. He learned stagecraft. He learned how a show was put together from the ground up. He learned what it is that actors and singers do, and what they need to do it better. He witnessed at first hand the atavistic spell that those old, belting, oom-pah music hall styles could weave over an audience. Most of all he learned he was good at it.

Four

IN 2010, a computer programme devised by True Knowledge Ltd of Cambridge, England, identified Sunday April 11, 1954 as the most boring day in history. It must have been a close run contest. In the Fifties the notion, much vaunted by the Lord's Day Observance Society, that anything liable to arouse a flicker of interest on a Sunday was Satan's work ran deep in the national psyche. The shops, with one or two fleeting exceptions, were closed. In England, the pubs were subjected to severely restricted opening hours. In Wales, they were shut all day. Some parks chained the swings and roundabouts lest a wanton child be tempted to seesaw straight down to Hell.

To drown the tedium, most people listened to the wireless. This meant *Two-Way Family Favourites*, a record request programme for our boys overseas, both regular and National Service, mostly playing the songs specifically tailored to the market – Petula Clark's 'Sailor' (. . . stop your roaming), Ann Shelton's 'Lay Down Your Arms' (. . . and surrender to mine), Frankie Vaughan's 'I'll Be Home For Christmas' (requested by Lance-Corporal James "Jackie" Keeling of the Royal Warwicks, BFPO 43 for Vera, Chuck, Dave and all the gang back home in dear old Blighty).

At one-fifteen, Billy Cotton, clearly aware of the effect that Ann Shelton and chained-up swings was having on the nation, would shout, at parade-ground volume, "Wakey-Waaaaak-hay!", which was the command for his band to launch an assault on 'Somebody Stole My Gal', at reckless speed and maximum volume.

His show, *The Billy Cotton Band Show*, ran on radio from 1948 to 1968. There were resident vocalists and usually at least one guest star: maybe Russ Conway, a hit-making pianist despite having lost half a finger to a bread-slicer, or, if you were lucky, on the TV version you might catch a glimpse of, say, Cliff and The Shadows, or Adam Faith. The highlight was always a comedy song, put over either by one of the resident singers or by Billy himself: 'I've Got A Lovely Bunch Of Coconuts', 'Oh! Oh! Oh! Oh! What A Referee' (. . . 'cos his little wooden whistle wouldn't whistle), 'Nobody Loves A Fairy When She's Forty', 'It Ain't The Cough That Carries You Off' (. . . it's the coffin they carry you off in).

Meanwhile, in another part of town, events were afoot to make life more interesting. Soho, London's bohemian quarter, haunt of whores, pimps, gamblers, piss-heads, musicians, artists, anarchists, foreigners and movie executives, was drowning in coffee. Coffee, often served as a frothy cappuccino in transparent Pyrex cups and saucers, had the great virtue of not being tea. Tea had served its purpose, sustaining the nation through the rigours of the Blitz and rationing. Coffee represented the new, hip, anti-establishment, international way of life that the aspirational – particularly the young aspirational – wanted to wrest from the post-war mess. The coffee bars usually featured that other symbol of chic modernism – Formica, laminate of the future. Tart the place up with a bullfight poster and a raffia-bound Chianti bottle, taint the air with Gauloises and every customer is a Hemingway, a Sartre, a Juliette Greco or Simone de Beauvoir. To be accepted in the world of the coffee bar, was to be part of a secret society. Dudley Sutton, probably most often recognised as Tinker Dill from the TV series *Lovejoy*, became one of the initiated.

"I was working at the Cat's Whisker in Kingly Street where the hand-jive was invented, and I remember sitting in Jimmy the Greeks' [in Frith Street] with Bernard Kops [playwright, novelist and poet]. And Bernard was telling me about Nietzsche and angst. And I said, 'What's angst?' And he said, 'It's like when you stand on the edge of a cliff and want to throw yourself off.' 'Oh, yeah,' I said. 'I've got that.'"

The coffee bars began to attract specialist crowds. The Macabre on Meard Street, decorated mostly in black with skulls for ashtrays, was a hangout for proto-Goths. Folkies and transvestites favoured the Nucleus on Monmouth Street; poker-players the heroically squalid A&A just off the Charing Cross Road.[20] One of the most achingly hip of them all wasn't in Soho at all. The Gyre and Gimble – the 'G' – was in John Adam Street, round the back of Charing Cross Station. It was a basement, with ill-matched furniture and benches around the walls. Regulars included Ironfoot John, a limping, caped and bearded philosopher; Ernest Page, civil servant during the day, astrologer by night; a clutch of guitar players and singers including Diz Disley, Tommy Hicks and Redd Sullivan; Dexy Dan, a drug dealer who sampled too much of his own product ever to be fully conscious. And Lionel Bart.

Three months after the most boring day of the century, on July 5, 1954, Elvis Presley, a white-skinned truck driver, on his third visit to Memphis Recording Services, having tried many songs in many styles in the hope of tickling producer Sam Phillips' fancy, began to mess around with an old Arthur 'Big Boy' Crudup number 'That's All Right'.

Eight days after that, on July 13, Chris Barber and his band assembled in Studio 2 at the Decca Studios in Broadhurst Gardens, West Hampstead, London. They recorded a few jazz standards, including 'Chimes Blues' and 'Stevedore Stomp'. While the rest of the band took a tea break, Chris Barber on double bass, the singer Beryl Bryden on washboard, and the band's banjo player, Lonnie Donegan, on guitar and vocals ran through a couple of numbers that had been going down well in their live shows. One of them was called 'Rock Island Line'.

Elvis and Lonnie were both white guys trying to sound like black guys, and each spawned a revolution.

'Rock Island Line' mouldered in Decca's vaults, and wasn't released as a single until January 1956, a full 18 months after the session, by which time, on the basis of live performances and rare album tracks, a grassroots enthusiasm for 'skiffle' – the name given to Donegan's style of music – had already seized the country.

Like the punk revolution 20 years later, skiffle was essentially "this is a chord, this is another, this is a third, now form a band" music, with the added advantage that it was much cheaper: no amps, no drum-kit, just an acoustic guitar or banjo, a washboard (still a fairly common household appliance, at least at your gran's), a broomstick-and-string 'bass', and a check shirt. Before long there was an uncountable number – sometimes it must have felt like trillions – of skiffle groups up and down the country playing church halls, works canteens, church halls, school hops, church halls, church fetes and church halls. And each new clone further diluted the white-hot passion of Lonnie Donegan's original until it was entirely subsumed by a generalised cheerless enthusiasm.

Meanwhile, the American product had begun to make its presence felt with a string of releases, not from Elvis, but from Bill Haley – a cuddly, Michigan-born 30-year-old – and his Comets, who looked and behaved like Senior Risk Actuaries letting their hair down at a conference in Findlay, Ohio. This was never proper rock'n'roll. It was Western Swing ineptly gene-spliced with Big Joe Turner and dressed in rayon, but all the same it pushed several of the right buttons and, throughout 1955, one or other of Haley's records was usually hovering in or near the top 20. The breakthrough came with the UK release, in October 1955, of MGM's *The Blackboard Jungle*, which featured Haley singing 'Rock Around The Clock'.

For tens of thousands of adolescents, here was an escape tunnel, a route to freedom from Billy Cotton, from chained-up swings, from the nineteen-bloody-fifties.

It all came together in 1956. The year of Suez, Hungary, the Montgomery Bus Boycott was also the year that 'Rock Around The Clock' found its way to number one in Britain, Lonnie Donegan's 'Rock Island Line' entered the hit parade on both sides of the Atlantic, and the first UK releases of Elvis Presley singles alerted the British public to the possibility that sexual intercourse might be more than a theoretical construct. It was also the year in which Lionel Bart sold his first song. For money. To Billy Cotton.

It was a mild little piss-take of what had become Lionel's adopted habitat.

> INTRO:
> *I've tramped all round London Town*
> *Without any dillyin' or dallyin';*
> *And now I can say – with a serious frown –*
> *The whole place has gorn Italian.*
>
> CHORUS:
> *Oh, for a cup of tea*
> *Instead of a cuppuchini!*
> *What would it mean to me?*
> *Just one little cup so teeny.*
> *You ask for some char, and they reckon you're barmy.*
> *Ask for a banger – they'll give you salami.*
> *Oh, for the liquid they served in the Army –*
> *Just a cup of tea!*
>
> (Break)
> *They've sold the tea urns –*
> *And bought a . . .*
> *Whhoooshh!!*
> *The train now standing at Platform Seven . . .!*
>
> 2nd INTRO:
> *Now there's Old Joe's Caff – it's not the same –*
> *The menu is all high-falooty;*
> *He's even decided to alter his name –*
> *'Le Café de Joe' sounds more snooty.*

(Samba break):
Why has ev'ry caff gorn airy-fairy?
Why is all the stuff contemporary?
Whitewashed walls like my own granny's airy . . .
Cactus to the left,
And aspidistras to the right
So that your coffee – when you get it –
Is all hidden out of sight,
And all the sugar there is brown
Instead of ordinary white,
And if I wasn't getting thirsty
I could keep it up all night,
But . . .

2nd CHORUS:
Oh, for a Rosie Lee
Instead of a black depresso!
Am I a minority?
Is there someone else who says so?
Oh, give me the chance and I'd happily swop
Every shop selling every drop
Of slop with the bottle with the froth on the top
For just one cup of tea!!

Despite its bid to outdo Cole Porter's 'I Get A Kick Out Of You' for maximum number of rhymes in the minimum number of lines ('flying too high with some guy in the sky is my idea of nothing to do' – a score of six – versus 'swop, shop, drop, slop, top' – five, but a trophy-winning seven if you include the half-rhymes 'bot-' and 'froth'), 'Oh, For A Cup Of Tea' did not set the world alight. But it did make Lionel Bart 25 guineas (£26.25). He could now call himself a professional songwriter.

The Soho crowd tended towards a cultural Stalinism in their approach to music. Folk singers like Ewan MacColl and jazz revivalists like Ken Colyer had strict rules about what kind of music was allowed and how it should be played. Even among backsliders and liberals, Billy Cotton was considered the archdeacon of cultural decadence and 'Oh! Oh! Oh! Oh! What A Referee' ('Cos his little wooden whistle wouldn't whistle') the death-rattle of capitalism. Lionel, a card carrying Unity-theatre Communist and leading light of the G&G beard and pullover set, must have been aware of the political and social implications of his sell-out. He should probably have been ashamed. He should probably have kept it a secret. But, being Lionel, he wasn't and didn't, and far from skulking in the shadows, blew the entire 25 guinea fee on a party – a grand celebration of his triumph and, the first of many, a grand celebration of Lionel.

When the major-league coffee bars closed for the night, there were various all-night gaffs where the party could continue. At the beginning of 1956, most evenings the Gyre and Gimble crowd would end up at a squat called the Yellow Door, once a house in a street of houses, now a lone presence in the middle of a bombsite near the Old Vic Theatre. It housed a floating tenancy, including at one time or another, Kenneth Haigh, the actor then just about to make his name in John Osborne's *Look Back In Anger*, Shirley Eaton, who was later painted gold in the Bond film *Goldfinger*, John Antrobus, the Spike Milligan collaborator, Davey Graham, the guitarist, and, most important of all to our gradually unfolding story, Mike Pratt, a guitarist and piano player, then working in advertising.

"Mike Pratt was the moving spirit in that place," remembered washboard-player Johnny Pilgrim, quoted in Pete Frame's *The Restless Generation*.[21] "If he wasn't holding court in the kitchen, he was in bed with some big-breasted bird. I remember going round there one day and he was licking marmalade off this woman's tits. I thought that was very impressive."

Ex-merchant seaman Tommy Hicks was on shore leave from the ocean liner the *Mauretania*. He and a shipmate, Ivan Berg, were invited to Lionel's party at the Yellow Door. They found a huge bonfire and a crowd of people. "The centre of their attention was a small man with a huge hooked nose, a Beatnik beard, and a wide picture hat. He danced around, brandishing a feather boa and a hurricane lamp, singing a song as flat as a pancake: 'A pretty girl is like a melody . . .'

"'That's my cousin,' Ivan said proudly. 'He's a printer in the East End, but he writes songs.'

"The cousin finished singing, and floated over to us. 'Who's the chicken?' he asked Ivan.

"'I'm Tommy Hicks, a shipmate.'

"'I'm Lionel Bart, a success.' He grinned."[22]

He told Tommy about Billy Cotton and the 25 guineas. They talked about Lorenz Hart and Cole Porter.

It's unlikely that the Yellow Door party was the first occasion that Bart and Hicks had clapped eyes on each other. They were both 'faces' in the coffee bars. Tommy's teeth could be seen from space, and he played his guitar and sang at the drop of a hat. He'd crossed and recrossed the Atlantic, and in the US seen acts and bought records that to most British punters were no more than rumours. Lionel would have spotted him a mile off and, seeing a possible route to a toilet full of Dresden, grabbed with both hands the chance to meet him properly.

"And there was Tommy Hicks, and he was in the merchant navy and he was sitting in the corner with his guitar, this big guitar, beaming away playing Chuck Berry and Elvis Presley stuff and I thought he's got a bit of a blow about him, knows all this material. And we decided to form a band called the Cavemen. [. . .] For five minutes I played washboard. It wasn't a long-lived band."[23]

Sometimes they described the band as a 'country and comedy' team.

The Goon Show, an anarchic radio romp starring Peter Sellers, Spike Milligan and Harry Secombe, was big that year. The Goons cut a single called 'I'm Walking Backwards For Christmas' which went to number four in the hit parade. On the B-side was 'The Bluebottle Blues' (with Maurice Ponke and his Orchestre Fromage). In much the same spirit, Tommy, Lionel and Mike threw together a theme song for the Cavemen. 'Rock With The Caveman' a piss-take of the rock'n'roll phenomenon – rock, stone-age-sounding music – geddit? There were also vague satirical Unity-esque references to the Piltdown Man discovery which had, a couple of years previously, been revealed as a hoax.

That summer, Tommy and pals had occasional weekends in Brighton, busking on the beach. Mike and Lionel may have acquired a London taxi and taken it for a long drive around continental Europe. Although this may have happened the year before. Or it might not have happened at all. References to the trip are fleeting and mostly second-hand, recalled years later. Alcohol is a popular beverage.

On July 14, 1956, Soho held a Bastille Day carnival. John Hasted, Communist, choirmaster and lecturer in atomic physics at University College London, had commandeered a flatbed truck and recruited members of the recently formed Vipers Skiffle Group to jump aboard and sing to the thronged pavements. The thundery showers that had been forecast held off until late afternoon. The Vipers abandoned the truck in Old Compton Street and sought shelter in a nondescript café called the 2Is – a wrestler's hangout run by two Australians, Paul 'Dr Death' Lincoln and 'Rebel' Ray Hunter – not the sort of place the in-crowd from the G would normally be seen dead in. They ordered coffee and continued to play. As the skifflers left the management asked whether they'd like to come back some time and play some more.

The Vipers started regular skiffle sessions in the basement of the 2Is. Within a month or so, they were packing the place out every night.

Lionel, with his flawless instinct for sniffing out the action, was an early arrival on the newly emerging scene. He and Mike Pratt got themselves hired to paint the place: black walls with decorative motifs, including two Cleopatra eyes above the tiny stage. They were paid two crates of beer.

By this time Tommy Hicks had acquired management of sorts who arranged a gig for him at the 2Is, inviting John Kennedy, a showbiz photographer to take some snaps and advise them on how to promote their discovery.

Tommy opened his set with 'Rock With The Caveman'. It was written as a spoof, but all the same it pinned the audience against the back wall of the little cellar. It also had a profound effect on Kennedy, and after a brief exchange with Tommy in the street outside (allegedly, Tommy: "What do you know about show business?" Kennedy: "Nothing, what do you know about singing?") a deal was struck.

First thing Tommy needed was a new name. He had previously toyed with Tom Hicks and Chick Hicks (people laughed). Tommy's granddad was called Thomas Stil Hicks. Between them, Kennedy and Tommy changed the 'Stil' to 'Steele'. Tommy Steele.

Kennedy made a call to the Sunday tabloid the *People* and with their collusion invited a bunch of chorus girls, models and their beaux to a party at a posh gaff in Wandsworth. Tommy played. Photographers were on hand to capture the carefully rehearsed awe of the onlookers. The models had been told to pretend they were debutantes and heiresses. That Sunday, the story was splashed all over the front page: big photo of Tommy under the headline 'ROCK AND ROLL HAS GOT THE DEBS TOO'.

It was an age when aristocratic endorsement still counted for something. If Lady Isobel Barnet was seen sucking on a Zube, then Zube's sales graph would show a little excited peak. Rioting Teddy boys had given rock'n' roll a bad name, but here the world could see debutantes dancing like spinning tops and announcing to the world that rock'n'roll was as healthy as the Badminton Horse Trials and as tasteful as Aspreys.

Kennedy consolidated his position by getting Tommy gigs at the Colony Club and the Stork Club – upmarket dining and cabaret places. Realising his lack of experience could cost him money, he recruited a friend, Larry Parnes, who, bored with running the family's dress-shops, was looking to get a toehold in some other business.

Hugh Mendl of Decca Records, impressed by the headlines, booked a recording session at Studio Three, Broadhurst Gardens, a tiny room next door to the big studio where Lonnie Donegan had recorded 'Rock Island Line'. Lionel was there, with Tommy's mum and dad and, according to Lionel, the family dog.

There was no written music. The musicians assembled were all used to busking 'head arrangements'. Dave Lee, the piano player, was best known as a jazzer. Adept at parody, he later wrote a string of comedy hits for Peter Sellers and as bandleader provided different-style-every-week arrangements for Bill Oddie's masterpieces on the radio show *I'm Sorry I'll Read That Again*. The sax player was Ronnie Scott, a modernist in the style of Charlie Parker and Dizzy Gillespie, who eventually opened the club that bore his name. With Tommy on guitar, the three of them, plus bass and drums, gathered around the mics.

The old time cave dweller lived in a cave
'Ssss'what he did when he wanted to rave
Took a stick and he drew on the wall
Man that fellah had himself a ball

Rock With The Caveman
Roll with the caveman
Shake with the caveman
Make with the caveman, oh boy
Break with the caveman
Stalactite, stalagmite, hold your baby very tight.

His way with women was rather neat
C-er-lub a girl right off her feet
You know the lyric writers never lied
'Swhere they got the saying 'starry-eyed'

Rock With The Caveman
Roll with the caveman
Shake with the caveman
Make with the caveman, oh boy
Break with the caveman
Stalactite, stalagmite, hold your baby very tight.

Piltdown poppa sing this song
Archaeology's done me wrong
British Museum's got my head
Most unfortunate 'cos I ain't dead

Rock With The Caveman
Roll with the caveman
Shake with the caveman
Make with the caveman
Break with the caveman
C-A-V-E M-A-N caveman.

Five

'ROCK With The Caveman' has been harshly judged by posterity as being too sexless, too clean, too knowing, too safe and too dissimilar to the 'genuine' American product to be called 'proper rock'n' roll', but it's a mistake to write it off too hastily. It mixes enough honk to satisfy rock'n'roll's requirements with enough quotes from the works of Charlie Parker, starting with *Ornithology*, to put a smile on the face of passing musos and anoraks. Mention that Tommy, Mike and Lionel's song was the first British rock'n' roll record and pedants will shout things like 'Tony Crombie' but it was certainly the first one that made any impact.

With extraordinary prescience, Colin MacInnes writing in 1957, for the intellectually heavyweight *Encounter* magazine, summed up Tommy's – and to a greater extent Lionel's – contribution, saying that Tommy had "a certain English essence of sentiment and wit. Perhaps one day Tommy will sing songs as English as his speaking accent, or his grin. If this should happen, we will hear once again, for the first time since the decline of the Music Halls, songs that tell us of our own world."[24]

While those who came after Tommy got much closer to the feel and spirit of 'proper' American rock'n'roll, The Beatles, six or seven years later, undoubtedly and world-beatingly brought us something of that "English essence of sentiment and wit." And what MacInnes meant by songs that "for the first time since the decline of the Music Halls tell us of out own world" were what Lionel was to give us in *Fings Ain't Wot They Use T'Be, Oliver!, Blitz!* and *Maggie May.*

Hysteria had been known in British theatres before. Johnny Ray, the deaf, bisexual, American 'nabob of sob' had terrified British parents when he played the Palladium in 1953. Their daughters had mobbed the stage door trying to tear the clothes from his back, the flesh from his bones and the hearing aid from his ear. The *Sunday Pictorial* asked its "famous Bobby-Sox Doctor, a distinguished medical man", to explain their behaviour. Hysteria was his diagnosis. He hoped that it would turn out to be a relatively harmless form of hysteria, but feared that, "Ray is a child playing with the key which can unlock, control, or divert the HIDDEN impulses in human beings."

Since then a handful of British-made singers – Dickie Valentine, Frankie Vaughan – had prompted the odd scream or suffered a torn shirt button, but none of them had come even close to unlocking, controlling or diverting any HIDDEN impulses. Not the frightening impulses, anyway. Tommy Steele did. He was the first all-British, full-on, scream-and-scream-till-I'm-sick, wet-your-knickers, worrying-marriage-delusions, stalk-the-bastard, tear-his-face-off, quick-out-the-back-way, Rock'n'Roll-God-Pop-Idol ever to cause a top bishop to ask searching questions in the *Sunday Express*.

"When Tommy Steele steps on to a theatre stage," said Trevor Philpott in *Picture Post*, "it is like killing-day at some fantastic piggery."

Tommy's follow-up to 'Rock With The Caveman' was another Bart-Pratt-Steele composition: a minor-key shocker called 'Doomsday Rock' ("If you're a sinner and you gotta string along / hit me daddy with a three-point prong"). It was banned by the BBC, which did its sales no end of good.

By Christmas of 1956, just three and a half months after his 'discovery' at the 2Is, Tommy was part of the nation's collective unconscious. The *Kent Messenger* of December 20, 1956, records: "A prankster switched on the record 'Rock With The Caveman' in place of 'Good King Wenceslas' in the procession through Ashford, Kent last night. Carollers walked to rock'n'roll." Unlike John Lennon, Tommy never claimed to be more popular than Jesus, but assumptions were made.

Lionel, meanwhile, found himself cast in the role of one of the lesser-known apostles. Asked about his songwriting skills in the *Daily Mail*[25], Tommy replied: "Oh yes, I've written nearly all my songs: 'Rock With The Caveman', 'Doomsday Rock', 'Rock Around Town', 'Wedding Bells' – I've got a new kind of rhythm in that one. I write them with two pals, Lionel Bart and Michael Pratt. They're old shipmates."

Hoping perhaps for a better billing than 'shipmate', in November 1956, Lionel wrote to the BBC:

Miss Scott,
Television Centre,
(Television Auditions),
Wood Lane,
London, W.12.

Dear Miss Scott,

This is in the nature of an application for a variety audition.

It is unlikely that you will have heard of me, since most of my work has been as a script writer and song writer. Currently, it would seem that my only claim to fame is having written most of Tommy Steele's Rock and Roll record material for the Decca Recording Company Limited.

However, I have in the past done quite a few cabaret spots actually performing my own material. And this is what I would like to do as an audition for you. I will, in fact, try to be funny and sing one of my comedy numbers that Billy Cotton has been featuring on his radio programme. It is called "OH FOR A CUPPA TEA INSTEAD OF A CAPPUCCINA" [sic].

Perhaps you can tell me what space of time I will be expected to fill at the audition, if and when.

Sincerely,

Lionel Bart.

His reply came a month later inviting him to a preliminary audition at the Nuffield Centre, Adelaide St, W.C.2. At 11.00 am on January 3, 1957. A BBC memo – for internal circulation only – describes the occasion.

NAME: Lionel Bart (Scriptwriter)
ADDRESS: 59, Gloucester Place, W1
TEL: AMH 3696
APPEARANCE: Thin, cadaverous, black-bearded young man aged 26, of extraordinary appearance with a low forehead and an enormous beak-like nose.
DATE OF AUDITION: 3rd January 1957
PERFORMANCE: Oh For a Cuppa Tea Instead of a Cappuccina (his own original comedy vocal featured by Billy Cotton)
TIME: 2 minutes
EXPERIENCE: Advertising artist by profession who writes as a sideline. Recent successes include 'Rock With The Caveman'
REMARKS: His underdeveloped light baritone voice adequate for comedy numbers and diction clear. He at present lacks the confidence, showmanship and experience to perform as a soloist and has no set act, but with his prolific mind should prove extremely useful providing material and possibly may develop himself as a "goon" type later.

Three days later, Barbara Scott (Television Booking Manager) sent a duplicated letter with the personal details crookedly typed. She said she saw "no immediate prospect of using your acts in our television programmes as at present planned," but mentioned that they had added his name to their list of artistes and thanked him for giving them the opportunity of seeing his work.

The conviction that the rock'n'roll craze, and thus Tommy's shelf-life, would be a short-lived business made it imperative for Kennedy and Parnes to move fast. The long-term goal, if they bothered with one, was eventually to get the boy into something legit, something a bit more long lasting – like an ice-pageant, maybe, or a conjuring act – but for now the rock'n' roll hot cakes still seemed to have plenty of warmth in them.

The success of *Blackboard Jungle* had prompted the rush release of a follow-up, this time dispensing with the 'social significance' and most of the other deadweights, like plot and characterisation, and concentrating on the rock. This first ever, dedicated rocksploitation movie starred Bill Haley & His Comets, along with Freddie Bell & The Bellboys and The Platters, and was called *Rock Around The Clock*. Its UK release brought about a great destruction of cinemas, general public disorder and invented a genre that continued to be profitable for the next five years or so with *Don't Knock The Rock, Twist Around The Clock, Don't Knock The Twist* and *It's Trad Dad*.

Kennedy and Parnes approached Nat Cohen and Stuart Levy, the colourful proprietors of Anglo-Amalgamated, film financiers and distributors specialising mostly in low budget, fast-turnaround shock and schlock B-features. A deal was struck.

Nearly 40 years later, in a BBC interview, Lionel was still worrying that the project might have been ill conceived. "They were going to call it *The Tommy Steele Story*. Here's this guy, he's only 20, he ain't even started his story. And I suggested they couldn't all be rock'n'roll songs if they were doing his story. He's a cockney kid, he's been in the merchant navy, so let's have some cockney songs, and let's have some calypso, so I wrote a calypso song called 'Water Water Everywhere'. I wrote some cockney songs as well. The film took about six weeks to make – made a fortune."[26]

The Tommy Steele Story is a run through of the lad's life so far, shot almost in semi-documentary style and thus replete with fascinating insights into not just post-war morals and mores but also the production techniques and grammar of low-budget British film of the period. For students of popular culture or film studies it's unmissable. Otherwise make sure the remote's to hand.

Lionel and Mike wrote 12 songs in either seven days or 12 days depending on which reports you read. Three of them are among the best that Lionel and Mike ever wrote for Tommy.

'A Handful Of Songs' constitutes the film's, and Tommy's, and the songwriters' pitch. They can do 'jazz and cha-cha-cha, calypsos and street vendor's cries, strains of old refrains, sleepy time baby lullabies'. The calypso, 'Water, Water', is a sailor's reverie mostly about food ('roast beef', 'fish and chips') and girls ('in the pin-up photographs'). Best of all is 'Butterfingers', one of a small handful of straight love songs that the team wrote. The music is from the same mould as, say, The Platters' 'Only You', but the 'whoops, I lost you' resignation of the title and the lyric saves it from the gag-inducing melodrama that was common pop song currency of the time (listen to anything by Ronnie Hilton). It's an object lesson in how a Teddy boy with any aspiration to be cool should talk about lost love.

'Water, Water' (as a double A-side with 'Handful Of Songs') and 'Butterfingers' both made the top ten. The film's soundtrack record was the first British product to make the number one spot in the UK album charts (begun just a year earlier), holding the position for three weeks, losing it, then regaining it for another week before being ousted by Elvis.

More important for prestige, the songs won three Ivor Novello Awards: 'A Handful Of Songs' for 'Outstanding Song of the Year'; 'Water, Water' for 'Best Novelty Song' and the whole handful for 'Best Film Score'. Lionel was an award-winning songwriter of top ten hits and movie scores. His dad was unimpressed: "When you can write a song like [Doris Day's] 'Que Sera Sera', then you can call yourself a songwriter."

With money in his pocket, the King of the Coffee Bars transformed himself into a man about town, a face in the clubs, a player in the music industry. He liked to be seen around with the best-looking girls he could find. Anne Donoughue was a dancer working as Anne Donati at the Windmill Theatre, London's top venue for risqué revue. One night he took her to see Tommy at the Chiswick Empire. Afterwards she invited them all to a party on the other side of town. They travelled in Tommy's getaway vehicle, a housepainter's van. It was cold and uncomfortable. By the time they got there the party was over. Bickering ensued. Lionel decided to call it a night and left Tommy and Anne at the Sabrina coffee bar. Tommy proceeded to nick Lionel's date. Three years later they were married. They've been together ever since.

Checking out the clubs one night – a ritual Lionel adopted to make sure he always knew what was new and who was who – he encountered a dimpled youth called Reg Smith playing guitar and singing.

"When I was at school," says Reg, "one of the boys had a ukulele and I asked this guy – I remember his name now, Jimmy Monday – I asked him to show me what he was doing and he showed me the chords, the Gs and the Cs and the As. My father was a bus driver and his employers used to give the workforce a free bus so they could go down to the coast. And I used to sit in the front playing my ukulele and they loved it. I'd been useless at school, I'd been a waster, so when the ukulele came along and I was sitting in the front of the bus, all I can say is that for once in my life I had self-esteem. But then, of course, I heard a guitar."

Reg Smith changed his name to the infinitely more glamorous Reg Paterson and, thanks to coming third in a talent contest at the Hammersmith Palais, secured a gig at the prestigious Condor Club on Wardour Street in Soho, which is where Lionel saw him. "It was upmarket. People like [racing driver] Stirling Moss and [Queen's sister] Princess Margaret used to go there. I was singing rock'n'roll. They paid me a pound a night and a bowl of spaghetti. I'd never had spaghetti before. They said, 'Would you like some of this?' And I got a pound as well, so I was doing all right."

Lionel heard the voice, felt the attitude, saw the dimples. By now he knew enough to know he was in the presence of rock'n'roll. He also knew that Larry Parnes was hoping to work the Tommy Steele trick a second time so, at the end of the set, he went backstage. But Reg had left the building. "I had to leave early because I had to catch the last bus. I used to go from the West End down to the Elephant and Castle and then the bus from there used to go to Greenwich."

Lionel told Larry about Reg. It's a measure of Lionel's standing as a man-who-knew that Larry without even bothering to check the lad out himself, learned his home address from the club, had a contract drawn up and the following morning drove his pink and grey Vauxhall Cresta out to Greenwich.

"It was one of the most incredible things," Reg says, "I used to go to church. Mostly it was a social thing. I was never religious at all, but it was a great way of meeting girls. So I came home on the bus and came in the door and my father said, 'There's been a man. He knocked at the door and he wants to sign you up.' And I said, 'Who's that?' and he said 'Well, he said he's a man called Larry Parnes.' I said 'Larry Parnes came to our house?' I knew he was Tommy Steele's manager. He was famous. 'He said somebody had seen you at the Condor Club and he's come round with a contract.' I said, 'You're joking!' And he came back again that evening with the contract. One day in your life – a total change."

Reg Smith had already renamed himself Reg Paterson and saw no reason to take the process any further. "Larry said, 'I want to call you Marty. I've just seen a film called Marty and it's a very popular film and the character in it he reminds me of you. He's quite shy at times.' And I thought it was a horrible American name, so I said, 'I want to keep Reg,' so he said, 'We'll toss a coin.' Fair enough, 'cos he was a gambler and I was a gambler to a certain extent, but he was a big gambler. So he said, 'All right, toss a coin.' And he won. So then he said, 'Now for the surname. I see you as someone wild. You've got a bit of a wild nature. A wild streak in you.' I said, 'Oh no, Marty's bad enough, but not 'Wild'.' And he said, 'Yes, I can see it. Toss a coin again.' I lost. And it wasn't until about three weeks later when I actually saw my name in print I thought, 'Wow, he actually got something right.'"

As Steel became Steele, so Wild became Wilde, the first of what was to become Larry Parnes' 'stable' of rock stars. All of them, on joining the stable, were first stripped of their civilian identities and issued with a new name. Usually this consisted of an out-of-the-ordinary, maybe American-sounding first name and a second name with a hint of adventure: Vince Eager, Duffy Power, Dickie Pride, Billy Fury. Only one stablemate put up so much such resistance to the rechristening process that, rather than adopting Larry's suggested Elmer Twitch, he was allowed to remain plain Joe Brown.

The Tommy Steele road to stardom was followed step by step. Just as Tommy had been booked into the Stork Club, Marty was booked into Winston's nightclub, off Bond Street. According to John Kennedy's press releases, Josephine Douglas, presenter of BBC TV's seminal pop shows *6.5.Special*, came into the club one night, saw Marty and booked him for the following Saturday's show. Johnny Franz, recording manager at Philips Records, watched TV that night, and got on the phone.

Marty's first record was 'Honeycomb', a Spanish-tinged country-ish dissertation on the habits of bees. It is not rock'n'roll. For the B-side, Larry put in a call to Lionel.

"I knew who he was, but I didn't really rate him because I wasn't a fan of that kind of song. 'Rock With The Caveman' – it wasn't my kind of thing. I was into something else. I wasn't over-impressed."

Nevertheless, Mr Parnes had told him he had to collaborate with Mr Bart, so they collaborated. Marty had been working on a song called 'Wild Cat'. He came in with 'a whole batch of lyrics' and Lionel helped him finish it. It's nobody's finest hour. "Just who are you purring to? / I ought to tell you to shoo / 'Cos you'll never ever stay true / Not you."

'Honeycomb'/'Wild Cat' did not make anybody an overnight millionaire. Not until his second release, 'Endless Sleep', and a lot more TV exposure did Marty become such a prominent teen-dream player that a photo-romance comic was named after him.

Lionel the talent-spotter never gave up. A couple of years after finding Marty, he 'discovered' Clive Powell playing piano in a club and introduced him to Larry Parnes. Larry signed him. Lionel had already rechristened him 'Bertie Beamer' but, in the teeth of the usual opposition, it was decided that his new name would be 'Georgie Fame'. He was sent on tour as piano player with Billy Fury's backing band, The Blue Flames. When Larry fired The Blue Flames, they became Georgie Fame & The Blue Flames and released a string of jazz/blues/pop songs, reaching the top with 'Yeh Yeh' in 1964. As singer, keyboard player, composer, arranger and producer, George Fame has delivered unbeatable quality ever since.

Tommy's second film, *The Duke Wore Jeans*, was a crack at something a bit more conventional than *The Tommy Steele Story* was ever intended to be – a proper film musical with comic routines and production numbers. It's a take on Mark Twain's *The Prince And The Pauper* in which Tommy plays both Tony Whitecliffe, the son of a Lord who prefers cows to marriage, and Tony's lookalike, Tommy Hudson, a layabout who agrees to act as a substitute groom at Tony's arranged marriage to the princess of Ritallia. Lionel and Mike get a 'story' credit, with script by Norman Hudis, who'd written *The Tommy Steele Story*.

It's not very good. The dance routines, like all such British dance routines before about 1975, give the impression that the dancers have never really done this sort of thing before although they're willing to have a jolly good try, only they'd prefer it if nobody was looking.

For *The Tommy Steele Story*, Lionel and Mike wrote 12 songs in 12 days. *The Duke Wore Jeans* sounds as if one wet afternoon was ample. They produced a clutch of songs that sound just like the sort you're supposed to have in this kind of film except that they lack anything approaching passion, originality, or even much in the way of craft. 'What Do You Do?', a 'cockney song' well within Lionel and Tommy's comfort zones, is probably the best of the bunch – "What do you do with no school tie on? /

No Oxford accent to rely on? / Sing a verse or two of Any Old Iron."
Two singles were released from the soundtrack. 'Happy Guitar' limped its
way up to number 20. 'It's All Happening' with 'What Do You Do?' on
the B-side failed to even make a top 20 appearance.

The film is not without its charm. After 20 minutes or so, its awkward
jauntiness can begin to suck you in, but then you remember that, when
The Duke Wore Jeans opened, *West Side Story* had just embarked on its
second glorious year at Her Majesty's Theatre in London, and you feel
inexplicably ashamed.

By the end of 1957, Lionel was driving a Ford Zephyr Mark II convertible
in pale blue, more than £1,000's worth of quality motor. From Jacintha
Buddicom, a poet and childhood friend of George Orwell's whose life
story lives up to the promise of her name, he had rented a chi-chi little
house in Pond Place, Chelsea. He was songwriter, 'shipmate' and match-
maker to the country's hottest star. He was trusted talent spotter and music
consultant to pop's most influential manager. His songs had been in two
movies. He was about to win three Novello awards. He'd been on the
telly.

But this was the man who'd scrabbled for the front seats at the Grand
Palais on the Commercial Road in order to be 'really close up to the actors
so you could really see the greasepaint', who'd leaned over the pit-rail to
watch the fiddlers and the drummers. "I had the buzz even then." The
buzz does not go away. Rock'n'roll and movies pay the rent on chi-chi
houses, but they can never entirely satisfy the buzz. So, between the
hits and the films and the telly, he'd also started work on his first stage
musical.

Wally Pone, King Of The Underworld, was Lionel's last venture with
Unity Theatre. It's an adaptation of *Volpone*, a social comedy on the theme
of greed by Ben Jonson, the 16th–17th century playwright, street-brawler,
filth-peddler and rival of William Shakespeare. The original concerns a
wealthy Venetian con-man, a virtuous wife and some ass's ears. Along the
way there is much use of disguise, deceit, reverses and revelations and it all
ends badly.

Apart from its title and setting, modern-day Soho, quite what Lionel
made of the story is something of a mystery. As far as can be ascertained,
no script survives. Some of the songs, though, have. 'G'Night Dearie' was
recycled for *Fings Ain't Wot They Used T'Be*. 'Oh, For A Cup of Tea', the
song that Lionel had sold to Billy Cotton, was also featured, but the text, it
would appear, has gone.

Wally Pone opened on July 18, 1958. The reviews were tepid. *The Times* wrote, "Nobody could feel that such people were dangerous to society [. . .] they are so preposterous that they become as quaint and lovable in their pretensions as toys or dolls. Mr Bernard Goldman plays Wally and Mr Morris Perry, Mossy: neither seem capable of hurting a fly. They are both sheer fun." The songs are not mentioned.

The audience reaction was worse than tepid. Colin Chambers, in *The Story Of Unity Theatre*[27], describes the problem. "The difficulty of attracting audiences and at the same time helping them to understand and enjoy the new and the challenging was starkly demonstrated by the poor reception given to Lionel Bart's provocative and original *Wally Pone*, based on *Volpone*. Bart set his story in the contemporary world of Soho vice barons and satirised the fashionable coffee-bar culture which preceded the Swinging Sixties. According to an internal bulletin, *Wally Pone* played to practically empty houses for ten weeks, and the report commented that all audiences seemed to want was Old Time Music Hall."

If Lionel had been hoping for a West End transfer that would go on to break all box-office records and a New York opening that would make him the toast of Broadway, he was sorely disappointed. There were lessons to be learned and applied to future work, though. Turn down the 'provocative and original', boost the 'Old Time Music Hall.'

Six

THE years 1959 and 1960 were two *anni mirabiles* of Lionel's life; when he breathed, spat and shat hits; when a Hit Parade without at least three Bart compositions was an aberration; when he conquered musical theatre not once, not twice, but three times – the third time producing a masterpiece that's still doing stonking business all around the world.

He quickly put the lapse that was *Wally Pone* behind him and returned to an idea he'd talked about with Tommy at their first meeting.

"He wrote a show called *Petticoat Lane*," said Tommy Steele in a BBC interview.[28] "It was a sort of a synopsis of a show that he wanted me to do with him: and listening to some of the songs he tinkered about with [. . .] there were things like 'Consider Yourself', little embryos coming out which were later to become the *Oliver!* score. [. . .] 'Course nobody knew he was working on this giant; [. . .] something that was going to become one of the milestones of British musical history."

Nobody knew and nobody seemed to care – not even when Lionel abandoned the orginal *Petticoat Lane* idea and ported the songs over to a tentative adaptation of Charles Dickens' *Oliver Twist*.

He had seven or eight songs, some of which he'd made into rough demo tapes with himself playing Fagin, his secretary, Joan Maitland,[29] and various passing nephews and nieces playing the kids. He touted them around various managements but could arouse little interest. "And then a man called Oscar Lewenstein got me an intro to go over and see Joan [Littlewood] and her oppo Gerry Raffles."

If Oscar Lewenstein noticed you, your life tended to change. At one time he had been General Manager of Unity, which is presumably how Lionel got to know him, and then became one of the founders of the English Stage Company at the Royal Court whose production of John Osborne's *Look Back In Anger* is – in the GCSE crib notes – generally regarded as the first sighting of British drama's New Wave.

Lewenstein's commitment to the theatre had been proved when, in 1955, while on a dodgy trip to Communist East Germany to negotiate British rights with the great German socialist playwright Bertolt Brecht, he missed his stop on the train and ended up enduring an all-night interrogation at the Russian Commandantura. The Russians, febrile with spy paranoia, were adept at making people disappear. If it ever occurred to Oscar that the rights to one production of *Mother Courage*, 20% of gross takings plus a separately negotiated one-off payment for a two-year option on a second production and/or transfer (UK territories only) might not be worth 35 years in the frozen Gulags, he does not record it in his autobiography.[30]

An introduction to Joan Littlewood and Gerry Raffles, in the world of avant-garde-socialist-art-theatre, was like an invitation to dine with the Gods: Joan and Gerry were the presiding geniuses of the Theatre Royal, Stratford, London E15 (never to be confused with the Royal Shakespeare Company, Stratford-upon-Avon, Warwickshire).

Lionel was a fan. Like anybody interested in new developments in modern theatre he had worshipped at the altar of Joan and Gerry, and seen and admired their groundbreaking productions. Joan and Gerry were not interested in *Oliver!* but they were interested in Lionel.

"They had about 16 pages of a script written by Frank Norman of a play called *Fings Ain't Wot They Used T'Be*. And they wanted to make it into a musical, or a play with a lot of songs, anyway. But we only had two and a half weeks to write it, rehearse it and stage it, and that was the game. I thought, 'well I'm up for this' and I just downed everything and I reported for work." So began Lionel's relationship with Joan Littlewood, the woman who became – arguably – first his making, then his breaking, then his consolation: the Saint/Devil/Mother who raised him up so that she might cast him down.

After a slightly tiresome sojourn as a scholarship girl at the Royal Academy of Dramatic Art, Joan Littlewood ran away to Paris, arriving just in time to enjoy the street riots of 1934 which left 15 dead. In comparison, London, when she returned, seemed lacklustre, so she decided to go to America. With £9 to her name, fares were a sticking-point, but a few shillings could be saved if she walked to Liverpool, so she did just that. She wore cheap shoes. Just outside Dunstable she was terrorised all night by howling wolves and roaring lions, not realising that she had bedded down next door to Whipsnade Zoo. In Manchester, the BBC came to her rescue with an invitation to give a talk on being a Lady Tramp. There she met a man called Jimmy Miller. They married.

Jimmy later changed his name to Ewan MacColl, wrote 'Dirty Old Town' and 'The First Time Ever I Saw Your Face', and sired – with his second wife Jean Newlove, not Joan – Kirsty MacColl, who wrote 'There's A Guy Down At The Chip Shop Swears He's Elvis' and sang with the Pogues on 'Fairytale Of New York'.[31]

He and Joan were an electric combination. In 1938 they formed a political theatre company – first called Theatre of Action, then Theatre Union, then Theatre Workshop – that staged extraordinary shows in unpromising places – church halls, barns, works canteens, off the backs of lorries with no subsidy, sponsorship or money-from-home.

After the war a public-school dissident, Gerry Raffles, joined them. He was 19, handsome, modestly debonair. Joan was by now 33, dumpy and tombstone-toothed. She nearly always wore a knitted hat. Yet Gerry fell head over heels in love with her and Joan saw no reason not to return the favour, especially since Jimmy Miller/Ewan MacColl had by now found love or a fair imitation of it in several other places.

In 1953, with MacColl long gone, Joan and Gerry arrived in London and rented the Theatre Royal, way out East, beyond even Lionel's old stamping ground. It was an old Victorian-built melodrama house that had been extended by incorporating a wet-fish shop. Right up until the Eighties it still smelled slightly of fish. But it was going cheap, so they cleaned it out and set to work. They did Shakespeare: *Twelfth Night, Richard II.* Their 1955 production of Ben Jonson's *Volpone* is more than likely where Lionel found his inspiration for *Wally Pone.* Their show was critically acclaimed, but financially the company steered perilously close to ruin.

Salvation came in the shape of an Irish republican alcoholic. Brendan Behan's *The Quare Fellow*, a tragi-comic depiction of Irish prison life – Behan had spent time in Mountjoy as a 'soldier of the Republic' – was a smash hit. Its transfer from Stratford to the Comedy Theatre in the West End produced a steady flow of revenue and paid a couple of bills. This was followed by two more smash hit transfers: Shelagh Delaney's *A Taste Of Honey* and Behan's second play *The Hostage.*

Joan was one of God's subversives, a pathological anarchist, unhappy unless she was taking something apart, blowing it up, testing it to destruction, kicking its head in. Tellingly, though, her production notes are written in a neat, coquettish hand. Sometimes different coloured pens are used. They are decorated with baroque borders – Paisley patterns and flowers. These are the signs of an intelligence that only craves chaos in the world that it might be more gracefully re-made; not a nihilist, but a true revolutionary. And when Joan's productions worked, all the shattered remnants of plot, character, diction, spectacle, thought and music would magically reassemble into something solid and sound, becoming theatre that avoided the curse of arse-boredom entirely, and appealed even to people who don't like theatre very much.

But these production techniques relied on a biddable author with a relaxed attitude towards the script and a special kind of actor. The standard (at the time) drama school output of nicely spoken gels and dim young men who could look as attractively rumpled in tennis clobber as they could devastatingly handsome in evening wear did not cut the mustard at Stratford. Joan liked misfits. She liked people who looked as if they'd just walked in off the street. Often her actors were people who'd just walked in off the streets. They needed to be able to improvise, to think on their feet, to make it up as they went along, to unquestioningly follow (in a thoroughly democratic, socialist way) Joan's often bizarre instructions, whims and notions wherever they might lead.

"Darling, marvellous performance, but your feet are waiting for a bus," she once told Victor Spinetti. Luckily he – possibly the only person in the world – knew what she meant.

She called actors "her nuts", "her clowns", "her children". Some hated it. Those who stayed regarded the experience as something between a "bit of a laugh" and "complete existential rebirth".

"Working with Joan," says Victor Spinetti, "was fabulous. It was the time I felt most alive. And I know Lionel felt the same. She gave him permission to be a genius. It was all right to be clever."

"She was a bully," says Dudley Sutton, "But I liked it. (Grim smile – indicates self) Masochist."

In the production office at Stratford, James Booth, RADA trained but nonetheless one of Joan's 'nuts', came across a few scruffy pages among the litter of paperwork, a script of a play called *Fings Ain't Wot They Used T'Be* by Frank Norman. James knew the name. He'd just read Frank's novel, *Bang To Rights*, about his time in jail.

To call Frank Norman a jailbird in such close conjunction with mention of Brendan Behan could lead to the erroneous conclusion that the two men were out of the same trap. Behan's crimes were the attempted murder of two policemen and conspiracy to blow up Liverpool. Norman was done for passing dud cheques. Also, Behan was from the back streets of Dublin. Frank Norman was from Croydon. They did have a taste for drink in common, though, as well as huge potato heads. By his own admission, Norman had never seen a theatrical performance when he wrote the script. It ran to no more than 15 pages or so and didn't make much sense, so clearly it would need more than a bit of a polish to make it audience-ready. Nevertheless, the spirit and language of the piece fired the imaginations of all who read it.

In *Joan's Book*,[32] her autobiography published in 1994, Joan Littlewood describes her first meeting with "our beloved, impossible Lionel" – the dialogue and the lilt of Lionel's speech being, one suspects, a brave stab in the general direction rather than the result of phonographic recall. He has read Frank Norman's brief sketches and is impressed by the demotic dialogue.

"'First time I've heard cockney as she is spoke' said Lionel

"'What are we talking about?'

"'*Fings Ain't Wot They Used T'Be*'

"'Is there enough to go on?'

"'Only needs songs, instead of verbals', said Li

"'Well, who's the songwriter round here, Baronet?'

"'I'll have to have a think out with Frankie first.'"

Joan's subsequent setting up of the 'think out' is described in Frank Norman's memoir of the production in *Why Fings Went West*[33], published in 1975.

"Joan chained smoked Gauloises.

"'It should be a musical. I've met this wonderful nutcase called Lionel Bart. He's agreed to write some songs.'

"Rehearsals started in January 1959. Lionel had already written a few songs or what he called 'top line and chord symbols' for the show. On the first morning the cast gathered for the famous extemporizing and with every day that passed the original conception of the play drifted further away until it was hardly possible to identify with the antics onstage at all. As the weeks went by more songs were added and once in a while I was called on to write a few pages of bad language."

He later referred to *Fings* as, "A play Joan Littlewood put on based on a line I wrote."

The basic story concerns Fred Cochran, a down-at-heel gangster, trying to make a comeback. Lil Smith, his loyal girlfriend, longs for respectability and keeps a marriage licence ready for her lucky day. Fred's gambling den (his 'speiler') provides a haven for the failures of the underworld: Paddy the gambler, Tosher the pimp with his 'brasses' Betty and Rosie, and Redhot, a sad little burglar who never manages to get warm. When Fred wins on the horses, he redecorates his place. At the grand re-opening trouble brews and a rival gangster, Meatface, is beaten in a razor fight. The play ends with a wedding. Lil and Fred are giving up crime to go straight; handing over the gambling den to the local copper, whose long held ambition is to go bad.

It was written off the back of the then recently published *Wolfenden Report on Homosexual Offences and Prostitution*, which, in a blaze of prurient publicity, paved the way for the passing, ten years later, of the 1967 Sexual

Offences Act, which legalised homosexuality between consenting adults. The report also recommended that London and other major cities should initiate 'clean up the streets' campaigns which led to a rise in the number of call girls and small ads in newspapers and shop windows advertising 'masseuses', 'models' and 'large chests for sale'.

It is a telling sign of the times that the Wolfenden Committee, throughout its three year sitting, in deference to the more delicate sensibilities of the lady committee members, referred to homosexuals and prostitutes as 'Huntleys and Palmers' – a popular manufacturer of biscuits. (Since Sapphism had never been illegal, there was no discussion of Lincoln Creams.)

But at least the report gave some indication that morality's tectonic plates were at last on the move, and *Fings* was doing what it could to give them an extra shove.

When actors who were there speak of *Fings*, their eyes mist over. Even making allowance for the possibility that the show's subsequent success may have cast a rosy glow over their memories, there is no doubt that the camaraderie, the creativity, the daring and the buzz were all quite exceptional.

"There was no money: all the actors were on about £15 a week,"[34] said Lionel, and I'm talking about people like Richard Harris, James Booth, Barbara Windsor and Yootha Joyce. There was no time either: we had just two weeks to put a show on – write it, rehearse it, stage it. I was sitting in the stalls writing the songs while the actors were improvising their dialogue with Frank Norman; when the songs came up, I ran onstage and taught them to the actors. It was an amazing two weeks."[35]

Actors would swap characters. They'd play it posh just for a change. They'd play it in mock Swedish. Anybody could contribute to the process. If a passing drayman, delivering to the theatre bar, shouted out a line or whistled a tune, it was up for grabs.

Lionel got stuck in: "I mean I was up there on the stage, improvising with the actors. We were like a family. And I had to report in every morning with at least two new songs which had developed out of their improvisations. I was great, teaching 'em the songs, doing a bit of dancing with them. They were all clowns. They had this incredible style of picking up from each other. If a chandelier fell down they'd use it."

There were four separate productions of *Fings*. The first, which opened in February 1959, was so successful that it was brought back in April, then revived again at Stratford later in the year in order to get it ready for its

West End transfer. It opened at the Garrick Theatre the following February, 1960. Songs and scenes came and went between productions. Actors came and went, too. The original cast included James Booth, Eileen Kennally, Edward Caddick, Glynn Edwards, Howard Goorney, Richard Harris, Yootha Joyce, Brian Murphy, Ann Beach and Carmel Cryan – all stalwarts of British theatre, film and TV for years to come.

Fings followed *A Taste Of Honey* and *The Hostage* into the West End. Three West End transfers had stretched the theatre's very limited resources. Bits of scenery and costumes had to be rationed out. At one point *Fings* lost its entire set to *The Hostage*. The theatre's pool of suitable actors was drained, too, and new contenders had to be press-ganged wherever they could be found.

The Sewell brothers, George and Danny, were having a quiet drink when the Theatre Workshop caught up with them. They were from Hoxton, now crushingly trendy, then a cradle of violence. Danny – the original Bill Sikes in the London and Broadway productions of *Oliver!* – had been a heavyweight boxer who won four out of his seven fights with a knock out. George – who later starred in *Get Carter*, *This Sporting Life* and every TV cop show going – had been in the Merchant Navy. After that, he'd worked for a bit as roadie for a rumba band and ended up as a travel courier. He was 35.

In the pub that night they got talking to Dudley Sutton, who'd been working at Stratford on and off for a couple of years. Dudley mentioned to George that Joan was looking for someone with his looks to appear in her new production. All his life Sewell was blessed with a face that no jury would acquit.

"I thought Dudley was joking and I pointed out that I wasn't an actor anyway,"[36] Sewell said later. "But Dudley seemed to think that this would be an advantage."

Out of curiosity mostly, George signed on as one of Joan's 'nuts'. "It was very interesting to work with Joan," he said. "I'd never worked with anyone else so I thought it was normal and it was only afterwards that I realised how revolutionary it was. A lot of the time we'd just sit around and chat. If you listened to a tape of that chat, you'd think 'What the hell's going on?' But I do know if you stopped that chat and then Joan said, 'Right, now we're all going off to burn down Buckingham Palace,' we'd have followed her with no hesitation."

Two of George and Danny's childhood friends, Michael and Bernard Weinstein, had already gone into show business as the double act Mike and Bernie Winters. Their touring with Tommy Steele and appearances on *6.5.Special* earned them the reputation, in the *Daily Mirror* at least, as "top comics for Britain's teenage TV audience."

It was Mike and Bernie who had been instrumental in getting Tommy banned from the Adelphi Hotel, Liverpool – an early experiment in what was later to be called 'the rock'n'roll lifestyle'. They invited most of a local hospital's nursing staff (and some of the doctors) to a party in Tommy's room, wrought havoc (in those days the Adelphi had neither TVs in their rooms nor a swimming pool in which to throw them, so physical damage was limited to, for instance, the denting of silver-service), and finally put a very pissed John Kennedy to bed in a stranger's room. The stranger, on arriving back at the hotel in the early hours, complained to the management. There is an unproven suspicion that, in revenge for the ban, Mike and Bernie spread the rumour that the Adelphi had once employed Adolf Hitler as a waiter.

Tommy's tour hit London was around the time that *Fings*, auditioning for its second, pre-West End revival. In their joint autobiography, *Shake A Pagoda Tree*[37], Mike and Bernie tell the tale of how they, too, were almost shanghaied.

"On our day off Lionel and Tommy invited us across to the Theatre Royal, near my home in Stratford, where Lionel was rehearsing *Fings Ain't Wot They Used T'Be*. I sat in the stalls with them and Joan Littlewood while they auditioned girls for the part of the prostitutes. Shirley Ann Field [a glamour model then in the process of transforming herself – with great success – into a serious actor] came onstage to try, and Joan told me to go onstage and do a scene with her. 'But I don't know anything about the show,' I said. 'Don't worry: just make it up,' she said. So I joined Shirley to say, 'Hello. You doing anything?' She said, 'Piss orf. Don't want any of you layabouts.' 'How much for a bunk-up then, love?' 'Joan said, 'Oh very good'. But she didn't mean Shirley, she meant me. I refused the 50 quid a week Joan offered me to take the lead because I was making more in films.

"When the rehearsals finished I invited Tommy and Lionel over to my house for a bite to eat. My wife Siggi was furious when we turned up. I only gave her a fiver a week housekeeping and all she had were two pork chops, one for her and one for me. We got to my pad and the three of us stood smiling in the hallway as I asked, 'Can you give Lionel and Tommy something to eat?' 'No way,' she said. 'I can't do it. Not on the money I get. They can go over the road and get some chips. How dare you come home late and bring people with you'. So she slung them out."

Bernie did make one invaluable contribution to *Fings*. He'd seen a couple of dancer/comediennes up West who'd be perfect for the 'brasses'. Barbara Windsor and Toni Palmer were working at Winston's nightclub – with Ronnie Corbett, Danny La Rue and rock'n'roll singer Vince Eager. "I told Joan, 'She [Barbara] is definitely the girl you are looking for. She's made for the part.'"

Barbara's and Lionel's paths had crossed already. She vaguely knew him from the 2Is and from her occasional stints deputising for Josephine Douglas on *6.5. Special*. Her career was going well, so having dragged herself out of an East End childhood she was leery about going back to the East End to work in a slum theatre. Also the audition came just a few days after her husband, Ronnie Knight, had been sentenced to 15 months for receiving stolen goods. She was shaping up for a fight.

The audition was held at Wyndham's Theatre, on the Charing Cross Road, where the *The Hostage* was running.

"Inside the stage door," Barbara says in her eponymous autobiography.[38] "under the dingy light of a brick passageway, I could make out the vague shape of a podgy lady in a woolly hat.

"'What do you want?' she asked.

"'I've come about the audition.' Then I found myself thinking out loud, '. . . but I'm not really bothered to be honest. [. . .] I've only come because my agent sent me.'

"So, feeling a bit cocky I told this cleaning lady I was 'West End' and didn't want to go out to Stratford East where the new musical would be.

"'Aren't you a cute little thing!' she said. 'Cheeky cow,' I thought!"

Barbara was auditioning for the part of Rosie, who, they told her, was an Irish prostitute. She told them she couldn't do Irish.

"Then a woman's voice came from the darkness at the back of the theatre. 'Do you know anything about prostitutes?'

"'Oh yes. I see all the Soho brasses on my way to cabaret.'

"'Why don't you give us a Soho tart, then? Show me what they do.'

"This was irresistible. I started moving across the stage. 'Allo mister, five bob for a wank, ten bob for an oral, and a pound if you want the full card trick – it's cheap at a quid.'

Then, without accompaniment, she sang *Sunny Side Of The Street*.

The woman at the back of the theatre spoke again.

"'Thank you, I'd like you to be my Rosie.' Finally she came up onstage and I was face to face with the podgy woman in the woolly hat.

"'Blimey, it's you – I thought you was the cleaner.'

"'I know you did,' said Joan Littlewood, 'That's what I wanted you to think. You were behaving naturally, so I got you at your best. You got your job at the stage door.'

"Funny the way you always land the jobs you don't really want."[39]

The bolshie mood persisted. Barbara and Toni Palmer were schooled in a theatre of sequins and smiles. It took time to adjust to a world where the director scrubbed steps and you were expected to make up your own dialogue.

"I arrived on my first day, carrying my tap shoes," says Barbara.[40] "And the first thing Joan did was tear up the script. 'This is a load of fucking rubbish' she said . . . with the writer there! Then we started improvising. I said, 'I hate this way of working.' She said, 'Why don't you just fuck off then?' So I said, 'I will.' I went up West and bought a dog. She loved that. She'd got a tongue on her, yeah. We had words quite a lot."

Compared to most of the riff-raff who washed up at Joan's, Miriam Karlin was a toff. She was from leafy Hampstead in North London, and RADA trained. She'd done more West End than most of that lot had had hot dinners – straight and revue. And films.

Miriam was also a life-long socialist and huge fan of Joan's as she told a BBC interviewer. "I longed to work for her. Joan rang me and said, 'I don't suppose you want to come down and work in my old place?' I was over the moon, but my agent sniffed and said, 'Don't expect me to pay your Fortnums bills come Christmas.'"

She was signed up for a tour of duty as Lil, the female lead.

"It was the first time I could legitimately improvise. Li [everybody called him Li] did wondrous music and the actors improvised the dialogue. The songs took off in an amazing way – that was all Lionel."

The improvisation brought change at a breathtaking rate. Frank Norman had written Tosher the ponce as an old man. James Booth reinvented him as a tearaway and Lionel provided him with a song *The Student Ponce*. The creative high led to all manner of burgeonings. Barbara, bolshiness forgotten, was troubled by the close working relationships – especially with James Booth, who she'd met previously when they were both working on the Jayne Mansfield film *Too Hot To Handle*. Booth was in a relationship, Barbara was married to a man in prison, so nothing serious could happen. Instead they had to settle for, in Barbara's words, 'a nice little ding-dong.'

As soon as *Fings* developed this life of its own, Frank Norman found himself superfluous to requirements. He later poured his frustration into a novel, *Much Ado About Nuffink*, a thinly disguised *roman a clef* about a young working-class writer whose play is taken up by an avant-garde theatre company. Here the actors are complaining about the director – in Frank's version, a man.

"'Christ knows how I'm ever going to learn my fucking part. These twelve-hour rehearsals are killing me; all I have time to do is go home, flop into bed, then get up and come back here.

"'How the hell does he expect us to study the script when we're on the go all day and half the night? He changes the cues so often I don't know where the hell I am,' said the first voice. 'I went for a piss this morning and came back to find he'd cut three of my lines in the street scene.'

"'Good job you didn't have a crap. You'd have found your whole part cut.'"

The piss/crap joke may have originated with Frank, but down the years has been attributed to practically every actor who worked with Joan about every one of her productions. We'll probably meet it again in later chapters.

The cast revelled in the cockney/Jewish/criminal slang, competing to see who could be rudest, boldest, funniest, most obscure. In a theatrical tradition that had largely confined 'working class' characters to the roles of comic charladies and 'Gor blimey, guv'nor' dustmen, it was like at last being allowed to take off the corset and let out a fart.

"Before long we were all talking *Fings*," says Joan in her autobiography. "'Fink I'll shoot round the manor and see what's buzzin' meant 'I'll take a stroll down the lane.' We had a ball – Li's tunes spilled out all over Stratford. The number 'Fings Ain't Wot They Used T'Be' became our theme song. We sang it on the way to Bert and May's at lunch time and the locals took it up and added their own words."

They teased Lionel about the tune which, rhythmically at least, bore a striking similarity to Rodgers' and Hart's 'Mountain Greenery' – a huge 1956 hit for Mel Tormé. Sometimes they sang one song to the tune of another. But they sang it. And every morning Lionel, having the time of his life and fizzing with ideas, would bounce in with new tunes and new lyrics, written in the same brutal demotic, already duplicated on Roneoed sheets.

He revived one of his best songs from *Wally Pone* for the opening number. 'G'Night, Dearie' left the audience in no doubt as to what sort of evening they should expect. It's an exchange between the two prostitutes Rosie and Betty and the policeman: the cop's verse a half tempo plod, "Proceeding in a Westerly direction, saw a lady importuning in the street"; the whores chorus a galloping shriek, "G'night dearie, g'night honey, d'you need any company?"

'Contempery' was a piss-take of the interior décor craze that had seized the 'never had it so good' nation sung by Horace Seaton (played by Wallace Eaton), the designer brought in by Fred for his club's makeover. 'Contemporary' was the vogue word: Lucienne Day fabrics, the spindly Acapulco Chair, anything made of pegboard, Woolworth's Homemaker china, the vinyl/asbestos tile – they all came under the heading of 'contemporary'. The song's full of show-off rhymes: "In my house I've got rubber plants and cactuses / believe me, sir I preaches what I practises."

The first production opened on February 17, 1959 to mixed reviews. While Bernard Levin in the *Daily Express* called it "a play of brilliant, bawdy irreverence", Caryl Brahms in the London *Evening Standard* mentioned that, "the play is punctuated with songs (if punctuation means stopped by) thrown into what ought to be the action like currants into dough and seemingly without much meditation. There were of course some good things in the picture of Soho cellarage [. . .] I wish I could have liked it better. I wish I could have liked it at all."

Audiences disagreed and for the whole of that first five-week run it played to packed houses.

And the changes kept coming. "On the opening night when the critics were in," said Lionel,[41] "Joan Littlewood got hold of me in the interval and told me to write a new song, find myself a costume and appear as a totally new character at three separate cues in the second half. Which I did. I found an old trenchcoat down in the basement and an old bowler hat, blacked a tooth out, got some spoons from the canteen, borrowed a pair of maracas from the drummer in the pit and I came on as Meatface. It was crazy but looking back on it, it was the most enjoyable thing I've done in my life, in terms of theatre."

"Who ran away with a blind man's hat?" runs the song Lionel improvised. "Meatface, Meatface / Who done a murder just like that? / Meatface, Meatface / When there's a fight, he stays well made / He's a proper villain with a razor blade / Meatface, Meatface."

And it was still a work in progress six months later on its pre-West End run. Barbara Windsor was pulled out of rehearsals for a meeting with Joan and Lionel.

"'Joan asked me to write something for you. Here it is,' said Lionel, handing me several pieces of paper with the words and music to a song on it. He called it 'Where Do Little Birds Go?'[42]

"'Who am I going to sing it with?'

"'No-one,' Joan said. 'I want you to sing it on your own.'

"I was astonished. All Joan's work was about ensemble; nobody ever got a solo.

" 'How do you want me to do it? Am I going to make an entrance? Dance? What?' I asked.

" 'No, I want you to sit on a stool and just sing it sweetly, like a little bird. We'll have all the lights down and just a spotlight on you. And keep still. Sit on your hands.' "

'Where Do Little Birds Go?', like many of the other songs in *Fings*, proved that Lionel had learned the lesson spelled out in the verdict on *Wally Pone*. Audiences didn't want 'provocative and original', what they liked most was Old Time Music Hall. The song and Barbara's perform-ance of it are but a short step away from Florrie Ford singing 'When The Fields Are White With Daisies' or Marie Kendall singing 'A Bird In A Gilded Cage'. The strategy paid dividends.

"After I finished the number on our first night at the Garrick and the lights went up, the audience were on their feet, almost as one, clapping and cheering wildly, and calling: 'More! More! More!' [. . .] I loved the response, of course, but had no idea how to acknowledge it or what to do next. 'I can't do any more,' I said weakly. 'Lionel hasn't written any more.' Then I gave them my widest smile and added brightly, 'Anyway the next song's even better.' "

Barbara herself acknowledges that it was the making of her career. The next song, 'Big Time', wasn't better. It was still pretty good, though.

Fings opened at the Garrick on February 11, 1960. The longest running British musical in the West End at that time was Julian Slade and Dorothy Reynolds' *Salad Days*. It was about a magic piano that forced people to dance. "I'm gay, I'm breathless and I'm jubilant and I'm dancing," they sang. And, "Aren't I clever, nobody ever / Saw such a saucy saucer." Set against this, *Fings* – described as *Guys And Dolls* with its flies undone – came across like the Sex Pistols at a Nolans gig.

"It was my first West End show but right from the beginning it was set to go," Lionel said, "There was huge laughter in the theatre, and it already had a kind of following before we even opened in town. It became a kind of cult for a while."

In the rush to join the cult, Frank Norman's name was all but forgotten. *The Daily Telegraph*'s headline read, "Songs The Strong Point Of Musical". "It has pace, it has movement, it has colour and it has consistent style," said *The Times*. "In short, if there is a better musical production in the West End now one would be hard put to name it (even including *West Side Story*)." The review's only gripe is with "Frank Norman's book", but it goes on to say, "Whatever one's reservations about the book there can be no doubt whatever about the rest of the ingredients. The songs by Mr

Lionel Bart fit reasonably catchy tunes to the unusually ingenious lyrics. [. . .] Mr Wallas Eaton, gracefully house-coated as a flighty interior decorator, and Miss Barbara Windsor, a 'brass' sadly wondering where the birds go in the wintertime, are sheer delight."

The comparison with *West Side Story* is significant. Bernstein's music, Sondheim's lyrics and Laurents' book had set the bar intimidatingly high. Critics were poised to pounce on anybody who had a go at reaching it. *Fings,* with its 'reasonably catchy tunes', didn't even try to jump. It simply limboed underneath the bar; too English, too rude, too music-hall, too common and too vulgar even remotely to invite comparison.

Not all the criticism was so glowing. Collie Knox, a well-known *Daily Mail* journalist, here writing for *The Woman's Mirror*, uses *Fings* as a stick with which to beat theatre in general, moral degeneracy and the modern world: "Collie Knox, looks at the West End Theatre and says, 'WHAT A SEWER!' Is this real life, or is it plain dirt?"

"We have the world's finest actors and actresses," he says. "It is shameful that they should be forced by economic necessity to waste their talents on this odorous muck. I blame much of the popularity of this spate of underworld epics on some of the younger critics – anything to be 'different' and 'clever clever'. Plays and musicals which are neither sordid nor erotic are attacked by these babies. When plays come on in which everyone sleeps in the same bed and which glorify promiscuity, uncontrolled sexual appetites, hopelessness and self-pity, we are urged to see a brilliant new study of modern times."

Noël Coward, too, was less than unstinting in his praise. In his diary for May 2, 1960 he noted: "Last Evening Coley [Cole Leslie, Noël's secretary] and I went to *Fings Ain't Wot They Used T'Be*, which is a smash hit saved by a true performance by Miriam Karlin. It is maddening as a show because, without the indelible stain of Miss Littlewood's effective but restless direction, it might have been very good. As it is, there are some very amusing lines but as, with the exception of Miss Karlin, almost the entire company is inaudible, the thing is ruined. Apparently Miss Littlewood encourages the not very experienced young actors to improvise and say whatever pops into their minds. The result of this freedom from convention is chaos. They all talk at once and the timing is lost forever."

Most punters weren't so picky and flocked to see the young actors say whatever popped into their minds. The enthusiasm and excitement that had built up steam among the cast in the rehearsal room tsunamied over the footlights. Everybody left the theatre 'talking *Fings*' and singing the song, not giving a toss about its similarity to 'Mountain Greenery'. More gratifyingly still, just as the audiences were getting into the mood for kicking up their heels with the pimps and whores, a force appeared dedicated to stopping them. There's nothing like a bit of opposition to bring an evangelical determination to pleasure-taking.

The Lord Chamberlain's office, still fighting a rearguard action against filth in the theatre, could refuse a licence to anything it deemed 'unsuitable'. Lord Scarborough, the Lord Chamberlain of the day, was a soldier and a conservative statesman. There is no evidence that he had any knowledge of or interest in the theatre, but on matters of theatrical censorship his word was law. There was no higher authority to whom one could appeal other than the Queen.

A script of *Fings* had been submitted to the Lord Chamberlain's office before its first Stratford run. It came back with all the "sod offs", "bugger offs" and "piss offs" blue-pencilled. His Lordship was particularly concerned about the character of Horace Seaton, the interior decorator, fearing the possibility that he might be portrayed as a Huntley.

This being Theatre Workshop, and Joan being Joan and the cast being the cast, by the time his Lordship's comments had been received, the script as submitted had been forgotten, rewritten six times and peppered every night with a score or more of unscripted ad libs.

His Lordship's Office was not pleased. In February 1961 the manager of the Garrick received a letter:

The Lord Chamberlain's Office,
St James Palace, S.W.1

Dear Sir,

The Lord Chamberlain has received numerous complaints against the play 'Fings Ain't Wot They Used T'Be', in consequences of which he arranged for an inspection of the Garrick Theatre on 1st February last.

It is reported to his Lordship that numerous unauthorised amendments to the allowed manuscript have been made, and I am to require you to revert to it at once, submitting for approval any alteration which you wish to make before continuing them in use.

In particular I am to draw your attention to the undernoted, none of which would have been allowed had they been submitted, and which I am to ask you to confirm by return of post have been removed from the play.

Act 1
Indecent business of Rosie putting her hand up Red Hot's bottom.
The dialogue between Rosie and Bettie. 'You've got a cast iron stomach.'
'You've got to have in our business.'
The interior decorator is not to be played as a homosexual and his remark
'. . . Excuse me, dear, red plush, that's very camp, that is,' is to be
omitted, as is the remark, 'I've strained meself.'
The builder's labourer is not to carry the plank of wood in the erotic place
and at the erotic angle that he does, and the Lord Chamberlain wishes to
be informed of the manner in which the plank is in future to be carried.

Act 2
The reference to the Duchess of Argyll [whose recent divorce
proceedings had alleged adultery with 88 men and included, in
evidence, a photograph of her giving Defence Secretary, Duncan
Sandys, a blow-job] *is to be omitted. Tosher, when examining Red*
Hot's Bag, is not to put his hand on Rosie's bottom with finger aligned
as he does at the moment.
The remark, 'Don't drink that stuff, it will rot your drawers', is to be
omitted.
Tosher is not to push Rosie backwards against the table when dancing in
such a manner that her legs appear through his open legs in a manner
indicative of copulation.

Yours faithfully

Barbara Windsor had never heard of copulation and had to ask Joan
what it meant. "Fucking, you silly cow," was Joan's reply.

Lionel said he'd never seen a funnier bit of material and wanted to substitute, possibly for Horace the decorator, a character who gets the sack
from the Lord Chamberlain's office for not being enough of a prude.

Miriam Karlin pointed out that the Lord Chamberlain had been to see
the play twice and, judging by his laughter, had thoroughly enjoyed it.
Princess Margaret and her fiancé Antony Armstrong-Jones had been to see
the show, too. Judy Garland went several times. Later in the year, the Lord
Chamberlain's boss, Her Majesty The Queen, went twice in two weeks.
As far as can be established, she raised no objection to the builder's
labourer carrying the plank of wood at an erotic angle and neither did she
demand to know the manner in which the plank was in future to be
carried.

In 1960, the novel *Lady Chatterley's Lover* went on trial. Literary and academic worthies queued to defend Penguin Books' right to print every one of D.H.Lawrence's 'fucks' and 'cunts' without being prosecuted under the Obscene Publications Act. During the trial the Chief Prosecutor asked the jury, "Would you want your wife or servants to read this book", and censorship stood revealed as being less about morals than about class and control. Worst still to the emerging Sixties mindset, censorship was becoming a bit of a drag.

There was talk of a Broadway production of *Fings*, but the slang and accents were a worry and back then subtitling technology was in its infancy.

It maybe could do with a bit of translation, or at least explanation, for modern ears, too. Without it, the dialogue can sound corny, the songs rumpty-tumpty humdrum, the slang hopelessly dated and the gender politics criminally offensive, but in its time *Fings*, in its subject matter, its production style and in the relaxed ensemble of the actors, was nothing less than revolutionary. Best of all for Lionel, it was, "A very true cockney argot.": words and music not in bastardised American or fake hoity-toity but in his language, the language he'd spoken since he was a kid. It was a London musical, his London.

The theme song that had spilled all over Stratford soon spilled all over the country. Max Bygraves recorded a version with the words cleaned up. It spent 15 weeks in the top 40, two of them at number five. The cognoscenti, though, still sang Lionel's edgy original lyrics:

> VERSE: *I used to lead a lovely life of sin*
> *Dough, I charged a ton!*
> *Now it's become an undercover game.*
> *Who wants to read a post card in the window*
> *'Massaging done?'*
> *Somehow the Bus'ness doesn't seem the same*
> *It's a very different scene*
> *If you know what I mean*
>
> CHORUS: *There's toffs with toffee noses*
> *And poofs in coffee houses*
> *Fings ain't wot they used t'be*
> *Short time low priced mysteries*
> *Without proper histories*
> *Fings ain't wot they used t'be*
> *There used ter be class*

Doin' the town,
Buyin' a bit of vice
And that's when a brass,
Couldn't go down
Under the Union price, not likely!
Once in golden days of yore
Ponces killed a lazy whore,
Fings ain't wot they used t'be.

Cops from universities
Dropsy, what a curse it is!
Fings ain't wot they used t'be
Big hoods now are little hoods
Gamblers now do Littlewoods
Fings ain't wot they used t'be
There used to be schools
Fahsands of pounds
Passing across the baize
There used to be tools
Flashing around
Oh for the bad old days
Remember
How we used to pull for 'em
I've got news for Wolfenden
Fings ain't wot they used ter
Did their lot, they used ter
Fings ain't wot they used ter.

Seven

PHILIP King was a playwright best known for his successful farces *See How They Run, Sailor, Beware!* and *Watch It, Sailor!* In 1956 he wrote a straight play about a vicar being falsely and spitefully accused of homosexual molestation by a young parishioner and called it *Serious Charge*. Mickey Delamar, a movie production manager and assistant director who sometimes pulled a project of his own together, acquired the film rights. Since much of the action revolved around a youth club, it seemed appropriate and, given its screaming popularity, financially prudent to include a few rock'n'roll songs in the score. Tommy was the reigning king of rock'n'roll so Lionel, his shipmate, Master of the King's Music, was the obvious source to provide songs and advice.

It was 1958. Lionel, still checking out the action on a nightly basis, had spotted in the 2Is a new kid whose sallow skin, gymnastic sneer, phallocentric choreography and oil-slick quiff would have made him a perfect and sexually-invincible Elvis-clone were it not for his face, which had the innocence of Bambi.

By this time everybody down the 2Is knew who Lionel was. He was the hitmaker. If he showed interest in you, you knew you'd touched the first rung of the ladder to the toppermost. In order to speak to the Bambi-faced singer, Lionel first had to get past the Bambi-faced singer's dad, "a small wizened man with a little attaché case." He discovered the boy's name was Harry Webb. He lived in Cheshunt, a remote London suburb, and he had a band. Lionel went to see them, taking with him his latest girlfriend, another Windmill dancer and *Playboy* centrefold called June Wilkinson.

"She was quite an outstanding girl in many ways," said Lionel, "and it was difficult for those lads to play when she was there."

The 'lads' were The Drifters, soon to be rechristened The Shadows. Harry Webb had recently changed his name, too, to Cliff Richard.

"He was being managed at the time by somebody called Ganjou, out of a circus act. There was a circus act called the Ganjou Brothers and Juanita and believe it or not they were Cliff's managers for five minutes and Mr Ganjou said yes, and Cliff's dad said yes and he was in the film singing these songs."

The film features Anthony Quayle as the vicar and Andrew Ray as his accuser. Cliff takes the very minor role of Curley Thompson, the younger brother of the Andrew Ray character, but does get to sing three Lionel Bart songs, 'No Turning Back', 'Mad About You' (which featured what must be one of the first uses of the Bo Diddley "shave and a haircut, two bits" beat – the backbone of Buddy Holly's 'Not Fade Away' and Cliff's later 'Willie And The Hand Jive' – on any British record) and 'Living Doll'.

Some accounts say that Lionel wrote 'Living Doll' in less time than it takes to sing it, others make a more realistic estimate of somewhere between ten minutes and the whole of a wet Sunday morning. It was, by Lionel's own account, inspired by an advert in the back of the *Sunday Pictorial* for a, "Darling Doll. She kneels, walks, sings and sits. Beautifully proportioned, lovely face, sleeping eyes, brushable hair, delightful wash-able dress, matching panties. 10/- deposit plus weekly down payments or cash payment of 99/6."

The 'Living Doll' Cliff sings in the film is an uptempo number, based on a riff similar to Elvis' more full-throttle 'King Creole'. Cliff didn't much care for 'Livin' Doll'. When told by his recording manager Norrie Paramour that a soundtrack single would have to be released, there was general dismay. But the pressure was on. 'Move It', written by Ian "Sammy" Samwell and at the time the best rock'n'roll song ever recorded in the UK, was Cliff's breakthrough, reaching number two. The follow-up had just scraped into the top ten. Two subsequent singles had barely made the top 20. Sales had more than halved. Cliff and The Shadows were looking for a guaranteed hit and feared that the *Serious Charge* songs were not going to reverse this slow slide into obscurity.

Bruce Welch, The Shadows' rhythm guitarist, remembers one historic night at Sheffield City Hall. "We were getting ready to work that night, and we were onstage talking about it, and we agreed 'Living Doll' was the best one, but we thought we can't do it like that, 'cos the original way it was done in the film it sounded like a BBC recording session. It was awful. And I was just sitting on the stage with a guitar and I said, 'Why don't we do it like this, like a country song.'"

It was Cliff's – and Lionel's, and Bruce's – first number one. It knocked Bobby Darin's 'Dream Lover' from the top spot at the beginning of August 1959, and stayed there until mid September. It even made the *Billboard* top 30 in America, and it won one of the four Novello Awards that Lionel picked up in 1959.

Much later in life, Lionel told pianist, composer and author James

McConnel that the secret of a good song is not to overcomplicate, to settle on one musical idea and one lyrical idea and limit the vocal range so that any Joe can sing it. By these and any other standards, 'Living Doll' is a brilliant song. The tune mostly consists of the same four notes, a boogie-ish saunter down a descending arpeggio on a major sixth chord repeated no less than seven times, with a four note twiddle at the beginning of each line and a three note variation on the end. The vocal range is a tenth – two notes over the octave – the range the average pianist can stretch to with one hand, thumb to pinkie. Structurally it's bare bones. Jet Harris's seven-note bass guitar solo is the intro.

The first verse sings like velvet and chucks rhymes at you with relentless vigour – "talking/walking", "please her/she's a", "eye/why/satisfy". With a first verse that good, a second verse could only spoil things, so we dispense with it entirely and move instead to the middle-eight. The lyrical conceit throughout the song plays with the literal and slang meanings of the word 'doll' – suspect in light of today's gender politics, but innocent enough back then. The middle eight, though, ratches the inherent creepiness of the conceit up several notches. Most people, if a friend invited them to admire a girlfriend's hair, then touch it, then confessed a desire to lock that girlfriend up in a trunk for fear that a big hunk might steal her, would try to keep things calm while furtively dialling 999. Cliff somehow gets away with it – just – before moving hurriedly on to the third verse, or rather the verse that would be the third verse if there had been a second verse and which is, anyway, no more than a welcome repeat of that excellent first verse. After the guitar solo, the middle eight is repeated, then, on the grounds that you can't have too much of a good thing, the first verse is reprised for a third time, Jet Harris repeats his intro, Hank B. Marvin hits the whammy bar on his recently acquired red Fender Stratocaster and it's all over. Perfect pop.

The song brought a change of direction for Cliff as he told us 32 years later when appearing on Lionel's *This Is Your Life*: "In '59 there was a massive change of tack that took place musically for me. I went into a different kind of music. And it started with a song that went . . . du du du du duu duu du (sings 'Living Doll')." No more the snarling Bambi, Cliff became a smoother, slicker, fountain-of-youth, all-round-family-entertainer Bambi – an image that's kept him in vineyards, swimming pools and Bibles for more than half a century.

'Living Doll' marks a watershed between rock'n'roll and soft pop – the pop of gentler melodies, slower tempos, swooping strings, Bobby Vee, calmer shoes and increased use of grooming products – that held sway until Mersey beat blew everything else out of the river. Not that it mattered much to Lionel. He had more shows to write.

It would be wrong, though, to leave *Serious Charge* without mentioning that its star, Andrew Ray, became, according to rock god Vince Eager, the butt of Tommy and Lionel's practical jokes.

"They were doing it all the time," he says, "no expense spared." It was Tommy and Lionel who, according to Vince, years before the TV prank show *Candid Camera* did the same thing, wheeled an engineless car into a garage and asked the mechanics to help them get it started. It was they who first replaced the regular one-gallon fuel tank in a Messerschmitt 'bubble-car' – a tiny three-wheeler with a 173cc engine – with a 20-gallon tank, then drove it into a petrol station and asked the attendant to fill it up.

But their most elaborate prank was one of the many they played on Andrew Ray. "What happened, apparently, I heard from Lionel, was that he and Tommy hired these actors to impersonate MI5 people, and they picked Andrew up from a West End theatre where he was appearing. And they took Andrew back to Lionel Bart's mews house which was done out like a war room, and they told him he was going to be taken to Poland the next morning, along with the other actors in the play, to do a special performance for the diplomatic service in Warsaw. Poland was, of course, still behind the Iron Curtain back then. They gave him these new lines he had to say in the play, which they told him was the key to the new code, and there'd be special people in the audience who'd understand this and get the code. So they had him brought to Lionel's house and he stayed the night and the following morning they blindfolded Andrew. They put him in a car which they'd hired – like, an army car – with extras in officers' uniform and the car took him to Northolt Aerodrome. And there was a Dakota waiting on the tarmac. And they put him on the Dakota and then when they were about to take off, Tommy Steele came on the intercom and said 'Fasten safety belts' and all that. And then they opened the door and there was Tommy and Lionel Bart as the pilots."

Sometimes Vince Eager winds people up.

Bernard Miles was a fine character actor who'd brought a poignant dignity to roles like Joe Gargery in David Lean's 1946 film of *Great Expectations* and the quietly heroic Chief Petty Officer Hardy in Noël Coward's *In Which We Serve*. On telly he'd taken the title role in *Nathanial Titlark*, an early sitcom, playing the oo–arr bucolic he had already established on the wireless. The monologues became a best selling record *Over The Garden Gate* – still available on Amazon.

He devoted himself to the theatre with a tireless, if often eccentric passion. Along with his wife, the actress Josephine Wilson, he opened the 'barn' in his St John's Wood back garden as a 200-seater playhouse and staged a string of ludicrously ambitious productions. For the Purcell opera *Dido And Aeneas*, he secured the services – God knows how – of the sopranos Elisabeth Schwarzkopf and Kirsten Flagstad, fresh from triumphs at the Royal Opera House, La Scala and the Met, allegedly paying the latter in beer. A recording of the Bernard's back-garden production, made at EMI Studios in Abbey Road, is still widely regarded as the definitive version.

A 200-seater in the back garden was only ever going to be a temporary measure, so Bernard and Josephine hatched a plan to build a completely new theatre on a blitzed site at Puddle Dock in Blackfriars, just over the Thames from the playhouses of Shakespeare's day. In October 1956, the City Corporation granted "Bernard Miles and other poor players of London" a lease on the land at a peppercorn rent.

The builder's estimate was £126,000. The Corporation promised 38%. The rest came from Bernard and Josephine's tireless fundraising. They threw barbecue parties on the building site. They staged races, featuring TV's glamour kick-dancers the Tiller Girls. They beguiled members of the public into buying individual bricks at half-a-crown a pop. And they shamelessly knocked, cap in hand, at the doors of their well-heeled neighbours – the City's banks, insurance companies and stockbrokers.

The Mermaid Theatre's design was based on the old Greek amphitheatre, 600 seats, shallow thrust stage and no pros arch, but incorporated the state-of-the-art technology of automated revolving stage, projection facilities and stereophonic sound. In keeping with the times, it shunned theatrical red plush and gold leaf in favour of bare brick modernism.

Lest this apparent austerity should deter the bow-tie crowd, the theatre also incorporated a top-drawer restaurant with stunning views over the Thames. Bernard reckoned he could price two meals and two tickets at a quid and still turn a modest profit.

He hired his team. Sean Kenny, an Irish architect who'd helped design the stage and auditorium and had worked with Joan on *The Hostage* at Stratford, was brought in as resident Art Director. Peter Coe, a 29-year-old who'd been artistic director at the Queen's, Hornchurch, and the Arts, Ipswich, became resident producer.

For the first production, Bernard himself did a rewrite job on an eighteenth-century play by Henry Fielding, *Rape Upon Rape; Or The Justice*

Caught In His Own Trap, turning it into a musical which he called *Lock Up Your Daughters*. He approached Laurie Johnson, who'd scored a couple of films and TV shows, to write the music, and Lionel Bart to write lyrics.

Work started in February 1959, straight after, or possibly overlapping, the intensive rehearsals for *Fings,* which opened on the 17th. The deadline was May. Having written one musical in two weeks, Lionel must have found the prospect of three months leisurely.

Nevertheless, according to Laurie Johnson, the pre-production 'think-outs' were dangerously engrossing: "One night, leaving Bernard's office after a late night meeting at the Mermaid, walking between Lionel Bart and the stage designer Sean Kenny, I fell like a stone into an ill-lit trapdoor in the stage floor. The three of us were engrossed in conversation when I simply dropped out of sight. Walking between them, I was there one minute, gone the next. The force of the fall broke two of my ribs."[43]

Rather than taking him straight to hospital, Lionel and Sean took him to the pub over the road and plied him with brandy. He quickly recovered at least the use of his writing hand.

"Songwriting is a partnership," said Laurie Johnson, "quite unlike composing orchestral music, which is a self-contained activity. Sometimes the lyric comes first, sometimes the melody. We kept in daily contact by phone and we met regularly at Lionel's mews flat or in my home. Sometimes Lionel might give me no more than a song title or a phrase, which I would take further and give some musical shape. Or I might give him a melody, or part of one and he would start writing a lyric there and then on his portable typewriter. He was very quick. Sometimes we wrote two songs in a day. We completed the bulk of the show – the major songs – in no more than two or three weeks."

The stage was huge, 90 feet deep and 60 wide, and without a pros arch looked even bigger. Sean Kenny's architectural imagination made great use of the space and the revolve. Since there was no orchestra pit, he concealed the musicians within the set, where, from time to time during the action, they could be glimpsed by the audience. Dominating the picture was a huge portcullis, which became at various times the wall of a prison cell, or an arch between two Hogarthian houses. His lighting plan – cramping the whole space into a dingy interior or opening it out with heavenly sunbeams – was breathtaking.

Bernard Miles, the showman, planned an extravaganza for the theatre's opening.

On May 29, 1959 the actor Jack Hawkins' daughter, Caroline Hawkins, dressed as a mermaid with a tail and a golden crown and wrapped in rugs was rowed down the river Thames. She was carried ashore into the theatre and onto the stage, where, amid cries of 'Shame!', the Lord Mayor stripped her of her tail to signify that from now on she was confined to shore. Then the Lord Mayor declared the theatre open.

These days the plot of *Lock Up Your Daughters* – or *Rape Upon Rape*, which was predicated on the notion that rape, or at least extreme sexual harassment, is all good clean *Carry On* fun – might be seen not so much as the basis of a rattling good night out as an argument for compulsory castration: Hilaret, on her way to elope with Captain Constant, is waylaid by a practiced seducer, Ramble, but before he can perpetrate the evil deed all three are arrested for affray and brought before the corrupt magistrate, Justice Squeezum. The Justice takes a fancy to Hilaret: his wife, Mrs Squeezum, takes a fancy to Ramble. Hilaret escapes Squeezum's clutches but later has to lead him on in order to get her lover freed from prison. And so on.

Laurie Johnson's music is the accomplished, sophisticated work of a man who knew his way around a suspended fourth, a ground bass and a phrygian half cadence. Thankfully, he makes no attempt at fake eighteenth-century flummery and instead mixes cha-chas with jazz ballads, patter songs and oom-pah. Lionel rises to the challenge with an aplomb that must have surprised anybody who thought 'Rock With The Caveman' was his best shot. Rhymes skitter, syntax throws itself off cliffs then, with cat like tread, lands on its feet. Comparisons were made at the time between Lionel's work on *Lock Up* and the lyrics W.S. Gilbert turned in for the Gilbert and Sullivan operettas. With hindsight, it's easier to see that where Gilbert's lyrics are Victorian mahogany sideboards, Lionel's are nifty little G-plan coffee tables with concealed drawers. Gilbert plants his fat rhymes proudly in your lap. Lionel hides his mischievously in places you never thought they'd be.

The showstopper was 'When Does The Ravishing Begin', a tongue-twister sung by Hy Hazell as Mrs Peachum: "Eeek! I shall swoon very soon for the fellow has me / Weak at the thought of the sport, and the fellow has me / Meek and as mild as a child / Til the fellow has me cheek, to cheek."

Bernard had stated in the theatre's manifesto that no show would ever run more than six weeks at the Mermaid before either transferring to the West End or coming off. The rule didn't last long. *Lock Up Your Daughters* ran from May to October 1959 and its success went a long way to recouping the building costs.

A Boston try-out for a Broadway transfer was staged the following

March and Lionel went over to supervise. After a couple of nights, he phoned Laurie Johnson, still in England, to say that a new song was needed for the second act. "I came up with the idea of a tango," Laurie wrote. "Lionel thought up the title of 'The Gentle Art Of Seduction'. He wrote the lyric fast – he had a mind like quicksilver – and called me back to dictate it over the phone. I composed the music and scored the number that same day, and it was flown over to the States the day after."

The Broadway opening was eventually abandoned because the show had 'encountered so many problems of staging and censorship'. But in 1962 it was revived at the Mermaid, then transferred to Her Majesty's Theatre on the Haymarket, where it ran for the best part of a year-and-a-half.

Lionel and Laurie won the Ivor Novello Award for 'Best Score for Film or Theatre of the Year' in 1960. Laurie went on to score more musicals (*The Three Musketeers*, *Pieces Of Eight*) films (*Dr Strangelove*, *Tiger Bay*, *East Of Sudan*) – and wrote most of the really good TV signature tunes (*The Avengers*, *World In Action*, *Animal Magic*, *This Is Your Life*, *Wicker's World*). When his daughter Sarah got married, Lionel was there. He sang 'Oh You Beautiful Doll'.

Tommy Steele's third film, *Tommy The Toreador*, released right at the end of 1959, was certainly more coherent than the first two, and included one of his best remembered songs. It's the story of a gullible seaman who, victim of happenstance and skulduggery, finds himself standing in for Spain's top bullfighter. Kenneth Williams' nostrils play the British vice-consul. Sid James and Bernard Cribbins, with baffling Japanese accents and a light smearing of Leichner No. 7 (Coffee Brown) play two Spanish conmen. Janet Munro, fresh from starring opposite Sean Connery in Disney's *Darby O'Gill And The Little People*, plays the love interest.

Most of Lionel's and Mike's songs – 'Where's The Birdie', 'Amanda', 'Take A Ride' – barely rise above the level of those in *The Duke Wore Jeans*, but then, like Gene Kelly singing 'I Got Rhythm' to street urchins in *An American In Paris*, or like Danny Kaye singing 'The Ugly Duckling' to the little bald boy in *Hans Christian Andersen*, Tommy settles himself down with a group of Spanish children and sings them a story that starts, "Once upon a time there was a little white bull."

'Little White Bull' credited to Bart, Pratt and Bennett (a pseudonym for Tommy Steele) was a Christmas hit in 1959. It won a Novello for 'Best Novelty Song', immediately became a favourite on BBC Radio's *Children's Favourites*, grew into a party piece and a misty-eyed memory for the Meccano generation, and is sometimes played at funerals.

Tommy The Toreador was the Cavemen's swansong. Even before the film opened, the press announced: "'Tommy Steele's songwriters, Lionel Bart and Mike Pratt, have split up', one of Tommy's co-managers John Kennedy said last night. 'I believe they didn't see eye to eye. There was some disagreement about the type of songs they were writing for Tommy and an argument about the size of their billing.' But 26-year-old [sic] Bart denied a rift in the team which turned out 30 songs for Tommy in 18 months. 'It's just that we thought it was time to give our partnership a rest,' he said at his Knightsbridge flat. 'I shall go on writing for Tommy. Mike is going to Spain to work on a serious play, but we are still good friends.'"

Later in life, Lionel told rock scholar Pete Frame[44], "My songwriting partnership with Mike Pratt wasn't running too smoothly, and I was writing more and more on my own. I was ambitious and wanted to do as much as I could, while Mike was often off on a jag, having a whale of a time, which was something I didn't really understand at the time. I understood it perfectly later on, when I was doing it myself – but back then, we were supposed to be working as a team and he was making every excuse not to work. I remember when we were putting songs together for *Tommy The Toreador* and he would be sitting there at the piano, smoking a joint, lost in dreams, or laughing his head off about something. He just didn't seem to be concentrating and I think that was when I snapped. I shouted 'I'm sorry, but I can't work with someone who drinks and takes drugs!' It's hilarious when I think about it because eventually I went off and made a far greater fool of myself."

Mike did go to Spain. He wrote two plays. When he came back he wrote gags and sketches for TV and revues, and still wrote songs, at one point collaborating with John Barry. He worked as an actor, too, did a lot of telly and a season at the Royal Shakespeare Company before becoming an international star as Jeff Randall in the TV hit series *Randall And Hopkirk (Deceased)*.

It has to be said that, with one or two exceptions, like 'Butterfingers' and 'Little White Bull', the collaboration between Lionel and Mike always seemed something less than the sum of its parts. By the end of '59, Lionel as a solo had had a number one with 'Living Doll' and had written two hit musicals. Mike hadn't.

Tommy was more than overdue to become the all-round family entertainer he'd always promised he'd grow into: international star of stage and screen – in *Half A Sixpence, Finian's Rainbow, Scrooge* and a score of other blockbusters – author, painter, sculptor, squash champion, composer, O.B.E. and husband.

Gerald Thomas, director of *The Duke Wore Jeans*, Norman Hudis and Peter Rogers, writer and producer of *Duke* and *The Tommy Steele Story*, and Nat Cohen and Stuart Levy of Anglo-Amalgamated, soon after *The Duke Wore Jeans* had opened, made *Carry On Sergeant* ('a regular *Carry On* with the call-up boys'), and spawned a franchise that would keep them in scotch and cigars for the next couple of decades.

Lionel's pals were doing well for themselves. He was gradually finding himself at the centre of a web of well-connected contacts. He was, as they said, where it's at. As Lionel Bart, hitmaker and man of the theatre, he was also establishing a distinct Bart brand image. The "thin, cadaverous" BBC reject was fast becoming an in-demand radio and TV personality.

In October 1958 he was paid seven guineas for a bouncy appearance on Tommy Steele's *This Is Your Life*. There was an interview with Donald Baverstock on the early evening magazine programme *Tonight* (five guineas); a chat about Tommy on the BBC Light Programme's *People Today* (five guineas). And then came the big one.

Juke Box Jury was a Saturday night fixture in which the week's new pop records were played to a panel of sages and celebrities watched by a studio audience. To be chosen as a panellist was as great, if rather more dignified, a celebrity accolade in 1960 as the front cover of *Hello!* is today. It was an accolade awarded to Lionel three times in all, the first on January 2, 1960, a week when three of the current Hit Parade hits were his own. And he went home with 30 guineas (£31.50) in his pocket.

And the work kept coming. He and Mike Pratt were hired to write songs for a movie called *The Heart Of A Man,* starring Frankie Vaughan, the larger than life Scouse crooner whose string of hits – 'Green Door', 'The Garden Of Eden', 'Kisses Sweeter Than Wine' – and liquid eyes had been making grown women swoon for nearly 10 years. Nothing of interest resulted except a long-forgotten Frankie Vaughan B-side called 'Sometime, Somewhere' and the start of a beautiful friendship between Lionel and the film's co-star, Anthony Newley.

Lionel had first encountered Newley on the cinema screen – he played the Artful Dodger in David Lean's *Oliver Twist* – and they became friends in the late Fifties, but it was 1960 before they had a chance to work properly together.

Warwick Films was a company run by partners Irving Allen and Albert 'Cubby' Broccoli. Eventually the partnership split when Cubby cosied up to Harry Saltzman, who owned the rights to the James Bond books, and made several fortunes. While it lasted, though, Warwick made some very respectable war films – *The Red Beret, The Cockleshell Heroes* – as well as the

Afghan adventures of *Zarak* (PILLAGE! PLUNDER! PASSION!) and the savage saga of *Odongo* (JUNGLE LOVE! JUNGLE THRILLS!).

In the spring of 1959, Allen and Broccoli had a surprise hit with a comedy, *Idol On Parade*, the tale of rock'n'roll star Jeep Jackson – played by Anthony Newley – and his conscription into the British army. Along with Newley, it co-starred Lionel Jeffries, Anne Aubrey, Sid James and the apparently omnipresent Bernie Winters.

Newley's idiosyncratic singing style – the role model for David Bowie's early Sarf London drawl – won him a contract with Decca and resulted in a string of hip hits. Early in 1960, his cover of Frankie Avalon's 'Why?' spent four weeks at number one.

Irving Allen was the lucky man who had Newley under contract so cashed in with a string of hastily made follow-ups to *Idol On Parade*. The first was *Jazz Boat*, starring much the same dream team – Newley, Aubrey, Jeffries and Bernie Winters, minus Sid James, but plus James Booth, star of *Fings Ain't Wot They Used T'Be*. The songs, provided by Joe Henderson, are perfectly serviceable but do little to exploit or explore Newley's vocal quirks.

For the third film, *Let's Get Married*, Newley recruited the more simpatico Lionel. "He'd come up to my drum and we'd think of some expression, like, 'I don't wish to know that – kindly leave the stage,' or, 'You're joking, of course.' Expressions that were happening around that time, that were hip," said Lionel. "And one of them was 'Do you mind?' And I thought that's not a bad song title, and I wrote this song, 'Do You Mind?'"

Recorded in March 1960, 'Do You Mind?' takes all the lessons about simplicity learned from the success of 'Living Doll' several steps closer to the Buddhist state of sunyata. It's minimalism, years before its time. It begins a capella. After the first line, Lionel himself joins in with finger clicks – the actual sound of one hand clapping. The two guitar players, drummer and double bass, when they eventually make their presence felt, are clearly under instructions not to put themselves out. Like 'Living Doll', 'Do You Mind?' dispenses with the extravagance of a second or third verse and instead repeats the first verse three times, alternating the repetitions with a bridge section. The tune is a nine-note phrase made up of just four different notes repeated with very little variation until it sticks. The bridge modestly wails in a way that, in comparison with the restraint of the verse, comes across like an explosion of passion.

For a while, in April 1960, 'Little White Bull', 'Do You Mind?', two versions of 'Fings' – one by Max Bygraves, the other a Russ Conway instrumental – and Adam Faith's 'Someone Else's Baby' with 'Big Time' (also from *Fings*) on the B–side, were all slugging it out in the same top 40. 'Do You Mind?' triumphed and became Lionel's second number one.

The following year, Newley scored a massive theatrical success on both sides of the Atlantic with *Stop The World – I Want To Get Off*, a show he wrote with Leslie Bricusse. One story has it that the title came from graffito. Lionel knew better. "You know, we used to come and swap song titles," he said, "and [Tony] was after doing something that involved four dancers – four girls – and himself going through a quest for life and – it seems what they were actually doing was *Peer Gynt* – and 'Stop The World – I Want To Get Off' was a title I was playing around with myself for a song and – if my memory serves me right – we decided to swallow it as a song and let him have it as a title for his show (chuckle). Tony might remember that differently."

As if this were not enough achievement for a single man in a single year (and we haven't even started on *Oliver!* yet), Lionel, by way of a retrospective, also released an LP of himself singing a selection of his works, with arrangements by Laurie Johnson. Called *Bart For Bart's Sake*, and including *Goon Show*-type jokey bits – "Side Two, or Side One if you play it first, you mad, controversial thing you" – it features songs from *Fings* and *Lock Up*, plus 'Newmarket Nightmare', the song that put the cat among the Stalinists at Unity, a couple of Noël Coward–ish cabaret–ish numbers and a delightful delve into modest filth called 'Why Can't We Do What Mr Kinsey Says'.

Gramophone magazine said, "The performance is bright and uninhibited but the style is limited, the best thing about it is the accompaniment directed, quite brilliantly, by Laurie Johnson."

Lionel can barely have noticed this or any other review. By the time they hit the newsstands, he was busy, busy, busy again, this time creating his masterpiece.

Eight

"WHEN I was a young kid in the East End," said Lionel, "there was a little sweet shop opposite our house where you could get a chocolate bar with a toffee in it for a penny. It was called 'Oliver', and the wrapper around it had a picture of a lad asking for more."

Lionel – accounts vary – never read Dickens' book, so the story behind the chocolate bar was first revealed when he and John Gorman, two National Servicemen bunking off, saw the David Lean film. Its plot – the one largely adopted by Lionel – is a significant improvement on Dickens' version, most notably in its masterly editing of tosh and its rewrite to keep Oliver central to the action right up until the end.

"I became enchanted with the story," Lionel told the *Daily Express* in 1994[45]. Key songs seemed to arrive in his brain uninvited. "First one I actually wrote was 'Where Is Love?' I was in my car, returning from somewhere. I have never spent more than an hour on a tune. Songs should be like sneezes. Spontaneous."

A sheaf of typewritten notes, heavily annotated in pencil, undated but clearly from a very early stage of the writing process, establishes that the outline of the scenes and the placing of songs were there from the start. In these notes, the only song in its final form is 'Where Is Love?' Others have either generic titles – 'Beery, Bawdy Song' – or working titles and a few sketchy lyrics. The opening, for instance, is the same procession of hungry boys in the workhouse, but instead of 'Food Glorious Food' he introduces a song with the working title, 'There's Gonna Be A Change In The Workhouse': "Gruel, gruel / it's wicked, it's cruel / Three times a day every day of the year / An onion twice a week / And half a roll on Sundays / There's gonna be a change in the workhouse / It's gonna be meat pies, chicken, gooseberry tart etc."

The bulk of the composition happened in July 1959. "I fled with a mate to a little fishing village in Spain called Los Boliches near Torremolinos, and I went with one brown Italian cotton suit and I rented a place for about £2 a week with a maid. And I wrote *Oliver!* there [. . .] all the Fagin material and the songs and the ballad 'As Long As He Needs Me', which I suppose is about my own dying love, but then I heard a little Spanish urchin on a beach singing 'Living Doll' in Spanish. And I thought bloody hell, what is that tune? And by coincidence, which I prefer these days not to call coincidences, I was discovered by a cub reporter for the *Daily Mirror* who said that 'Living Doll' had been such a success and you should come back."

He also received a letter from his secretary, Joan Maitland.

Dear Li,

LIVING DOLL NO 1 ......!!!!!

Hal thinks the sheet music sales will also go to number one . . . Hail to Britain's leading composer.

"When I came home, I made a demo tape of the songs. I hawked them around various theatre companies and impresarios, but they all turned me down. They said that, with it being full of orphans and workhouses, it was much too downbeat."

Twelve managements turned it down, including Joan Littlewood and Gerry Raffles at Stratford East. Peter Rogers, executive producer on *The Tommy Steele Story*, turned it down as a movie idea with Tommy playing the Artful Dodger. When Lionel played the tape to Jack Hylton, biggest of all the producers, Jack fell quietly asleep. Another, unnamed producer thought it needed a gimmick and ". . . suggested in all seriousness that we should consider using an all black cast. At that point I had seriously to consider his suggestion."

The difficulty of the sell was perhaps a reflection not so much on Lionel's work as on the state of the British musical. In 1960, new musicals came and went with breathtaking speed, leaving the twitching corpses of flops knee deep all over the West End: *When In Rome, Kookaburra, Johnny The Priest, The Dancing Heiress* all opened and closed, some faster than a blinking eye, some kept on life support for weeks before the kind thing was done. Even the more successful shows – Julian Slade's *Follow That Girl*, Wildeblood and Greenwell's *The Crooked Mile* – succumbed to the inescapable malaise. The public did not want the kind of musicals it was being given, and possibly did not want musicals at all.

Oliver! eventually found its way to the desk of Donald Albery, scion of a theatrical dynasty and owner of four West End theatres. Albery had earned himself a reputation for bringing experimental productions – most notably Samuel Beckett's *Waiting For Godot* – into the West End and making them pay. He had already worked closely with Joan Littlewood and Gerry

Raffles, engineering the transfers of *A Taste Of Honey* and *The Hostage*, and reckoned that, if he screwed the costs down, he could stage *Oliver!* for £15,000.

Albery's first choice to direct *Oliver!* was Joan Littlewood. With too many irons in the fire already and not much of a taste for fancy West End formalities, she turned it down. Another idea was to give it to Vida Hope, an old pal of Lionel's from the Unity days whose direction of Sandy Wilson's *The Boy Friend* helped it towards a 2,000-performance run in the West End and another 500 on Broadway. The safest suggestion, and the one Albery finally settled on, was the tried and tested *Lock Up Your Daughters* team of director Peter Coe and designer Sean Kenny.

"Coe had an enormous ego," says Lionel in a private memoir. "He always used to dictate that his name was in a box on all the posters and he always had my stage directions struck out of the script. Directors as a rule don't like the writer's stage directions especially when they're as detailed as mine used to be. He used a lot of them, but he didn't have them on the actor's script – that's a real ego thing."

Kenny was an Irishman straight from the pages of the *Táin Bó Cúailnge*, who could enchant with his glowing heart and reverent credulity, drink oceans, eat herds, and, when roused to battle, build walls of corpses. The eldest of nine Tipperary brothers, he trained in Dublin as an architect, then kitted out a 30-foot shrimper and, with three friends, set sail for America. They survived a hurricane. Maybe Sean ate it.

In America he sought out the revolutionary architect Frank Lloyd Wright.

"He was having breakfast with his students. 'I'm the man from Dublin,' I said. 'Good,' he replied. 'There's a pick and shovel outside the door. Go build your own house.'" So he did. In the shape of an umbrella.

He helped Frank Lloyd Wright design the Guggenheim Museum in New York. Many people have mentioned that the building looks like a Sean Kenny stage set, although it's hard to know who influenced whom.

Sets for a double bill of Sean O'Casey's *Shadow Of A Gunman* and Theresa Deevey's *Light Failing* at the Lyric Theatre, Hammersmith, were among his first theatre designs. They got him noticed, inevitably, by Joan Littlewood, who hired him for *The Hostage* at Stratford. Then, as already told, Bernard Miles hired him for his new Mermaid Theatre, which is where Kenny first worked with Lionel.

"Let's get the theatre out of its coffin," he said, in the programme notes for *Lock Up Your Daughters*. "Let us rebel, fight, break down, invent and reconstruct a new theatre. Let us free the theatre from the cumbersome shackles of outmoded traditions." And unlike many theatrical bigmouths, Sean Kenny could walk the walk, too.

His designs are spoken of wherever theatre design is discussed as the work of God. He hated static scenery. For *Oliver!* he designed and engineered an extraordinary assemblage of rough wooden beams and blocks which moved seamlessly and apparently of their own volition, to create streets, thieves' kitchens and Regency interiors. Of the show's nightly five curtain calls, at least one was for the set.

In 1966 he married Judy Huxtable, actress, deb and model. When mutual waywardness brought that to an end, he lived with another actress, the commensurately heart-stopping Judy Geeson. But his true milieu was not the boudoir but the pub. He told stories. He floated ideas. In the early Seventies he dreamed of laser palaces with David Bowie and would have built them, too, except that death took him, at the improbably young age of 40, in 1973. Lionel adored him.

Lionel's original casting suggestion for Nancy was his good friend Alma Cogan, the 'girl with the giggle in her voice'. Alma was an immensely popular singer, mostly of novelty songs, whose presence in the cast would have guaranteed ticket sales. But even if Alma could have summoned the gravitas required for poor, defiant Nancy, the baggage she brought to the proceedings would always have been a problem. An audience that is secretly baying for 'Never Do A Tango With An Eskimo' in the midst of 'As Long As He Needs Me' is an audience that has, quite literally, lost the plot.

Auditions were held at Wyndham's Theatre, owned by the Alberys. Lionel sat in the middle of the stalls with Peter Coe. A young singer walked on to the stage and said her name was Georgia Brown.

"No you're not. You're Lilian Klot," came a voice from the darkness. She and Lionel were from the same streets. They'd known each other when they were kids.

Georgia Brown/Lilian Klot was a jazz singer who had caused something of a stir when she took the role of Lucy Brown in the 1956 Royal Court production of Bertolt Brecht and Kurt Weill's *The Threepenny Opera*. In the following year she replaced Bea Arthur in the New York production of the same show, which starred Weill's wife, Lotte Lenya, as Jenny. Though lacking the celeb status of Alma Cogan, there was no doubting her A-list credentials as a performer, and after she'd belted out an impressive audition there was no doubting she was Nancy either.

Fagin was more of a problem. Again, the box-office benefits of a big star name could not be ignored, but Rex Harrison, Sid James and Peter Sellers all turned the part down. Lionel was keen on Max Bygraves, who'd had a hit with the bowdlerised version of 'Fings Ain't Wot They Used T'Be'. Like Alma, he was best known for novelty songs, raising the alarming possibility of an audience pining for 'Never Do A Tango With An Eskimo' in the Nancy scenes while hankering in the Fagin scenes for Max's ever-popular 'Gilly Gilly Ossenfeffer Katzenellen Bogen By The Sea'.

Ron Moody caught the theatre bug doing student revues at the London School of Economics and then formed an association with the writer Peter Myers, appearing in a series of revues – *Intimacy At Eight*, *For Amusement Only*, *For Adults Only* – establishing himself as a versatile actor, comedian, mime and singer who could negotiate an operatic aria as deftly as a knees-up. A self-confessed workaholic, he often ran from the theatre as soon as the curtain came down to do a nightclub cabaret spot. In 1958, his skill as a vocal mimic led him to the High Court of Justice as a witness in the matter of *Sim v. H.J.Heinz Co. Ltd and Another*. The case, one of the earliest of its kind, revolved around Ron's impersonation of the cadaverous actor Alistair Sim in a baked bean advert. Sim believed that "if he allowed his voice to be used in this way he was doing something beneath his dignity as an actor". Moody acknowledged that "in the past [he] had given performances in which he simulated the voice of Mr Sim" but denied that he had used his impersonation on this occasion. Sim's request for an injunction was refused: a legal triumph for the freedom of the bean.

In 1959, Ron went legit in the first London production of Leonard Bernstein's *Candide*, a work generally considered a musical triumph but a cruel disappointment if you're expecting another *West Side Story*. *The Times* called it "flat-footed" but was impressed by Ron's performance as the Governor of Buenos Aires.

Gerry Raffles got in touch with Ron to discuss the possibility of his coming into *Fings*. During the course of the discussion, *Oliver!* was mentioned. Ron's agent got in touch with Peter Coe and an audition was arranged.

Ron did his cabaret act, then read through one of Fagin's scenes. "I told him [Coe] I didn't know what to do except to imitate Alec Guinness's towering performance in the film," Moody says in his memoir *A Still Untitled (Not Quite) Autobiography*[46], "and he said I should do that and I did and still he looked interested." Asked to sing something, he treated them to a full-on operatic romp through *Nessun Dorma*. "Vincero," he sang, climbing to the money note. "Vincero." I shall win. I shall win.

Lionel, possibly still hankering for Max Bygraves, walked out. Even more worryingly, he announced to the press that he was thinking of playing the part himself – "just for kicks".

Nevertheless, Ron was recalled. This time he did a scene with a little boy playing Oliver, learned and sang 'You've Got To Pick A Pocket Or Two' and was given the part. Moody wanted £150 a week, but would have settled for £100. Albery, still intent on bringing the whole thing in for £15,000, offered him £85, take it or leave it. Moody very reluctantly took it, although afterwards it was revised to £95.

Danny Sewell, ex-boxer, ex-Parisian nightclub bouncer, ex-South African emerald miner, brother of George and friend of Mike and Bernie Winters, was typecast as Bill Sikes. The young Michael Caine, who'd set his heart on the part, cried for a week.

After what was billed as a nationwide search for an actor over the age of 12 and under the height of four foot ten to play the title role, Keith Hamshere was chosen. Keith had once performed a song and dance routine with Old Time Music Hall star Bud Flanagan on the *Crazy Gang Show*, otherwise growing up in Ilford had been fairly uneventful.

Martin Horsey, aged 14, whose father ran a coffee stall in Bermondsey, was chosen to play the Artful Dodger.

Barry Humphries was fresh off the boat from Australia, where he'd already established himself as a Dadaist, actor, painter, writer, animateur and comedienne. He became Fagin in the 1967 revival of *Oliver!* and again in 1997, but in this first production he was cast as Mr Sowerberry, the undertaker.

Tony Robinson, *Black Adder*'s Baldrick and guiding spirit of the *Time Team*, was there, too, as one of the kids.

Rehearsals started in early May at the Mary Ward Settlement in Bloomsbury and, after a couple of weeks moved to the Prince's Theatre (now the Shaftesbury) where a rough mock-up of the set had been erected. Although the hours were long, Peter Coe's command of logistics meant that the marshalling of 16 principles, nine 'workhouse boys and Fagin's gang' and 12 'Londoners' on and around the huge set took place with military efficiency.

Changes were made. When the Act I finale needed beefing up, Lionel produced a new song – or rather he recycled one: the tune of 'Be Back Soon' had made its first appearance, with the title 'Be A Man John Bull', years earlier in the Unity Theatre production of *Cinderella*.

Much rehearsal time was spent trying to pitch the mood of the piece, to adjust the balance of comedy and melodrama, and to find the characters. Is Nancy a downtrodden bimbo or a gutsy survivor? Should Fagin be played evil or a comedy rogue, or can he be both? Ron Moody's memoir gives a blow-by-blow account of the process: "However much of a clown Fagin might be, a mushroom cloud of panic would explode within him at the merest threat of the 'drop' [the gallows]. The deep, deep dread that if Oliver 'peaches' [informs], they're all dead! A whole piece of Fagin's character had fallen into place."

But the same pages also reveal a major flaw in the conception and structure of *Oliver!* that might have been the making of it, but occasionally threatened to reduce the whole production to a seething mush. *Oliver!* had two leading roles. There's nothing dramatically wrong with having two leads in a show, but it's dicey. Even dicier is a situation in which it's uncertain whether there are in fact two leads or one lead and a support and, if so, which is which? Nancy or Fagin? The rivalry between Moody and Brown grew first into a feud, then into a full-scale war of attrition.

"Joan Thring [publicist] comes in with the press photographers to have publicity for Georgia and the kids," Ron records in his diary for May 17, 1960.

"What is this? The Georgia Brown show? They don't want Moody and we haven't started yet?" The possible advantages of the burgeoning rivalry are apparent in the next line. "Ah, well, it's the notices that will count, so I must just concentrate on working hard!"

The root of the problem seems to have been Ron's wish to work with somebody less "intense and heavy" than Georgia, and – she never kept a diary so this is to some extent guesswork – Georgia's impatience with Ron's mercurial ad libs and extra bits of business. "I just didn't take to Georgia," Ron says. "It happens in shows. A show is like a small village with gossiping neighbours." And as time went on the village grew less like Camberwick Green and more like Midwich, Village of the Damned.

It is customary for a new musical to 'try-out' in the provinces – sometimes in a couple of different theatres – before coming into the West End, allowing time for problems to be ironed out and cuts and changes to be made before fully exposing its underbelly to the fangs of the big-time critics. Even if it had been financially viable to dismantle and erect Sean Kenny's massive set, there were few stages in the country big enough, and with the right sort of machinery to contain it. The Wimbledon Theatre had one such. For its try-out, *Oliver!* was given just two weeks at Wimbledon. The west London location screwed costs down further by doing away with the hotel bills that come with a show on the road.

As soon as rehearsals moved down to Wimbledon and the cast saw the set for the first time in its full glory, and saw how the moves and routines they'd worked out at the Prince's came to life, and felt the flow of the music, and the magnificence of Eric Roger's orchestrations, the buzz started to grow as well as the inevitable doubts – is it this good? Are we fooling ourselves?

John Junkin, a friend of Lionel's from Theatre Workshop at Stratford East who later appeared in *Maggie May*, recalled going back after the first try-out.

"Some friends, I think from the Workshop, asked me if I wanted to come down to Wimbledon to see Lionel's new show. So we went down to this large barn like place – I think it had been an old musical hall theatre – not knowing what was going on and suddenly this incredible piece of magic started. We sat there with this lovely tingly feeling – like goose bumps – coming over us. As it went on you got higher and higher, the songs, I remember, hitting you like blows – 'Food Glorious Food', 'Who Will Buy?', 'As Long As He Needs Me' – two great numbers by Ron Moody as Fagin – 'You've Got To Pick A Pocket Or Two' and my favourite 'Reviewing The Situation'. And it built and built. Wonderful sets – wonderfully different approach to musical theatre. And at the end of it we went back – there was a very basic canteen backstage – and when we got there they were all huddled together, Georgia Brown and Ron and Lionel and everyone and I can remember their almost disbelief when we rushed in and almost erupted with the praise, pouring out. They said, 'Is it really that good?' They didn't realise because they got too close to it in the development. Even Lionel, not a man renowned for his lack of confidence, was very tentative in accepting our praise. But we were right – they went in at their peak and it was obviously a hit."

Despite the general high, changes continued to be made. Mostly they were small. The ovation given to 'You've Got To Pick A Pocket Or Two' created an eggy moment, with Ron and the lads standing onstage trying to stay in character while the applause thundered on, then recovering themselves sufficiently to carry on with the action. Accordingly the song was moved to the end of the scene, allowing the applause to take its natural course. Other changes were more radical. To cover a possible technical hold up in Act I, Lionel provided a whole new song – 'That's Your Funeral' – for the Sowerberrys and Mr Bumble. It's not one of his best and although, "Then the coffin, lined with satin / Large enough to wear your hat in," usually raises a smile, Mr Bumble's line "I don't think this song is funny" indicates the general view.

Lionel the "artistic genius whose talent must be nurtured". (COURTESY THE LIONEL BART FOUNDATION)

Thinking about Nietzsche, angst and frothy coffee, early 1950s. (COURTESY LIONEL BART FOUNDATION)

With John Gorman, outside G&B Arts, with hope in their hearts and holes in their shoes. (COURTESY JON GORMAN)

"Who ran away with the blind man's hat? Meatface." *Fings Ain't Wot They Used T'Be*, 1959. (COURTESY THE LIONEL BART FOUNDATION)

The late Fifties intellectual. (COURTESY THE LIONEL BART FOUNDATION)

Reinventing theatre and knitwear with Joan Littlewood. (COURTESY THE LIONEL BART FOUNDATION)

The ladies' man (1) with Alma Cogan and matching teacups, 1961.
(HARRY HAMMOND/COURTESY THE LIONEL BART FOUNDATION)

The ladies' man (2) with Georgia Brown and matching macs, 1962.
(DEZO HOFFMANN/REX FEATURES)

Reinventing youth culture with Tommy and Anne Steele, and Jess Conrad, 1959. (COURTESY THE LIONEL BART FOUNDATION)

Reinventing menswear with Robbie Stanford, 1963. (COURTESY THE LIONEL BART FOUNDATION)

Congratulating old pal John Gorman on his uncanny likeness to Rolf Harris, mid-1960s. (COURTESY JON GORMAN)

With Cliff, studying a photo-strip based on a song he wrote for Tommy Steele in a comic possibly called *Marty*, 1959. (COURTESY THE LIONEL BART FOUNDATION)

Picking a winner with Frank Norman and cap, 1959. (IDA KAR/NATIONAL PORTRAIT GALLERY)

"Stick to the white notes." The one-fingered pianist with Marty Wilde, 1960. (PICTORIAL PRESS)

Playing "rock , paper, scissors" with Judy Garland and a perplexed Noel Coward at the *Maggie May* first night party, 1964. (DAILY MAIL/REX FEATURES)

Lunching with John Lennon, 1964. (EVENING NEWS/REX FEATURES)

"Mucking in with the family." With Mick Jagger, 1964. (TERRY O'NEILL/REX FEATURES)

The ladies' man (3) with Marianne Faithfull and matching secret smiles, Savoy Theatre, 1964. (BENTLEY ARCHIVE/POPPERFOTO)

Lionel, while *Twang!!* crumbled around him, banging the drum in celebration of *Oliver!* becoming Britain longest-running musical, 1965. (TRINITY MIRROR/MIRRORPIX/ALAMY)

The Moody Man of Mohair with his original nose. (COURTESY THE LIONEL BART FOUNDATION)

The score as a whole, though, has become entwined in our DNA. Stop strangers in the street and ask them to sing a song from *Oliver!* Most will at least be able to hum the first line of 'As Long As He Needs Me'. Some will manage a fair chunk of 'Consider Yourself' and a small, but pleasing minority will sing through the entire score with great glee and gusto while buses are missed and banks go bust.

As anyone will know who's seen a school production performed by tone deaf Goths accompanied by the poor mad music teacher exacting yet more revenge on a broken piano and still been thrilled, the songs are bulletproof. Lionel has taken the *Wally Pone* advice to boost the Old Time Music Hall more to heart than ever. These are songs that demand thumbs to be shoved under braces and winks to be bitten off.

When the actor Dudley Sutton began to write songs of his own, he sought Lionel's advice. "Stick to the white notes, Duddles," Lionel told him. "The black notes are only there to get you out of trouble." For most of the *Oliver!* score, Lionel either ignored his own advice or courted trouble.

'Where Is Love?', the song that came to Lionel while he was driving, "like a sneeze, spontaneous", was the root from which all the others sprang. "It's the premise of the piece," he said in a private memoir. "In a way they're all searching for love and I did try to put a third dimension on to Fagin who is also searching for love. I'd read a book about Charles Dickens by that time, about his own life and how he was searching for love which he didn't really find."

For the first five bars it adheres rigorously to the 'white notes' rule. Then it strays further and further, exploring the outer limits of the black notes before coming, quite suddenly, home.

Ray Lamb, Head of Music at the Sylvia Young Theatre School, has taught 'Where Is Love?' to generations of the kids who've starred in *Oliver!* "It sounds easy," he says, "because it's a well-written song, but it isn't. There are some very unusual chord changes, and phrases that can catch you out because they're similar to other phrases but not quite the same. The range is challenging, too. A lot of the boys we find will sing up to a C, but it goes up to a D just at the end."

The lyric – Lionel preferred the more robustly Brechtian phrase 'songwords' – set the style for most of *Oliver!* by pruning back the verbal extravagance and show-off rhymes of *Lock Up Your Daughters* to plain words and simple sentiments.

Claims have been made that 'Where Is Love?' is Lionel's ultimate *cri de coeur*: that the search for true, lasting and loyal love, perhaps to compensate for a perceived lack of love in his childhood, was a lifelong obsession. The validity of the claim is incontrovertible although any notion that such an obsession made Lionel in any way unique or even unusual, or that it fuelled the engine of his creativity, is, of course, nonsense. The obsessive search for love is shared by every postman, headmistress and shepherd in the world. It does not, however, provide them with the means to write hit songs.

The related psychobabble, that starvation of affection in early childhood leads the performer to seek pseudo-love of a cheering crowd and the adulation of the masses, is one that's been applied to every entertainer since Thespis of Icaria. Admittedly, the roar of the crowd can – and often does – induce a high pleasant enough to result in dependency problems, but in the main show business is a job, not a mental illness. Those who speak direct from their hearts into the hearts of millions can do so not because they feel the pain more acutely or live closer to the edge than mere mortals, but because they're good at the job. And if they do live closer to the edge, if they drink more, snort more and fuck more than the average postman, headmistress or shepherd, it's mostly because, if they're that good, they can afford to and the opportunities present themselves more often. But the job security's rubbish.

The lyricist Gene Lees has criticised 'Where Is Love?' for stretching the first 'Whe-e-e-ere' over five notes, as if the song would be improved by changing it to, "Where on earth oh where is love", or "Where oh where oh where is love," or "Where the hell d'you think is love". As Lionel told Mark Steyn, "He should hear Johnny Mathis's cover version: at the end of it he makes about 20 syllables out of the word. I mean, what's he going to do? Start giving Handel a hard time for the *Messiah*?"

Less pedantic listeners who have no qualms about the "Whe-e-e-e-ere" might nonetheless balk at the "is it underneath the willow tree?" which, setting aside the unlikelihood of a boy born and raised in a workhouse being much cop at tree identification, does seem an alien intrusion of poshness – an evocation of Desdemona in Shakespeare's and Verdi's *Othello*, or maybe Ko-Ko's 'Tit Willow' from Gilbert & Sullivan's *The Mikado* – in the otherwise comfortingly familiar ambience of 'hot sausage and mustard.'

The technical quibbles are tosh, anyway. Oliver's in the dark, put to bed under the counter in Mr Sowerberry's shop. He's surrounded by coffins. He's afraid. He sings himself a lullaby because there's nobody else to sing it, negotiating the major sevenths and tricky modulations with his sky-clear, pitch-perfect treble. There's optimism in the tune, too, and courage as it soars bravely up to that high D. Feel free to blub and to wonder at the majesty of schmaltz.

'Consider Yourself' was another of the first batch of songs. "The moment I wrote that tune, it was in the morning," Lionel said,[47] "a lovely morning bright and sunny and my secretary had come in about 9.30. I said, 'I've got this great song where the Dodger welcomes Oliver.'" At the time, Lionel was living at Reece Mews in South Kensington. "I wanted to sing it and dance it, but the mews house itself was too small so I had to go out into the street. I knocked at my next-door-neighbour Francis Bacon's door and sang a chorus to him." Francis Bacon, then about 50 years old, is one of the most important British painters of the twentieth century. He was a heavy drinker. His reaction is unrecorded.

"I was just walking around the streets singing this daft song, adding lyrics, and it reminded me of once when I was about 12 or 13 on the way back from learning my bar mitzvah and I went off with this stick against the railings whistling and singing every bloody march I knew, and it was like Souza time really, '76 Trombones' with *The Music Man*. And that's how I felt when I wrote 'Consider Yourself'."

Some of the songs, Lionel told Mark Steyn, were composed in a *Tom And Jerryish* way, with the rhythm suggested by the character's walk. "The song 'Oliver' was really the Beadle's walk, a kind of dum-de-dum. Fagin's music was like a Jewish mother-hen clucking away."

The Fagin songs are, for obvious reasons, the most self-consciously Jewish in *Oliver!* Ron Moody detects hints of 'My Yiddishe Momme' in 'Reviewing The Situation'. The musicologist Jack Gottleib[48] finds the same song has roots in a Hebrew chant, 'Havdalah (Separation)'.

'As Long As He Needs Me' is as white-note simple as 'Do You Mind?' until the fourth line introduces the verse's sole breakout from white to black: ray, me, fah, si, soh soh, si being the black note between soh and lah. The single si, a flattened sixth, introduces a hint of the exotic. It's a gypsy note, a Hungarian note, a Jewish note. It lets the darkness in, undercutting the white note certainty of the rest of the song with a moment of doubt and pain and regret.

The lyric has the same ambiguity. This is the mixed-up manifesto of a battered wife and an anthem for all battered wives: a mess of self-justification, apology, excuses for the abuser, heartbreak and defiance, constantly shifting its point of view and mode of address, a middle-of-the-night anxious churning of the same thoughts, round and round. The first verse, "As long as he needs me / oh yes he does need me / in spite of what you see / I'm sure that he needs me", is a chant, a mantra of obsessive self-delusion. In the end it's the defiance that wins out. The hell, she's got her pride, but, God, it's vilely misplaced.

The knockout blow is delivered by the key change. The last verse goes up not a half step, not a whole step, but one-and-a-half steps, putting the singer in a new vocal range which, if the key's properly set in the first place, should be her belting range. This provides the money note – on that last 'needs' – in Georgia Brown's case a high C, which brings the audience to its feet and leaves them feeling that the ticket would have been cheap at twice the price.

Shirley Bassey's version of the song entered the hit parade in August 1960, just a couple of weeks after the show opened, and stayed there until December nestling for five weeks at number two. In September of that year Lionel chose it as his fourth choice on the radio biography-through-music show *Desert Island Discs*. He calls it his favourite song from *Oliver!* and adds, enigmatically, that he wrote it for someone very special to him. John Gorman suggests that the "someone very special" was his mother and the song is about her less than always amicable relationship with his father. This is impossible to substantiate and hard to believe – anyone who knew Yetta smiles at the idea that she might have been the victim of a bullying husband, or any other sort of victim. Lionel's claim that it was about his "his own dying love" is even more enigmatic. Love for whom?

The start of June 1960 brought terrible weather. Ascot was a washout. A hailstorm whitened the turf at Lord's and the belltower of Beccles church was struck by lightning. But towards the end of the month it brightened up. Temperatures soared to the extent that at Sheffield Assizes, Mr Justice Streatfield gave permission for counsel to remove both wigs and gowns. By the 30th, central London was a sticky, sweaty place to be.

Advance bookings for the New Theatre in St Martin's Lane (subsequently rechristened the Albery, now the Noël Coward) were disappointing: only £130 worth of seats had been sold. There were empty seats even on this, the opening night. So Lionel had every reason to sweat. Nevertheless a decent turn-out of celebs – Rex Harrison, Lionel Blair, Judy Carne, Alma Cogan, Jess Conrad, Max Bygraves, Morris and Yetta Begleiter – smiled and waved at the cameras. According to Yetta, the Duke of Windsor – formerly Edward VIII, the King who abdicated in order to marry a divorcee – was there, too; but she may have been mixing him up with Rex Harrison, the way mothers do.

Lionel betrayed his nerves in an interview, given earlier in the day to Herbert Kretzmer for the *Sunday Dispatch*, "Let me tell you, mate, if anything goes wrong on the stage tonight, I am going to walk out of the theatre and wander around Trafalgar Square until it's all over."

His 'date' that night was 'starlet' Jackie Lane, who later became one of Doctor Who's assistants and, later still, Tom Baker's agent. Lionel insisted on an aisle seat.

He had been working long hours – rehearsals, meetings, rewrites. "So, I'm tired out and I'm sitting about 12 rows back in the stalls on the aisle. [. . .] I knew the lighting and I was very good at leaving to go to the bar or whatever and then coming back without the audience or the performers seeing me. I could just do it in a moment thanks to the distraction of the lighting.

"Bearing in mind that there had been so many changes made, we had only the ten days at Wimbledon, we kind of opened cold at the New Theatre, no previews. And literally a few nights before that we had to completely change the ending of the show. After the murder at London Bridge and the chase of Bill Sikes and the dog, I'd written a scene back at the workhouse where the Artful Dodger is saved and Oliver brings him back to his benefactor with a handful of goodies for the kids, and it was a short scene with bits of reprise songs in it. Well the fact of the matter is, mechanically we couldn't strike London Bridge, so we had to kill all the bits of dialogue and sing those reprises – and that's how the sung curtain call came about, leading to the vocalised curtain calls you often see these days.

"Well, I'm in the stalls in my little escape-hatch seat and here comes the opening number."[49]

The woodwind trills. The brass undercuts it with a five-note fragment, repeated. The curtain goes up to reveal the inside of the workhouse. Over the stairway, the words "God Is Love" are cut out in crooked letters: below that is a bare wooden table flanked by benches. The orchestra settles into a walking vamp. The boys file in. The stage lightens. They sing. "Is it worth the waiting for? / if we live to eighty-four / all we ever get is grooo-el." The audience relaxes. Smiles break out. By the time Oliver asks for more, it looked like everything was going to be okay.

". . . and straight into the next scene which is when they capture Oliver and put him in a cell. And onto the next little domestic scene between Bumble and the widow at the workhouse and a song called 'I Shall Scream'. One of the twin revolves is supposed to come forward a bit to establish a domestic scene, and that little domestic scene revolve didn't come as far as it was meant to. I should think the only people who knew were the actors, myself, Sean Kenny and the director. But I thought doom and disaster were about to take place and that was my cue. Under cover of darkness, I raised myself to a stoop, eased my seat up, and fled quietly into the street. I went to see old Nelson in Trafalgar Square."

Lionel also went around the corner to the Garrick where *Fings* was still playing and, jumpy and restless, popped in to see Barbara Windsor who did her best, in between her own entrances and exits, to calm him down.

"I came back down St Martin's Lane and as I was approaching the New Theatre I heard this rumbling noise. The nearer I got, the more threatening it sounded. And it was coming from the theatre itself, as ominous as any mob noise sounds: Ban the Bomb, Zeig Heil, whatever. And I thought, 'They think it's bloody awful.' And at that moment Donald Albery, the owner came hobbling towards me." Albery had a wooden leg. "And naturally enough I presumed he was trying to take me away from danger – but following him was a very tall commissionaire with the gold braid and the hat and all the ushers and usherettes and I thought, 'There's been a disaster here' and I tried to rush back to Trafalgar Square. They grabbed me and said, 'You've got to go in,' and I said, 'I'm not going in there,' and I was actually forced out of the wings to an absolute uproar. The company were all onstage. I didn't know they'd already taken about 23 curtain calls. They'd sung all the reprises of 'Consider Yourself', the house lights were up in the theatre, the entire audience was standing, and it wasn't an organised clapped standing ovation, you knew it was genuine. I was just pushed onto the stage and I didn't know whether to sing or whether they'd sung the songs, and everybody was baying, 'Speech, speech, Author'."

There are several contenders for the title "Pinnacle Moment In The Life Of Lionel Bart". This is the first.

"My mum was in, on that first night, out in the dress circle. So I thanked her and I thanked Charles Dickens. I remember shouting something like, 'Thank you mum. Thank you Charles.' Though, according to the newspapers, I managed to shout, 'May the Good Dickens forgive us.' To which a voice from the gallery riposted, 'You've done a wonderful job.' And at that minute the band started again. The company all sang 'Consider Yourself', but still the audience wouldn't leave, and in the end the entire stalls, or as many of them as could, came up onto the stage. I've never seen it happen before or since except when they did it in *Hair*. Just went on and on. I don't remember too much more about that night because it was just loads of faces – joyous faces is all I can remember."

"What a night!" Ron Moody recorded in his diary. "I don't think I've ever felt so relaxed and at home onstage. The show has a smash hit reception with 17 curtain calls, Lionel Bart makes a speech and I feel for him! Little Yiddle makes big time! And I have a great cheer at the end, establishing me, in all humility as the star of the show. [. . .] We moved around backstage in a force field that crackled and fizzed around us."

Herbert Kretzmer, journalist and lyricist, was in on the excitement, too. "Bart stood backstage at the New Theatre being kissed, back-slapped and hand pumped in a delirium of congratulation after one of the most ecstatic first night receptions London has witnessed since *Oklahoma!* came to town. Bart accepted the idolatry with a series of thin, nervous grins. Sweat filmed his forehead. He glistened like a garden gnome after a shower."

The next morning word had got round. The box office took £600 before lunch.

Plaudit war broke out among the critics. *The Daily Herald* splashed, "Oliver Twist? Give me More!" *The Sketch* noted there was, "A warming wonderful thing to hear last night – resounding, uproarious cheers for a British musical." Milton Shulman in the *Evening Standard* praised Bart's "zestful and unabashed blending of Tin Pan Alley, Yiddish folk melodies and the rhythms of the Old Kent Road. They not only buttonhole you; they practically slug you." The *Daily Mail* declared that the music had "the vivacity of a cockney Offenbach, the grace and simplicity of early Rodgers". The *Mail* and the *Standard* both praised the "sweet-looking, sweetly singing" and "cherubic" 13-year-old Keith Hamshere. Everybody agreed that the set was perfect for what *Tatler* described as "a roaring transpontine melodrama". Equally unanimous was the praise for Ron Moody: "exemplary – like Ivan the Terrible in a ginger wig," (*The Observer*); "a dustbin Boris Godunov, a kitchen sink Rasputin," (*Daily Mail*).

Only *The Guardian*'s Philip Hope-Wallace bucked the trend, sneering that it had "the atmosphere of the London Christmas matinee", and though he conceded that it had "a certain gutter-sparrow charm", his summary called it "a sad disappointment, a starveling musical from the workhouse".

Noël Coward recorded in his diary for Sunday July 31, 1960: "I saw *Oliver!*, the new musical of Oliver Twist, and found it really remarkable. The best English musical I've seen for years. The boys are wonderful and Miss Georgia Brown a whacking new star. Production and lighting beyond praise, lyrics bit weak, but music charming and cheerfully devoid of imitated Americanisms. It was a thoroughly rewarding evening."[50]

"I didn't wait up for the reviews that night," Lionel said. "But I do recall waking up the next morning in bed at Reece Mews where my staff just brought all the morning papers in to me. The phone never stopped, and I guessed I realised then that I'd made my niche somewhere and it probably began to dawn on me that I was famous."

The cracking and fizzing of the forcefield, the resounding, uproarious cheers and the transpontine roar did nothing to still the insistent clamour of war. Fagin and Nancy. Moody and Brown. Bayonets were sharpened. Artillery summoned.

The *casus belli* was summarised in an interview Ron Moody gave to *The Times*. "For me, making the show work was getting belly laughs – like most variety artists. But the straight actor believes you fix your performance in rehearsal and that's it. [. . .] And I kept developing Fagin, changing Lionel's words until I got the laughs. So he got cross with me. He said: 'You have to change the words back to how they were on the first night.' I said: 'If you do that, you won't get any laughs.' Instead of being grateful, Lionel was offended.

"Georgia Brown, who played Nancy, did not appreciate my improvisation. In fact, she was very hostile to it. Now I can see I was at fault for not being more considerate, but when we were doing the show I didn't think it was my job to be considerate to other people. My job was to make the show work. When I look back, I think I could have been kinder. I don't really like how I was then."

Each engagement is forensically analysed in Ron's diary, liberally referred to in his *A Still Untitled (Not Quite) Autobiography*.

"October 6th: Georgia does all she can to kill my laughs; let her do what she likes. She can't win."

"It was the comedian versus the method actor; the anarchist versus the neurotic. The buzz of hate between us was brilliant for the show."

As the battleground moved increasingly to the stage and the antagonists trod on lines and sabotaged business, the benefits of hate became less apparent. At one point Donald Albery called in a representative from the Independent Theatre Council to help negotiate a peace settlement, threatening disciplinary action unless hostilities were at least scaled down.

An uneasy peace descended only when Ron's involvement in his own TV show made him too busy to care. He left the production a few weeks later, a year, almost to the day, after its opening.

That first production of *Oliver!* ran in the West End for 2,618 performances, the record for a British musical until *Jesus Christ Superstar*.

Where there's a hit there's a writ. Peter Maurice, the publisher of Lionel's Tommy Steele songs was among the first to weigh in hoping for a piece of *Oliver!*, claiming 50 per cent of the royalties on the grounds that Lionel wrote *Oliver!* while he was still under contract to Maurice. This was a matter of lawyers and letters and contracts that didn't much concern Lionel. More damaging to his reputation were the accusations of plagiarism.

In America, Ira B. Arnstein, described by Jack Gottlieb as "a crackpot composer", brought obsessive plagiarism suits against popular composers, including five against Cole Porter. Lionel was, on several occasions, threatened with copyright suits, sometimes by spurned lovers trying to get even, or chancers looking to make a few quid, sometimes with more justification. There are just 12 notes in the chromatic scale, eight if you "stick to the white notes". The permutations that make musical sense are even more finite. Statistics alone are enough to ensure that the same combinations of notes will crop up time and time again. If the composer is deliberately writing within a genre, it's even more likely. The first line of Lennon and McCartney's 'Can't Buy Me Love' is just a breath away from George Shearing's 'Lullaby Of Birdland'. The first five notes of Clare and Conrad's 'Ma He's Making Eyes At Me' are identical to 'Un bel dì', Cio-Cio San's aria from Puccini's *Madama Butterfly*.

Keith Richards, of The Rolling Stones, talks about the songwriting process as identifying a hole where the song should be – as if the entire canon of world music is a huge jigsaw puzzle and the composer's job is merely to identify and manufacture the missing pieces. 'Yesterday' came to Paul McCartney pretty much in a dream. At first he was reluctant to claim ownership, convinced it was merely a tune he'd remembered but couldn't quite place. He played it to everyone he met, including Lionel, asking them to identify it. Good tunes are like that. They sound as if they've always been there.

There are murkier reasons, too, for the accusations of plagiarism – or at least of being "derivative" – often levelled at Lionel.

James McConnel, the pianist and composer who worked with Lionel in the Eighties and Nineties, detects snobbery at work. The two big British musical hits of the Fifties were *The Boy Friend* by Sandy Wilson (Harrow and Oxford) and *Salad Days* by Julian Slade (Eton and Cambridge). How could it be possible that Lionel Bart (Dempsey Street Mixed Infants and St Martin's Scholarship), a slum kid who couldn't read music or even play a musical instrument, could have a bigger hit than either of them? Cheating seemed the only plausible explanation. If he's not stealing the tunes outright, he's taking proper tunes (written by properly educated pianists of good family), twisting a couple of notes and calling them his own.

On the other hand, Lionel always liked to work collaboratively, thriving on the creative buzz of bouncing ideas around, showing off his speed and versatility. Sometimes, though, he enjoyed the collaborative buzz a lot more than he did the subsequent sharing of credit.

We've already mentioned that 'Be Back Soon' was a recycled version of 'Be A Man, John Bull', the Unity song from *Cinderella* for which Lionel and Jack Grossman had provided the songs.

Jack Grossman remembers his contribution to 'Be A Man, John Bull' as being rather more than a couple of notes, but, rather than sour a friendship with unpleasantness, chose to shrug his shoulders and give Lionel the benefit of the doubt. The subject was never referred to again until, 30 years later, Jack was having dinner with Lionel.

"Lionel said, 'You know, Jack, you used to write some pretty good stuff.' And I said, 'Well, yeah, thanks very much, Lionel.' And he said, 'You know I think I pinched some of it.' I laughed and Lionel said, 'You know what? I think I stole some of my own stuff, too.' That's chutzpah, that is."

Joan Maitland, Lionel's secretary, was another pal from the Unity days. She worked with Lionel on the development of *Oliver!*, on the book, and singing the original demos of the six songs he recorded and played to Donald Albery. She could also read and write music, so provided the lead sheets.

Another Unity member, Harry Landis, says: "Joan came to me and said, 'Guess what Lionel's asked me? He wants to do a musical about Oliver Twist. He wants me to do the dialogue from the book by Dickens – the book of the show – and he's going to do the lyrics and music.'

"So they settled down and she spent weeks doing that and they got a finished product together and he presented it to Donald Albery. And of course, from Lionel's point of view, that was it. If Donald Albery's interested then it's all me. She's out of it in spite of all that work. So Joan comes to me and says, 'What am I going to do? He's trying to cut me out of it and I did all that work'. So anyway, I introduced her to some people in the business who looked after these things – some financial people – the sort of people who took 20% of your income when you got your songs published and they threatened him with the courts. The last thing he wanted was it out in the open because he didn't want anyone anywhere ever to think of that, so he did a deal with these people. It came to a lot of money. Next thing I know I get £300 in tenners in an envelope from Joan to say thank you very much."

It has to be said that Harry's love for Lionel – for all sorts of reasons personal and political – is less than unconditional. Other, possibly more reliable sources, including John Gold, the lawyer who administers Lionel's estate, have suggested that Joan typed out some of the dialogue from the book, wrote out the lead sheets and so, in recognition of her contribution, Lionel gave her a cut of the show, which her family still receives. The truth probably lies somewhere in between the two. Certainly the event caused no permanent enmity between Lionel and Joan. She happily came to the first night of *Oliver!*, wrote the book – with full credit – for *Blitz!* and later, with her husband Jack Maitland, provided the book and lyrics for the musical version of *Tom Brown's Schooldays* which enjoyed a short but respectable West End run in 1972.

In Lionel's *Desert Island Discs*, Roy Plomley, the urbane host, remarks that Lionel was the first man to write book, lyrics and music for a West End show since Ivor Novello. In reply, Lionel goes a little vague and mumbles something about not being all that genned up about theatrical history.

Claimants to Lionel's copyrights are emerging all the time. "There was a chap, he was a chiropodist in Barnet," says Marty Wilde. "I can't remember his name but he was a stunning chiropodist and one day he's doing my feet and he said, 'Erm you knew Lionel Bart didn't you, Marty?' So I said, 'Yes, I did.' So he said, 'I used to write the music for him.'"

Turns out that Lionel used to use the same chiropodist and, while chatting one day, discovered that the chiropodist played a bit of piano, so while the feet were soaking, he took to dictating his latest melodies for transcription. The honourable chiropodist was not claiming copyright, but all the same leaving relative strangers with your unpublished works written in their hand is an open invitation for lawyers to come and take your trousers off you.

When the initial *Oliver!* hysteria was over, and the critics had put their plaudits away, and the audiences had booked all the seats for months ahead, and the cast had grown tired of bowing, Lionel sat down and wrote his thank you letters.

To Peter Coe, he wrote: "Now that the critics have stopped chirping, let me thank you for having so much patience with the most meddlesome author and composer since W.S. Gilbert or Sean O'Casey. Everyone says we are a great team so I guess we must be pretty useful. Here's to the next battle. Take a good holiday and forget *Oliver!*"

To Sean Kenny he wrote: "Now we have both been recognised as geniuses by the people who've given themselves the authority to recognise genius, may I say that I knew before them and, if anybody deserves that sort of label, you do. Let me join in the tribute to the greatest stage designer in the world. If you refuse to do my next show, I'm retiring. Much love, Lionel Bart."

Sean did work on the next show. And the one after that. But not the one after that – and that was the one that came close to forcing Lionel into retirement.

Nine

*F*INGS had made Lionel man-of-the-moment: *Oliver!* made him a certified A-lister, courted by the glitterati.

We find him, for instance, holidaying in Cannes soon after the *Oliver!* opening, and lunching with Pablo Picasso. Did Lionel approach Pablo or Pablo approach Lionel? Picasso's passion for the bullfight is well documented, but none of his biographers mention this passion encompassing 'Little White Bull'. Picasso's English was as limited as Lionel's French, Spanish and Catalan, so how they communicated is another puzzle that will never be solved. Anyway, en route to the restaurant, they were accosted by an English teenager who recognised Lionel. "He was a pretty astute kid," said Lionel. "I thought he was on the game." The boy spun a "cock and bull story about how his parents had stranded him there". Lionel was impressed and gave the boy £30 – in 1960 a week's wages for, say, a bank manager. As Picasso and Lionel ate, they watched the boy successfully panhandle punter after punter. Eventually Lionel went over to congratulate him, get his £30 back, and tell him, "Gimme a call when you're back in London; you're a hustler and I think maybe you'll get on somewhere . . ." Three years later the boy, Andrew Loog Oldham, became the manager of The Rolling Stones. He and Lionel remained life-long friends.[51]

Despite his less than enthusiastic response to *Fings*, Noël Coward went backstage after the performance to congratulate the cast. He almost certainly went round to congratulate the cast when he went to *Oliver!*, too, joining the throng of celebrities queuing to shake hands with Georgia Brown and Ron Moody. But, strangely, neither at *Fings* nor at *Oliver!* does Noël seem to have run into Lionel – at least according to Lionel, who says of their first encounter: "I was sitting in my flat in Kensington when the phone goes and this voice says, 'Hello, this is Noël.'" The only Noël Lionel knew was Noël Harrison, the son of Rex Harrison, but the voice didn't sound right. "I said, 'Noël who?' And the voice replies, 'Coward, you cockney cunt' – which is alliteration, right? However, he said, 'Pack a toothbrush and come to Switzerland.' Which I did.'"

Amanda and Elyot swapping terse one-liners on the terrace at Deauville in Coward's *Private Lives* seems a world away in time, space and manners from Fred and Lil trading insults in *Fings*, but in fact Coward and Bart had much in common. Despite his impeccable consonants and Royal connections, Noël was the son of a not-very-successful piano salesman. His mum had to take in lodgers to make ends meet.

In his early career he'd done time as an *enfant terrible*, playing fast and loose with moral boundaries and trampling on all those bourgeois notions of good taste. His 1924 play, *The Vortex*, a sex'n'drugs'n'Oedipal-overtones shocker, was accused of "assailing the moral welfare of the nation" and being a threat to public order, and was granted a licence only after Noël had personally charmed the scowl off the Lord Chamberlain at a private meeting.

Both Lionel and Noël were multi-taskers, although Noël added actor and singer to the roster of writer, composer and lyricist they shared. Neither had received much in the way of formal musical training. Noël could busk at the piano using several fingers at a time but, like Lionel, usually used an amanuensis to write down his tunes and make sense of the harmonies.

Both were gay and both shared a taste for sharp dressing, fancy smells, civil behaviour and filthy talk.

Before 1967, being gay was a complex and dangerous business. If the police caught you at it, they'd send you, like Oscar Wilde, to prison. If you were in the public eye, you could be as camp as Liberace, and with luck your fanbase would put it down to extravagance, exuberance, theatricality. But any hint that you actually did it brought outrage and disgrace. Worst of all was the possibility that your mum and dad and your brothers and sisters might find out.

"My dad was in denial of all that," says Lionel's nephew Sammy whose dad, Harry, known as Bunny on account of his habit of rabbitting on, often had cause to worry about the welfare of his kid brother. "My mum told me a story about him. Lionel came round sometime in the Fifties, before I was born, and she said to my dad, 'I think your Lionel's . . .' – I don't know what word she would have used in them days. And dad said, 'No, no, no, my brother's not like that.' And mum said, 'I think he is.' And dad wouldn't have it at all."

Most people were brought up to understand, if they understood it at all, that arousal by your own gender was a sure sign you were a monster, a disgusting pervert. In the arts, however, particularly the coffee-bar-bohemian wing of the arts, there was something of a cachet attached to homosexuality. It meant you stood out from the ruck and probably had a good deal of angst. This didn't necessarily mean you were considered any less of a 'disgusting pervert', it just meant it was cool to be a 'disgusting pervert'. Still, it took bottle to own up.

At Unity, Lionel had girlfriends. Harry Landis remembers him going out with an Isobel Pepper. Muriel Walker[52], also at Unity, remembers him being very keen on a friend of hers. On the Soho coffee bar scene he was rarely without a Windmill lovely on his arm: we've heard already of his involvement with June Wilkinson, the *Playboy* centrefold whose bongos had so frightened Cliff and The Shadows, and Anne Donoughue, the beauty that Tommy Steele married.

Indeed, many of the old Unity gang still remain sceptical about Lionel's gay credentials. Back then, according to his Unity co-writer Jack Grossman, there was, ". . . no hint. While I was at Unity with Lionel there was simply no hint whatsoever. And I don't think *he* knew." There is even a lurking suspicion, shared by Muriel Walker, that he 'assumed' the gay persona the better to fit in with the likes of Larry Parnes and thereby further his professional career. If the theory's true and he was faking it, then his deception was eminently convincing.

Eric Williams, an interior designer, raconteur and one-time gigolo, first met Lionel in 1952. He was 21 and Lionel 22. "He tried to pick me up," says Williams. "Actually I suppose he succeeded in a way. We became friends, but not in the biblical sense. I had a friend called Nick who worked on the boats and he was exceptionally handsome. And he knew Lionel very well because Lionel had been chasing him forever. He didn't get anywhere with Nick because Nick wasn't inclined that way either but he introduced me to Lionel." Lionel told Eric about his first sexual experiences with the boy in the tent at the Victoria Boys' Club camping trip. As far as Eric knows, Lionel never slept with a woman his entire life.

At Unity, Lionel did make a half-hearted attempt to come out. Harry Landis had a girlfriend back then who had a television. Lionel, tellyless at the time, used to come round to watch. One night, "He told me he thought he was gay. I said, 'Where do you get that from?'

"'I just feel it. I think I'm gay.'

"He didn't say 'gay', of course, I think he must have said 'queer'. He wanted to tell somebody that he had these inclinations and he didn't know who to tell. I played it wrongly, of course. These days you say, 'Well, if that's how you feel, go for it.' But you didn't do that in those days. You said, 'Don't be daft. Don't be silly. You're all right.'"

Jack Grossman insists that Harry also added, "Or, if you really feel like that, why don't you announce it in the *Jewish Chronicle*?"

There were few role models for the awakening homosexual. "In those far off days," said Quentin Crisp, "a homosexual was never anyone you actually knew and seldom anyone you had met." Even the more famous role models were barely recognised as such: Frankie Howerd? Who would have guessed? W.H. Auden? Never. Burgess and MacClean? What, both of 'em?

Lionel's encounter with Quentin Crisp at St Martin's must have intrigued, but the Stately Homo's full on lilac-haired resplendence required a level of full-time commitment that Lionel could never have matched.

Larry Parnes, manager of a stable of pedigree rock'n'rollers, had managed to combine – for the times – overt homosexuality with a busy schedule and regular-coloured hair. What he lacked was much in the way of taste or restraint. His mode of dress might not have passed muster at the more conservative gentlemen's clubs (Suede!! Mohair!! Baines, fetch my gun), but was conventional enough for the time.

Parnes' taste in cars and interior décor, on the other hand, would have raised eyebrows and possibly horsewhips. He liked pink. He drove a pink and grey Vauxhall Cresta. His bedroom was a riot of fluffy pink with lambskin rugs and pink lacy lampshades.

He had made a career out of finding good-looking young men, dressing them, posing them, 'grooming' them – the word was used then without the present-day connotations – for stardom. In other words, he lived in the sweetshop. To have expected restraint would have been like telling Hugh Hefner at the *Playboy* Mansion that he could look but never touch.

Muriel Walker, Larry Parnes' (and later Lionel's) secretary, enjoyed a distinguished career. She worked on Unity's in-house magazine *New Theatre* before moving to Italy, where she became the actress Anna Magnani's personal assistant. Back in England, Lionel introduced her to Larry, who was hiring. She took responsibility for the day-to-day running of the Parnes empire and the well-being of the lads in the stable. "I used to deal with the mums a lot. They were always worried. Sometimes I'd have to phone up and get insurance for the boys' cars and I'd say, 'Under 21, rock'n'roller, sports car,' and they'd laugh. There was always a troupe of boys in and out of Larry's flat, of course, but not the boys themselves. He always separated business from pleasure – road managers, perhaps, hangers on and helpers, but not the boys."

Vince Eager remembers it different. "He fancied all of us plus loads of matelots and marine boys down Piccadilly every night."

Nine

Most of Larry's stable – Tommy, Marty, Duffy Power, Dickie Pride, Joe Brown – were Londoners. If the gig was within driving distance of London, afterwards they'd go to their own or their parents' homes. Vince Eager was from Grantham in Lincolnshire. Larry was not going to put his hand in his pocket to send one individual home to Grantham. Neither was he prepared to shell out for a hotel room, so it was assumed that, when in London, Vince would stay at Larry's pink flat in Gloucester Road, Kensington. Vince at this time had but a sketchy understanding of human sexuality in all its diversity but Kenny Packwood, Marty's guitarist, took a moment to bring him up to speed on one or two points pertinent to Larry.

In those days of cramped housing and Abbot & Costello it was not considered unusual or compromising for two grown men to share a bed, so Larry's showing Vince the pink master bedroom and indicating which side of the bed was his could not in itself have been considered grounds for complaint. All the same, Vince was suspicious.

"I spent an hour and a half in the ensuite bathroom," Vince told Sue McGregor in BBC Radio 4's *The Reunion*, "and after brushing my teeth I got into the bed and what I did was very crafty for one so young. I actually got in between the top sheet and the duvet as opposed to getting in between the two sheets and I was lying there and I was scared stiff. I was shaking. And I felt this hand come across and of course it couldn't get any further because of the two sheets. And he said, 'Oh you've got the . . . er . . .' And I said, 'No, I always sleep like this.' And I grabbed one of these lacy pink bedside table lamps and I just put my hand on it. I just went like this so that he could see it. And he turned over and went to sleep. I didn't sleep all night but he did. And why he called me 'Eager' I don't know 'cos I certainly wasn't that night."

Relations became less strained when the rock'n'rollers and Mr Parnes relaxed into the roles of 'Bash Street Kids' and 'Teecher' – with Vince as 'Danny' and Billy Fury as 'Plug'.

"Billy and I created mayhem. I took it in turns with Billy to crawl into Larry's bedroom at night. He'd be in bed with some matelot or whatever and we'd sneak in on the carpet with the sheepskin rug and we'd take pound notes 'cos we wanted to go out and we didn't have any money. It was bad enough taking the money but we also took his car and the trouble with it was the gear change was on the steering wheel and I couldn't find reverse so everywhere we went we had to make sure we parked so we didn't have to reverse out."

The pink promiscuous Parnes role model could never have worked for Lionel. He was a respectable East End boy. He didn't want his parents coming round for tea and seeing pink lacy lampshades. And he was, most of the time anyway, a lover not a lurcher.

Marty Wilde first got to know the man who'd 'discovered' him when Lionel took him for a drive around the West End in the Ford Zephyr Mark II convertible (all the early rockers shared a passion for cars and can remember marques and colours with unerring accuracy), showing him his favourite theatres and clubs and buying him coffees. No pass was made or lewd talk exchanged. On the other hand, Marty also wearily remembers Lionel and Larry gossiping about boys like 'tatty schoolgirls'.

Vince Eager, asked whether Lionel ever made a pass, is quick to reply, "No, no, never," as if such an idea was absurd. But he suggests that the reason may have been not that Vince was so unattractive, or Lionel so backward in coming forward, but that Lionel's interests lay elsewhere. He was spoken for.

The object of Lionel's affections declined to be interviewed for this book, possibly preferring his grandchildren to hear reminiscences from his own lips rather than by post from Amazon, but many of Lionel's friends mention that he was a 'steady' from the late Fifties into the Sixties and may even have been the love of Lionel's life.

Few of Lionel's paintings or drawings have survived, but there is, in a private collection, a sketch he made of the young man sleeping. Its creation was clearly an act of devotion. When Lionel talks about going to Spain "with a mate" to write *Oliver!*, when he says 'As Long As He Needs Me' was written about "my own dying love", there's little doubt who he's referring to.

"There were people who came and went," says Eric Williams, "but this was the only one. It was all madness mixed up with sex and not sex and rejection and not rejection. He often didn't get anywhere with boys he fancied. Then when he started to get somewhere was when he used his celebrity and his power and money to get laid and he hated himself for that. That's not the best way to get laid. We all know that doesn't work. You might get laid, but that's not the name of the game. He never believed that he could be attractive to anybody. He never believed that anybody would ever want to go to bed with him. It was all in his mind and it was not true, but you couldn't convince him."

"He was a peculiar person," says Marty Wilde, not a man to over-dramatise. "He could be very intense. You got a tremendous sense of foreboding sometimes. He had very dark eyes and he could be this brooding person."

Anybody in search of a method for combining relatively overt homo-sexuality with public discretion, a productive career, an exuberant – camp even – sense of style that would never encompass pink fluff or lacy lampshades, a wide, nurtured and influential set of friends, a degree of control over self-doubt and depression, and the art of eloquent smoking could do no better than to study the life and work of Noël Coward. Lionel was lucky enough to study at the feet of the Master.

Following up the invitation, the "cockney cunt" travelled, with afore-mentioned boyfriend in tow, to Les Avants – otherwise known as Chalet Coward or Shilly Chalet – Noël's place near Montreux in Switzerland.

Noël Coward had been the embodiment, promoter and protector of the Noël Coward brand since the end of the First World War, when he never let his status as an unknown pauper diminish his imperious attitude towards auditions or rehearsals. With advancing years – he was 60 when he first met Lionel – the *enfant terrible* of the Twenties with the silk dressing gown, diseased morals and cocaine eyes had matured into a balding Buddha, fervid patriot and dispenser of clipped rent-a-quotes. He was also desperately unfashionable, an archetype for the smart and angry and modern of what not to be. During the Fifties he had, like Fat Elvis, wowed the supper crowds in Las Vegas with his staccato songs and untarnished charm, but he hadn't otherwise had a worthwhile hit in 15 years. He was a dinosaur and a joke, and continued to be regarded as such until the 1962 revival of his *Private Lives* began to make it okay to like Noël again.

The secret of being Noël was constant vigilance and rigorous organisa-tion. His best work, like Lionel's, was often produced in a rush – *Private Lives* was reputedly written in just four days. Noël had learned early on that the actual production of plays, songs and musicals was a relatively minor part of the job. The remaining hours and days and weeks were taken up with the daily grind of selling your work and yourself – the kind of thing that has become so familiar to the present day inhabitants of *Hello!* and *OK!*

'Branding and marketing' for Noël meant nurturing old and establishing new friends, acquaintances and contacts, attending and hosting an endless round of lunches, dinners and drinks parties, composing sheaves of letters of thanks and congratulation, and selecting thoughtful gifts. His diary entry for May 5, 1961 records encounters with "Dickie [Lord Louis Mountbatten], Walter and Biddy [Monkton], Molly Buccleuch, [Douglas] Fairbanks Jnr, Princess Margaret [the Queen's sister], Tony A-J [Armstrong-Jones, soon to be the Queen's brother-in-law], the Duchess of Kent, Irene Browne, Lionel Bart, Tony Richardson, Vivien [Leigh], Jacko [Merivale], Bobbi Helpmann [choreographer, actor and director], etc."

'Keeping the product up to date' meant seeing every new play, musical and film, being aware of every passing fad and formulating an opinion to be wittily summarised wherever hats dropped.

'Maintenance of plant and equipment' involved, as well as the time-consuming rituals of grooming and tailoring, frequent medical check-ups and cures to minimise 'down-time', and long expeditions to exotic places to reinvigorate the mental health.

Most tricky of all was the problem of 'trade secrets', the art of giving the public the complete picture they demand while remaining, where it matters, a very private person. In Noël's case this discretion was a matter of vital importance. A slip could have landed him in prison. The knack was to induce a species of Orwellian double-think. Everybody knew Noël was gay, but pretended they didn't. Or they knew, but imagined that, unlike all the other 'bad' homosexuals, he was one of the rarer examples of a 'good' homosexual – somebody who managed to love his own sex and assume many of the stereotype characteristics of the homosexual without being 'depraved' or 'monstrous'. Or best of all, they didn't want to know because it's none of their bloody business.

It was a high-wire act in which one could never quite trust the safety net. When John Gielgud fell in 1953 – arrested for 'importuning for immoral purposes' – his career was saved, in Britain at least, by the kindness of his fellow actors and the generosity of his audience. Others weren't so lucky.

Towards the end of his life, when it was legal, not to say de rigeur, to be gay, Noël was asked why he didn't formally 'come out'. "There are still a few old ladies in Worthing who don't know," he replied. More likely the old ladies knew, but would rather rummage through a knitting bag than a human soul.

The rules of celebrity were, to Noël, as a natural as breathing. It was the job he was born to, and most of the time he enjoyed it.

Another secret was acquiring the right staff. Nobody could hope to run an industry as complex and as labour intensive as Noël Coward Inc. alone. Noël was blessed with an entourage, a 'family', of efficient and loyal friends; people who, again intuitively, understood how the business worked and who were as protective of the brand as he was. That first time Lionel went to visit, the inner circle consisted of Cole 'Coley' Lesley, Graham Payn and Lorn Loraine.

The difference between Noël and Lionel was principally one of entitlement. Though both were from modest backgrounds, Noël's mother was a Captain's daughter. She knew she was 'better than this'. Her beloved Noël was groomed for stardom from birth, never doubting his right to fame, wealth, adoration and pampering. Lionel's parents were immigrants inured to the idea that every crust and every breath had to be snatched from the jaws of malevolent fate. You fight or you go under. Keep smiling, keep talking, keep moving and you're in with a chance that nobody'll notice you've strayed beyond the green baize door into the carpetted bits. All his life Lionel tried to rid himself of self-doubt and insecurity, to do away with the notion that all the other hitmakers were somehow 'proper' whereas he was just trying it on, that one day he'd be 'found out'. His friendship with Noël, along with all its other benefits, provided a comforting wodge of self-affirmation. Noël had been called 'The Master' since his twenties: Lionel seemed happy to play the acolyte.

Noël's diary for October 21, 1960 records: "Lionel Bart arrived today for the weekend. He is a curious creature, not actually very prepossessing looking but rich with talent and a certain Jewish-looking charm. In looks he reminds me of Jed Harris when younger, but with more sympathy."[53]

The comparison is not flattering. Jed Harris was a Broadway producer of "sinister looks". He reminded Noël of a praying mantis. Laurence Olivier used him as a model for his Richard III.

Nevertheless, the visit went well, despite Lionel's boyfriend having a cold, and laid the grounds for a warm friendship with Noël and Coley.

Their letters are not exchanges of carefully crafted bon mots between celebrities, written with one eye on future publication and posterity: they are prosaic, boring even, litanies of domestic and professional trivia, private jokes and schedule management. "I shall be at the Connaught from December 13th through 20th so let's hope we can meet. I long to hear about *Blitz!*"

The Master writes thank you notes as conscientiously as a well-schooled nine-year-old: for a cigarette box, a "rich, red, gorgeous script cover" and a pair of "sneaky sneakers. Absolute heaven. You are a dear kind boy. Ta muchly, love Noël."

Coley's letters are written in the comfortably suburban style of a Home Counties mum writing to an undergraduate son: "I did enjoy your visit and now that you know the way you must come again as they say. I do hope [your friend's] cold is better and please give him lots of love."

One year, for his Christmas card, sent to everybody, Lionel came up with a design that incorporated the word, "Noel" hundreds of times and signed "love Lionel". In reply, Noël handmade a card with "Bart, Bart, Bart" written all over it and signed, "love Noël".

That first visit led to many more at Chalet Coward, and at Blue

Harbour, Noël's first house and later guesthouse in Jamaica. After one such study, Cole Leslie sent Lionel a wallet of holiday snaps with a note attached: "Please pass some of these [photographs] on to [your friends] as a souvenir of that very happy day and give them my love. We liked them both very much and in case they wonder why I have taken so long explain that the negs with the reorder form got themselves right down as far as they could get between the upholstery of the car and have been lost for months. Aren't inanimate objects awful sometimes? I love you, but you know that, Coley."

"I look like Margot Fonteyn after the last waltz," Lionel replied when he saw the snaps.

This acceptance by Noël, Coley and Graham had an instant and lasting effect on Lionel. A week after the first visit, he boasted of it to the London *Evening Standard*.

"'I don't know that it's ethical to tell you,' he says eagerly, 'but Noël said I was the greatest English composer since himself [. . .] I can tell you, man, it was inspiring. Positively. He showed me the first act of his musical and I told him about my plans. I think he puts me on a level with himself. Gave me a present of a rhyming dictionary, he did. Never use one myself but he said he did and so did Cole Porter. [He] wrote a dedication in it: 'Do not let this aid to rhyming / Bitch your talent or your timing.' Seeing Noël and the way he lives gave me a taste for gracious living. I want to have a villa in the south of France and a penthouse in New York – in addition to my place in London."

And he wrote:

> "*Dear Noël,*
> "*Thanks for your note. I must tell you at this point I get a great charge out of receiving correspondence from you because you write as you speak and I can sit up in bed reading your words aloud in a rather bad imitation of your voice and there you are almost in the room.*"

"Noël brought him to meet legends such as Marlene Dietrich at his Savoy suite," the *Daily Express* reported.[54] "Dietrich remarked that with his thick sideburns he looked like an 'Egyptian Beatnik'. In his naivety, Lionel pointed out the little piece of cotton dangling from her blue Chanel suit, mistaking it for a laundry mark. Coward quashed him: 'That's not cotton, you twit, it's the bloody French *Legion d'Honneur*.'"

When asked about his influences as a lyricist, Lionel cited Lorenz Hart, sometimes W.S. Gilbert, and always Noël Coward. Noël gave him

masterclasses in songwriting and stagecraft. He offered him financial coun-
selling, including advice never to invest in your own shows – a tip that
ultimately, and disastrously, Lionel failed to heed. He offered guidance –
and more importantly example – on how to conduct one's love life. And
he showed him how to use time management and delegation to optimise
one's talent, enjoy one's wealth and keep the blues at bay.

Lionel listened and tried, with mixed success, to learn and to gather an
entourage just like Noël's. He was lucky in his secretaries, from Joan
Maitland and Muriel Walker in the Fifties and Sixties, to Brenda Evans at
the end of his life. They were his friends, his custodians, his confidantes
and his helpmates who kept his feet on the ground and chaos at bay. The
rest of the entourage was more problematic. There was often a boyfriend
around, too, a "flavour of the month" as Jon Gorman later called them.
One, an American, came with two huge messy dogs called Romulus and
Remus. Others stole.

Other friends were never a problem. Everybody loved Lionel. Early in
his career his network of contacts was exponentially broadened when he
met, befriended and, like everybody else in the world, fell in love with
Alma Cogan, the reigning Grand Vizier and Social Secretary of the
Showbusiness Freemasonry.

Alma had been singing professionally since she was 14. By the early
Fifties she was a permanent feature in the hit parade, recording mostly
novelty/comedy songs – 'Never Do A Tango With An Eskimo', 'The
Banjo's Back In Town', 'Sugartime' – which she embellished by chuckling key syllables in the same sort of way as Buddy Holly later hiccupped.
She dressed like a Disney Princess, in hooped edifices of tulle and satin and
sequins and sparkles, wider than she was tall.

For three years running, between 1956 and 1958, she was voted *New
Musical Express*'s 'Outstanding Female Singer', and then again in 1960. But
her popularity offstage was even more impressive. To know her was,
apparently, to love her.

Though it seems to have had an instant and mesmerising effect on all
who met her, the exact nature of Alma's appeal is hard to pin down. On
film and disc she seems no more jolly and vivacious than most of her
equally enthusiastic contemporaries, but mention her name to any one of
those contemporaries and there is still that intake of breath and inward
smile. "She was . . ." they say, ". . . bubbly."

The same is true of Lionel. His friends find it easy to enumerate his
faults, to condemn his lies, his egotism, his irascibility, his insults, his child-
ishness, his need to control, but then comes the intake of breath and the

inward smile. Noël Coward once said he would "rather spend five minutes in a four-ale bar with Lionel Bart than a year's yachting cruise with the Oxford Debating Society".

'Charismatic' is a word often used to explain the appeal of people like Alma and Lionel. It means, "No, I don't understand it myself, either, but I have a terrific vocabulary."

Alma's flat, in Stafford Court on Kensington High Street, which she shared with her mum Fay and her sister Sandra, was Grand Lodge of the Showbiz Freemasonry. Here she threw parties that might have been considered risibly demure in a Hampshire convent but still attracted showbiz's biggest hitters from both sides of the Atlantic. "For one party," Alma's sister Sandra Caron records in *Alma Cogan A Memoir,* "we decided on a country and western theme, and covered the furniture in checked gingham. When people arrived they were greeted by trays of hot dogs, crisps and pickles."[55] The guests, who had whale of a time, included Peter O'Toole, Leslie Bricusse, Anthony Newley, Joan Collins, Alan 'Fluff' Freeman, Sir Joseph Lockwood (Head of EMI), Lionel Blair, Shelley Winters, Albert Finney and Judy Garland.

Every night was open house. People 'went on' to Alma's. Another entry from Noël Coward's diary reads: "Lunched with Vivien [Leigh] at Tickeridge. She was fine and gay. I went to Brighton to see Larry [Olivier] and Joan [Plowright], and dined with Terry [Rattigan] and Robin [Maugham] and finished up at Alma Cogan's in London at 12.30, where I met two Beatles."

Guests would have a drink, a cup of tea. Fay would make sandwiches. They played parlour games. They played cards. Fay was a reckless gambler.

Lionel first encountered Alma in the early Tommy Steele days and was as impressed by her charisma as she was by his. By 1960 they were inseparable. Muriel Walker remembers Alma popping into Lionel's house in Reece Mews "nearly every day". And Lionel says, "I was always up at the flat. Fay was an attraction there on her own. She always had a poker game going with the likes of Tommy Steele, Sean Connery and Stanley Baker, or she'd just be making sure everyone had enough to eat."

Seen dining together in London's trendiest night spots, soon Alma and Lionel were linked romantically. Will they, won't they? The two teases added grist to the rumour mill when, in August 1960, Alma's latest record, 'Train Of Love', had as its B-side a song called 'The "I Love You" Bit', a duet with one Ocher Nebbish, a transparent disguise for Lionel. The song is a woman's complaint to a man who, though he passionately declares his love – 'I love you, I love you' – at every opportunity, seems unwilling to take the relationship any further: towards the altar, for instance, or, perhaps in Lionel's case, towards the boudoir.

Morris and Yetta never gave up hoping that their youngest boy would one day bring them grandchildren. In a 1961 interview with the *Daily Express,* Yetta describes her Lionel as, "A very good boy. Our seventh child, God bless him." He had just moved them into a ground floor flat in Stamford Hill, "after I fell downstairs". "Now he wants to buy me a mink coat but I said: 'Lionel, a mink coat would be too heavy for me at my age and besides I have a beaver lamb.'"

"Mrs Begleiter," the *Express* goes on, "would be even happier if her son showed some sign of getting married. 'He says it wouldn't be fair on a girl,' she explained, 'because he has to travel and be out late at night. Lionel would never be unfair to a girl. He is as generous with his love as with his money. Last time he was here, he came back and knocked on the door. I thought he had forgotten his money or something. But he said: 'Momma, I forgot to give you two kisses. He's a good boy.'"[56]

Ten

JOSEPH Heller, the American writer, whose debut novel *Catch-22* is mentioned in most 'Top 100 Books of All Time' lists, once said, "When I read something saying I've not done anything as good as *Catch-22* I'm tempted to reply, 'Who has?'"

Oliver! was always going to be a tough act to follow. It never occurred to Lionel to go down the 'same winning formula with diminishing returns' route by following *Oliver!* with *Copperfield!*, *Expectations!*, *Curiosity!* and *Rudge!* He always needed to move on, to try something different. Re-inventing yourself and your style can either be taken as a sign of restless artistic questing or galloping insecurity. In Lionel's case it was probably a bit of both.

Four days after the *Oliver!* opening, with three hit shows (*Oliver!*, *Fings* and *Lock Up Your Daughters*) running in the West End, Lionel was struggling to come to terms with his new found fame, power and potential wealth and not making a very good job of it. He outlined his dilemma in an interview with Herbert Kretzmer for the *Sunday Dispatch*.

"'I'm always worrying,' he said, 'about what comes next. It's a dodgy lark, I tell you. Some people get dizzy with success. Not me. I get apprehensive. That's it. Apprehensive.'

"The ivory telephone rang at his elbow. Bart spoke into the mouthpiece. 'Who wants seats for the show? Lord Whom? Okay, tell him he can have two.'

"Bart replaced the phone, lit another cigarette. 'Where was I?' he said, 'Oh yes, success.'

"Bart rubbed his nose with his knuckles. 'The phone never stops ringing. I am inundated with offers. People want me to write songs for shows, songs for films. But listen, mate, I've got to know what to take on, what to turn down. It's a headache. I have just rejected a Hollywood offer to write all the songs for Elvis Presley's next picture. I need something big and exciting to be working on. I can't repeat myself, see? That's fatal. Everything I do must be bigger and better than anything I've done before. That's my kick, mate.'"[57]

To satisfy his "kick" for "bigger and better" he therefore decided to re-stage the Second World War, this time improving on the original Hitler-Churchill co-production by adding a ragamuffin chorus, a lovely wedding and his own mother. The title *Blitz!*, by his own admission, he stole from Hermann Goering.

If *Oliver!*, a tale of displaced lives and the search for love, is partly autobiographical, *Blitz!* is avowedly so, a point made by Joan Maitland – now fully credited as writer of the book – in the programme notes.

"During the ten years I have known him," she says, "the idea of this show has always been in his mind, and the character of Mrs Blitztein, which embodies so much of the spirit and courage of his own mother, had become so real to him that during our writing sessions it was almost as if Mrs Blitztein 'wrote' her own lines.

"The theme of the show galvanised both of us, but sometimes the remembering was painful. We both have personal recollections of the horror of those days, when the Blitz turned everyone's life upside down and each family bore its share of lives lost and hopes blasted. Mrs Blitztein would always change the mood rapidly, and set us both laughing.

"Lionel was only a child during the war and was repeatedly parted from his mother and family. The memory obviously still moves him very deeply, and the evacuees song 'We're Going To The Country' is, I think, one of the most poignant moments in the show.' "

It opens with air-raid sirens – a sound which, less than 20 years after the real thing, could still chill the blood. They were played loud. People overhearing in the street outside would often look nervously around and hurry their steps. Onstage the cast takes shelter in an Underground station. Fires break out. Masonry crashes.

Lionel described the plot as "three human stories inside an epic canvas; the major human conflict – the major plot – personifies the spirit of London and how that spirit developed during the period of the piece."

It's set in Petticoat Lane and, like *Romeo And Juliet* and its progeny *West Side Story*, revolves around two feuding families: the Blitzteins run by Mrs Blitztein, 'The Queen of Petticoat Lane' who sells pickled herrings, and the Lockes run by Alfie Locke, ARP warden and friut'n'veg man. Carol Blitztein and Georgie Locke fall in love. People die. Children are evacuated. Carol goes blind. There is a desertion, a marriage, and in the end when Mrs Blitztein is buried in rubble it is her arch-enemy Alfie Locke who digs her out.

Many have criticised the plot as sentimental, to which more measured voices reply, "Of course it bloody is. It's a musical."

In its size, scope and naked appeal to patriotism, *Blitz!* has similarities to

Noël Coward's 1933 extravaganza, *Cavalcade* – a digest of British history from 1899 to 1929, seen from the point of view of one silver-spoon family. In keeping with the then emerging spirit of the Sixties and his own ingrained if often subliminal socialism, Lionel's patriotism is shot through with irony: the song 'As Long As This Is England', a prescient celebration of multiculturalism, is sung principally by an Irishman, a Chinese and a Jew – but, as was discovered when Union Jack underpants and Kitchener kitsch began to appear in the shops a couple of years later, even the most ironic patriotism can still possess the power to stir the blood and moisten the eye. When, in *Blitz!*, bombs fall and first generation immigrants stiffen lips and exhibit pluck, there is audible sniffing in the audience.

The set came before the script. Long before Lionel sat down with Joan Maitland and a typewriter, he was taking Sean Kenny on recces to the East End with sketch pad in hand.

"For me it was a new experience," Sean wrote in the programme notes. "It was the first time I had come close to wartime London, for I was at school in Ireland at the time, and the Blitz to me was something far away. We began with a series of sketches, ideas of places, ideas of people, ideas of situations and stories began to centre round Petticoat Lane and the tenement buildings. We saw lots of photographs, newsreels, newspaper cuttings and films made in London during the Forties period."

Sean was by now at the hub of the emerging Sixties scene. His studio was at 18 Greek Street, Soho, above the Establishment Club, the satirical cabaret run by Peter Cook and Nick Luard. He worked in a fog of cigarette smoke to a Miles Davis soundtrack.

"Hope all goes well with you and the sun never goes in," he wrote to Lionel on October 20, 1961. "Since you left I have been doing a series of oil sketches on *Blitz!* and from these we should get a good feeling of colour and atmosphere. The strange thing is from them one gets a strange feeling of waiting, or people waiting for something to happen. Also I think we can be overall fairly unrealistic and brush realism in with our details – shelter signs, posters etc. . . . all good wishes, Li, and hope to see you soon full of ideas, yours ever, Sean."

The 'brushed in' details identified the main locations – Victoria Station, Petticoat Lane, Bank Underground – but the main bulk of the set consisted of five mobile revolving house units and a 36 foot span bridge, weighing 10 tons, which had to stop accurately at various levels up to a height of 24 feet. There were also several flying pieces, some of which weighed a ton. Nobody had attempted anything on this scale before. Stage technology had to be reinvented. Moving the houses with tracks and mains-driven motors, in the conventional way, was out of the question. Apart from many other considerations, the cables would end up as spaghetti and trip up the dancers. A complete new system relying on battery-powered motors assisted by hidden stagehands had to be devised. More difficult still was the problem of radio interference. In the pre-computer age, each scene change had to be 'talked into position'. Any breakdown in communication between stage manager and the stagehands would result in maimings and death. Standard walkie-talkies tended to get picked up by the house sound system and their signals turned to white noise by the electric motors. The Multitone Electric Company had been developing a more sophisticated system for use in hospitals and was persuaded to adapt their technology for Sean's specialist needs. It worked. Nobody died. In addition to the tons of moving metal, there were smoke guns, explosions, fires, a fireman's hose that would inflate on cue, a powerful wind machine. . . .

The overall budget for the show was £60,000 – four times as much as *Oliver!* Two-thirds of that – £40,000 – went on the set. And that's not including the running costs incurred by having a small army of stagehands on the payroll to operate everything, or the cost of having the stages of two theatres reinforced to take the additional weight.

In the summer of 1961, during a trip to Stockholm with Donald Albery to see the Swedish production of *Oliver!*, Lionel made his initial pitch for *Blitz!* In October, Albery visited the offices of Apollo Music, Lionel's recently formed music publishing company, to hear a tape of the music. He greenlit the show to go into the West End, ideally on V.E. Day, the anniversary of the end of the war in Europe.

Lionel wrote to Noël Coward, who was in New York where his own show, *Sail Away*, opened a few weeks earlier. "Pleased to hear about *Sail Away* and I'm looking forward to receiving the cast album from you. I've prepared a pretty slick stereophonic tape recording of the songs from *Blitz!* and as soon as you come into town let us fix a date as I want you to hear it right now. I'm in the midst of director problems on the show, but come hell or high water I plan to get the thing staged in the West End by May 8, VE day, even if I have to direct the darn thing myself."

The "director problems" were a matter of finding the right person. Peter Coe was busy – in 1962 he directed a well-received *Macbeth* with Christopher Plummer at the other Stratford, the Shakespeare Memorial Theatre, at Stratford-upon-Avon, followed by another Dickens-inspired musical, *Pickwick*, in which Harry Secombe sang 'If I Ruled The World' at a volume that ensured the world heard his wish.

Eleanor 'Fiz' Fazan was a dancer and choreographer who'd also enjoyed success as a director in two shows produced by Donald Albery: *Share My Lettuce*, a revue written by Bamber Gasgoigne and starring Kenneth Williams and Maggie Smith, and *Beyond The Fringe*, written and performed by Peter Cook, Dudley Moore, Alan Bennett and Jonathan Miller. Scraps between those four uppity Oxbridge satirists had required the mediation skills of a hostage negotiator but, after *Oliver!*'s difficulties with Peter Coe, Ron Moody and Georgia Brown, whether even this would be enough to qualify Fiz for a Lionel Bart musical was a matter of doubt.

Toni Palmer, cast as the glamorous Elsie, Mrs Blitzstein's lodger, thought not. "We had two directors. We had Eleanor Fazan, who was totally the wrong person for that show, and then Lionel took over. . ." Speaking almost 50 years after the event, the memory of Lionel taking over still causes Toni to laugh immoderately. She tries to speak but isn't quite ready. Then she manages, "and that was even more chaotic. You see, Lionel didn't have that kind of brain to be a director, he wasn't practical. I don't think he ever boiled an egg. He couldn't make a cup of tea. He never did anything like that." There is a short pause then, "Lionel took over . . .," and the laughter starts again.

Lionel had had one previous brush with directing.

At the end of 1958, a young writer named John McGrath had enjoyed some critical and commercial success with his play *The Tent* at the Royal Court. A year later, another of his plays, *Why The Chicken?*, a confrontation between a social worker and a Teddy boy gang, had caused a stir at the Edinburgh Festival. The play's appeal to Lionel was obvious. Ever since *Blackboard Jungle* and *Serious Charge*, delinquency had been coining it at the box office.

He acquired the rights and planned a London production with a Sean Kenny set and himself as producer, director and composer of incidental music. Among the cast were two young hopefuls, Terence Stamp and Michael Caine. It was Lionel who ensured that his two debutantes were properly welcomed into the showbiz Freemasonry by taking them, one night, to Stafford Court and introducing them to Alma – a form of showbiz bar mitzvah. Michael Caine helped Fay clear up. "What a nice tidy boy you are," she said. "For an actor."

Lionel also wrote a title song, 'Why The Chicken?', and had it recorded by Dave Sampson, a young singer 'discovered' by Cliff Richard down at the 2Is. Neither record nor show set the world on fire. The record sank without trace. The show struggled through try-outs at Streatham and

Golders Green, after which a West End transfer was deemed economically unwise.

Thankfully John McGrath survived the fiasco, went on to co-create the long-running TV cop show *Z-Cars* and to write, produce and direct movies including *The Billion Dollar Brain* and *Carrington*. As founder and director of the 7:84 Theatre Company he also established himself as one of the most original and influential theatrical voices of the twentieth century.

With doughty Dunkirk spirit, Lionel refused to let a setback like *Why The Chicken?* affect his will, his courage or his confidence to turn "bigger and better" into "biggest and best".

So he became director of *Blitz!* Eleanor Fazan was associate director, an arrangement which – as one suspects from that disingenuous "darn" in his "even if I have to direct the darn thing myself" protestation to Noël – was almost certainly Lionel's steely intention all along.

Teddy Green, the choreographer, had just finished work on the Cliff Richard film *The Young Ones*. Lionel thought his credentials were ideal: "If he can teach Cliff to dance, he can handle my dancers."

Early signings to the cast were two members from the original 1939–45 Blitz production. Hermann Goering and Adolf Hitler were, of course, dead, but Winston Churchill was alive and apparently available and so was that other pivotal figure of the British effort, 'the Forces Sweetheart', Vera Lynn, hit singer of '(There'll Be Bluebirds Over) The White Cliffs Of Dover', 'When You Hear Big Ben' and 'We'll Meet Again'.

In the Act I air-raid-in-the-underground scene, the protagonists turn to the BBC for news and comfort. To make the moment special, Lionel recruited Vera to record 'The Day After Tomorrow', his own pastiche of a wartime song, but a pastiche so accurate that many ticket-buyers mistook it for the real thing; indeed, some insisted they could remember singing it as their troopship steamed out of Portsmouth.

Lionel (or a secretary) also sought permission from Sir Winston Churchill to use his wartime speeches. Graciously, Sir Winston's secretary replied: "You may use extracts of his recordings in one of your plays [. . .] and if you wish to make a donation for using these recordings, Sir Winston suggests Save The Children."

Two legends, one of them for the price of a hefty bung to a worthy charity. Result.

Finding the rest of the cast proved more of a headache. In an interview with the *Daily Herald* Lionel was reduced to asking the reporter for casting suggestions.

"If you know anyone who can play a fat cockney mum and sing like

Ethel Merman, there's a part waiting for her. I went to chat with Tessie O'Shea about it the other day and she auditioned me. I couldn't get a word in edgeways."

Mrs Blitztein eventually went to Amelia 'Millie' Bayntun, a woman built for strength not speed, who, in keeping with Lionel's predilections, had served time with Joan Littlewood at Theatre Workshop. Millie was a Bristol girl with the round vowels and perfect consonants of the middle classes. To prepare for *Sparrers*, Joan fixed her up with a few elocution lessons after which she was able to speak cockney (and, for *Blitz!* Yiddish/cockney) well enough to convince Lionel she could be the real thing. Later, in the TV cop show *Dixon Of Dock Green* and a string of films including several *Carry Ons*, she made a delightful career out of her faux-Bow credentials.

Bob Grant, another Stratford lag, who later turned up as Jack Harper in the TV sitcom *On The Buses*, was cast as Alfie Locke.

Harry Landis, Lionel's old Unity pal, was an early choice to play Harry Blitzstein, but suspects that, at this stage in the game, Lionel might have been a bit full of himself. "He got me to go up and see him and he was sat in the stalls with Georgia Brown. They treated me like some amateur. 'Could you do this . . .? Could you improvise some . . .?' and I thought, 'Blimey, Li, it's me. What's all this?' Anyhow I left." It was some time before the *Blitz!* office got back to Harry's agent, offering the part. "But she just said, 'Sorry, he's signed up to the BBC for 12 weeks now.' So . . ."

So, the part went instead to Tom Kempinski, a gaunt-faced young actor, who later became a prolific and esteemed playwright. His *Duet For One* ran (twice) in the West End and on Broadway and the film version earned Julie Andrews a Golden Globe nomination.

Appropriately for such an autobiographical piece, many of the *Blitz!* songs revive the spirit of the childhood singalong. 'Mums And Dads' is a coach-party song of counter melodies – this side of the coach are the mums, that side's the dads, and the mums sing this and the dads sing that, and when you sing both tunes together, whaddya know they sound nice. 'Who's This Geezer Hitler?' could be one of the mucky songs Lionel made up in the playground in exchange for turns on roller skates. "They say he had a father and the father had his fun / He stayed around to see how long it laar-sted / Then Adolf came along and his papa went on the run / And that's why poor old Adolf's . . . flabbergasted." And everyone falls over laughing because the naughty man nearly said a rude word.

Elsewhere he seems to have chucked his "stick to the white notes" rule completely out of the window and fallen into the sophisticated embraces of spiky chromaticism. The third line of 'We're Going To The Country', the evacuees' song, could come from something alarming by Schoenberg played at an unsociable hour on BBC Radio 3. It's difficult to sing and difficult to hear, but dramatically it works a treat – adding an ominous colouration to what would otherwise be a cheery song about cows.

The modes and rhythms of the synagogue can be heard everywhere. 'Bake A Cake', Mrs Blitzstein's Yiddishe Momme eulogy to the healing power of Mrs Beeton's recipes, starts with an uncompromising 'doh doh fi' – the 'fi' being the black note between 'fah' and 'so'. 'Doh' to 'fi' is a magic interval, the flattened fifth, the tritone, the diabolos in *musica*, the devil in music. Desperate to resolve itself to the 'soh' it's an interval of hopeless yearning. Sometimes in the synagogue it is the sound of the ram's horn, the shofar, sliding up to 'soh'. Leonard Bernstein explored its strangeness endlessly in the *West Side Story* score – in the Jets' whistle, the first two notes of 'Maria', in 'Somewhere' and 'I Feel Pretty'. In 'Bake A Cake' it is also the sound of a virtuoso violinist preparing to dazzle. And it is the sound of Mrs Blitzstein defiantly nailing her colours to the mast: "I am Jewish! I bake cakes!"

Blitz!'s budget allowed for a larger orchestra than was available for *Oliver!*, permitting, for instance, a Count Basie-style big-band arrangement on 'Who Wants To Settle Down' and the exotic tinklings of a cimbalom (a sort of Hungarian zither played with mallets) on 'Bake A Cake'.

Bob Sharples, composer, arranger and conductor of endless movies and TV shows, was hired as orchestrator. At least that's what it says in the programme – 'Orchestrations by Bob Sharples'. Lionel, shooting his barrow boy mouth off again, denied the claim.

"I've made the orchestrations," he told *The Times*, "although I've not written down the dots. I have planned the orchestrations with Bob Sharples, my musical director. First I made a tape of the entire score (singing some of it myself and with other singers to help) with a small group – piano, bass and strings – to accompany. We've gone on from there and fortunately there is a very good rapport between Bob Sharples and me. We get the rhythm and pointing I need. Then we get the harmony. Then we go on to the texture. If we don't get it right we scrap it and start again – that may be an expensive method but we've found that it works."

It might work for the music, but the bald statement, 'I made the orchestrations', and relegating the role of Bob Sharples to that of a tradesman brought in to write down the dots can't have done much for the 'rapport'. Such things can, and did, come back to bite.

The Donmar Warehouse these days is a busy theatre in Earlham Street, Covent Garden. Then it was a disused banana-ripening depot recently acquired by Donmar, a company set up by DONald Albery and MARgot Fonteyn as a putative rehearsal space for the London Festival Ballet. But before the Festival Ballet was moved in, the *Blitz!* set was outlined on the floor and rehearsals began.

Lionel's directing was occasionally whimsical. "I remember spending hours with a stirrup pump," says Toni Palmer, "and I knew it'd be cut. We were supposed to be in the underground putting a fire out – we had a stirrup pump drill or something, me and this other girl, and Lionel had us practising with this thing for hours. I said, 'Why are you doing this Lionel, it's never going to be in the show?'"

She was right. It wasn't.

But with Fiz Fazan, Teddy Green, Sean Kenny, Barry Busbridge, the stage manager, and George Rowbottom, the company manager, to oversee the practicalities, Lionel could revert to his *Oliver!* role as senior fusspot and general morale booster. This was playing to his strengths. And it was the role he continued to play long after the rehearsal period was over. When he couldn't be there in person, he sent letters.

"I want you to know that the performance I saw last night was very heartening to me," he wrote more than a year after the show had opened. "I appreciate that this audience may not have been one of the better ones, but even so your performances do great credit to a company who have nearly completed a year's run." The fussput then takes over. He wants more "visual spontaneity" in the curtain calls. He's worried about the wearing of neckties and carnations in the wedding scene. But finishes with a cheering "Thank you", not to mention a "Keep it up" and a "Let's show 'em".

The try out was scheduled for April 13 at the Regal Cinema, Edmonton. Donald Albery and Sean had looked at about 20 venues. This was one of the few with a stage big enough for the set. Even so it was not ideal. The set-building had to be scheduled around film shows, bingo sessions and Saturday morning kids' clubs.

"When I was about 14 or 15, I remember sneaking off from school and borrowing my father's dinner jacket to go to the world premiere performance of *Blitz!* at the Regal, Edmonton," says Sir Cameron Mackintosh, producer of *Cats, Les Misérables, Phantom Of The Opera*, as well as most of the other musical hits of the past 40 years, including four West End revivals of *Oliver!* "I've never seen anything to this day as extraordinary as that production, so one was totally aware that Lionel Bart was absolutely the giant of musical theatre at that time." [58]

Princess Margaret liked it, too. The show's West End opening was at the Adelphi on May 8, but the Princess, along with her new husband Antony Armstrong-Jones (about to become Lord Snowdon), attended a charity preview the night before. It was a technical disaster to the extent that the last scene couldn't be played at all, which didn't really matter because by this time nobody could see the stage anyway – the result of a hyperactive smoke gun.

"I thought it was wonderful," said the Princess, smiling radiantly. "I enjoyed every minute of it." Though remote, the possibility that the smoke gun was spiked has not been discounted.

The show ran for a respectable 18 months and recouped its costs in the first four, but the initial reviews were mixed. *The Times* spent most of its column inches showering Sean's set with praise, then split the rest between compliments for Amelia Bayntun, Toni Palmer and the chorus of kids, and a damning assessment of the plot and songs.

Noël Coward, who came with Elaine Stritch, Gladys Cooper and Coley, wasn't too keen, either. "From the production point of view it was marvellous," he tells his diary, "but alas the book and the direction were bad. The music and the lyrics are fairly good but the whole thing is overwhelmed by Mr Sean Kenny's moving sets which never stay still for a minute. It got pretty bad notices on the whole. I am sorry for Lionel Bart, he has rich talents, but in this he aimed too high. It probably won't do him any harm to fail a little. God knows we all have to go through it from time to time."[59] His own show, *Sail Away*, starring Ms Stritch, had opened on Broadway in October 1961 and closed in February 1962. Noël's final comment on *Blitz!* – slightly altered almost every time it is quoted – was, "Twice as long and twice as loud as the real thing."

The Daily Telegraph, on the other hand, was so enthusiastic it lapsed momentarily into tabloid-speak, squeaking: "It's going to be a whacking, walloping hit."

Kenneth Tynan in *The Guardian* was most scathing: "Mawkish where it tries to be poignant, flat where it means to be funny, and secondhand where it aims at period authenticity." But, again, he goes on to marvel – not in an entirely approving way – at the set. "In *Blitz!* there are distinct signs that the sets are taking over. They swoop down on the actors and snatch them aloft; four motor-driven towers prowl the stage, converging menacingly on any performer who threatens to hog the limelight; and whenever the human element looks like gaining control, they collapse on it in a mass of flaming timber. In short, they let the cast know who's boss. They are magnificent and they are war: who (they tacitly enquire) needs

Lionel Bart? I have a fearful premonition of the next show Mr Kenny designs. As soon as the curtain rises, the sets will advance in a phalanx on the audience and summarily expel it from the theatre. After that, the next step is clear: Mr Kenny will invent sets that applaud."

Lionel never seems to have been nettled when Sean stole his thunder. "It was a most massive set," he said, years later. "I mean, when *Oliver!* opened, [they said] 'You come out of the theatre whistling the sets.' Well, on *Blitz!* one of the critics said that this time the sets come offstage and applaud themselves. It's been a great pleasure and a great joy for me to be able to work with Sean. He was a giant. I've seen him destroy sets because a kid said it didn't work and he'd throw it away. And he'd do amazing sets in restaurants on plates and serviettes. And he'd write poems in draughtsman's handwriting. And he's an inspiration."[60]

The writs began to fly not long after the show opened. In a complicated wrangle, Bob Sharples, the orchestrator, dismissed by Lionel as the man who wrote down the dots, sued Donmar Productions, Donald Albery's company, claiming that he had composed some of the show's music. Lionel countersued to clear his copyrights and reputation. Alex Murray, formerly Alex Most of the Most Brothers, also claimed he had composed some of the music for the show. All the claims were eventually settled, but mud sticks. The feeling, rarely directly stated but often present between the lines, that nobody without benefit of birth or musical education could possibly be so successful without somehow cheating, became more prevalent. Lionel's immodesty didn't help either. British achievers are supposed to be diffident. His irresistible urge to talk things up, particularly in the press, was earning him a reputation as a show-off clever-dick. There were sneers behind hands. And a burgeoning desire to see him take a pratfall.

"It's a fatal thing when an artist does what's expected of him. To me, art is a search, and if you start repeating yourself you perhaps believe that you have found yourself, and then surely there's nothing more to say and little more to do." Lionel says in the *Blitz!* programme notes, which, to some, might as well have read, "Kick Me."

The 'search' that is 'art' had luckily not entirely distracted Lionel from pop. Marty Wilde's chart career, having reached a nadir with 'The Fight', his mid-1960 release that climbed to number 47 and fizzed out, had since been on the up and up. 'Little Girl' reached number 16. 'Rubber Ball', his cover of Bobby Vee's American hit, went top ten. Surely all he needed to make that final push to number one was a Lionel Bart song.

The song, 'Hide And Seek', a tale of a young man who is tired of playing games with a young lady and hopes for some token of her commitment to the relationship in the near future, was recorded in a style reminiscent of a John Barry/Adam Faith single, with jaunty strings and a catchy twist beat. Marty worked on the song with Lionel, but had his doubts from the start: "You see that's more of a show tune than a rock'n' roll thing and it was a bad feeling all round, 'cos when I was promoting it I just knew it wasn't gonna work. Philips [the record company] had a wonderful promo man, a press man called Paddy Fleming who was a lovely guy, and Paddy was working his nuts off to get this song a hit and I thought, 'No, Paddy, no.'"

Marty's instincts were right. 'Hide And Seek' stalled at 47. What did Marty care? The previous November his wife, Joyce – the best looking of *Oh Boy*'s glamour in residence, the Vernons Girls – had given birth to a beautiful baby girl, Kim, and was pregnant with a son, Ricky. Twenty years later, Marty and Ricky would write a song and Kim would record it. 'Kids In America' went number one in most of the world but was denied its rightful position in the UK by Shakin' Stevens. Two years before 'Kids In America' hit the charts, Shakey had recorded 'Endless Sleep', Marty's hit from 1958. Lionel was Kim's godfather. That's how tiny the Rock Pool is.

At the end of 1961, like every musician worth his or her salt since the choirs of angels over Bethlehem, Lionel had a crack at a Christmas number one. For weeks the virtues of 'Give Us A Kiss For Christmas', written and sung by Lionel Bart, were puffed up in *Melody Maker* and *New Musical Express*. It got airplay, too, like 'Little White Bull' becoming a favourite on Uncle Mac's Saturday morning radio show *Children's Favourites*. But even though, remarkably, there were no other season-specific songs around that year, Lionel was kept from the top spot by Frankie Vaughan's 'Tower Of Strength' and 66 other records. Still, like so many of Lionel's songs, it made its mark. The number of people who can, given the right stimuli, surprise themselves by singing through the whole of 'Give Us A Kiss For Christmas' with not a word out of place is a stunning testament to the power of recovered memory syndrome.

Eleven

THE Sixties were a bigmouth time. Working-class lads – some faked the working class bit with a put-on accent and an invented dad with pneumoconiosis, but most were genuine lads – took advantage of a temporary fashion for limited egalitarianism, a fad for identifying rudeness with wit, *Chatterley*-stoked rumours about the working-man's sexual vigour, the creeping influence of Richard Hoggart's *The Uses Of Literacy*, and their big mouths to blag their way into jobs, parties and knickers formerly considered way above their station.

As well as the mouth you needed the props – the threads, the wheels, the pad – the quantities and quality depending on the audacity of the blag. Novelists and playwrights, for instance, selling to 'new directions' publishers and out-of-town theatres needed little more than ten Woodbines and a jacket that smelled of light engineering. A composer/lyricist/author selling £60,000 musicals first of all to cash-sensitive West End producers and then to 1,500 ticket buyers a night for as long as possible needs a truckload of magnificence and an ocean of flair.

Clouds of perfume prepared the way for Lionel's arrival. You could smell him coming.

"*L'Heure Bleue or 'the bluish hour' was created by Jacques Guerlain in 1912,*" goes the ad copy. "*The fragrance is velvety soft and romantic, it is a fragrance of bluish dusk and anticipation of night, before the first stars appear in the sky. The top notes are opening with spicy-sweet aniseed and fresh bergamot that gently lead to the heart of rose, carnation, tuberose, violet, and neroli. The soft and powdery floral notes are resting on a base of vanilla, Tonka bean, iris and benzoin. The perfume is mysterious, elegant and timeless.*"

For most of his life this was the mysterious, elegant, timeless smell of Lionel Bart. Sometimes, when he was in the mood for a more gourmand nuance, he would switch to Guerlain's Mitsouko: "*the opening is long, like a play of all beautiful notes, and, of course, this fragrance is not for ordinary day use. On the skin it sounds as if it starts from far away, without any allusion to its intensity and sensual side. Mitsouko is one of the well known aromas of chypre olfactory group with cool top notes and oak moss in the base. But it also has a note of a juicy peach, which gives a clear and quite gourmand nuance.*"

He not only wore Guerlain, he championed its virtues wherever he went.

"He gave it to everyone, girls and boys alike," says Toni Palmer, who was in *Fings* and *Blitz!* "We all got it on the first night – we all got a bottle of that for a present and we all stank of it. It is the strongest, it's not like a man's perfume." In 1961, a bottle of Mitsouko was his Mother's Day present to Yetta.[61] Other sons are content with chocolates and flowers but for Lionel nothing short of the chypre olfactory group would do.

It was a generous gift. On December 16, 1964, according to a receipt in Lionel's archives, a bottle of *L'Heure Bleue* cologne, size unspecified, from Swan and Edgar set him back £4 12s 6d (£4.62). As if for comparison purposes another receipt is filed next to it establishing that lunch for three at the Ivy (including a litre of rose wine at 17s 6d) came to £6 5s (£6.25).

Lionel invented his own language at an early stage of the game. Tommy Steele describes him, back in 1958, speaking in a hybrid of East End, Hollywood and Noël Coward. To this at some point was added the 'jive' talk popularised by clarinettist Mezz Mezzrow in his autobiography *Really The Blues*, another essential read for the Soho coffee-bar set, and some rock'n'roll slang learned from Little Richard lyrics and Bill Haley films. The result is close to the language parodied by Mike Myers in the Austin Powers films.

"It's been 'Go, Bart, Go!' ever since I was a kid in the East End," he told Donald Zec in the *Daily Mirror* in 1962. "If you really want to know the truth – it's the kicks that matter, nothing else. I just want to write musicals. I want to stand up and shout to the biggest audience I can get. If they want to listen that's okay, man. If they don't, well that's still fine by me, baby."[62]

He wanted to stand up and shout to the biggest audience he could get, but though he often stood up – and jigged and dived and gestured – he rarely shouted. Everyone who knew him impersonates the voice when they quote him. It's unavoidable. It's a whisper, a hiss. It could be gossipy-confidential or deadpan-funny or conspiratorial like a spiv's sales pitch or scary in the manner of Marlon Brando as Don Corleone but it was never less than arresting, forcing his audience to lean forward slightly and listen to nobody but Lionel.

Harry Landis reckons the voice and the language were developed, deliberately or otherwise, as a class eradicator; an alternative to the various registers of 'telephone voice' and 'interview voice' that most people adopt. Neither posh nor cockney, it enabled him to rub shoulders with cab drivers and princesses without ever feeling out of place. "The quiet voice," as Harry puts it, "disguised his true persona which was a cockney loudmouth."

The voice he had sussed, but Lionel's looks brought self-doubt and anguish. Eric Williams, Lionel's friend from their early twenties until the end, was party to most of the fears and phobias. "Lionel always thought he was ugly," he says, "to the point of no return when he was in his twenties and thirties. He wasn't ugly. He just didn't look like Errol Flynn. Lionel had marvellous eyes." Everybody mentions the eyes, which could be variously smouldering, liquid, troubled, brooding or intense. The difficulty came with the ears, which were a little simian, and the nose, which, even before it had been bashed around in the Victoria Boys' Club tent-pole incident, had had a puffin-like quality. An early extravagance as soon as the money began to flow was a nose-job, followed by another nose-job when the first proved unsatisfactory. "It was an improvement," says Eric Williams, "because he had a real big sort of Fagin conk and it didn't help."

Lionel's mother wasn't so impressed. "Cost him £150," she said. "It's a family joke. I keep asking him: 'Lionel, where is the long nose?'"

But he could wear clothes like a supermodel. He cared. At G and B Arts, the £30 he and John Gorman had forked out for new coats and shoes at Dunn & Co was considered a priority business expenditure. Even when he had holes in his shoes, the uppers were polished and the hair combed. "He was always shaved and neat," says Toni Palmer, "but then again he was a good Jewish East End boy and he was brought up like that to be tidy and neat and do things properly."

Lionel was among the first to glimpse those first rays of glamour when they peeped above the horizon to brighten the post-war monochrome world. Unity was a worker's theatre, but it was nonetheless a theatre. "His friends from the theatre arrived at our factory from time to time," says John Gorman in *Knocking Down Ginger*, "bringing Bohemian colour to an already colourful business. A young aspiring actor, Ivan Berg, made regular visits roaring up on a cerise painted Vespa, while the stage designer and director Bernard Sarron came with his Siamese cat on a gold chain. And when the money began to flow from the first Tommy Steele hits, Lionel's life-style changed. He was able to indulge his love of stylish clothes, to spend hours at the hairdressers, where they razor trimmed his beard and scented him with cologne."

The great menswear revolution of the Sixties began in homosexual Soho. Bill Green, working under the name of Vince, was a photographer specialising in artistic studies of the male physique. In the early Fifties he diversified into fashion, opening Vince's Man's Shop in Newburgh Street.[63] It was here that, according to John Gielgud, "Chelsea homosexuals, artists and muscle boys" could indulge their taste for skintight, sudden hues, soft pastels, the peek-a-boo and the see-through. An early advert featured a young Sean Connery posing in a matelot vest and thigh-hugging jeans. The new pop stars, advised by their pink, promiscuous managers to search for something different, sexy and shocking, raided Vince's rails. In 1957, one of Vince's assistants opened a store of his own just around the corner selling essentially the same gear but targeted at a broader demographic. He expanded and eventually owned nine shops, all on the same street – Carnaby Street. There's a plaque high on the wall there now, celebrating his name: John Stephen, 'The Modfather', the designer who dressed the Sixties and brought jobs and overtime to his factories in Glasgow where the Paisley velvet hipsters were sewn.

In 1959, a reporter for the *Stratford Gazette* wrote: "For a man in the four figure wage bracket, Lionel certainly doesn't dress like a successful composer. He wore light grey suedes, tight rust-coloured jeans, no tie and a navy blue turned-up-at-the-collar overcoat." There speaks a reporter too thick even to register he was sitting on the cutting edge of style; someone who obviously imagined that successful composers, like all the other successful people he'd encountered, would dress like the Duke of Edinburgh; who little realised that, five years later, light grey suedes, tight rust-coloured jeans, no tie and a navy blue turned-up-at-the-collar over-coat would be *exactly* the kind of thing successful composers would wear whatever their gender. Lionel liked to be achingly hip.

The day after *Blitz!* opened in 1962, London's *Evening Standard* described his suiting and booting in fetishistic detail: "light-green peaked *Oliver!* hat, light-green man-made-fibre suit, navy shirt stitched with white (no tie), navy Paisley silk handkerchief and navy suede shoes."

The *Daily Mirror*, in 1964, said Lionel owned "40 suits, 25 pairs of shoes, two pairs of cowboy boots, 40 shirts, scores of hats and four over-coats. 'My cufflinks are always white gold. I won't touch anything else.'"

His nephew Sammy has one of his uncle's Gieves & Hawkes suits – a work of art to which the final notes of *L'Heure Bleue* still cling. Gieves & Hawkes was a very traditional Savile Row firm, founded in 1771 and a royal favourite. More often, Lionel preferred to patronise the newer showbiz tailors, Dougie Millings, who dressed The Beatles, and Dougie Hayward, "the Rodin of tweed". There is a series of photographs of another celebrity tailor, Robbie Stanford, fitting Lionel with an extraordi-nary adventure in gentlemen's outerwear. This is a suit of Lionel's own design: he could paint, draw, compose, write – he'd have been a fool not to have at least one crack at haute couture. The suit is a three-piece in a green worsted fabric. The waistcoat has sleeves. The jacket does not. The sleeveless jacket slips over the sleeved waistcoat. The style didn't catch on. Undeterred by this early disappointment, a couple of years later he was seen sporting a midnight-blue eight-button baratthea suit with "tighter-than-tight" trousers and, on his feet, patent-leather boots with Cuban heels. "I design all my own clothes and get my tailor in Shepherd's Bush to make them up for me."

His handmade shirts had cutaway cuffs. Beneath the cuff his initials were embroidered – a detail that only his laundry would see but which emphasised that for Lionel perfect clothes do more than make you look good: they make you feel good, too.

Towards the end of his life Lionel, diabetic and comfort-eating, was the subject of a *South Bank Show* documentary. For his interview with Melvyn Bragg he wore an off-white crew-neck sweater in an open-knit. Even though the sweater is almost certainly cashmere, on any other overweight man in his mid-sixties it would look like a sack containing used sports equipment. On Lionel it looks magnificent.

"He always wore hats," says Ron Pember in a BBC interview, "a wonderful variety of hats. Pork pie cum trilby types. Frank Sinatra type hats at an angle across his head." He also favoured broad-brimmed varieties in velour and velvet. Muriel Walker possesses one of his early stunners in ginger fur. "Every day at rehearsals for *Blitz!* it would be a different hat," adds Pember, who was in the original production. "I recall one afternoon Lionel didn't turn up for rehearsals and everyone was wondering where he was. The rumour went round that he was in hospital, having one of his hats removed."

The accessories were good, too. "Talk about cool," says his friend David Charkham. "He had a watch. It was the size of a silver dollar – in fact it was a silver dollar and inside the silver dollar was a watch that came out. It was so cool." He even had a cooler kazoo than most people. "He composed a lot of stuff on that kazoo, but it wasn't like the little plastic ones. It was a big brass one and it used to sit on his piano."

"As soon as Lionel received his first cheque from his publisher," says John Gorman, "he promptly put down a deposit on a new car, an ice-blue Zephyr convertible with a power-operated hood. For Lionel it was a conspicuous and potent symbol of success. [. . .] It also profited the youngest of our lads in the firm for Lionel would extravagantly pay him five shillings to wash his car during the dinner hour."

The stakes were gradually raised. By 1960 the collection boasted a Mercedes Benz convertible with a built-in telephone, a Volkswagen Karmann-Ghia ("for nipping around town") and a Riley Pathfinder. Later he added a two-door Bentley Continental in blue – registration LB 3. At one point he also owned LB 1 and LB 2, but sold all three number plates to the Lebanese Embassy when times got tough.

The fastest four-seater sports coupe in the world was the Facel Vega, originally a Franco-American hybrid built in a Paris suburb – an arresting alliance of *séduisant* bodywork wrapped around a huge Chrysler engine. In its ten-year production run between 1954 and 1964, only a handful – 1,500 or so – was made. Picasso had one. Danny Kaye had one. Tony Curtis had one. The King of Morocco had one. The President of Mexico had one. Ava Gardner had three.

On January 4, 1960 the French goalkeeper and existentialist writer, Albert Camus, whose novel *L'Etranger* was another of those essential reads for anybody interested in coffee and angst, was on his way back to Paris from a holiday in the south of France in a Facel Vega being driven by his friend, the publisher Michel Gallimard. In Villeblevin, 60 miles short of their destination, the car, travelling at an estimated 112 mph, hit a tree. Camus and his publisher were killed.

This then was an existentialist's car: a car that, as well as having bodywork that brought even the auto–illiterate to orgasm, was a throbbing metaphor for the Meaninglessness of Life and the Absurdity of Existence. So it went without saying that Lionel Bart had one. In blue with white leather upholstery. Later Ringo Starr had one, too, although David Charkham suspects that Ringo might have bought Lionel's secondhand.

Victor Spinetti, the actor and director who starred in *Fings*, three Beatles' films and most other things that were worth seeing, was once given a lift in the Facel. "I'd never seen such a car," says Victor. "The dashboard was like a fighter plane. And I remember we were driving up Wardour Street and he said, 'I'd like to block Wardour Street off from one end to the other and have all the faces that I fancy in this street, and then every face, I'd have every one of them – every one.'"

Here then is the second contender for Pinnacle Moment In The Life Of Lionel Bart. It is 1962. Even though the Sixties have not properly been invented, you are driving around the streets of London behind the wheel of the car that killed Albert Camus while wearing a green Robbie Stamford suit with the long-sleeved waistcoat, glancing occasionally at your silver dollar watch and scenting the streets with *L'Heure Bleue*. Your own songs, the songs that you wrote, are pumping out of the in-car

45 rpm disc player. Maybe you're even talking on the car-phone. Wardour Street is crammed with every face you've ever fancied. You beckon one of them – some blonde and beautiful beau or a top star of stage, screen and television – to the passenger seat, gun the engine and whisper in your trademark hiss, 'Go, Bart, Go.'

Twelve

DAVID Merrick was a sensational Broadway producer, but a very unpleasant human being. Some say his moustache was waxed, but they may be exaggerating. A publicist in the Barnum mould – Max Bialystock from *The Producers* could have been inspired by him – when his 1961 show *Subways Are For Sleeping* was ill-received he sought and found New Yorkers with the same names as the top critics, invited them to the show and used their laudatory quotes in subsequent ads. The ruse was rumbled almost immediately, but the stunt itself provided enough publicity for the show to turn a modest profit. Similarly, to bring a little controversy to the 1957 Broadway production of John Osborne's *Look Back In Anger*, he hired a woman to rush the stage and slap Kenneth Haigh, playing Jimmy Porter. It hurt like hell but sold seats. His biggest successes – *Gypsy, Hello Dolly, 42nd Street* – made the record books for longest runs, highest grosses, most awards and the rest.

Merrick had a reputation for being a bully, an egotist and a skinflint who famously believed that it is never enough merely to succeed, you also have to watch others fail, too. Victor Spinetti, whose reputation for getting on with people is as renowned as Merrick's reputation for misanthropy, enjoyed his little idiosyncrasies

"I used to go and see him and sit in his office, this red office, and he had this toy: a trick cyclist that was on a wire. It was up there in the corner and there was a special thing to wind it down and as you were doing an interview with him he'd play with that and bring it all down to the desk to try and distract you."

A bidding war had broken out for *Oliver!*'s US rights soon after it had opened. Merrick won. All the same, he wanted to be sure that *Oliver!* had staying power before risking money, so waited till it had run a couple years in the West End before staging an American production – and even then, he sent the show on a lengthy five month tour before bringing it to New York.

Oliver!'s American premiere was at the Los Angeles Philharmonic Auditorium on August 6, 1962. From there it hauled itself to San Francisco, Detroit, Toronto . . . 11 cities in all. Georgia Brown, Barry Humphries and Danny Sewell all went over from the original cast, as did Peter Coe to direct and Lionel to infuriate and be infuriated by Peter Coe and generally supervise. Ron Moody had quit the London production several months previously so Fagin was played by Clive Revill, the banana-faced actor who as well as distinguishing himself in the UK with the Royal Shakespeare Company had been a regular on Broadway since his appropriately Dickensian debut as Sam Weller in a 1952 production of *Mr Pickwick*.

Lionel had already been subjected to a minor mauling in America with the death 'on the road' of *Lock Up Your Daughters* and was disenchanted. America is "a big flavourless peach," he told the *Daily Mirror*, "all palaces and no conversation. Everybody, everything is so beautiful, but I found the beauty was a mask that disguised a lot of evil and a pathological yearning for a fast buck."

Eventually the show found its way to New York and opened at the Imperial Theatre on January 6, 1963. Joining the cast was the most recent of the Artful Dodgers from the London production. This was David Jones, who had not long celebrated his seventeenth birthday and who, as Davy Jones, went on to achieve megastardom in The Monkees – the band and the TV show. In interviews he speaks fondly of his time in *Oliver!*, but then again for most of his life he's been too busy singing to put anybody down.

Lionel kept huge scrapbooks into which he – or his secretary – pasted his press-cuttings. There are cupboards full of them. One entire book is devoted to *Lock Up Your Daughters*. The *Oliver!* books fill a whole shelf. But there is practically nothing on *Oliver!*'s Broadway opening: a couple of business letters from Lionel to the producers and from the producers to Lionel; a souvenir programme; but no press cuttings at all. The reason being that the papers were on strike.

The New York City newspaper strike started on December 8, 1962 and went on for four months. There may be some benefit to be gained by opening a bad show during a news blackout. With no critics to savage it there's a chance that it might recoup its costs before word gets around that it stinks. But an average or a great show, starved of publicity, can easily and unfairly shrivel and die.

Oliver! had word of mouth on its side. Even before the 11-city tour, a groundswell of rumour and legend had been building among musical theatre aficionados who treasured their bootleg copies of the London cast album. Indeed, the US publishers grew so concerned by the prevalence of these bootlegs that they rushed through a cast recording in Hollywood just two weeks into the pre-Broadway run. It would be ten years or more before *Jesus Christ Superstar* and *Evita* fully realised the marketing advantages of releasing the album before the show has opened, but *Oliver!* was there first. By January 5, 1963 the newly recorded album had risen to 28 in the *Billboard* LP chart. Two weeks later the same paper (immune to the strike) reported: "*Oliver!* [. . .] arrived on Broadway with a running head in record shops. The RCA Victor *Oliver!* album, made with the American cast [an odd description for Georgia, Barry, Danny and Clive] now stands in the 20th position on the mono LP chart and is likely to have the same kind of long-run sales the show is bound to enjoy at the box office."

Also on *Oliver!*'s side was its country of origin. Though it would be another year before five thousand fans – each bribed with a dollar and a free tee-shirt – brought Beatlemania to JFK, clues that the British were coming, were all over the place. Just across the street from *Oliver!*, at the John Golden Theatre, *Beyond The Fringe,* the Alan Bennett, Peter Cook, Jonathan Miller and Dudley Moore revue was packing them in, while a few blocks away at the Ambassador, Anthony Newley was doing good business with the title Lionel claimed credit for, *Stop The World, I Want To Get Off.* Perhaps more significant, riding at the top of the *Billboard* singles chart was 'Telstar', played by The Tornados (from London, Sunderland, Kidderminster and Dortmund, Germany) and produced by Joe Meek in his makeshift studio on the Holloway Road in London.

The 1948 David Lean film of *Oliver Twist* had initially been banned in the USA on the grounds of anti-semitism. In London, Moody's Fagin, too, had been the subject of doubts and criticisms. The complaints had been taken on board. "A comparison of the British and American cast albums," says the *Billboard* review, "will show that, somewhere in mid-Atlantic (or mid-Merrick), the classic characterization of Fagin has received an [. . .] ethnic housecleaning. Revill substitutes some inventive mugging and stage business, however, and manages to create an Aryanised Fagin who would be welcome at a fund-raising rally for B'nai B'rith." Georgia's clearly the star: "When she's onstage belting out 'Oom-Pah-Pah' in the show's Hogarthian smoke-filled cabaret of the Act II opening, or romping through 'It's A Fine Life' in Fagin's fusty lair, she's Britain's answer to Judy Garland."

Which brings us neatly to the third contender for the title Pinnacle Moment In The Life Of Lionel Bart. You don't have to be gay for this to be a compelling fantasy: it is the Broadway opening of a musical for which you are sole author of book, lyrics and music. As you enter the theatre, everybody, ushers included, breaks into applause. The curtain goes up, the audience goes quiet. At the end they clap and scream "Author, Author".

You go backstage with your date for the evening. She whispers a few words of encouragement and pushes you onstage. Eventually, after the congratulations and the champagne and the supper, your date takes you to the top of the Empire State Building and says, "This is your town, what colour do you want it painted?" Your date – and here comes the crunch – who entered the foyer, sat beside you, pushed you onstage, drank the champagne, took you to the top of the world – is none other than Miss Judy Garland.

By the time of *Oliver!*'s Broadway opening, Lionel and Judy were old friends.

On November 18, 1959, Judy had been admitted to hospital suffering from acute hepatitis. Her death was widely predicted, not least by her doctors. When she was considered well enough to leave hospital, more than three months later, the doctors were still giving her five years maximum. They also told her that in all likelihood she would never sing again. As if.

Nine years before that, when her life and career had been on the skids, she had rediscovered her mojo in a series of smash hit concerts in the UK, finishing with four sell-out weeks at the London Palladium. If she could do it once, she could do it again. In July 1960, she flew to London. She was greeted, cosseted and entertained by British friends, including Noël Coward and Dirk Bogarde, and saw all the shows worth seeing. One that particularly caught her fancy was *Fings Ain't Wot They Use T'Be*.

Miriam Karlin, then playing Lil, remembers one afternoon at the Garrick Theatre, between the matinee and the evening performance. She was sitting in her dressing room when the phone rang. "I was very grand," she told the BBC. "I had a phone in my dressing room. And Lionel was on the phone and he said, 'Oh, Mim, listen, I'm bringing Judy Garland tonight to see the show and we're going to a party afterwards at Douglas Fairbanks'. Will you come along as well?' And I thought, 'He's going mad.'"[64]

Judy came to see *Fings* "five or six times".[65] She went to see *Oliver!* too. At the end of August, Ron Moody records in his diary. "Judy Garland is in but Bart takes her in to see Georgia and not me – the little sod."

London and Lionel worked their magic. At the beginning of August the woman who would never sing again felt well enough to record 20 songs at Abbey Road.[66] Before leaving the US, she had also agreed to a couple of concerts at the London Palladium. Three days before her visit to *Oliver!*, she annihilated the Palladium audience with two hours of 'Trolley' and

'Swanee' and 'Rainbow' and strutting and tears, to which the audience replied by making more noise than 'Rock-a-bye Your Baby With A Dixie Melody'. A week later she did the same thing again. These proved to be try-outs for her Carnegie Hall concert the following April – described even by diffident commentators as "the greatest night in show business history".

Over the next couple of years, whenever Judy was in the UK or Lionel in the US, they were together. Rumours flourished. When it was reported on both sides of the Atlantic that Judy was seeking a divorce from her husband Sid Luft in order that she and Bart might become one, the couple's "just good friends" protestations were, as they always are, taken as incontrovertible evidence that they were monogramming silverware. Even more shocking was the possibility that Lionel, who was caught jetting to Majorca just hours after Alma Cogan had set off for the same destination, might be a two-timing cad.

These are the busy years, the in-demand years, when Lionel's progress is a blur. Now he's in New York, now he's in London, now he's in the south of France, now he's in Majorca and sometimes he appears to be in two or three places at the same time. Here he is walking Judy Garland up a theatre aisle. Now he's seen sharing a joke with Cary Grant or Pablo Picasso. And now he's in a Bedfordshire marquee judging the Woburn Abbey Easter Bonnet parade.

Oliver! ran for nearly two years on Broadway and, after a nine month tour, came back again for a mini-run lasting a couple of months. It won three Tony awards – Lionel for Composer and Lyricist, Sean for Scenic Designer, Donald Pippin for Conductor and Musical Director – and was nominated for a clutch of others, including Georgia for Actress in a Musical and Clive Revill for Actor in a Musical.

On February 9, 1964, just over a year into the run, ticket sales received a further boost when *The Ed Sullivan Show* hosted an evening of British acts and invited the *Oliver!* cast to take part. David Jones and company sang 'I'd Do Anything'. Georgia Brown sang 'As Long As He Needs Me'. 'Two Ton' Tessie O'Shea, a singer and ukulele player from Cardiff, then appearing at the Broadway Theatre in Noël Coward's *The Girl Who Came To Supper*, sang a medley of show tunes. And this was the night, of course, when The Beatles, amid more hysteria than was generated by the Lindbergh baby kidnapping and the Wall Street Crash combined, made their first US TV appearance. The show attracted a record 73 million viewers.

Thirteen

IN December 1961, Leslie Mallory, for the *Daily Herald,* spoke to Lionel and reported: "As soon as *Blitz!* is mounted he wants to get on with what he calls 'a folk opera set in Liverpool.' Do you know anyone from Liverpool?' he said. I thought of the best television playwright in the country. 'Alun Owen,' I said. Bart was up like a flash, snapping his fingers. 'Get him on the blower,' he told his secretary. 'Alun? Hello, dad. Listen. I've got an idea. It's a gas. When can we meet? Tomorrow?' In three minutes a tentative thought brewed into a coherent plan. That is the way Mr Bart does business."

Mallory's story is one of many told about the genesis of *Maggie May.* The fact of the matter is that nobody seems able to remember, least of all Lionel himself whose efforts to piece it together much later in life for the *South Bank Show* reduced him to a series of semi-coherent stumbles and mumbles. The various elements involved in the different versions seem to include the following:

1. Georgia Brown. "The true inspiration for *Maggie May,*" Lionel says in the same *South Bank Show* interview, "is Georgia Brown. I'd known her since we were babies." Georgia's achievement – in turning herself from Lily Klot, a snot-nosed East End kid, into Georgia Brown, accomplished jazz singer and respected interpreter of the Brecht/Weill canon – was almost as impressive as his own. Not long after the opening of *Blitz!*, in May 1962, she went into the studio with the Ted Heath Orchestra to record an album mostly of music-hall songs – 'The Honeysuckle And The Bee', 'If You Were The Only Girl In The World', 'Ta-Ra-Ra-Boom-Dee-Ay' – with jazz/swing arrangements. The album was 'devised and presented by Lionel Bart', who also contributed the sleeve notes and added some extra lyrics. His Nancy, he decided from the start, would be his Maggie May.

2. Kazantzakis. Georgia told Lionel about a book she'd been reading; *Christ Recrucified,* a novel by Nikos Kazantzakis, which was filmed in 1957 under the title *He Who Must Die.* The plot revolved around a passion-play staged in a Greek village in which the local prostitute – a

146

tart with a heart – is given the part of Mary Magdalene. Maggie May, Mary Magdalene. MM.

3. Harry H. Corbett. In 1957, Harry H. Corbett, the Theatre Work-shop regular who became a household name as Harold Steptoe in TV's *Steptoe & Son*, recorded a collection of sea shanties with Joan Littlewood's ex-husband, Ewan MacColl, and folksong collector Bert Lloyd. Released as an LP, *Songs Of The Sea,* they intrigued and inspired Lionel to try something different. Corbett also loaned, gave or introduced Lionel to other folk records.

4. The Irish Republican Army. In 1959, Brendan Behan's *The Hostage* was given a short run in Paris. Most of Joan's company at the time, including Lionel and Frank Norman, and half the set of *Fings* went over with it. Every night, after the curtain was down, Brendan liked to get fighting drunk, and ended the run, gloriously, in prison, having picked a fight with Air France. When Brendan was not fight-ing, he liked to sing. He had an extensive repertoire of Irish rebel songs.

5. Roller skates. The song, 'Maggie May', was one of Lionel's reper-toire of dirty songs that he used to sing as a kid in exchange for turns on roller skates.

6. *Porgy And Bess.* Gershwin's musical of love, betrayal and death among the dirt poor of South Carolina had always been Lionel's gold standard. The docks of Liverpool had – for Lionel – something of the same dark, alien quality that Gershwin found on Folly Island. Just as Gershwin was able to plug into the Gullah musical traditions of those islands, Lionel could immerse himself in Scouse/Welsh/Irish folksong.

.7. Alun Owen. While *Fings* was coming and going at Stratford, another play in production was *Progress In The Park,* about four kids in Liverpool, written by Alun Owen, a Welsh/Liverpudlian former actor and comedian. It transferred first to the Royal Court, then to the Saville Theatre. Owen's TV play, *No Trams To Lime Street* – about three sailors on shore leave in Liverpool, broadcast in October 1959 – is still regarded as a milestone in TV drama.

However the elements fell – and maybe Leslie Mallory's version of how it happened is pin-sharp accurate – the upshot was that Lionel decided to collaborate with Alun Owen on a musical called *Maggie May,* sort of based on the old song, ever so vaguely influenced by *Christ Recrucified* but with a folkish/sea shantyish score.

The most extraordinary part of the story is that the bulk of this coming together took place in 1961, a good 18 months before The Beatles' first record, and two years before the Mersey took over from the Seine as the world's most fashionable inland waterway. Planning a Liverpool musical two years in advance of Liverpool becoming the coolest place on the planet, in order to have it ready for production at the exact moment that Merseymania reaches its zenith seems evidence of either time travel skills, or prophetic powers to rival those of Nostradamus, or a superhuman finger-on-the-pulse, riding-the-zeitgeist with-it-ness. Blind luck was Lionel's explanation. "After *Oliver!* and *Blitz!*," he told the *Daily Express*, "I was desperately trying to get away from London. It started as an accident."

It was both an accident and an opportunity for apparently exploring some unfamiliar musical styles, while still rooting himself deep in his comfort zones. "After doing some research, I found that most of Liverpool's folk music had Irish Celtic roots. Now it's common knowledge, or should be, that the Irish are actually the lost tribe of Israel, so it's a good job I remembered my bar mitzvah music. However, I was lost on the chat. So I told my mate, designer and genius, Sean Kenny, who, without further ado, took me and my rough storyline to Alun Owen, who had already established himself with plays about Liverpool."

George Gershwin spent time living without running water or electricity on Folly Island, collecting his musical material for *Porgy And Bess*. Not to be outdone, Lionel sometimes claimed to have conducted extensive field trips to Liverpool: "I spent a year there to get the feel of the music. Really aping my idol in a way, George Gershwin, when he went to Catfish Row for a year to get his influences for *Porgy And Bess*. I thought I'd do the same thing. And Brian Epstein lent me this little flat in Liverpool. It was freezing. Had to keep putting shillings in the meter and it was freezing."[67]

Judy Huxtable, Sean Kenny's girlfriend, provides a possibly more reliable memoir. She joined Bart, Kenny and Owen on one of their Liverpool field trips. Judy Garland joined them, too. She was in Britain to shoot *I Could Go On Singing* with Dirk Bogarde, a movie which, by her own assessment, was "a pile of shit". Her mood, not helped by a separation from her husband and a custody battle over the children, had brought on several on-set tantrums, at least one suicide attempt and, in protest at there being no toilet facilities for the star's private use, a piss in a waste-paper bin.

"I feel particularly excited to have the chance to meet Judy Garland," says Huxtable. "She and Lionel are very close. At night in Liverpool, we troop to the Cavern to watch The Beatles perform. They are brilliant and we all agree they will go far. Afterwards we come back to our hotel.

Lionel has taken a suite and Sean and I go upstairs to join him. Everyone but me starts drinking. There's a piano in his sitting room . . . and Judy starts singing songs from her repertoire. She doesn't want to go to bed and we stay up all night listening to her."[68]

In August, Judy Garland and Lionel both flew to California – Judy to vacation on Lake Tahoe, Lionel to supervise the *Oliver!* opening in Los Angeles.

"Alun had to go solo for six months," said Lionel. "When I returned he presented me with a giant script and as he handed it over he said, 'I know it's long, boychick, but I've written a lot of material for you to make rhyme into songs. In any case you've got to learn a whole new language.' I said, 'Whaddya mean, a whole new language?' Then he went on about the dialect, saying it was part Irish, part Welsh and part catarrh. Then I asked him if I had to catch catarrh? He told me to drop dead, and that was the beginning of a beautiful friendship."[69]

Still the work was constantly interrupted by Lionel's commuting between London and New York. *Oliver!* on Broadway needed his intermittent presence, to schmooze, smooth, charm, hype and be Lionel.

One of the people he first schmoozed and later befriended was the composer Richard Rodgers, then 61. *The Sound Of Music,* his most recent in a string of hits trailing back to 1925, was nearing the end of a three-and-a-half year run.

Lionel was ticking off heroes; first Noël Coward, now Richard Rodgers, who though not a hero as such, had for almost 20 years breathed in the smoke from a hero's cigar. Lorenz Hart, always cited as one of Lionel's most important influences as a lyricist, had written effortless, sophisticated, clever, edgy, poignant words to Richard Rodgers' music from 1919 until his death in 1943. The hits began in 1925 with 'Manhattan', and rolled off the production line with the regularity of Fords but the glamour of Bugattis, year after year: 'Blue Moon', 'My Funny Valentine', 'I Could Write A Book', 'I Didn't Know What Time It Was', 'The Lady Is A Tramp'. There is not a lyricist in the world who would not give up a limb and a first-born to have written 'Bewitched Bothered And Bewildered'. "Vexed again, perplexed again, thank god I can be oversexed again."

Hart was also a Jewish homosexual who became an alcoholic and died at the age of 47.

Richard Rodgers' new lyricist, Oscar Hammerstein II, blew away Larry Hart's dark and edgy influences and nurtured a product which dealt less with oversexed persons of deliberately ambiguous sexual orientation and more with bright golden hazes on meadows, happy talk, June's proclivity for bustin' out all over and schnitzel with noodles. Their first show, *Oklahoma!*, ran for five years. Their last, *The Sound Of Music*, achieved the apparently impossible by featuring nuns and Nazis in the same show without a single accusation of tastelessness or erotic ambiguity. In 1960, a year after *The Sound Of Music* opened, Oscar Hammerstein succumbed to stomach cancer.

The prospect of a Rodgers and Bart musical partnership, according to Lionel, was mooted over the course of a year. They discussed an adaptation of *Moll Flanders*. Working methods eventually tore them apart. "I wrote a song in *Maggie May* which is a lullaby ostensibly being written there and then by this hooker to her sleeping lover," Lionel told Mark Steyn in 1990. "[Richard Rodgers] said, 'It works . . . but there are impure rhymes.' I said, 'That's because she's not a very good lyric writer.'"

Rodgers went on to collaborate with many lyricists, including Stephen Sondheim, but disappointingly there is no Rodgers and Bart songbook. Neither, as far as we know, did Lionel ever sing to him, in exchange for a turn on his roller skates, "Crabs on my rectum and sperm on my nipples / something and something like raspberry ripples . . ."

A more serious distraction from *Maggie May* came from a pullover mishap.

Polo necks were all the rage on the streets of London in 1963. The tight black polo neck, for years the trademark of the French existentialist, moved in from the East, while at the same time the similar but subtly different 'tight turtle-neck' of the American preppy moved in from the West. They met in one of John Stephen's shops in Carnaby Street. Made from bri-nylon, they were a second skin which clung to a man's nipples in an unfortunately anti-erotic way. Worn under a jacket they became first a semi-formal then a formal alternative to the necktie.

Lionel was trying on the preppy version in a New York menswear outlet when his head got stuck. Half in and half out he caught sight of himself in a mirror. Inspiration struck. His next show would be based on Victor Hugo's *The Hunchback Of Notre Dame*. He set to work immediately, giving his secretary the task first of producing a 12-page précis of the book, then getting hold of a copy of the 1939 Charles Laughton film (not an easy task in pre-video days), hiring a projector on which to run it and transcribing the dialogue. The project – at various times called *Hunchback, Quasimodo, Hunch,* and probably *Hunch!* – was to occupy him on and off for the rest of his life. It is diverting, if pointless to speculate what a different place the modern musical stage might have been if his hand had moved a little to the right on the bookshelf of world literature and, instead of picking out *Hunchback,* settled instead on Victor Hugo's weightier *Les Misérables.* Lionel Bart's *Miz!* might not have been more successful, but would certainly have been more fun than the Bublil/Schönberg version ("With home-made blades and hand grenades / we assemble for a knees-up on the barricades").

By mid-1963, it was apparent that *Maggie May*, not *Hunch,* was his front runner. Scousers had taken by storm the Toppermost of the Poppermost. Billy J. Kramer & The Dakotas, Gerry & The Pacemakers, The Swinging Blue Jeans, The Merseybeats, Cilla Black and, most notably, The Beatles had occupied the charts, put their feet up on the furniture, stolen drink from the fridge and left the back door open to let some of their pals from Manchester in, too. Liverpool was no longer a busy port in the north-west of England. It was Fab Fab Fabbersville, the capital of Fabland at the centre of the planet Fab. At Guildford breakfast tables, 14-year-olds were demanding "chip butties" because they were "gear". They were growing their hair, which they pronounced "hur". Behind the bicycle sheds they were lighting up "ciggies". And their heels were Cuban.

No sooner had Lionel and Alun got back to work on *Maggie May* than "we had to stop halfway through it. John Lennon phoned me and said, 'Can I have a lend of your writer. We got to do this film, *A Hard Day's Night.*'"

On October 31, 1963, *The Times* made the official announcement: "Mr Alun Owen is to write an original screenplay for The Beatles who are shortly to make their first film produced by Mr Walter Shenson and to be distributed by United Artists. Shooting is to begin early next February."

The luck of the Lionel. Not only had Liverpool, location of his musical, become the centre of the universe, his collaborator had practically become the fifth Beatle. "So, I lost Alun for a while. I just did some more songs, and it grew. And finally we had a script and a score."

Blitz! is 'big and exciting', *Maggie May* is 'arty and earthy'. It is also epic in scope, it steams with religio-political thematic nuance and includes a wildcat strike, a religious procession, a union traitor, a corrupt demagogue, a 'beat-club', a toadying publican, a spectacular death, a singing milkman, some of Lionel's finest songs and another breathtaking Sean Kenny set.

The action starts back in the Forties with Maggie May and Patrick Casey as children taking part in a Holy Week passion-play, then jumps forward to the Sixties. Maggie has become a prostitute – who calls all her clients Casey so we know she's still holding a torch for her childhood sweetheart – and Patrick is off at sea. When Patrick comes home to Liverpool, he finds himself forced into leading a strike at the dockyards. Maggie and Pat are reunited but, during a final act of defiance by the striking dockers, Pat is killed.

At the beginning of 1964, clutching the new script, Lionel flew to New York to present it to Georgia Brown. He explained to her how it was based on the Nikos Kazantzakis story that she had told him about: how the Maggie character was Mary Magdalene and Casey was Jesus.

Georgia had been playing Nancy every night for three years, so could be excused for being reluctant to sign up for another musical. She was a star on Broadway, almost certainly being wooed by other Broadway producers, record labels and Hollywood. She could have had any one of a number of reasons for turning down a show Lionel had specifically crafted for her, but the one she gave – or at least the one Lionel always said she gave – was that she "didn't want to play second fiddle to Jesus".

Various names were suggested for the 'Jesus' part – Peter O'Toole was front-runner for a while, but since the success of *Lawrence Of Arabia* the film industry had become his demanding mistress. Next on the list was Albert Finney, a bookie's son from Salford, whose triumphs in Karel Reisz's film of Alan Sillitoe's *Saturday Night And Sunday Morning* and Tony Richardson's film of Henry Fielding's *Tom Jones* had established the gold-seal bankability of his battered baby-face. He had just opened around the corner from *Oliver!* in John Osborne's *Luther*. He said no, too.

It was a short step from Albert Finney to Rachel Roberts. The two had co-starred in *Saturday Night And Sunday Morning* and the film had won her a Best Actress BAFTA. Three years later she won another Best Actress for *This Sporting Life*. She was also one of Joan Littlewood's 'nuts' having played in John Marston's Jacobean comedy *The Dutch Courtesan,* which was rehearsing at Stratford when *Fings* was running. And if that wasn't enough, her much publicised 1962 celebrity wedding to Rex Harrison (a close friend of Lionel's) made it a racing certainty that her name on the posters would sell tickets. She was good for the part, too; big, blonde and brassy. On the downside, she did have a reputation for storminess and liked a drink.

Lionel tracked her down to Portofino in Italy, where Rex had had a house built, and found her "having intensive voice training from Signor Tutti Frutti or somebody." She said yes.

In April, *The Times* announced that Casey would "probably be played by Mr Tom Bell." That never happened either. Eventually the part went to Kenneth Haigh, who had known Lionel since the pre-Tommy Steele days when they both used to hang out at the Yellow Door. In 1956 he'd played Jimmy Porter in the first ever production of John Osborne's *Look Back In Anger*. Like Alun Owen, he came trailing a small cloud of that most valuable commodity of all in 1964, Beatle dust, having played a minor part in *A Hard Day's Night*.

More Beatle-dust, far more, came billowing in with John Junkin, the character actor who, as 'Shake' the put-upon road manager, possibly had more lines in *A Hard Day's Night* than any individual Beatle. He was recruited to play Eric Dooley, one of the dockers.

Though Edna Everage was beginning to make her presence felt on TV and at the Establishment Club, Barry Humphries found time in her busy schedule to play the Balladeer, a shadowy chorus/narrator figure.

The money, £70,000 – a ten grand increase on *Blitz!* – was stumped up by Bernard Delfont, brother of Lew and Leslie Grade, all born Winogradsky and from identical eastern European/Brick Lane stock as the Begleiters. Indeed Morris and Yetta may well have seen not only the boys' parents, Isaac and Golda Winogradsky, singing at the Pavilion on the Mile End Road, but also Bernard himself, whose eccentric dancing made him a minor musical-hall star in the Thirties. All three Winogradsky boys had built themselves showbiz empires – Bernard did theatre, Lew (now known as Grade) did TV and Leslie (also known as Grade) was everybody's agent.

It would have seemed perverse to set anything in Liverpool without at least a nod to the 'beat scene', so Alun and Lionel incorporated a club and band into the script. By this time Liverpool bands, good ones, were thin on the ground, Brian Epstein having already hoovered up most of them.

Auditions were held at Delfont's Talk Of The Town nightclub, although Alun had a group in mind, anyway. The Nocturnes were a resident band at the Blue Angel club, one of Alun's preferred hangouts when he was in Liverpool. It was here he earwigged phrases he could lift and install in a script.

"In fact my girlfriend, Virginia," wrote Bill Harry, editor of *Mersey Beat*, "told him she had heard Pat Davies, Ringo Starr's girlfriend and Cilla Black's mate, utter the words, 'Who knitted your face and dropped a stitch?' And he used it in the musical."

The Nocturnes got the *Maggie May* gig and, for a while, it felt as if the big time was close enough to spit on. The press celebrated them as the first beat group to appear in a West End musical, they rubbed shoulders with the showbiz elite, guested on Eamonn Andrews' TV show and scored a record contract with Decca. Brutal disillusion soon followed. The record contract stipulated that their first single had to be 'Carryin' On', their song from the show. When the record bombed, their contract was cancelled. Even worse, though offers came in, the demands of the show – seven nights a week and two matinees – severely limited their availability. "Eventually the offers dwindled away," said Dave Elias, the band's keyboard player. "We were cocooned in this musical show. We managed to do a few Saturday morning shows but that was about it."

Other Blue Angel regulars did better. Geoff Hughes was an actor, working as a car salesman. Alun got him a part in the show, and he never looked back. He went on to play Eddie Yates in *Coronation Street* and Twiggy in *The Royle Family*.

In the end it's Ted Kotcheff, the director, you feel sorry for. He was a Canadian, primarily a film and television director, who later went on to make *The Apprenticeship Of Duddy Kravitz, First Blood* and *Weekend At Bernie's*. He had been brought in because, as director of Alun Owen's TV play, *No Trams To Lime Street,* he had proved his ability to make Scouseness happen in a dramatic context, but musical theatre was not his natural milieu and here he had to deal with (a) Lionel, never known to take a back seat and having directed *Blitz!* keener than ever to grab the wheel and try a couple of handbrake turns, (b) Sean, whose set as usual was an awe-inspiringly magnificent logistical nightmare, (c) Rachel, and (d) from time to time Rachel's husband Rex Harrison.

During rehearsals just before the out-of-town opening, Rex flew in from Rome where he was filming *The Agony And The Ecstasy,* playing the Pope to Charlton Heston's Michelangelo, and snuck into the theatre. While Ted Kotcheff was sorting out a bit of business, a voice from the darkness at the back of the stalls advised, with all the weight of papal authority, "I wouldn't do that if I were you."

Spats were frequent. So were accidents. John Junkin remembers there being a "very high casualty rate", but "nothing defeated Lionel. He never lost that bubble, the ability to gee people up, give them that extra bit of energy."

The 'bubble' could also be interpreted as 'constant and unwarranted interference in every aspect of the production' or, to use John Junkin's again more charitable words: "He had, in the nicest way, tunnel vision. What he wanted was a show in the West End that was a hit. He was always there, giving notes, nagging – never showing a lack of confidence in your work or his own."

When Lionel's 'bubble' met Rachel's 'difficult' the explosion was atomic.

"We had our battles during the try out," said Lionel. "I gave her a hard time. 'Look dolly, it's not a hymn singing class, you know,' I remember bawling her out. She was good but she was difficult. Sean Kenny was designing the show. Rachel had to appear high up on one of the mobile sets. 'She might fall,' I said. He gave me a wink, 'We'll risk it.'"

The collaboration between Lionel and Sean once again produced a magnificent monster. They goaded each other to creative excess. "Sean was a hundred years ahead of his time," said Lionel. "We had one of the only composer-designer-author relationships ever. We swopped drawings before I even wrote a note of a show. Sean's attitude was, 'It can be done.' I'd do a drawing. He'd do a drawing. He'd write a three-line poem which would set me up to do a huge momentum song that would travel through four different sets inside one number onstage. In *Maggie May* there was a song that started out inside a pub, went on to the streets, went on to the Mersey Ferry, the pub became a ferry and then the ferry went across the Mersey and then we'd be on the other side of the Mersey, all inside one number. This was a huge innovation."[70]

Richard Mills was Bernard Delfont's assistant. "It was a typical Sean design," he says, "very complex interlocking machinery, all driven by electric motors. I was very nervous of this and asked him if we could have some manual winches as back up. His reply was, 'Richard, one day they are going to land a man on the moon and they're not going to winch him up.'"

"The joke going round the company," said John Junkin, "was, 'How's your girlfriend?' 'Oh, she's no longer with us. She got eaten by a Sean Kenny set.' We rehearsed for six weeks and then went to Manchester and the opening night in front of the critics was the first time we had all the songs and all the costumes and no one knew whether they could make all their changes. The stairs backstage were littered with semi-dressed, exhausted dancers."

On the streets of Liverpool many of the posters advertising the show had already been redesigned by wags who had replaced the 'B' in 'Bart' with an 'F'. Lionel liked that. Just the sort of thing he would have done.

Lionel's date for that Manchester opening was, once again, Miss Judy Garland, in Britain after a disastrous tour of Australia, a suicide attempt in Hong Kong (pills), another soon after her arrival in London (wrists), a triumphant 'Night of 100 Stars' at the Palladium, during which the audience shrieked, "Sing, Judy, sing" and a pissed John Lennon shrieked, "Fuck off, Judy, fuck off."[71]

After the show in Manchester, everybody commuted to Liverpool for a party at the Blue Angel. Judy played the One Armed Bandit for a while, then decided she had to sing and called for an accompanist. Despite the place being packed with musicians and 'Over The Rainbow' being in the repertoire of any self-respecting group at the time, there were no takers.[72] One legend has it that after a while Judy's mood turned ugly. She argued with Allan Williams, the club's manager, who promptly barred her. This story is also told about Judy at the *Hard Day's Night* after show party, and about Judy having a drink after appearing at the Empire. It may, of course, have happened on all three occasions. Or it might never have happened at all.

"Judy heard the music before she saw the show," said Lionel.[73] "She said, 'I got to record those songs.'" At the Manchester opening, "she was cheering away and a great person to have in an audience. Then about four weeks afterwards we decided to make this record of four of the songs. And she was quite remarkable. We spent a couple of days. [. . .] And I'm there with the arranger, Harry Robinson, and she wanted to be told about phrasing and routining in great detail. And I thought she was having me on at first, but I thought, 'Okay, I'll make some suggestions.' And she was just a joy to work with because the session the following weekend, on the Sunday, she pitched up with a couple of large hampers of smoked salmon and caviar and champagne and wine for the big band. And she did everything virtually in one take. I've never seen anything quite so professional."

She recorded four of the songs: 'The Land Of Promises', 'Maggie, Maggie May', 'It's Yourself' and 'There's Only One Union'. They were released on an EP (Extended Play 7″ vinyl record) and later turned up on the CD compilation *Classic Judy Garland – The Capitol Years 1955–1965*. They're weird records. Judy sings lines like, "The TUC is free to see just how my membership expands" with so little apparent comprehension the words might as well be in Tagalog.

Maggie May is Lionel's most accomplished score. It's "Celtic music", as he puts it, "all married to ancient Hebrew music." The influence of Kurt Weill is in there too – possibly an indication of its origins as a vehicle for Georgia Brown.

'I'm Me' could have come straight from *The Threepenny Opera*, 'Casey' from *Mahagonny*, but both have an English twist, a lilt to the rhythm that makes them unmistakably Lionel. Most impressive is the score's consistency. In comparison, *Blitz!* and even *Oliver!* show signs of being a ragbag of assorted styles – music hall for this one, synagogue for this, torch song here, pop song there. *Maggie May* has beat songs, jazz songs, muckabout songs, but musically they're clearly all drawn from the same source – this Celtic/Hebrew/Kurt Weill/Folksong mix, perhaps more comfortably described simply as 'Lionel Bart music'. It would perhaps be too dismissive of the *Oliver!* score and the *Blitz!* score to suggest that, at last in *Maggie May*, Lionel had found his style, his voice; nevertheless plot, lyric, tune, attitude and personality here find a singularity and a cohesiveness they had never known before.

A few nights after the Manchester opening, Lionel was given his first chance to shine onstage since he sang 'Meatface' in *Fings*.

"I remember one of the dancers," says John Junkin, "Fred Evans, who played a small part as a milkman, had a song to sing, 'Shine You Swine', and he'd been having problems with his throat. No one bothered to tell us, but that night we were standing by ready to go on and Fred's music was being played and into the spotlight in a jacket and a hat four sizes too large came Lionel and he played the milkman. And he enjoyed himself enormously. What he looked like – Fred was twice his size – was . . . well."

The West End opening was at the Adelphi Theatre on September 22, 1964. The red carpet was the most gaudily decorated of Lionel's career.

"We mingled with Lionel and his 'fiancée/mate' Alma Cogan," says Andrew Loog Oldham.[74] "Peter Sellers and Britt Ekland were there, as were Roy Moseley and Anthony Perkins; Noël Coward and Binkie Beaumont . . ."*

". . . and Rex Harrison and Sybil Burton. [. . .] Rex Harrison looked embalmed and embarrassed. He had the expression of a man who wished he'd never crossed the Strand and left the safety of his quarters in the Savoy. Rachel Roberts – wife number four in a tally of six – was *Maggie May*'s not-so-lady-like leading lady, a boisterous diva who had been carrying on so much backstage over the past few weeks' rehearsals that leading man Kenneth Haigh looked at her with a murderous glint in his eye. Rachel had turned her actress's insecurity into a twister of a Welsh tornado and had the production, cast and crew by the balls, which she squeezed and twisted. [. . .] Judy Garland was swaying in the wheeze with her latest gay betrothal on one arm and the ghost of prescriptions past on the other. Kenny Lynch [. . .] wondered why so many whores would spend good money to see another one gone bad."

---

* A week or so before the opening, Noël had sent Lionel a telegram: "Dear Li, Do I ask too much? May I please buy four seats for the first night for *Maggie May* on the 22nd? If that's impossible I would be grateful for two." All it lacked was an enclosed Postal Order to make the humility utterly sincere.

Lionel, dressed in a high cut eight-button double-breasted suit with a deep collared shirt and a tiny satin bow, came with Alma wearing high heels, an outsize satin bow and her hair bouffed higher than Judy Garland. Alma's sister Sandra was there, too.

"We arrived at the theatre to be greeted by Lionel [. . .] I'm sure he did not even see us, such was his state of nerves. Amidst all the hubbub we tried to take our seats and get settled before the curtain went up – it was late as it always is on first nights. We had no sooner achieved a reasonable degree of comfort than Alma felt a tap on her shoulder. We then heard the unmistakable clipped tones and rolled r's of the Master himself, Noël Coward. 'Madam, would you kindly rrremove your busby.' After much laughter and many apologies we began what must have looked like a ridiculous game of musical chairs, our striking appearance only adding to the general hilarity and excitement of the moment."

Maggie May was better received than *Blitz!*, certainly by the first night audience. They applauded "with an enthusiasm even more deafening than Mr Ray Jones' most vigorous orchestrations," said *The Times* critic. "And in point of fact there is a good deal to be rapturous about." Then, like a Lower Sixth Former reviewing the School Play for the Mag, the same critic makes sure everybody's sterling effort gets a mention. "Mr Sean Kenny's sets – streets, warehouses, docks, a ferryboat and New Brighton Fairground – are [. . .] toughly, accurately and overpoweringly atmospheric. Mr Paddy Stone's choreography takes modern teenage dance as its starting point and is always lively and unusual. Mr Ted Kotcheff's production is always explosively vigorous. Mr Owen's dialogue, as we expect, is made of the tough derision that is Liverpool's natural speech, a disguise for its innate sentimentality. Miss Rachel Roberts and Mr Kenneth Haigh find opportunities for subtleties of acting rarely suggested by their lines. Mr Bart's ultimate destination is, of course, a sort of folk opera with its music created from the eclectic anthology of styles with which he works. In the amount of music he has composed for *Maggie May* he is probably nearer to his aim than any earlier show."

The *Express* praises "Miss Roberts, with her mouth twisting like sheet metal" and says that "Mr Haigh is in his best, offhand, leaping form – including a dangerous looking high dive off an electrified dockside crane."

"I went to the opening of *Maggie May* which is a smash hit and, on the whole, deserves to be," Noël wrote in his diary. "Personally I wouldn't care to see it again on account of being allergic to strikes and squalor, but it is very well done."[75]

The show ran profitably for more than a year and was a success by any standards except . . . *Blitz!* opened and closed; *Maggie May* opened and closed and all through it *Oliver!* kept on running. The sets and casts got bigger, the orchestras got louder, the music more ambitious, but nothing could come close to that first monster hit.

From the start, Rachel Roberts' days were numbered. "Her contract was for a limited run, six months I think," said Lionel.[76] "She opened big in London, but she got tired. She also started drinking. She got pissed out of her mind one night, forgot to put her girdle on, and came out from the wrong side for one of her duets. Afterwards we all met, Bernard Delfont who was presenting it, Ted Kotcheff who directed it and Alun Owen who wrote it. None of them dared face a tigress like Rachel to tell her what they thought of her bloody awful conduct. I was pushed forward.

"I knocked on her dressing room door, very nervous.

"'Come in,' she said. You could hear how pissed she was. I told her I thought her conduct was disgraceful.

"'Do you think I'm drunk?' she said.

"'Darling, I've tripped over the empties outside.' I'd a huge pile of money with me, from the box office or somewhere. I shoved it at her. 'If I were you, Rachel, I'd take this and catch the folk while they are still outside and offer them their money back. You were fucking awful.'

"Well, home I go, very choked, and get into bed, and about 2.00 a.m. the phone rings. It's Rex. Blazing angry.

"'I hear you've been bloody rude to my wife. What did you say to her, you little homosexual runt?'

"Well, I got really angry at that. 'Here,' I shouted at him down the phone, 'Who the hell are you calling little?'"

A couple of years later, when Rex Harrison was playing Doctor Dolittle, Anthony Newley said, "'I dunno whether Rex could actually talk to the animals, but he was certainly married to one."

When the curtain went up on February 18, 1965, Georgia Brown walked on to the stage as Maggie. The audience was taken by surprise. There had been no announcements in the press. Even Bernard Delfont's office – though they must have been aware of Rachel's leaving – seem to have been caught a bit off balance by Georgia's appearance, leaving open the possibility that Lionel had masterminded the whole thing as a coup, making sure he got his Maggie – the proper Maggie for whom the show was written in the first place – onstage before anybody had a chance to argue.

The switch certainly did the show no harm. Ticket sales still flourished, but if Lionel had been hoping that Georgia's presence would give *Maggie May* the fillip it needed to turn it into another *Oliver!*, he was disappointed.

Joan Littlewood had meanwhile become a film director, having adapted *Sparrers Can't Sing*, a Stephen Lewis play that had been given a bit of a working over at Stratford, for the big screen. It was a cockney tale of love and betrayal for the filming of which Joan had hired her full complement of 'nuts' and 'clowns', including Barbara Windsor, James Booth, Victor Spinetti, Brian Murphy, Yootha Joyce, Glynn Edwards, Avis Bunnage, George Sewell and the rest. Lionel must have been feeling left out because when he read in the *Daily Mail* that the film was over budget and behind schedule (two increasingly common characteristics of Joan's projects, as Lionel was soon to learn the hard way) he rang Joan and said he had an idea for a song called 'Ain't It A Shame Sparrers Can't Sing' and she could have it for 50 quid.

Barbara Windsor tells it different. "I played this soppy little bird called Maggie," says Barbara Windsor, "and one day Joan phoned me up and she said, 'I've got a rough cut of the film and I want to show it to Li-Li, why don't you come along.' There was just the three of us went to see it. And we sat there watching it and when it finished, Lionel had tears in his eyes. He said, 'I just loved it. I love this film, and I'm going to write you a song. And he wrote me 'Sparrers Can't Sing' and I sing it over the titles. And it went to about number 30 in America. Isn't that strange?"[77]

Cubby Broccoli, the producer of Anthony Newley's *Idol On Parade* and *Jazz Boat*, had done well for himself. *Dr No*, the adaptation of an Ian Fleming novel he'd co-produced with Harry Saltzman, eventually made those who had a stake in it the best part of 60 million pounds. It also made the line "Bond, James Bond" number 51 in *Premiere* magazine's Top 100 Movie Quotes and Ursula Andress's bikini a cultural icon which 50 years later was sold at auction for £41,000.

The follow up, Cubby decided, would have, as well as guns and girls, a hit theme song. Obviously he'd get the best in the business to provide it, so he called Lionel and commissioned him to come up with a tune that would vaguely fit over the existing James Bond theme and a lyric that would name-check the title without giving away the plot.

Matt Monro, "the singing bus driver" (he had briefly driven a Number 27), was George Martin's great pre-Beatles discovery. Martin had encountered him doing a Frank Sinatra parody for *Songs For Swinging Sellers,* a record he was producing for Peter Sellers, and was so impressed he started recording him for Parlophone. Their second record, 'Portrait Of My Love', went to number three. A deal with Warwick Records in America, and a US tour, put the follow up, 'My Kind Of Girl', into the US *Billboard* charts at number 18.

Russian tunes and Jewish tunes are near neighbours, and Lionel, as he'd proved over and over again, could do Jewish in his sleep. He'd also had some experience with the Bond-style bass line, having used something very similar for the opening of 'Food Glorious Food' (without ever accusing Monty Norman or John Barry of plagiarism). All the same he pushed the barriers of his comfort zones and excelled himself. 'From Russia With Love' is a sneaky, sinuous tune – a spy tune that dodges round corners for eight bars before jumping out with a leap from major to minor. The lyric is sinuous, too, stretching syntax and rhyme across the musical lines. In accordance with the remit, it mentions the film's title as frequently as is seemly and, far from giving away the plot, makes no mention of it or anything related to it. Matt Monro inhabits the song like he's lived there all his life and John Barry's arrangement gives it stick with the cimbalom (the instrument he'd possibly first encountered in the *Blitz!* orchestra pit) and arguably the best ending of any Bond theme.

On November 20, 1963, President John F. Kennedy, who had already nominated Fleming's novel as one of his top ten favourite books, had the film privately screened at the White House. The following day he flew to Texas. The day after, while riding in a motorcade down Dealey Plaza in Dallas, he was shot and killed. This means there is a distinct possibility that the last song JFK ever heard on this earth was a Lionel Bart song.

John Barry decided to compose the theme of the third Bond film, *Goldfinger,* himself, and brought in Anthony Newley and Leslie Bricusse to write the lyric. At their first meeting, he played them the first three notes of his tune. Newley and Bricusse, unprompted and in unison, finished it for him. "Wider than a mile," they sang – the second line of Henry Mancini's then-current hit, 'Moon River' – proving yet again that Lionel was not the only composer to have to face down accusations of plagiarism.

Fourteen

HE had the car, the clothes, the chat, the talent, the haircut, the props. The only thing lacking was the pad. Even when "it's the kicks that matter, nothing else", you need a place to call home.

The dinky little mews cottage in Pond Place was replaced by an even dinkier one just up the road in Reece Mews. This was centre of operations throughout *Oliver!*, *Blitz!* and *Maggie May*. As a venue for meetings, which it frequently became, it was impossibly cramped. But there was little time for house-hunting, as Lionel told the London *Evening Standard* in October 1960. " 'Searching for a new house in the centre of London – you would have thought it wouldn't be all that difficult to get something nice for £40,000 but those agents haven't come up with anything that's right. Course my needs are a bit peculiar. I need a big place with a triple garage, a large room for parties and a private sun terrace. One don't want to feel frustrated when the sun comes out, do one?' "

It was 1963 before Lionel found the sort of thing he was looking for. He took his secretary, Muriel Walker, to see it. "It was a shell," she says. "It was dingy and a bit smelly and there was an old woman there and a bit of a scullery. And I said to Lionel, 'Are you taking it?' And he said, 'Yeah.' He needed a prestigious residence."

The house, in Seymour Walk, off the Fulham Road in Chelsea, was formerly known as St Dunstan's Priory and had been built around 1905 on land that once backed on to a farmhouse owned by Jane Seymour – the third wife of Henry VIII. A previous tenant described it as an "Edwardian monster" bedevilled by bad stained glass that he had removed. Though his accountants and lawyers advised against it, Lionel bought it for £55,000 and then proceeded to remodel it at a further cost of £140,000.

The actor Peter Arne was put in charge of the rebuilding. An odd choice. His previous experience included running, 20 years earlier, a dodgy construction business in South Africa which fraudulently took a small fortune from the novelist Mary Renault. Twenty years later he would be bludgeoned to death by an Italian vagrant. But his dealings with Lionel – apart from a builder subsequently suing for non-payment of bills – seem to have been relatively straightforward. And the house did not fall down. The interior decorator was Beaudoin Mills – who later became Shirley Bassey's manager. It would appear that Mills' taste was never allowed to intrude on Lionel's preoccupations and peccadilloes. Lionel had strong views, for example, on the subject of wallpaper and would dispatch couriers to Paris in search of an exact colour nuance.

As the builders and decorators moved in and out, speculation in the neighbourhood ran high. Dismay was widespread when they watched a huge cast-iron stork being hoisted with great difficulty, but little apparent sense, to the chimney-top.

Homes And Garden featured the property in September 1968: "From the noises of the street the visitor is translated into near ecclesiastical tranquillity, an effect heightened by the soft background music and clusters of tall gothic candles. Somehow it is difficult to imagine how those brash, raucous songs which have played so emphatic a part in the post war show business scene could have been composed against this gentle background."

The main room came straight from *Citizen Kane*'s Xanadu: huge, with a vaulted ceiling, high, gothic windows and a baronial fireplace. To one side, the bay window was draped in white, like a medieval tent. To the other stood the grand piano. This was the big piano. There was also a little piano. When asked why he had two pianos, Lionel replied, "The big one's for the heavy stuff, the little one's for the light stuff."

Overlooking the main room was a minstrels' gallery from which, at the push of a button, a cinema screen descended, one of the many gadgets that littered the house: remote controlled curtains, air con, concealed TVs and sound systems and a tape recording system on which he could record his musical thoughts from any one of 15 different locations in the house.

Behind the minstrels' gallery was the master bedroom, protected by soundproof screens. From his bed he could, and sometimes did, watch the ebb and flow of a party in the big room below, like a recumbent puppeteer. The chairs in the dining room were high backed thrones, made to Lionel's design. Suits of armour lined the main staircase and the huge chandeliers had been rescued from the set of *Becket* where they had lit Canterbury Cathedral. French doors led out to the garden.

Some gardens take centuries to develop and mature. Muriel Walker says the Seymour Walk garden happened "virtually overnight. I came into work one morning and there's this garden with a fountain and grapes in tubs growing all round. A complete garden. A team of gardeners had come in and made this instant garden."

In the summer house, according to *House And Garden,* Mr Bart liked to play "ping-pong with his friends."

To maintain tranquillity in Lionel's bleached pine study, the telephone bell had been replaced by a flashing light. "Every room had its own décor," says Muriel. "And I used to say the night before, 'Which room are we working in, Lionel?' So I'd know how to dress for the following day to match the colour scheme. My office downstairs had pale green silk walls. In the downstairs loo, the floor, the walls, the ceiling were all mirror tiles." The mirrors could be alarming, "One day, an actor called George Cooper came flying out of this loo and he said, 'There's 60 bald old men in there looking at me.'"

The visitors' book reads like a social register. To choose a couple of pages at random: The Rolling Stones' manager signs in as "Andrew Loog Oldham – to name but a few," beneath which two wags have added, "A few what? Keith Richards" and "Beds – Mick Jagger".

Below that, Alan 'Fluff' Freeman, the legendary DJ, writes, "And I didn't come to do his washing", a reference to his appearance at the time in TV ads for Omo detergent. Turn the page to find the signatures of Sean Kenny, his actress wife Judy Huxtable, Lionel's G and B Arts partner John Gorman (who adds, cryptically, "Worth a hundred grand"), Terence Stamp, Christopher Stamp (brother of Terence and co-manager of The Who) and Alma Cogan.

Elsewhere Lyndon B. Johnson (President of the USA, 1963–1969) has recorded his presence, although it's more likely that another of The Rolling Stones did it for him.

"Michael Caine and Terence Stamp came for breakfast every morning," said Lionel.[78] "My [former?] next-door neighbour, Francis Bacon, showed up regularly. Peter Blake and Lucien Freud were long-time friends. And a typical party would also draw Princess Margaret, The Rolling Stones, Cassius Clay – there would be 600 people there from all walks of life."

The Beatles were regular visitors, too. John Lennon found the mirrored lavatory an ideal spot to get stoned. Then he liked to lie on a sofa and rip cruel piss out of anyone who came near.

Rumours began to spread that Lionel's 'Fun Palace' was home to orgies and excesses not seen since Caligula went properly barmy. "There was no permanent orgy," says Eric Williams. "He'd have a party about once every two weeks. People like Stanley Baker would be there. And Alma Cogan. And Nureyev. He had a statue of two naked men Greek wrestling and Noël Coward was there. Coward always had a wonderful way of making an entrance and an exit and on his way out he stands and looks at the statue and says, 'Now, *stop it* you two.'"

A gathering that pauses to listen to Noël's latest bon mot does not sound like one at which horses are being buggered by libertines drunk on virgin's blood.

The story of a glass bowl, placed near the exit and filled with ten pound notes so that guests who found themselves short of cab fare home could help themselves, is fairly well substantiated; the existence of a second glass bowl filled with cocaine, less so. And anyway, since some of the guests would not have known cocaine from a sherbet-dab, the risk of someone dipping a lolly and finding more in the way of sweet fizziness than they'd bargained for would have been worrying.

"I didn't take part in all that kind of thing," says Toni Palmer, actress, dancer, singer and owner of the longest legs in show business. "I mean, I was married and lived at home and cooked the dinner. If I thought it was going to be like that I just left. Not very interested in all that."

Even the unstably prurient, of course, panting to know, could never learn the secrets of what went on in Lionel's private apartments behind the minstrels' gallery and the soundproofing. One can only hope that whatever went on it brought, like *Oliver!*, pleasure to millions.

Sammy Bergliter, Lionel's nephew, a child at the time, found even some of the more thought-provoking details a source of innocent wonder. "The house had 27 rooms[79] and a sauna which you got to through a secret passage in the back of the wardrobe. It's the sort of thing kids just love. One of the rooms in the house was pitch black and Lionel used it for meditation. It was a bit scary so I'd just glance in and creep past. Sometimes he'd send his chauffeur, Jim The Lim, to fetch me. I saw the Fun Palace as a fantasy life, while my life at home in the East End with my mum and dad was the reality. I remember he had a TV built into the wall and to get it out you were supposed to use the remote control. I didn't know this and I pulled the door off. I was horrified and ran to his housekeeper. She said don't worry and she was right. Lionel just shrugged and said he didn't want his home to be treated as a museum."

The housekeeper lived with her husband in a cottage in the garden. "At Reece Mews he had a housekeeper called Mrs Glue," says Muriel. "Lionel called her 'Sticky'. But she wasn't very good. The live-in housekeeper at Seymour Walk was Mrs Glue's sister, Esther, and she was very, very good. And her husband Tony liked to think of himself as a valet, but he did things around the house. He always wore a blazer. He was a kind of military type and he'd always address Lionel as, 'Sir'. And he'd say, 'Don't call me sir, call me Lionel.'"

It is one thing to own a 'prestigious residence', another to convince yourself that you are the kind of person who is entitled to live in such a house. The Big Talk was always as much for Lionel's own benefit as it was for the press. Not long after he moved into the Fun Palace he drew up a daily schedule.

LIONEL'S BASIC PROGRAMME
8.30 Breakfast in bed with newspapers and telegrams.
Deal with outstanding correspondence. Relay to Muriel all outstanding
work to be typed.
The telephone bell in the drawing room should have been switched off last
thing at night. However, as soon as the soundproofed screens for the
master bedroom rise, cleaning of the drawing room, bar and terrace can
carry on without disturbing Lionel.
10.00–12.00 Writing and composing period. Lionel should be
undisturbed during this period, therefore study and drawing room should
have been cleaned by 10.00 am. Also hammock on the terrace should be
uncovered by this time, cigarettes, ashtrays etc. should be put out on
sunny mornings only.
12.00–1.15 Lionel with Muriel in the office. Deal with all outstanding
phone calls. Deal with outstanding correspondence. Relay to Muriel all
outstanding work.
1.15–3.00 Lunch. Furniture, cigarettes, ashtrays etc. should be laid out
in the main garden by this time on sunny days only.
3.00–4.30 Rest period. This period should be used for shopping,
painting in the studio or just sunbathing in the garden.
May have lunch appointments in town in which case lunch should be
served for guests and staff here as usual. However, Lionel should always
endeavour to return home for the rest period.
4.30 Sign all outgoing correspondence. At this time he will receive visitors
– business, social or newspaper reporters.
5.30 Dress for the evening.
6.30 Visitors for cocktails.
8.00 Dinner will be served. On the occasions Lionel goes out to dinner,
dinner will still be served for staff and guests.
When Lionel is operating this basic programme he will retire at 1.30 am
at the latest.

Asked whether Lionel adhered rigidly to this regime, Muriel smiles knowingly.

However grand the house and the regime, Muriel herself never broke faith with the principles to which she adhered back at Unity. "There was a day when we were at Seymour Walk and Lionel said to me, 'Princess

Margaret's coming to tea today.' So I said, 'Right, Lionel,' and I got my coat and I said, 'Bye. Sorry, I don't do curtseying to anyone.' And he never got over it. He was always telling people that. 'She wouldn't meet Princess Margaret.'"

"Meanwhile," the *House And Garden* feature concludes, "he claims that he is well content with this mildly spectacular, highly theatrical, metropolitan working pad – St Dunstan's Priory that was is now a house of warmth and space which offers its mercurial, volatile owner full scope for decorative ideas and a much needed peaceful retreat for his work."

The world that met under Lionel's roof had become as mercurial and as volatile as its owner. Traditionally the great divide in show business was between 'Variety' and 'Legit'. 'Variety' was comics, singers, ventriloquists, contortionists, eccentric dancers, illusionists, jugglers and Henry Vadden, the man who caught a cartwheel on his pickelhaube. 'Legit' was anybody appearing as Hamlet at the Old Vic or Daphne Pink in *Watch It Sailor!* at the Northampton Repertory Theatre. There were even two trade unions: VAF (Variety Artists' Federation) for the contortionists, Equity for the Hamlets.

By the mid-Fifties, variety was dying on its arse. TV was largely to blame. Why would anybody take a bus into town and pay two-and-a-kick to sit in a dog-eared theatre watching a handful of acts one tenth as good as those they could watch in the comfort of the home for free? Then, even as the Last Rites were being read, rock'n'roll provided a jolt of electricity which, temporarily, gave variety the illusion of life. For a while everything seemed back to normal. The teenagers who revived those moribund variety theatres were forced to sit through a series of comics, jugglers and old-style band singers before being allowed to scream at Tommy, Marty or Cliff. They didn't complain. They belonged to a generation that had never been allowed so much as a smell of pudding before they'd properly finished their dinner.

Variety knew no snobbery, artistic or otherwise. As soon as it had been established that the rock'n'rollers made money and rarely spat on the carpets, they were welcomed into the wonderful world of showbiz. But the rockers grew more and more impatient at being classed with the dog acts and contortionists. In the records of Elvis and Little Richard they had found an epiphany, a clarion call, a revolution. There was a yawning gap between what they felt inside and what they saw onstage as they waited.

Showbiz, in the broadest sense imaginable, had always had its dissident wing: trad-jazzers like Ken Colyer, modernists like Tubby Hayes, folkies like Ewan MacColl, bluesmen like Cyril Davies, who put art above commerce, rage before beauty and beards below chins.

The Beatles were grammar school boys. John had been to art college. In Germany they had befriended posher kids who had photographed them in arty half-shadow, put them in existentialist polo necks, de-greased their hair and cut it into the Sorbonne/Caesar style. They knew if they wanted success they'd have to do what Mr Epstein said and play the showbiz game, but from the start they were edging away, redefining the terms, renegotiating the stylistic deal.

Andrew Loog Oldham, the hustler who'd tried to chisel £30 out of Lionel and Pablo in Cannes, had, as Lionel had predicted, done well for himself. With his finger welded to the pulse, he'd worked for Mary Quant and John Stephen, Joe Meek, Bob Dylan and The Beatles, then become the manager of The Rolling Stones. Having already spotted that the irreverence manifested by those cheeky Beatles might be the tip of an antisocial iceberg, he encouraged his new charges to be defiantly anti-showbiz and, if possible, demented sociopaths. It worked. The turning point, according to Keith Richards, came on July 4, 1964, the day The Rolling Stones went on *Juke Box Jury*. The idea of having a panel made up of the members of one beat group rather than a random clutch of celebrities had been tried with great success sixth months before with The Beatles. They had said Beatle-ish things, clowned around and generally endeared themselves the way they always did. The Rolling Stones were merely surly. They didn't like any of the records. They were taciturn. They gave chairman David Jacobs a hard time. This was not show, but it certainly did the biz. By the end of the year the market had been whipped up to full spending power, surliness was the new black, and a million kids were chanting "We Don't Need No Alma Cogan".

Nevertheless Alma's flat and Lionel's house remained places where the two worlds collided, where apparently Keith Richards and Noël Coward could trade gags while John Lennon confessed his burgeoning doubts about the value of war to Frankie Vaughan. And there is much evidence to suggest that this fanciful idyll isn't far from the truth.

Paul McCartney first introduced himself to Alma Cogan in 1963, when he spotted her at the Establishment Club. He had a recording contract. They were in the same business. He was from Liverpool. He could talk to anybody. "Hi, Alma, I'm a singer, too."

On January 12, 1964, Alma and The Beatles found themselves on the same bill at the Palladium and The Fabs, in the way that everybody did back then, went on to Alma's after the show. It was the first of many visits that Paul describes in Barry Miles' biography:[80] "I saw a documentary about John Betjeman, who said that when he got out of college there was a country house to which he was invited. And he said, 'There I learned to be a guest,' and that's what happened to us at Alma's flat."

Alma's mum, Fay, became, in Beatlespeak, 'Ma Macogie'. For a brief time a flame of unfulfilled romance burned between Paul and Sandra. They all called Alma 'Aunty Alma' except John, who called her 'Sarah Sequin' and, if rumours are to be believed, was her long-time lover: an affair complete with false names – John was a married man – disguises and steamy trysts in anonymous hotels. Meanwhile, Brian Epstein, The Beatles' manager, though gay, decided that Alma would be his wife. She was in show business. She was Jewish. It would be a match made in heaven. He even took her to Liverpool to meet his parents.

But no matter how close the miscegenation between old showbiz and new rock, it was becoming increasingly apparent that full integration could never happen, and might not even be desirable.

"At the time," says Keith Richards, "just like anything else in 'popular entertainment', they thought, it's just a fad, it's a matter of a few haircuts and we'll tame them anyway."

Tony Calder, Andrew Loog Oldham's business partner, remembers a party at Lionel's where Noël Coward sang from the minstrels' gallery, "and I thought 'who the fuck is this guy with his *Mad Dogs And Englishmen*. Li Baby. Noël Baby. Bart and Coward Baby.' I wasn't interested in that scene."

Lionel might have wanted to keep a foot in both camps, but he had made himself such an integral part of the old showbiz world – Li Baby, Noël Baby, Alma Baby – that there could be no escape. And besides, he was in his mid-thirties: a grown-up – a sympathetic, funny, friendly, supportive grown-up, who wore the hippest clothes, knew the hippest clubs, threw the hippest parties, but a grown-up all the same. Great man to have on your team, though. Lionel had the contacts you needed to get ahead, knew where the bodies were buried and who was shagging whom. He was unfailingly generous with his time and money. And he seemed to know – or used to know – the secret codes required to break into the charts.

Andrew Loog Oldham, though by now aged in experience, was still only 19 – too young to vote, take out a hire purchase agreement or sign a contract. A year or so after taking on the Stones, he was managing Marianne Faithfull, too. Wary of signing her over to one of the big companies, he was keen to finance her recording sessions himself, thereby retaining control over the master tapes which he would then lease on to a major – a nifty bit of footwork pioneered by Phil Spector in America and Joe Meek in Britain. This would require capital to hire studios and musicians, and a grown-up to sign the contracts.

"Oh, I got jumped on with that one, absolutely," said Lionel. "I became the official manager of Marianne and The Rolling Stones for a short space of time and I was their publisher. It was a family."

With Andrew he formed two companies, one for recording and one for publishing, and generally mucked in with 'the family', helping the young-sters with their homework: giving (according to Lionel) Mick Jagger a hand with some of his first efforts as a songwriter – 'As Tears Go By' and 'Satisfaction'. In return, Mick gave Lionel a hand with 'Carryin' On', the Nocturnes' song from *Maggie May*. "But Mick didn't take credit for that, it was a family affair."

Lionel was generous with his money and with his talent, providing a song, 'I Don't Know How', for Marianne's first single. A studio was booked and a small orchestra.

Like everybody, Andrew loved Lionel. He was indebted to him for setting him up, staking him, looking out for him. He owed him big time. But . . . "The Lionel Bart song was awful," said Marianne. "It was one of those songs that needed the proper register. My voice was just plain wrong. We did take after agonising take."

"The Bart song was the biggest piece of dogshit you've ever heard in your life," said Tony Calder, "so they [the musicians] went for a break. Came back with 20 minutes left of the session and started on 'As Tears Goes By'. Then the cor anglais comes in. I said, 'It's a smash'; [. . . Andrew] said, 'Don't tell Lionel.'"

In the end, Lionel's song didn't even make the B-side. It was allowed quietly to vanish.

"I need something big and exciting to be working on," Lionel had said after *Oliver!* "I can't repeat myself, see? That's fatal. Everything I do must be bigger and better than anything I've done before. That's my kick, mate."

The world had turned. Whatever came next not only had to be bigger and better than anything he'd done before, it had to be nothing like any-thing anybody had ever done before.

"Let's get the theatre out of its coffin," Sean had said. "Let us rebel, fight, break down, invent and reconstruct a new theatre. Let us free the theatre from the cumbersome shackles of outmoded traditions."

Oh, shit. Here comes the bad part.

Fifteen

"I T started out as a shambles," said Muriel Walker, "and finished up as chaos."[81]

On August 27, 1964, a month before *Maggie May* opened in the West End, Lionel signed a contract with Brookfield Productions Ltd, Peter Sellers company, giving them, for an undisclosed advance, a piece of his next musical – the title and nature of which was still to be decided. United Artists, the American film distributors who'd backed *A Hard Day's Night*, took a piece of the action, too, in exchange for £130,000 – nearly double the entire budget of *Maggie May*.

Lionel was thus spoiled for angels. And for ideas. He was unsure whether to go with the polo-neck-inspired *Hunchback Of Notre Dame* he'd come up with in America, or a brand new idea based on the legend of *Robin Hood*.

He knew – from Unity and from Stratford, from the New York experimental companies, La Mama and Living Theatre, from the sparkle of his own first nights, particularly *Oliver!'s* first night – that theatre could be and should be something more than a social outing consisting of two long periods of relative tedium relieved by a 20-minute break for drinks. Theatre should be an *event*, a celebration, a party.

The creative fervour of the *Fings* rehearsals still looms large in the memories of those who were involved. That was a party, all right. Lionel called in the woman who had made it all happen.

Since *Fings,* Joan Littlewood had gone from strength to strength. Her *Oh, What A Lovely War!* had just closed on Broadway, where it had hoovered up a bagful of awards. But, like Lionel, she was always dreaming of something bigger and better. She had made plans for a massive arts centre, "a laboratory of fun", in the East End, and she had ambitions to go fully international with even grander projects in Hammamet, Tunisia. All of this would require enormous sums of money – the sort of amounts you get from a massive hit in the West End and on Broadway.

Joan takes up the story in her autobiography, *Joan's Book*, although her unwillingness to name either the show or Lionel indicates her distaste for the whole venture and the depth of her ultimate disillusion.

"I found I was under contract," she says, "to one or two good songs and no script, not even the outline of one. Where was his secretary? The one who'd adapted the book for his last 'sure fire' successes [Joan Maitland?]. He couldn't have found backing with nothing. I knew I had a reputation for salvaging any old thing, but I needed something to go on, if only an outline. Worse still, our composer had undergone some sort of sea change since I'd worked with him. Success and other drugs had persuaded him that he could do anything, including playing poker. A series of all night sessions set in – poker not work."

The reference to drugs deserves examination. There is only hearsay evidence to suggest that Lionel was in an altered state at this time. Muriel Walker, his secretary at the time, says she never saw any evidence or behaviour to suggest he was particularly pissed or stoned, and he was certainly never out of control. It could be that his enthusiastic embrace of the hip and the new caused Joan Littlewood, and others, to assume that drugs would automatically be involved.

On the other hand, if he wasn't doing at least the odd pill it would have been a miracle. Miriam Karlin reckons he was into something or other back when they were working on *Fings*: "One realised that sometimes he was rather spaced out but then in those days a lot of us were – this is the ghastly part, that we were all on some sort of pills and things."[82]

The world was swimming in uppers and downers. Doctors prescribed them for tiredness, insomnia, obesity, anxiety, paranoia, depression, disillusion, angst, you name it they had a cure. You didn't have to be 'on the scene'. Sheet metal workers and laundresses were popping mouthfuls of Preludin, Dexamyl and other barbiturates to keep them thin, happy and well-rested.

"We used to go and get them for our friends' mothers on a Friday night," says Jon Gorman, son of Lionel's RAF friend, John. "Everyone had pills. It was just how it was. It wasn't drug taking. It was just pills."

And if one pill didn't cure whatever ailed you, the answer was to take four. And if for any reason no doctor was to hand with a prescription pad, gentlemen with interesting aftershave and obsessive briefcases were happy to fill a paramedic role. When the uppers made you a little too up but you suspected a counteracting downer would make you just that little bit too down, you could back off just the right amount by the use of reefer, by now known as 'pot', which was illegal, but only in a Lord Chamberlain sort of way. Georgia Brown had been smoking pot since forever and had, according to many sources, introduced Lionel to the five-skin spliff somewhere between the 'I'd Do Anything' and the 'Oom-Pah-Pah'. Cocaine was good for a party. Heroin was addictive and made you play bebop. Cigarettes gave you cancer, but not for ages. Alcohol was sewn into the fabric of human existence. "Would you like a drink?" "Whisky and coke, please." Glug, glug, glug. And you're out on the town.

"So I'd turn up with a pad and a stylo," Joan continues, "and find him at the card table unable to tear himself away and losing, night after night. There were three of them with him, dab hands at the game. [. . .] Each morning one or other of them would send a note round, claiming what he was owed.

" 'How are you going to pay all that?' I asked one morning 'With dolly mixtures?'

" 'I'll cut him in on the show. He's good at gags, used to write the best soap opera in the States.' "

'He' was Harvey Orkin, an American writer who had written for a while on the Phil Silvers *Sgt. Bilko* series. For a time he was also a theatrical agent, numbering Richard Burton and Peter Sellers among his clients. In Britain he'd started a third career as a TV pundit on *Not So Much A Programme More A Way Of Life*, one of the follow-ups to *That Was The Week That Was* and the programme on which the word "fuck" was first heard on British TV.

And now he was co-writing a Robin Hood musical he'd won a piece of with a pair of tens or some such. "Life deals the cards," said Voltaire, "but it's up to you to play them."

By May 1965, Lionel and Harvey had a rough outline of a show they called *Twang!!* (with two exclamation marks) and could begin casting. The backers wanted major stars of film and TV. Joan wanted her usual crew, 'my nuts', 'my clowns'. Joan got her way and her usual crew – James Booth, Barbara Windsor, Bob Grant, Eric Hooper, Maxwell Shaw, Howard Goorney, Kent Baker and Bernard Bresslaw – were signed up.

A slight sticking point came when James Booth, every inch the leading man, decided he'd prefer to play Prince John, the Baddie, rather than Robin. Lionel tried to talk him round. Joan tried to talk him round. They told him he was the only man for the role. They told him that Lionel would build the part up, that he would get all the best lines. Eventually John Bryan, the show's producer, outlined a new concept for the part – a Robin Hood that would be a cross between Errol Flynn and Bugs Bunny. It was an offer no actor could refuse. Booth was Robin.

It has to be said that at this stage the script made little sense. The essential idea was to do a rollicking romp through Sherwood, combining the bawdy laughs of a *Carry On* film with the attitude and spontaneity of *Fings*. Initial ideas of combining this with forests of showgirls in a Ziegfeld-style spectacle were, at Joan's behest, abandoned. Although nothing was set in stone. As Joan said, "We don't have to commit ourselves in advance to a storyline."

Still with plot, character, diction, spectacle, thought and music in a fluid state, a set designer was brought in. It wasn't Sean.

Sean had defected to Anthony Newley. *The Roar Of The Greasepaint – The Smell Of The Crowd*, Newley's allegory on class warfare, was running, with a relatively modest Sean Kenny set, at the Shubert Theatre on Broadway. Pretty much straight after that, Sean was booked to production design the film version of Newley's *Stop The World – I Want To Get Off*, being shot at Elstree and Pinewood. He would have no time for *Twang!!*

For the want of Sean – or possibly to spite Sean – Lionel had a meeting with the anti-Sean.

Oliver Hilary Sambourne Messel was the uncle of Princess Margaret's husband, Antony Armstrong-Jones, and had excelled in designing sets for the Royal Ballet. Forty years earlier he had been a 'bright young thing', one of the Ivor Novello/Noël Coward set described by Cecil Beaton as "terrible homosexualists". Back then, one of Messel's party pieces had been a shadow-play in which he mimed gross seductions and the administering of enemas. During World War Two he had served as a camouflage officer, disguising pillboxes in Somerset which he transformed into the most extravagantly camouflaged pillboxes ever seen in a theatre of war. Here was a faux haystack, a castle, a folly. And here – what japes – a common roadside caff. Unlike Sean Kenny, Messel did not tend towards the Harland & Wolff school of theatre design. Two-ton towers, revolves and mobile beams seldom featured in his imagination, but he was terrifically good at foliage. He was also the gentry's interior designer of choice.

"They're changing the style at Buckingham Palace," Lionel wrote in 'Contempery', one of the *Fings* songs, "Oliver Messel is full of malice."

Now, the man Lionel had been taking the piss out of five years earlier was the man he wanted for Sherwood. Messel was, after all, terrifically good at foliage. And he'd done a couple of jobs for Noël in the past, so came highly recommended.

In his contract, Messel was given complete visual control over the sets and costumes. At this point in his career Lionel was accustomed to having complete control over everything. So was Joan.

A *Carry On* style romp, directed by Joan Littlewood, with sets by Oliver Messel, makes as much sense as an Alvin & The Chipmunks album, produced by Van Morrison and conducted by Herbert von Karajan. And it gets worse.

174

Paddy Stone had been the choreographer on *Maggie May*. For that, he had constructed a dance routine which consisted almost entirely of jumping up and down on the spot. It was sensational but painful. In later life many of those involved suffered back and knee problems. But Paddy would tolerate no slackers. He was an exacting man. A perfectionist.

Joan had little patience with choreographers. She had nothing against expressive movement that led to the freeing of the feeling body, but wasn't at all keen on the "two-three-kick-turn-one-two-HANDS" school of dance.

Lionel Bart, Joan Littlewood, Oliver Messel, Paddy Stone. The dream team.

A strong producer could perhaps have fused these disparate elements together, acted as a go-between, kept everything on schedule and on budget. In July, John Bryan, the producer from Brookfield Productions, went off to work on a film – *After The Fox* starring his boss, Peter Sellers – leaving his second-in-command, Timothy Burrill, in charge. Burrill had already proved he was a safe pair of hands in the film world: he went on to become a distinguished film producer – responsible for Polanksi's films *Tess* and *The Pianist* – but *Twang!!* was going to require a producer of long experience, saintly patience and a Christ-like way with miracles.

Bernard Delfont seemed not only to possess all three qualities but, as the producer of *Maggie May,* had already known and withstood Hurricane Lionel. For a piece of the action and a salary, he agreed to act as a 'supervisory producer' and sent his own assistant, Richard Mills, into the lions' den as his eyes and ears. Richard appraised the situation: "Oliver Messel, the designer, had by now started to panic. He didn't know what sets he was supposed to be designing. Joan had told him not to worry – the shape of the show would soon be fixed. Oliver patiently explained that first of all he had to know what all the scenes were; then he had to design them; then they had to be approved; and then, they first of all had to be built; and then painted.

"I pointed out to Joan that the time scale for this, for a major musical, even if everyone worked flat out, was five or six weeks. 'Well in that case,' said Joan, 'since Oliver knows we need at least a forest and a castle, let him design those, then he can do whatever he wants with the rest of the sets, and I'll improvise the book around them.'

"Since there was no alternative, I conveyed this to Oliver, and between us we worked out what the other scenes might be; village green, banqueting hall, drawbridge, Maid Marian's bedroom, battlements of the castle etc, etc. Slightly mollified, this he proceeded to do."

Oliver began sketching. On a visit to the theatrical costumiers Monty Berman Ltd, he learned to his consternation that *Twang!!* was not the only Sherwood-based show in town. Bermans was already running up a set of Robin Hood costumes for *Babes In The Wood*, the Christmas pantomime at the Palladium, starring Frank Ifield as Robin, Arthur Askey as Big Hearted Martha, and Sid James and Kenneth Connor as the Robbers. Even more disturbing, *Babes In The Wood* was to be produced by Leslie A. McDonnel and Leslie Grade in association with *Twang!!*'s new producer, Bernard Delfont.

Bernard saw no conflict of interest in his producing two West End Robin Hoods simultaneously and told Lionel that if *he* thought it was a problem, he should consider postponing *Twang!!*

"The opening date hadn't been set yet," says Richard Mills, "and we needed to establish the date of the first rehearsal. In those days, a musical would usually rehearse for four, or at the most five, weeks. 'Since you're making it up as you go along, will five weeks be enough rehearsal time?' I asked Lionel. 'Oh no, we need three or four months,' he replied.

"After I recovered my composure, I explained that this was out of the question, since, after four weeks of rehearsal pay, the artists all had to be paid full salary. Lionel suggested to me that we wouldn't officially rehearse; we would just invite all the principal performers to a three or four month party at his large house, [. . .] and there they could make it all up with Joan. Not having a lot of choice, I told him we would go along with it, if the artists agreed. Since they were all part of Joan's company, 'my nuts', as she called them, from Stratford East, they did.'"

The rehearsals/party at Seymour Walk did go on for months, Joan, Lionel, James Booth, Alfie Bass, Howard Goorney, Max Shaw, Bob Grant, Phil Newman, Bernard Bresslaw and Arthur Mullard dutifully turning up day after day. Arthur Mullard dropped out early on the grounds that he liked getting paid. Alfie Bass, Lionel's songwriting champion from the old Unity days, had originally been asked to play Sammy The Tailor – a role that changed into a character called Rip The Tapper and ended up being Will Scarlett. He left, too, deciding it wasn't for him. Ronnie Corbett, a diminutive performer who'd been at Winston's nightclub with Barbara Windsor and Toni Palmer, was asked to take his place. George Cooper, who was originally supposed to play King Richard and who had had four songs written for him already, became Friar Tuck when Joan cut the King's part entirely.

On warm days they sat out on the terrace to read through the latest version of the script, which was typed out with lots of blank spaces for improvisation. No one was allowed to take it home to learn their lines for fear they'd get attached to them. Act I gradually came together, but as the days turned into weeks it seemed that there might never be an Act II at all. Lionel seemed unruffled.

"Instead of getting the script right," says Richard Mills, "Lionel seemed to be more interested in what the front of house sign should look like." He had plans to cover the Shaftesbury Theatre with a neon target (very mod, very Who, very Jasper Johns) and have neon arrows shooting into it from the other side of the road. It took a long time to talk him out of it on the grounds of cost, electrical engineering practicalities and road safety.

Tim Burrill, the assistant producer, would pop into Seymour Walk from time to time to check on progress. Joan would immediately weave him into her improvisations. He was a tree, a peasant, a horse, a whore. Joan took a shine to him.

Meanwhile Paddy Stone spent four days at the Shaftesbury Theatre auditioning dancers. Even though *Hello Dolly*, auditions were being held at the same time around the corner at Drury Lane, a thousand hopefuls turned up. Very few of them reached Paddy's exacting standards.

"Paddy had a very short fuse," said Richard Mills, "many times stopping just short of physically assaulting his dancers. He did actually throw a chair at one."

At the auditions, he asked one of the dancers how far she'd come.

"'180 miles, Mr Stone, from Liverpool'

"'Well you should have auditioned in Liverpool. I could have smelled you from there.'"

Summer came. Lionel left for America. Joan took herself off to Tunisia to tend her various projects there. Oliver Messel went on a tour of Europe with his old friend Claudette Colbert. Paddy Stone had a previous engagement in Japan, where he was staging the spectacular *Takarazuka Dancers of '65*.

In August, Joan returned from Hammamet with a 'find': a young Lebanese actress called Nadia Telas, and announced, "Ladies and Gentlemen, say hello to our Maid Marian." The briefest try-out revealed that Nadia's singing voice did not exist. Toni Eden, a band singer who had been in the second cast of *Blitz!*, was hurried in. Joan insisted that to be absolutely historically accurate – the essential conflict being that between the Norman English and the Anglo-Saxon English – Maid Marian should be as Norman as possible. "So, brush up on your fucking French."

A script was assembled from the various drafts and fragments produced so far and a read-through organised. The shortcomings were apparent even to passing cats and earwigs: no proper storyline, coherent style, characterisation, structure, through-line or reason to exist.

Joan decided that the only way she was ever going to get a workable version of the script was to write it herself, so moved into the United Artists offices on Shaftesbury Avenue and started work.

"Joan doesn't think much of the things that I've done that she didn't stage," Lionel said, reflectively. "She walked out in the intervals of *Blitz!* and *Oliver!* and thought *Maggie May* was a right load of old rubbish."

On September 8, Joan had finished her script and ordered another read-through. Resplendent in white plastic boots, red tea-cosy hat, tailored jacket and Gerry Raffles' raincoat, she announced to the assembled company that the show at last had a theme, a concept, a *raison d'être,* a mission. "We're taking the piss out of *A Midsummer Night's Dream*," she said.

At this point the plot went something like . . .

Robin Hood and his Merrie Men, in a variety of preposterous disguises, attempt to break into Nottingham Castle in order to prevent a marriage between the nymphomaniac court tart Delphina and the hairy Scots laird Roger The Ugly, arranged for the purpose of securing the loan of Scottish troops for bad Prince John. Then some other stuff would happen.

A mild hysteria settled on the company. Before the read-through, Joan announced that anyone who was bored should feel free to leave. Many did. Harvey Orkin arrived late and waited patiently to recognise something he or Lionel might have written. The moment never came, although the script was liberally dotted with references to songs Lionel had written, half written, considered or spoken of. The cast, too, felt cheated. All their improvisations and practically everything else they had contributed at Seymour Walk had been ignored. The whole two months had been a waste of time. Joan asked for honest opinions. There was a pause. Somebody said, "Oodles of songs and crappy jokes."

Joan brushed off their doubts: "It's a lot of twaddle, but we'll muddle through," she said. She laid the blame for any shortcomings firmly at Oliver Messel's door: "We're hidebound by Messel's Edwardiana. The whole scheme's wrong."

On September 20 rehearsals for *Twang!!* officially began at the Fourth Feathers Youth Club, just off Baker Street. Three rooms had been hired: one for the dancers, one for the actors and one for the singers.

Since communication between director, designer, composer, choreographer and authors had effectively broken down, each worked on his or her own show.

Lionel had engaged Ken Moule – another veteran of *Fings* – to work as musical director and orchestrator. It immediately became apparent that he was going to have to do the work of at least three people. Lionel wanted him at Seymour Walk to work on the new songs which came and went in a heartbeat. Joan wanted him with her to play for the actors while they rehearsed: "Would you mind, Ken? It helps the children get into the mood." To start work on the orchestrations he needed information about moods and transitions and action before and after each song. Does she glide to flutes, or skulk to trombones? Does the finish want cymbals for glory or oboes for the grave? Nobody knew.

Paddy Stone's temper was forever frayed. "You can be a poof if you like, but I don't want you to be a poof onstage. I want strength, strength, strength." One dancer conceived such a loathing of Paddy that he didn't trust himself to handle the prop swords. A handful of tranquillisers every morning was all that was standing between him and homicide. A few went over the wall and auditioned for *Hello Dolly!*

If Paddy enraged, Joan bewildered. When she took rehearsals everything went to Lololand. Dancers who had spent their professional lives working with "two-three-kick-turn-one-two-HANDS" were asked to pretend they were contestants for the Miss World Competition and act out the characteristics of the countries they represented.

"During one rehearsal," says Barbara Windsor, "one of ten statuesque showgirls who had to run through a make-believe forest dressed as a reindeer asked her [Joan], 'What do I do here?'

"'Just do your own thing, dear' said Joan.

"She actually told a showgirl to 'do your own thing'. Have you ever seen a showgirl do her own thing? They're lovely girls but dense."

Even the actors were tired of improvising. Joan had them playing cowboys and Indians to get in the mood. She called it "parallels" – finding your way into a scene by playing it in many different genres, styles and emotional pitches. It can be a useful technique for shaking the falsehood and dramatic clichés out of a scene and finding the bare bones of what's required to make it come alive. As long as there's a coherent scene there in the first place. And the actors aren't bleary and leery and weary.

To get at the truth of Barbara and Toni's 'To The Woods' duet, Joan asked them to pretend to sit on a park bench and imagine they were waiting for a rock group to pass by riding motorcycles on their way home from a party. She told the Merrie Men to pretend they were the Viet Cong and the Sheriff's men were the Americans.

The first batch of Oliver Messel's costumes came from Bermans. They were heavy, hot and cumbersome. Paddy, already doubtful of his dancers ability to move with any grace or sparkle, now discovered that in costume they could barely move at all. The costumes would have to be redone, redesigned, remade.

Joan, always a firm believer in the adage 'a cast that plays together, stays together', decided to throw a party. Her birthday, October 6, provided the excuse. She sent invitations, marked 'Top Secret', to selected members of the cast and crew instructing them to turn up at the Fourth Feathers at seven o'clock in the morning. A breakfast of grouse and game pie and champagne had been prepared. By ten everybody was drunk and it was decided to move the party to Regent's Park. Joan played Pied Piper, with a transitor radio strapped around her neck. Bye-laws categorically forbid the playing of music in the park. Joan was chased by a park keeper. "It's a ship's radio," she shouted, suggesting that to switch it off would endanger those in peril at sea. After their little run in the park, Joan decided her 'nuts' were good and ready to rehearse so led them back to the Fourth Feathers. The usual improvisations were adapted to the mood of the day: "You're Richard Burton and you've just been thrown out of the Hilton. Show me what you'd do." To a dancer she said, "Imagine you've just woken up and you're sick or something and didn't want to come into rehearsals, but you did, and Lionel walked in with great news. We're all going to America. Show me what you'd do." The dancers still weren't quite in tune with Joan's modus operandi. After a long pause, one of them said, "But . . . if I was sick, I wouldn't have come into rehearsals."

A few days later, Lionel organised another, more formal birthday party for Joan. She didn't turn up until one in the morning. "Lionel had to cut the cake himself," says Muriel Walker. "He was terribly hurt."

By this time, rehearsals had moved from the Fourth Feathers to the Shaftesbury Theatre to prepare for the try-outs in Manchester. Lionel sat on one side of theatre, Joan on the other. From time to time he would wander over for a word. Joan would send him away with a flea in his ear.

Barbara Windsor could see that all was not well with Lionel. He was "giving Joan rewrites that made little sense. It all got too much for Joan. In the middle of a blazing public row, she screamed at Lionel, 'It's that fucking LSD, isn't it?'"

"I said to Jimmy [Booth], 'That's not fair. We're all in it for the money, aren't we?'

"'She doesn't mean that, stupid,' he said.

"'What does she mean then?' The only LSD I knew about came in my wage packet. It was the abbreviation for pounds, shillings and pence.

"Jimmy said he'd tell me later, but I was so intrigued that I buttonholed

Joan after the row had died down and asked her, 'Is it all about money?'

" 'No, you silly cow!' she said 'Don't you know? He's into acid.'

"I was none the wiser.

" 'The rubbish that makes people hallucinate and believe they can fly out of windows.' "

Again, only hearsay suggests that Lionel had tried acid, but most people in Lionel's position at this point in history would have. Acid, LSD, Lysergic Acid Diethylamide, was very much the new drug in town. The Beatles had discovered it a few months earlier, when George Harrison's dentist spiked his and John Lennon's coffee. Timothy Leary, the great San Francisco acid guru, wrote that it could bring "the transcendence of verbal concepts, of space-time dimensions, and of the ego or identity", but failed to address the question of whether such transcendence was a good thing or a bad thing for musical theatre.

Joan reserved a special place in her heart for Harvey Orkin. She called him 'The Orchid' and liked to toy with him.

"Harvey," she would say, "I need some funny lines. Go and write me some funny lines." Disconsolate but obedient, Harvey would find a quiet place to write some funny lines. Joan would read them.

"This isn't funny, Harvey," she would say.

"I see," he'd say.

"You don't like me, do you, Harvey?"

"No."

"So why have you put up with me?"

"Because I thought you were talented."

A sure sign that a show is in trouble is when indiscriminate shagging breaks out among the cast and backstage staff. In these early weeks of October, indiscriminate shagging broke out among the cast and backstage staff.

"Everyone felt," says Barbara, "they needed all the love they could get to lift their spirits."

On October 19 the new, redesigned costumes arrived from Bermans. Oliver Messel – who had dressed Norma Shearer as Juliet and Vivien Leigh as Cleopatra, who was described by fellow designer Desmond Heeley as "one of the greatest set and costume designers England has ever produced" – organised a dress parade onstage. Joan didn't like the frocks and tunics. She sat in the stalls, hating their poshness, their newness, their Messelness.

"Howard, take that off and wear it inside out," she said. "We have better costumes than this at Stratford East."

Paddy Stone hated the costumes, too. Before they had been heavy, hot and cumbersome. Now they were heavy, hot, cumbersome and tight. They were particularly tight in the crotch. The dancers couldn't leap.

Oliver Messel grew sad. He was saddened by Barbara's candy-floss hair. He was saddened when they cut a hole in one of his turrets so that Barbara could stick her candy-floss head through it and sing a song. He was saddened when he found a note from Joan to the wardrobe department reading: "S.O.S., for Gods sake, come to the rescue of the visual effects and destroy these ghastly colours. Crepe them in black."

On October 20, after another day of fighting with Joan, Lionel wrote four letters – to Bernard Delfont, Harvey Orkin, Paddy Stone and to Joan – saying that he refused to take any responsibility for *Twang!!* He considered it not to bear any relation to anything he created. He would agree to his name being used only if he was given complete control.

On October 21, extracts from the letter appeared in the *Daily Mail*.

Joan called a meeting of the cast and arrived carrying her luggage. She had just checked out of her room at the Savoy. She was leaving. On top of her dirty laundry lay a bunch of dying flowers and a large buff envelope, stuffed with dog-eared papers. The envelope was marked, 'LIONEL'S FINAL FUCK UP'.

The actors asked her to stay. She agreed on condition that she be given complete autonomy. The actors agreed. Joan suggested they consult with other members of the company and put it to the vote.

The dancers didn't want Joan back, but since the alternative seemed to be for the show never to open, and since all the jobs at *Hello Dolly!* had already been taken, they reluctantly went along with the actors.

Paddy Stone said he would agree to her coming back as long as there were no more radical changes to the script.

The feelings of the company were conveyed to Bernard Delfont and, with his blessing, Joan was reinstated.

Lionel was not consulted.

"After that," says Barbara Windsor, "she was like Hitler."

John Bryan, the original producer who popped back from time to time for news of the latest disasters, was banned from rehearsals. When asked why, Joan replied, "All money men are cunts."

A band call revived spirits. With full orchestrations, the songs sounded substantial. Was there perhaps a possibility that the audience might not notice that the structure the songs were attached to was an insecure assembly of ill-matched scraps and patches in urgent need of underpinning? Could the songs carry the show on their own?

There was a cost to this optimism. Ken Moule had been playing for rehearsals all day, rehearsing late into the night, then going home to write and rewrite the arrangements. And now he was conducting the orchestra. The following morning he collapsed. A new conductor was engaged.

Three days later, the whole circus was shipped off to Manchester for a November 3 opening at the Palace Theatre. The theatre, a huge 2,000-seater, had been dark for some time. It was cold. The sets went up and the cast started rehearsing and carried on until two in the morning. The following day it was again two before the cast was sent home, and even then Joan carried on rehearsing a scene with Barbara Windsor and Philip Newman in Barbara's dressing room. At three, she decided it needed a complete rewrite.

Lionel, chatting with Benedict Nightingale of *The Guardian,* appeared quietly confident and gave no sign that anything was amiss. He was good at this sort of thing. He joked about the problems they'd had with the Lord Chamberlain's office, who "had declared that the women must not remove their chastity belts in full view of the audience and wanted a refer-ence to the Holy Grail to be removed. 'He also asked us to take out a few words, four-letter words,' said Mr Bart. 'So we've substituted some six-letter words which mean the same thing. But,' Mr Bart continued wryly, 'the present show did not bear much relation to the script the Lord Chamberlain saw; scenes have been added or altered and, under Joan Littlewood's direction, the cast has been encouraged to improvise and ad-lib. 'If someone in the audience coughs one of the cast might make up a scene about it,' said Mr Bart." As far as the press – and often the cast and crew – were concerned, Lionel never experienced a moment of doubt, fear or indecision. His friends knew better.

Alma Cogan was, by this time, semi-engaged to Brian Morris, the owner of the Ad Lib Club, the place where the showbiz aristocracy liked to party. "Brian found that he had limited claims on Alma's time," says Alma's sister Sandra Caron. "One day he arrived to take her out. She was on the telephone. She stayed on the telephone without a break for the next two hours.

"'What on earth have you been talking about?' he stormed. 'Nothing is worth two hours on the telephone.'

"'Yes it is,' she said. 'That was Lionel Bart. His show is in trouble. He needs reassurance.'"[83]

November 3 came round. Opening night. Again, they rehearsed with-out a lunch break until 6.15. Even then Joan gave notes until curtain up.

Richard Mills, John Bryan, Timothy Burrill and Bernard Delfont sat in a grim line, in row F.

"After the musical had lurched its way through the first 25 minutes," says Richard Mills, "Bernie rose from his seat and said, 'I'm going to the bar'. Ten minutes later, John Bryan joined him. We then reached a moment in the plot where Barbara Windsor had to deliver the sort of line that everyone in show business dreads when a show is not going well. 'I don't know what's going on here,' said Barbara. 'Neither do we,' came a loud voice from the stalls. Barbara stepped forward to the foot-lights, and addressed the audience. 'I'm awfully sorry that it's a bit of a mess, but we are working on it, and I'm sure we'll get it right. Now back to the plot.' At this moment I turned to Tim Burrill, and found that he had left as well."

Barbara's aside to the audience upset Ronnie Corbett. "He couldn't forgive me for coming out of character onstage, and refused to speak to me when I came off.

"'What could I do?' I asked him. 'I couldn't ignore it.'

"The whole show was so terrible that Jimmy Booth told me he couldn't face going onstage for the finale. He was too fed up, too humiliated, to confront an audience that was now baying for his blood. 'Bollocks you are, Jim,' I said. 'We've done our best. It's not our fault the show's a mess.' So we all went out for the big finish and performed to the backs of hundreds of people flocking to the exits. By the time we got to the end of the last number, the theatre was empty."

"Lionel sat in Row E and clapped enthusiastically but more or less alone," says a typescript found in Lionel's archives, unattributed, but almost certainly not by Lionel. "After the show, he got up onstage and told the cast, 'Now I'm going to get a grip on this show. I'm going to put my stamp on it. Joan and I will do it.' He announced he was going to scrap two songs, cut 45 minutes, write four new songs and tighten up all the ad libs. 'First night audiences are always kind of guinea pigs. I smell success, the greatest success since *Oliver!*'"

The critics showed no mercy. The *Daily Express* called it "a nose dive not an arrow-flight. Not *Twang!!* but Thud!" The *Daily Mirror* came up with "*Twang!!* goes clang." "Flop!" said *The Guardian*. "The kindest description of this rambling, inconsequential and distressingly, intolerably, wickedly long show is simply, pantomime. It begins with a line of peroxide girls, wiggling and bellowing every possible rhyme to *Twang!!*, moves on to the Merrie Men doing a sort of Music Hall turn: and continues with a great number of presumably related episodes which I will not relate since I can't remember them." However, the reviewer knew where to lay the blame: "The guilt ultimately must belong to Mr Bernard Delfont, who is presenting it all. He is allowing us to see a tawdry unfinished show and he is using us poor provincials as guinea pigs, using us to help decide what changes must be made before the all important opening in London."

The following morning, Delfont called a meeting in his room at the Midland Hotel. Joan arrived half an hour late and immediately launched an attack. She blamed the poor rehearsal facilities. She blamed the costumes, the draughty theatre, the non-existent book. She accused Harvey, Oliver and Lionel of incompetence and obstinacy, adding that Lionel had never known his limitations. She got up to leave. As her parting shot she mentioned that at least she had always got on with Paddy Stone and given him her consistent support. "That's not true," said Paddy. "You are a fucking liar, Joan."

It was naturally assumed that Joan's eventual exit from the room was her resignation from the show. But when Lionel, Harvey, Paddy and Bernard arrived at rehearsals that afternoon, there she was, halfway through an oration about the overall turpitude of British theatre. Educationally, psychologically and sociologically Britain was, apparently, far behind the rest of the world. When she'd finished, she told the cast that from now on they'd have to direct themselves because she was leaving.

For the next two days Joan stayed locked in her hotel room, with two security men guarding the door, and the press baying for an interview. Then she disappeared.

All great stories need a blood sacrifice, ideally just before the denouement, usually for purposes of atonement, redemption or retribution. Jesus died to save our sins; Obi-Wan to facilitate Luke's escape from the Death Star with Han, Chewbacca, Princess Leia, R2D2 and C3PO. It is ironic that Joan's blood-sacrifice, her resignation and disappearance at the exact moment when all seems lost, lends to the real story of the making of *Twang!!* exactly the kind of narrative integrity so culpably absent from the show itself. Thus life not only imitates, but often improves on art.

Students of gender politics might also have noticed the imbalance at *Twang!!*'s top table – Joan (1), Lionel, Oliver, Paddy, Richard, John, Timothy, Bernard, Ken (8). They might also have noted that when a sacrifice was called for, it was the woman who took the scapegoat role; and that in subsequent written accounts of the *Twang!!* shenanigans, Joan is almost invariably portrayed as the villain of the piece. What can you do? It was 1965. Sexism didn't even have a name. *Mad Men* would have been a documentary series. Betty Friedan was a lippy housewife. And besides, no matter how hard you try to picture Joan as a victim of gender politics – and it is difficult to see her as the victim of anything, even unstated and largely unconscious but nonetheless ubiquitous psycho–socio–economic forces – for all her genius she couldn't half be a divisive, manipulative pain-in-the-arse sometimes. "She used to encourage you so far down the tightrope," John Junkin said, "you were bound to fall off in the end."

It was by now impossible to open a newspaper without reading about *Twang!!* General Elections have been given fewer column inches.

"Every day we were besieged by the press, who were waiting for the company at the stage door," says Richard Mills. "In the morning when we came in to rehearse, there were between 15 and 20 reporters. They had smelt blood; they thought this was going to be the biggest disaster in theatrical history – they were right. Every day, there were stories on the front pages of the national press, recounting some new piece of disaster they'd sniffed out."

After a brief interregnum when the director's crown was forced onto Paddy Stone's reluctant head, Lionel staged a lightning coup and seized the reins of power.

"Now we were really in the shit," says Richard Mills. "And it just got deeper and deeper."

The making of *Twang!!* had had its blood sacrifice. Clearly what the show now needed was a deus ex machina – a god who would descend from the flies, wave a magic wand and turn everything into *Oliver!* Bernard Delfont thought he knew just the man for the job.

Burt Shevelove was an American writer and director, who'd worked in radio, TV and the theatre. In 1962 he'd had a huge hit with *A Funny Thing Happened On The Way To The Forum*, a slaves'n'sandals romp based very loosely on the works of Plautus. Shevelove and Larry Gelbart had co-written the book, with music and lyrics by Stephen Sondheim. It ran for two years on Broadway. The London production, starring Frankie Howerd, inspired the long-running TV series *Up Pompeii!*

A Funny Thing was, it seemed, all the things that *Twang!!* was trying to be – an assembly of top-class tit and knob gags ("bawdy, irreverent humour") wrapped up in a ludicrous but nonetheless lucid plot held together with knockout songs and draped in gauzy showgirls. What's more, Shevelove had a reputation as a show-doctor – a man who could come in, spot the fatal flaw, rewrite these scenes, cut those, fire him, hire her, move a couple of songs around and bob's your uncle it's a hit.

He arrived – deus ex machina – on Saturday November 6, having told Bernard Delfont, "I can only promise I can make it less bad." He spent Sunday studying scripts and consulting with principals. On Monday morning he addressed the troops and put it to 'em straight: "You didn't just bore the audience on opening night. You antagonised them. The show will definitely be more organised now."

Not if Lionel had anything to do with it. He had plotted his own course of action to save the show and was not about to be sidetracked.

"Lionel and I would sit upstairs watching the performance every night," says Lionel's secretary at the time, Muriel Walker, "and I would take notes and then go backstage and give them to the performers. After that we would go back to the Midland Hotel where we were staying and over supper Act I Scene I would be rewritten. I would go back to my room and type it all up on to stencils. Then the next morning I would go into the office at the Palace Theatre and run off the scene and distribute it to the actors. And the next night we would do the same thing for the next scene. But the problem with that was that the redone scene had little to do with the others." Or, for that matter, with Shevelove.

After one particularly intense argument between Lionel and Burt, Lionel quit, "That's it. I'm off on me holidays." He was back in a couple of hours.

The flood of new scenes, new business, new lines were a performer's nightmare. They wrote dialogue on the backs of trees, castles, limbs, costumes and the floor. "I was keeping a running budget on the estimated costs of the show," says Richard Mills, "and what the final financial implications would be, if and when, we transferred it into London. [. . .] Each day, I would phone Bernie, give him an update on the additional costs, and suggest that we close the show down. Each day, Bernie said, 'Let's give it another day.'"

Bernie's patience ran out on November 19. Richard Mills got the nod.

"'Right, that's it – we're out of here'. I was packed and on a train to London within the hour. Bernie phoned John Bryan, our co-producer, and said, 'We're pulling the plug – are you joining us?' John Bryan's attitude was – well you're more expert in these matters than me, so let's forget it."

Lionel's last remaining backer was United Artists. He pleaded with them to put up the extra cash needed for the West End opening. Will they, won't they? In the press, the Munich Crisis was never so hotly debated.

"The overriding subject of speculation within the company for the past four weeks," said Benedict Nightingale in *The Guardian*, "has been; is the show going to the West End or not? Decisions have been announced, postponed and postponed again. In the meantime the show has been in a continual state of disrepair."

And in another report, "If things came to an unexpected crisis he [Lionel] would be prepared to bear the cost of backing it himself."

"Never," Noël had told him (now with a touch of reverb), "put money into your own show."

Somewhere a deep and heavy bell should toll to signify both that this is the eleventh hour and that doom visits those who in their vanity and folly would defy Noël Coward.

On November 20, the day after Delfont and Brookfield pulled the plug on *Twang!*, *Oliver!* celebrated its 2,284th performance, which put it into the record books as British theatre's longest running musical.

A celebratory procession left the Old Curiosity Shop in Portsmouth Street at the back of Kingsway at 2.20 p.m. and arrived at the New Theatre, where *Oliver!* was playing, at 2.50. A carnival float, decorated with an *Oliver!* theme, carried the kids from the show. In front of them marched the band of H.M. Irish Guards, by gracious permission of Her Majesty the Queen. Leading the whole procession, playing a big bass drum, was Lionel Bart.

The Irish Guards had cost him £120; the design and build of the float, £140; coaches and taxis to ferry the children, £21 17s 6d; telegrams to newspapers had cost £6 6s 3d; Panadol, 6s 9d.

During a manic episode, sufferers from Bipolar disorder can experience delusions which lead them to believe that they are possessed of super-human powers, that they are 'chosen', that they are unstoppable. There is no evidence that Lionel was ever diagnosed with Bipolar disorder.

Much the same mood – without the delusional element – can be induced by your show, the one you wrote, becoming the longest running British musical.

It can also be induced by a noseful of cocaine.

And it can be induced by being an East End son of an immigrant tailor who has to spend every waking moment proving that he's as good as if not better than every other fucker on the planet.

In exchange for his West End opening, Lionel signed a deal with United Artists effectively giving them 50 percent of all his profits from music publishing for the next ten years. He had to bring *Twang!!* to London, he announced, "just to show the knockers".

On November 28, the circus moved to London and rehearsals started for a West End opening at some unspecified date. The changes kept coming. Numbers with intricate dance routines that had taken weeks to rehearse were unceremoniously dropped. A major plot change switched Barbara Windsor's love interest from Elric Hooper's Alan-A-Dale to

Bernard Bresslaw's Little John. Bresslaw was six foot six. Barbara barely five foot. "Whenever I have even a faintly serious love scene in a show," said Barbara, "someone always wants to put a gag in it."

The cast's morale found new depths. Confusion was the biggest complaint. The actors never had time to draw a bead on who they were supposed to be, or what style they were supposed to be playing.

"The difference between Joan and Burt," said Ronnie Corbett, "is that with Joan you always knew who you were supposed to be, but never where you were going. With Burt, you don't really know who you're supposed to be, but you always know where you're going."

Some decided the best place to go was home. George Cooper (Friar Tuck) walked out and never came back.

Oliver Messel walked out and flew to his home in Barbados, where he stayed mostly for the rest of his life, decorating the homes of his simpatico neighbours. There is a colour, still used extensively for Barbadian shutters, known as 'Messel blue'.

Bernard Bresslaw walked out for a bit, but came back again. So did Burt Shevelove. Harvey Orkin took to criticising Shevelove's dress-sense. "Burt, my God, you're wearing a brown suit with a grey face."

On December 10, Lionel handed Burt a letter. In it he said they were half way to developing a uniquely new form of musical comedy. He said he had written 18 of the 23 songs in a strong burlesque music hall tradition and that three of the mood ballads were meant to involve the deeper thoughts of the romantic leads. He wanted to emphasise that the dialogue and sections of the songs should be sung, in turn, to God, the world and no one in particular. He hoped that Burt would take these insights on board and implement the changes during the last week of rehearsals.

There is no evidence to suggest that the following morning Burt went in and told Ronnie Corbett to sing his songs, in turn, to God, the world and no one in particular. But Lionel's letter must constitute part of the growing body of circumstantial evidence in support of Joan's contention that he was transcending verbal concepts and space-time dimensions. Or he might just have been shitting himself and burbling.

The first dress rehearsal started with James Booth hitting Maxwell Shaw (Prince John) in his duodenal ulcer and forgetting to pull the punch. It finished with Burt telling the cast, "Lionel and I disagree over the finale, but we'll have an argument tonight and I'll win and I'll give you the new dialogue tomorrow."

Twang!! opened at the Shaftesbury Theatre on December 20, 1965. Sean Connery, days before the premiere of his new James Bond movie,

Thunderball, was in attendance, as were Millicent Martin and David Frost and a host of others.

The curtain was late going up and technical gremlins caused the house lights to flicker on and off throughout the first half.

Lionel, in protest at Burt's cutting of two "mood ballads", had inserted a note in the programme saying, "Lionel Bart wishes to announce that two song items 'Unseen Hands' and 'Writing On The Wall' are now in a new show called *Son Of Twang.*" A shiver must have run through cast and crew – a sequel?

The first half was slow. At the interval there was sporadic applause. In the second half, the booing began. Lionel suspected it was an old-fashioned claque – a group paid to laugh, applaud or in this case boo – arranged by Joan. If this was the case, she could have saved her money. The curtain call was given to an almost empty house. "We took our final bows in a crescendo of boos," said Barbara Windsor. "Many people, it was clear, had just come along for the sport."

The critics arranged a crucifixion. Milton Shulman in the *Evening Standard* called it "the worst musical of 1965", an opinion more recently updated by the *Telegraph* which called *Twang!!* "the seventh worst musical of all time". The *Mirror* complained that "the only memorable tune after the interval was the National Anthem." *The Stage* called it "a show without a single witty line, a single memorable song, or a single arresting situation. The story line is as clear as a tattered cobweb and the book (full of exchanges like 'Use guile', 'I haven't got any') suggested provincial pantomime at its worst."

The words "thin", "boring", "painful", "dull", and "lumpy" crop up frequently. "The basic trouble is this," said Benedict Nightingale in *The Guardian*. "Everyone's trying to do a spoof but haven't decided who or what they are spoofing."

Lionel, determined to talk it up, kept the soundbites coming: "People liked it," he told *The Guardian*. "There were 200 laughs – 150 of them solid laughs – which makes it about my funniest yet. I heard every note and every word of the lyrics. All it needs now is lightening up – more speed."

Wearing a yellow sweater and black hipster trousers, he told the *Daily Sketch* he'd been fielding calls all day from Paul McCartney, David Frost, Brian Epstein and many others saying what a fantastic hit he had on his hands.

It had been agreed from the start that Burt Shevelove would leave as soon as the show had opened in London. His last act at the Shaftesbury was to pin a note to the theatre's bulletin board, addressed to the cast: "We all stood on tiptoe and nobody gave us a kiss. How sad."

It was not a happy Christmas.

"I had to keep nagging before Christmas," says Muriel Walker. 'Lionel, do something about your Christmas presents.'

" 'Yeah all right, all right.' Christmas Eve came. 'Mu, could you, er . . .'

" 'What . . .?' So I had the car with the chauffeur, and I went to Harrods with a list of people and I had a day to buy all these Christmas presents – an average of five pounds. Buy the presents in a day [and] get them all to a collection point."

Muriel did well. For Lionel's nephew Sam she got a building kit for £3 17s 0d. For Rita, a blue beatnik's set. Gemma and Anthony Orkin, Harvey's kids, got a ceramic dressing table set (£5 9s 0d) and a Pinocchio puppet (£1 15s 0d) respectively.

One hopes that, as Lionel signed each Christmas card, he sent a prayer to heaven / that *Twang!!* would keep on running / until nineteen sixty-seven.

When the cast reassembled on December 27, Lionel had taken over. He addressed the troops: "It is my decision at this stage to inject energy and pace into the show to make it audience proof and live up to the great praise I have publicly bestowed upon it. [. . .] We are about to salvage and transform this piece – into a fast moving ensemble entertainment. I stress the word ensemble. Ensemble speed. Ensemble sense of fun. Ensemble style and attitude towards taking the mickey out of the Robin Hood myth. Ensemble understanding of what each scene and song is supposed to achieve plot wise. If we convey this sense of fun to our audiences – we will have audiences for a long time to come. [. . .] It is my intention to build this show into the most popular entertainment in London by the beginning of March. If by that time there is any artiste here who doubts his contribution within the ensemble we will be prepared to consider their resignation as soon as they can be swiftly replaced. I expect my cuts and amendments to be received unequivocably – without remonstrance of any kind."

At the beginning of January, he was having to write a personal cheque for £4,000 every Monday to keep the show open.

On January 12, he gave in, announcing that "unless a miracle happens" he would close the show in three weeks.

The miracle never came. Three weeks and three days later, on January 29, 1966, it was over.

Sixteen

"WHAT was Lionel frightened of?" asks Eric Williams, his lifelong friend. "I think he thought he was going to be found out. I think David Niven said he thought he was going to wake up one day and somebody was going to find out he was just David Niven and he'd be found out because he never believed he could do it anyway."

"Some people say Lionel got what he deserved," adds Richard Mills. "His sense of self-importance cost him all his money and most of his future royalties. From being the 'Golden Boy' of British musicals, whose mere name could open any door, he became someone who producers shied away from."

"Lionel got what he deserved" has become the accepted version of the story, although exactly what crime he'd committed to deserve his punishment is seldom specified. Phrases like "his sense of self-importance" and 'ideas above his station' are sometimes bandied.

The Ancient Greeks called it hubris – the crime of assuming so much pride and arrogance that it presents a challenge to the gods: a crime so prevalent that one god's sole duty was its punishment and her name was Nemesis.

Everybody likes a good story and here was, literally, a classic. Lionel was guilty of hubris and was laid low by Nemesis. It makes a satisfying narrative that pleases our atavistic sense of justice, confirms our understanding of cause and effect and shortcuts the need for grey detail.

Twang!! left his reputation, never rock solid, in fragments. In the business, people whispered that he was 'difficult' – a word that can be a compliment when you're producing hits but when the flops come turns quickly into a synonym for 'pariah'. And, perhaps worst of all, his name found its way on to the comedy agenda. He became a bit of a joke.

On January 22, 1966, a week before *Twang!!* closed, a three-day party at the Longshoreman's Hall in faraway San Francisco climaxed when the punch was spiked with acid and six thousand 'hippies' (a name first coined a year or so earlier) danced with erratic limbs to music provided by The Grateful Dead and Big Brother & The Holding Company. A butterfly had flapped its wings and within months if not weeks the flotsam and jetsam cast up by the resulting tidal wave began to fetch up on Lionel's doorstep.

Lionel could never have been a hippie: his hair was too wiry, his appreciation of tailoring too acute and his standards of hygiene too demanding. But the hippies' relaxed attitude to sex and – in light of *Twang!!* – their contempt for worldly success must have had their appeal.

The hazy calibration of the dial that runs from 'open heartedly generous' via 'soft touch' to 'victim of theft' had always confused Lionel as much as it delighted the agents, publishers, accountants, lawyers and sharks who rushed to his side with loaded Parkers when extortionate cheques or small-print contracts were to be signed. Now it delighted the hippies and other hangers on, too.

The Fun Palace had always been a place where pleasure-seekers, musicians and other happy, smiley people could find a welcome.

For a time, Julie Driscoll, who went top ten in 1968 with Dylan and Rick Danko's 'This Wheel's On Fire', found a place to rest her head at the Fun Palace. Justin Hayward, later of The Moody Blues, lived in the staff cottage for a while with his girlfriend Anne Marie Guirron and the two of them "sort of looked after Lionel". Julie, Justin and Marie were undoubtedly perfect and appreciative house guests. Indeed, Marie liked so much to put things neatly away that Lionel christened her "Miss Tidy-Doll". Others were not so orderly.

Like The Beatles' Apple Corps on Savile Row a couple of years later, Seymour Walk developed a reputation as a place where public-spirited hippies could free an unfortunate breadhead of troubling possessions and thus set his soul free. "We are stardust," they sang, "we are golden, let's go and have a sandwich round at Lionel's."

An even worse drain on Lionel's resources and patience than the hippies were the boyfriends. He loved obsessively and obsession tore his generosity completely off its hinges. He showered his favoured ones with clothes, perfume and cars. One lucky chap found himself the recipient of not one, but two Morgans. If the presents didn't suit, the boyfriends would occasionally help themselves to something that did. One, Anthony Haydon, who moved to the house in 1967 – although whether his role was boyfriend, pal, assistant, hanger-on or all of the above was never made clear – eventually, as will be seen in the next chapter or so, helped himself to a vanload of valuables.

And the parties went on and on.

At Wembley, two days before Lionel's 36th birthday, Bobby Moore sent a long pass to Geoff Hurst. The referee was looking at his watch.

Spectators were coming on to the field. They thought it was all over. The fifth goal of the match, England's third, had been controversial. Did it cross the line or didn't it? Determined to lay all doubt firmly to rest, Hurst hit the ball so hard you could almost see the whizz lines behind it, just like in a *Roy Of The Rovers* cartoon.

After the match, Tina and Bobby Moore celebrated quietly with a few friends at their home in Essex. "It wasn't anything fancy, just a few drinks and a bit of music for a couple of hours," Tina says.[84] "After everyone left, it all felt a bit flat, to be honest. Bobby poured himself a lager while I cleared away the glasses." But then "we got a telegram from the composer Lionel Bart, inviting us to a party with Tom Jones and Joan Collins." Nobby Stiles, Jackie Charlton, Tom Jones, Joan Collins and a chorus of hippies, boyfriends and hangers-on all scented with the 'soft and powdery floral notes' of *L'Heure Bleue*. If Lionel's devices that could record sound from twelve different points in the house were running that night, tragically the tapes are long lost.

In February there had been a momentary panic when Alma was admitted to hospital with what they thought was a grumbling appendix. Later in the year she went on a tour of Sweden. After the last concert, she passed out. She was stretchered back to the UK and, on October 5, installed at the Middlesex Hospital. During exploratory surgery following the appendix scare, cancer had been diagnosed. The doctors had told Brian Morris, her fiancé, but he had kept it quiet, not even telling Alma.

The depths of Lionel's desperation can be seen in two telegrams sent by Noël Coward in response, one assumes, to impassioned pleas for help and consolation. Noël was at his home in Jamaica, discussing *Star!*, the biopic of his one-time stage partner, Gertrude Lawrence.

> October 9, 1966
> *Dearest Lie, I'm heartbroken and am unable to help you. From Monday onwards house full of film executives discussing Gertrude Lawrence movie hotly followed by more guests till end of November.*

This must have elicited a still more impassioned plea from Lionel, causing Noël to telegraph again, later the same day.

> October 9, 1966
> *Really dreadfully sorry. Please understand terribly sad about mutual friend. Please give loving messages and my fondest love to you.*

Alma died on October 26.

The archives contain holiday snaps: Lionel and Alma having a laugh, Lionel and Alma and the other Lionel (Blair) in a restaurant somewhere hot, Lionel and Alma and Tommy Steele in a boat in Venice. There are postcards – from Athens, from Italy, from the south of France – "It's better than Portsmouth, Almee." She always signed them 'Almee'. There's a flexidisc – one of those thin plastic records that used to come free with magazines – this one recorded in Japan and inscribed in Alma's hand, "Just a little thing I did in a studio here – give it a listen." Unplayable now. Alma's first night telegram for *Maggie May* is clearly the work of somebody more intimate with at least the titles of the songs than Rachel Roberts probably was. "Day don't all make the same size promises but I do dat today. It'll be the greatest qvelly (*sic?*) may. I know 'cos I'm me and I will love a man and it's yourself I love. Almee."

"When she died, he couldn't cope," says Muriel Walker. "He couldn't even cope with the idea of the funeral. He went off to America."

There were shows to sell in America and films to plan and people to see and besides, travel is the traditional cure for heartbreak. New experience drives away the old and leads to a forgetting.

Until 1956, Tangier, in Morocco, had enjoyed the odd political status of being an 'international zone' jointly administered by Britain, France and Spain. It made it an oddly lawless place – *La Ville De Plaisir* where "you could get anything you wanted if you paid for it. Do anything, too, for that matter – it was only a matter of price." For uptight northern Europeans, whose every move was circumscribed by post-war austerity, rules and regulations, it was a blessed escape. For homosexuals it was heaven. Even after losing its status in 1956, the police and authorities feared the economic consequences of a clampdown too much ever to wag the finger with anything other than a token fierceness. Lionel went there twice in 1967 and found the real Xanadu of which the Fun Palace could only every have been a Mattel copy.

York Castle had been built by the Portuguese in the 15th century to defend Tangier, which they had recently conquered, from Moorish attack. When the British acquired Tangier, they too used the castle as a military base, the Moors at that time being led by a mastermind with the delightfully appropriate name of Gayland. In 1961, the castle was acquired by the interior designers Charles Sevigny and Yves Vidal who worked their magic turning it into "one of the most beautiful houses in the world". While the likes of Kenneth Williams and Joe Orton made do with a room at the Rembrandt in town, Lionel rented York Castle standing proud above the kasbah. It was the beginning of a fantasy, entertained for the rest of his life, that he would buy the place as a permanent holiday home. "What d'you want to do something like that for?" Brenda Evans, his sensible secretary used to say in the Eighties. "You'd only want it to impress somebody."

In 1967, he was at the castle in April, and again in August. On both occasions he found himself in Tangier – entirely coincidentally – at the same time as the actor Kenneth Williams. The two had met years before when Williams was working on the revue *Pieces Of Eight,* and because of Kenny's involvement in the *Carry On* films, they had many friends, including Barbara Windsor and Bernard Bresslaw, in common – if, that is, Lionel could still number the *Twang!!* cast among his friends.

"Went to Magoga & were joined on the beach by Mochta," Kenneth tells his diary on April 1. "Several Moroccans shout out 'You fuck Moroccan boy tonight' and other disgusting slogans. Got the bus back to G. Hardy for lunch and there was Lionel B. and loads of friends. We were all introduced. Lionel asked me & L to dinner tomorrow night."[85] Details of the dinner are not recorded.

On the second visit they spent several days together, Lionel talking about the plans for an *Oliver!* film and charming Kenneth with gossip about Rachel Robert's drunkenness in *Maggie May* and the Rex Harrison "little homosexual runt" anecdote. It could only ever have been a holiday friendship. Kenneth liked to shriek. Lionel whispered. Kenneth was a confusing mix of campery and prudery, erudition and vulgarity, exhibitionism and self-disgust but, if his diaries are anything to go by, in Tangier the campery was let off the leash and allowed to scamper. He complains of "Tange" being filled "with yr. actual silly queens and naf polones." Lionel "hated all that campery," says Eric Williams (no relation to Kenneth). "He never did any of that. He was a bloke and he was very masculine in every way."

Back in England, despite all setbacks, there were signs that Lionel was still reassuringly A-list. The most important, most exclusive party of that year was not a glitzy occasion. There was no red carpet, no flashbulbs, no haute couture, no diamonds, but you knew that an invitation meant you were in the most inner of all inner circles. You were la crème de la crème.

Brian Epstein had bought himself a country house at Kingsley Hill in Sussex. As a housewarming, and to celebrate the upcoming release of The Beatles' latest LP, *Sergeant Pepper's Lonely Hearts Club Band*, he decided to host a little garden party. John, George and Ringo, with wives, were in attendance (Paul had a previous engagement), together with the usual entourage, Mick and Marianne, Robert Stigwood and a few others. It was a family affair. Lionel was included in the family.

It was a beautiful summer day. The new album played over and over. Everybody got high. "The minute you walked through the door you got dosed," Lionel says in Bob Spitz's *The Beatles – The Biography.*[86] "The boys were making the rounds serving tea out of a china pot that had been generously spiked with acid." John spent most of the afternoon sitting in his Roller, out of his brain, with Derek Taylor, The Beatles' former press officer, also out of his brain, listening to another new release, Procol Harum's *A Whiter Shade Of Pale.* Cynthia, John's wife, was taken badly by the acid and stood at an upstairs window contemplating suicide. Brian, too, went off after a bit. Inconsolable about Paul's absence, which he now took as a deliberate slight, he wept and raved.

Meanwhile Lionel was having a lovely time. "The whole party appeared to be tripping like mad," he said, "everyone was dancing around to the flame of a candle."

On July 26, the Sexual Offences Act 1967, decriminalising homosexual acts between consenting adults in private, was made law. "It's getting better all the time," The Beatles sang from every open window during that hot Summer of Love.

On his 37th birthday, three days later, Lionel gave an interview to the *Daily Mirror.* Still being, for official purposes, an 'eligible bachelor' he did not, of course, see fit to mention the new law, but spoke instead about his difficulties getting *The Hunchback Of Notre Dame* – "the most spectacular conception for the stage I've ever dreamed of" – launched and into orbit. He insisted that his difficulties in interesting backers had nothing to do with the failure of *Twang!!* "Almost every producer in the world is scared of it," he said. "Maybe they'll put the show on after I die and then discover what a winner it is."

The interviewer or sub-editors appended an opening paragraph to the piece, and a headline. The headline read: "Whatever Happened To Lionel Bart?" The opening paragraph read: "There was a time when the magic of songwriter Lionel Bart sparkled from every hit parade. But not any more. It's over three years since a Bart composition appeared in the charts. Since the crash of *Twang!!* eighteen months ago, little has been heard of him." The coolest man on the planet, still cool enough to be invited to the coolest party of the year, had become – at least for *Daily Mirror* readers – no more than a "Where Are They Now?" curiosity.

On August 9, a few days before Lionel's second visit of the year to Tangier, Joe Orton, the playwright and close friend of Kenneth Williams, had his brains hammered out by his partner Kenneth Halliwell who then topped himself with 22 Nembutals.

A couple of weeks later, Epstein was dead.

Brian and Lionel had naturally bonded. They were both rich, gay, Jewish, showbiz, sharp dressers and quietly spoken, so why wouldn't they? But there was something disturbingly hardcore about Brian. Lionel had his troubles with boys, but they were nothing compared to Eppy's. Pick-ups regularly beat the shit out of him, although nobody – possibly not even Brian – was ever quite sure whether this was an act of criminal violence or part of the service. On one occasion, two rival pick-ups beat the shit out of each other, then they beat the shit out of Brian's flat, then they beat the shit out of Brian. He was a heartbreakingly troubled man.

When The Beatles decided they'd had enough of touring in 1966, Brian had felt marginalised, useless, rejected by the boys he had made into the biggest stars in the history of show business and whom he loved so dearly. He was also dependent on near fatal doses of barbiturates to put him to sleep at night and amphetamines to keep him awake during the day. It was the pills that saw him off. The coroner recorded a verdict of accidental death, but everybody knew, really.

A friend whose life in so many ways ran parallel to Lionel's own had met a terrible end. And this less than a year after he'd lost Alma. Overcoming two such deaths in such a short space of time would have required deep reserves of emotional resilience.

Many of the full-time hippies in San Francisco took their health and their drugs very seriously. They ate mung beans and brown rice. They smoked a little grass but concerned themselves with its provenance. Alcohol was a crude poison, for the most part to be shunned. Acid was a ritual you took part in maybe once a week. You prepared carefully for your trip. There were casualties, of course, who ended starving, hysterical, naked, but it was the inexperienced, weekend hippies who really clogged the psychiatric wards; they were the ones who "throw themselves in front of moving cars, strip naked in grocery stores and run through plate-glass windows."[87]

Often the problem was "the widespread tendency to mix two or three drugs at the same time. Acid and alcohol can be a lethal combination, causing fits of violence, suicidal depression and a general freak-out that ends in jail or a hospital."

In October, Lionel was in court. George Warne, one of the builder/ decorators who'd worked on the Fun Palace, was suing for unpaid bills.

The press had a lovely time reporting the details of the violet lavatories and electric curtains meticulously catalogued by counsel and judge, trumpeting them as examples of his spendthrift vulgarity. They really did have it in for poor Lionel.

He had decided to sell the place, anyway, telling the press, in strict accord with the new hippie ethos, that he was tired of owning things. "It belongs to the past, and I belong to the future."[88] "What's the point of staying there? A bachelor in a six-bedroomed house? Besides, unless I move the hippies will be making this their headquarters. I'm getting besieged by the flower people. I wake up some mornings and I don't recognise some of the faces still hanging around . . ."

Bertrand Russell had first found fame in 1910, collaborating with A.N. Whitehead on the three-volume *Principia Mathematica* which explored the fundamental axioms of mathematics through a system of symbolic logic. As a Cambridge academic he had tutored the logical positivist Ludwig Wittgenstein and assisted in the publication of his *Tractatus Logico-Philosophicus*. He founded a school, married four times, shagged Lady Ottoline Morrell, wrote the excellent *History Of Western Philosophy* and, as a pioneer member of the Fabian society and a lifelong pacifist, was regarded as a good guy by the beatniks and hippies who cheered him when he spoke at anti-nuclear demos.

In his eighties, he had published three books of short stories and, deciding that they could form the basis of blockbuster musicals, approached Lionel Bart.

His front-runner was a story called *Satan In The Suburbs* which he and Lionel discussed for a while. But by 1967 both had gone off the *Satan* idea. Lionel reckoned it was too similar to *Damn Yankees*, and Russell thought it was old hat and was keen to get started on something completely fresh. "I was knocked out that he asked me," Lionel said, "and tremendously impressed that a man of that age should want to play new games."[89]

For now, the collaboration could be taken no further due to both men's prior commitments: Lionel had a movie to promote, Bertie had to set up the Vietnam War Tribunals with Jean-Paul Sartre. The next gap in either diary wasn't really until 1970, by which time Bertie was dead.

Seventeen

THE filming of *Oliver!* started with trouble and ended in triumph.

The squabbling broke out as early as 1962; arguments about who had sold which rights to whom, under what circumstances and with what conditions. Essentially Lionel wanted the film to be made by Brookfield Productions, the Peter Sellers/John Bryan outfit that eventually backed *Twang!!*, while Donald Albery favoured Romulus Films, producers of *The African Queen, Room At The Top* and many others. The execs at Columbia Pictures, the huge Hollywood corporation that had distribution rights, enjoyed throwing their weight around, too. It went on for years.

Everybody wanted Peter Sellers to play Fagin but he said he wouldn't unless Brookfield got the contract and eventually a High Court judge (the details are hard to follow) ruled that Sellers wouldn't be that good in the part anyway. Peter O'Toole, who said he'd already been promised Fagin, fell out with everybody. Arg followed barg. Small print was scrutinised, artistic considerations weighed and after many barristers had made enough to send even their youngest sons to Eton, a deal was put together between Romulus Films, Warwick Films (the company responsible for *Jazz Boat* and *Idol On Parade*, although where they sneaked in is anybody's guess) and Columbia.

By 1966, the project had a director on board. Lewis Gilbert was an East End boy, ten years older than Lionel. He had been responsible for some of the best British war films – *Reach For The Sky, Carve Her Name With Pride, Sink The Bismarck*. In 1965 he made *Alfie*, which won multiple Oscar nominations and launched Michael Caine's Hollywood career.

"If I was born to make a film," Lewis said on *Desert Island Discs*, 40-odd years later, "it was to make *Oliver!* I longed to make *Oliver!* and Lionel Bart said to me, 'nobody else will do it. You will do it. [. . .]' That was a film that I longed, longed to make."

Lewis was a busy man. For most of 1966 and the start of '67 he was otherwise engaged directing the fifth Sean Connery Bond film, *You Only Live Twice*. All the same he made sure there were enough holes in the schedule to accommodate planning meetings for *Oliver!* His frequent absences from the Bond set were noticed. "Which film are we working on today, Lewis?" Cubby Broccoli would ask.

Lionel's preparation for these meetings was rigorous. He worked hard to give Vernon Harris, Lewis's trusted screenwriter, a fund of ideas and suggestions. A 20-page document dated January 23, 1967, concerns itself with anti-semitism. "I would here reiterate my strong insistence that FAGIN in my version of *Oliver Twist* should not be portrayed with any-thing approaching Dickens' ghetto-joke image of a Jew. The melodies of his songs are quite sufficient to tell us the background of his heritage without the use of and accompanying Jewish gesture, attitude or verbal inflection. He has lived in London all his life. He is therefore a Londoner. His dialect, accent, argot and language should be that of a London cockney (i.e. Stanley Holloway, Frankie Howerd). His physical image and demeanour should be that of some kind of zany chicken with red hair and beard sticking out spikily awry, out from his bright-eyed face. I have endeavoured to make the rhythm and tempii of his songs/dialogue akin to that of a chicken – sometimes timid, sometimes violent – always scared of violence. Erratic, nibbling and pecking for goodies that are thrown his way, but always looking this-way-and-that-way to see that nobody is watching. This chicken-like figure of a man – a mother hen protecting the little villains and pick-pockets who are his chicklets; sometimes with mock violence; sometimes with a matriarchal quality, at which moments he becomes a broody hen."

Lionel also provided new scenes for the screenplay, new snatches of dialogue and three brand new songs: 'Bullseye', for Bill Sikes, 'I Know You Know I Know', and 'Checkmate'. None of them made the final cut.

Just as everything seemed to be going well, *Alfie* came back to bite Lewis Gilbert. In order to finance *Alfie,* Lewis had sold his soul to Paramount Pictures and now, they decided, it was time to collect. Lewis found himself contractually obliged to direct an an adaptation of a Harold Robbins novel called *The Adventurers,* a stinker starring Charles Aznavour and Candice Bergen.

"I messed it up," he told Kirsty Young on *Desert Island Discs,* "because I signed a contract where the chap said to me, 'Oh, don't worry, you can do *Oliver!*' Then he reneged on it." Lewis couldn't even bring himself to name *The Adventurers.* "It's too hurtful for me to say that I gave up *Oliver!* to do *that* film."

Lewis's forced defection left the *Oliver!* team stranded. "I said, 'Well, there's plenty of directors around, surely. It's a wonderful subject. By the way, Carol Reed is available.'"

Carol Reed, too, felt he was born to make *Oliver!* In 1960, he had tried to buy the film rights, but found the price too steep. As an illegitimate son – there were many more – of the great Victorian actor/manager and founder of RADA Sir Herbert Beerbohm Tree, Carol had showbiz in his veins. In the early Thirties, he went to work for Associated Talking Pictures at Ealing Studios and rose up the ranks until he was trusted to direct a film all on his own. This was *Mr Midshipman Easy*, with Hughie Green, later TV host and surprise grandfather of Peaches Geldof, in the title role. Reed's most celebrated work before *Oliver!* had been his collaboration with the producer Alexander Korda and the writer Graham Greene on *The Fallen Idol* and *The Third Man* – both multi award-winners in the Forties. It was Reed who found himself wrangling Rex Harrison in *The Agony And The Ecstasy* while Lionel was wrangling Rachel Roberts in *Maggie May*. Compared with Rex, a chorus of 84 London kids was going to be a breeze.

In 1938, the whole of America had been whipped into an hysterical frenzy over the search for the perfect fiery beauty to play Scarlett O'Hara in *Gone With The Wind*. Auditions were held in small towns and blighted suburbs. Hopes were raised. Thousands of midwestern stenographers with average to good profiles were certain that they were the one. In the end the part went not to some unknown but to Vivien Leigh, the English star whose husband was the great Laurence Olivier.

The Romulus/Warwick/Columbia publicity machine tried to apply the same hype to the search for the perfect Oliver. Though the headlines that resulted failed to ignite much more than a flicker of interest, 2,000 – some estimates say 5,000 – hopeful mothers combed their son's hair with water and joined the queues. As it had been with Vivien Leigh, so it was with Mark Lester, an eight-year-old stage-school child with an actress for a mother, an actor for a father and an already impressive CV. His face, criticised by those who would prefer an Oliver with more gumption, could melt the hearts of long-dead polar explorers, but he did, as we shall discover, have one potentially ruinous flaw.

Some of the Artful Dodgers seen onstage had set a high standard, but by 1967, they all looked, sounded or were too old for the part. Or too busy. Davy Jones, the original Broadway Dodger, was a Monkee. Steve Marriott was lead singer with The Small Faces. Phil Collins, though still four years from joining Genesis, was a jobbing actor.

In his younger days, Phil had played football in the park with two brothers from up north named Jack and Arthur Wild. Phil's mother, June, ran the Barbara Speake Stage School along with Barbara Speake herself.

She saw something in the boys and talked their parents into sending them to her school, promising to find them enough acting work to pay the fees. As good as her promise, she worked them hard, eventually securing Jack a job in the *Oliver!* cast. He was 16 when the film came out, but still didn't look a day over 12, and though he had never played the part onstage, he was more than ready for the Dodger.

Harry Secombe was a veteran of *The Goon Show*. A broad man, much given to sudden shrieks and raspberries, he had found a home for his loud Welsh-tenor voice in the musical *Pickwick,* which had run to great acclaim in London. When it transferred to Broadway, the show had not been a commercial success but had nonetheless netted Secombe a Tony Award – enough to make him a safe bet for Mr Bumble The Beadle on both sides of the Atlantic.

For a while, Richard Burton's name had been thrown into the hat as a possible Bill Sikes. Richard and his wife Elizabeth Taylor liked, whenever possible, to work together. Elizabeth wanted to be Nancy. At Seymour Walk one day, she followed Lionel to the lavatory, locked the door and sang at him for a very long time. She was not given the part. And neither was Richard Burton given the part of Bill.

Since the beginning of the Sixties, Oliver Reed, Carol's nephew, had been for all intents and purposes on the staff at Hammer Films, playing an innocent man who turned into a savage beast in *Curse Of The Werewolf,* the victim of an innocent man who turned into a savage beast in *The Two Faces Of Doctor Jekyll* and an innocent sailor who turned into a savage pirate in *Pirates Of Blood River*. His wide experience of being chased over rooftops by villagers and townspeople bearing flaming torches made him, not Burton, the obvious choice for Bill Sikes.

Carol Reed wanted Shirley Bassey to play Nancy. Columbia expressed concerns that a woman of colour being murdered by a white man could throw up all manner of problems, particularly in the southern states. Georgia Brown was an obvious front-runner. Judy Garland was mentioned, too. Words like 'earthy', 'feral', 'brassy' were bandied, but Columbia decided that young, clean and glamorous would play better for the family audience. Shani Wallis was shiny and slim. Her teeth were crisp and her skin unblemished. She had appeared to great acclaim in the West End and on Broadway. Her face was known from frequent television appearances in the UK and the US. She fills the screen with her bright vivacity in a way that makes the criticism of those who hanker for the dark side, the smoke and the danger, seem churlish.

The role-call of prospective Fagins seemed to grow day by day: Peter

Sellers, Laurence Olivier, Peter O'Toole, Laurence Harvey, Dick Van Dyke, Alec Guinness and Bruce Forsyth were all considered. At the eleventh hour it was acknowledged that, despite Lionel's (and presumably Columbia's) concerns about the 'ghetto-joke' stereotype, the Fagin in everybody's head was the one they'd seen at the New Theatre in 1960. Even so, Ron Moody says he wasn't entirely certain the part was his until the first day of filming.

Most jobs on a film set involve short periods of intense, panic stricken labour followed by long periods of hanging about, keeping quiet and staying out the way. It's a tedious process and unless you have a particular interest in hairy men fiddling with bits of wire while less hairy men stare intently at the sky like religious meerkats there's not even much to watch. Lionel was never much good at keeping quiet or staying out of the way. Even less so when the entire process, from first day of shooting to royal premiere, took more than a year.

"When we came to make the film, I didn't see much of Lionel," said Ron Moody.[90] "It was written or adapted for the cinema by Vernon Harris and he basically took the same script, [. . .] the same plot as the musical and there wasn't much to do except adapt it for the screen."

Not until the final stages of editing did anyone dare mention what must have been the elephant in the room throughout the shoot. Mark Lester could not sing. His voice would have to be dubbed.

It was hushed up at the time and the secret kept for 30 years.

Two weeks before the royal premiere, John Green, the music supervisor, conductor and arranger, was given the task of finding a kid who could sing 'Where Is Love?', 'Food Glorious Food', 'Consider Yourself' and the rest, record him lip-synched to Lester, splice it all together and not tell a soul. He auditioned 200 piping trebles. None of them were up to it. The rest of the story could have been adapted from, say, *Singin' In The Rain* (on which John Green had also worked), or *42nd Street*.

One day, John's daughter Kathe, 20 at the time, was waiting for her dad to finish work. Standing behind him in the studio, she began to hum 'Where Is Love?'

"My father twirled around in his chair," she told the *Daily Mail* in 2004, "and said, 'Who made that noise?'" She nervously owned up and her father immediately sent her off to learn the songs. Kathe had a perfect-pitch voice, and she could learn fast. "I knew nothing about lip-synching," she says. "But I did a lot in a week-and-a-half and Columbia loved it."

Columbia gave her £400 and threatened her with dire consequences if she spilled the beans. "My word was my bond," she said, "and I never told anyone." In fact the story didn't come out at all until the film's DVD release in the late Nineties.

Kathe had no particular ambitions as a singer. She worked as a model for a while, then ran a horse therapy centre in Florida.

"It was an improvement. I couldn't sing," Mark Lester said. "I have no idea why I was picked. My singing was atrocious and I couldn't dance."[91]

The film premiered at the Odeon, Leicester Square, on September 26, 1968. Lionel's old pal Princess Margaret turned it into a proper royal premiere.

It won six Oscars, including Best Picture, and was nominated for another five. Lionel got Best Original Score. Carol Reed got Best Director.

"And I happened to be in Hollywood at the time," said Lewis Gilbert on *Desert Island Discs*, "and I walked into the hotel and there was Carol Reed. He rushed over and he threw his arms around me and he thanked me for recommending him to do the film, but . . . I mean, he was a great director, anyway. That's show business."

It is difficult to understand why the six Oscars seemed to provide so little solace for the humiliations of *Twang!!* They represented, after all, a level of recognition unprecedented in the history of British cinema and musical theatre, yet far from providing Lionel with the long-awaited balm of self-assurance and a new creative certainty, triumph seemed only to have provoked more restlessness.

If *Twang!!*, in the David Niven way, had exposed him as the fraud he always thought he was, the six Oscars can only have revealed what fools the members of the Hollywood Academy were for being taken in. And the more the great ones of Hollywood smiled, the more they dressed in their pretty frocks and made their heartfelt fatuous speeches, the more foolish they became. East End kids don't play games like that. East End kids blow things up. Even if it entails a little self-destruction.

And besides, the *Oliver!* score was something he'd written nearly 10 years ago. Times had changed. He'd changed. It was 1968. Outside the world of the Hollywood glitterati and the offices of silver haired men in Lockes' and Henry Poole, owning up that you'd written several successful book musicals was like hanging a sign around your neck saying, "I am old. I am straight. I am on the discard pile," when all you ever wanted to do was Go, Bart, Go.

"Pop music, and by that I mean the really honest kind, is the only thing happening today," he told Ian Dove for *Billboard*, the American music paper.[92]

He outlined various projects he was working on: developing a Sean Kenny scenario for TV or film (possibly a musical adaptation of *Gulliver's Travels* that Sean had devised as that year's Christmas show at the Mermaid); working with "British singer Julie Driscoll and organist Brian Auger" on "a film version of *Saint Joan* with the organ sound as the voice of God"; collaborating on an experimental theatre project with Tom O'Horgan, the producer of *Hair*, which Lionel admired immensely ("I think it represents the future of theatre"); and he had made a new album "and one interesting aspect is that the LP is being used as the basis of a film. Bart sees this kind of mixed media approach as a signpost for the future. 'The soundtrack can come first and be used as the basis for the movie rather than the other way round.'"

People didn't write musicals any more. They wrote concept albums. Frank Zappa's *Freak Out!*, The Beach Boys' *Pet Sounds*, The Beatles' *Sergeant Pepper's Lonely Hearts Club Band* were not just collections of three minute sweeties, but 40 minute entities, with themes and ideas. The Moody Blues' *Days Of Future Passed* was the story, told in song, of a day in the life of Everyman. It spawned two hit singles – just like *Fings* and *Oliver!* had done. And the band had performed the entire album live as a quasi-theatrical stage show.

The Moodies were Lionel's pals. He'd known their manager Alex Wharton, since, as Alex Most, he'd been half of the Most Brothers at the 2Is. Their singer/guitar player/songwriter Justin Hayward had lived in his back garden. Deram, the Moodies' record label, had recently been set up by Hugh Mendl, the man who had first recorded Tommy Steele. Honeybus, another Deram signing, had enjoyed a top ten hit with 'I Can't Let Maggie Go', written and sung by Pete Dello, who worked with Lionel's publishing company Apollo Music. These people were practically family.

A plan began to form.

Isn't This Where We Came In? – Through A Looking Glass With Lionel Bart is a concept album consisting of 13 songs, approximately divided into the seven-ages of man and subtitled 'Pre-Birth', 'The Child', 'The Seeker', 'The Hider', 'The Lover' and 'The Finder', written in a range of styles from oom-pah to progressive jazz. One of the songs, 'Dreamchild', had appeared in *Twang!!* Another, 'May A Man Be Merry?', should have appeared in *Twang!!* but was cut at some stage in the rehearsal process. Others possibly came from early drafts of *Hunchback*, *La Strada* and anything else he had in the goody bag. In between the songs were snatches of dialogue, off-the-wall comments and introductions. The credits read like a Who's Who of everybody worth having in British pop, jazz and comedy – arranged by John Cameron, Harry Stoneham on piano, Paul Jones on harmonica, Kenny Wheeler on trumpet, Danny Thompson on bass, cameos from Kenny Lynch and Willie Rushton, backing vocals by Madeline Bell, Rosetta Hightower, Leslie Duncan and the Mike Sammes Singers.

"The more times it is listened to," said *Billboard*[93], "the greater the appreciation, but it should appeal to those who enjoy something special and unusual." In the late Sixties, rock critics tended to hedge their bets, terrified that the feedback freakout they condemn might turn out to be the next big thing.

The best tracks are fine examples of curious but beautifully crafted late Sixties pop. Even the bursts of progressive jazz are quality bursts of progressive jazz. Think Bonzo Dog meets Alan Price meets Ian Dury meets Albert Ayler meets Singalongamax and you're in the approximate neighbourhood. The sleeve is cutting edge even by *Sergeant Pepper* standards and features, as its centrepiece, a real mirror, suggesting that, though the album could be understood as Lionel's experiment in autobiography, its real subject is you the listener. To stoned hippies this sort of thing was dynamite.

The innovative printing was a G and B Arts job, executed by the company Lionel had started 20 years earlier and which was still run, as a thriving business, by John Gorman. These days he had his teenage son, Jon, working at his side. "My dad designed that album and put it together for Lionel," says Jon, with justifiable pride, "and we printed on mirror foil which was unheard of in those days."

Cutting edge in every respect, then. Pity about the sales.

The six Oscars may have done little to instil calm or confidence, but they had established Lionel as a major Hollywood player. Universal offered him a contract to write, produce and possibly direct two pictures: one based on the Edmond Rostand play *Cyrano de Bergerac*; another, *Ruggles Of Red Gap*, based on an English-Butler-In-The-Wild-West comedy which first saw light as a strip cartoon before becoming a 1935 vehicle for Charles Laughton. The Cyrano idea – obviously appealing to a two nose-job man – was one he'd toyed with before, as a potential Broadway musical with Peter O'Toole as the big-nosed Frenchman.

Lionel travelled to California the pretty way, via Jamaica, and took the opportunity to drop in on an old friend. "Today Lionel Bart came over from Port Antonio where he is composing in the rain," Noël Coward records in his diary. "He was very sweet as usual."

Hollywood did not take to Lionel quite so agreeably. The Universal execs did their best to treat him like a king, plying him with presents, bungalows, servants, secretaries and gofers. Lionel took the piss. It's an understandable reaction. Faced with a roomful of faceless executives whose job it is to pamper for profit, the spirited individual feels that he or she has no alternative but to nudge their tolerance until cracks emerge, and then worry the cracks until the whole edifice of smiles and presents crumbles to rubble.

Maybe the rot set in when he expressed a wish, rather than working on *Cyrano* or *Ruggles*, to develop his *Hunchback of Notre Dame* idea. The exec asked him who his ideal set designer would be. "Somebody like Pieter Brueghel or Gustav Doré," replied the boy from St Martin's College. The producer turned to his secretary. "Check to see whether either of those two guys are available."

"He had this big office," says Victor Spinetti, who'd been told the stories many times. "And he'd be sitting there . . . 'What d'you want in the office?' 'Well, I fancy . . .' and he'd make up things he didn't really want. He'd say things like, 'I want a big painting of a ship' or something. And it would turn up. 'I want two chairs' and 'I want this' and 'I want that.' And he told me, 'I went in that office and I sat there for a bit and I never picked up a pencil or a pen.'"

Thinking up new and outrageous demands was always going to be more fun than writing *Ruggles Of Red Gap*.

"I asked them for a giant teddy bear," he told Jack Tinker for the *Daily Mail* in 1989.[94] "It had to travel in the front seat of my chauffeur driven car."

He called the bear Spencer, which was short for Spencer Tracy. Breaking point, he found, came when he demanded that Spencer should have his own headed notepaper. "They said even Paul Newman didn't have his own notepaper."

Meanwhile he had rented a house on Pacific Ocean Drive at Malibu, where he threw a party. What seems to have happened is that Lionel played host to some friends' teenage children. The teenagers invited other friends to stay. Lionel soon found himself "besieged by hippies", just as he was in Seymour Walk, and left. The hippies trashed the place entirely before leaving themselves.

Three years later, in an English court, the owners of the house, Si and

Marilyn Litvinoff, sued Lionel for $2,325 to cover damage done to and thefts from the house and $3,500 in lost rentals while the house was off the market for repairs and refurbishment. The list of missing and damaged items mentioned a painting on glass called *Girl On Watermelon* and valued at $200, a radio, a TV, a collection of early shaving mugs, a fireplace brush, a lithograph called *Confessions Of A Mutinous Man*, an electric blanket, a yellow ashtray and a plastic polka dot cushion. The glass in both shower doors was smashed. There was $102 worth of broken windows. And God only knows what had happened to the garden hose.

Lionel didn't bother mounting a defence.

Otherwise 1968 was a year of heartache and distress. Judy Garland died. She had moved to London just after Christmas 1967 and married her latest husband, Mickey Deans, first in church and then at Chelsea Register Office. The wedding reception at Quaglino's was a bleak affair. They had rented the entire restaurant but the few guests who turned up barely filled a couple of tables. Lionel was in America. The newlyweds took a house in Chelsea. Judy's health was not good and her concerts, which these days invariably started anything up to an hour late, were lacklustre affairs. At the Talk Of The Town, people threw bread. One Sunday morning in late June, Mickey found Judy dead on their bathroom floor. The inquest followed the same pattern as Brian Epstein's. The coroner recorded a verdict of "accidental death" caused by "incautious self-overdosage" of barbiturates.

By October, Hollywood had owned up that they'd had enough of Spencer, and Lionel had owned up that he'd had enough of Ruggles. "So in the end I was packed off in disgrace," he told Jack Tinker, adding, as if to explain the entire curious episode, "I supposed I didn't like myself."

Back in England, he appeared as a character witness in a burglary trial. The offence had taken place six months earlier at his house in Seymour Walk. On the morning of May 16, Lionel's housekeeper at the time, Alex Payne, discovered that the house had been ransacked. He phoned the police. When they arrived, they were admitted by Anthony Haydon, a debonair 21-year-old who let them in but said he was just on his way out. The police did nothing to stop him.

According to the *Evening Standard*[95], "Clocks, paintings, antiques and film projectors worth at least £2,000" had been stolen. The housekeeper said that the "thieves had apparently spent most of the night at the home. [. . .] They drank bottles of whisky and other spirits from the bar as they went about their business of completely ransacking the house and stealing all they wanted." They had got in by breaking a glass panel in the back door. The mystery was that "almost every window and door in the house is wired to the burglar alarm which cannot be seen by anyone. This was not let off."

Realising they may have made a boo-boo, the police tracked down the man who'd answered the door, Anthony Haydon, and made an arrest.

In court, Lionel protested Haydon's innocence. He said that he had known him for two years or so. They had been travelling companions. Haydon had been an employee and had lived at Seymour Walk on and off. He had trusted him with his financial dealings. Lionel's faith in Haydon, already shaken by the charge sheet – as well as the Seymour Walk job, Haydon was up for two other robberies and various other offences – must have been destroyed entirely when Haydon was found guilty and his record was read out. He had six previous convictions. Lionel had trusted, maybe loved, and been abused.

Understandably, he couldn't wait to get shot of Seymour Walk and let it go at a knock-down price. He had bought it for £55,000, spent an estimated £140,000 remodelling it, and now got rid of it – accounts vary – for either £100,000 or £115,000. Either way he'd taken a worrying hit.

By the end of the year he was back living at the little house he'd continued to rent in Reece Mews.

And the upsets kept on coming.

La Strada is a 1954 film by the Italian director Federico Fellini in which Anthony Quinn plays Zampanò a circus strongman, who buys a slow-witted girl, Gelsomina, played by Guilietta Masina, from her mother, dresses her in a clown costume and teaches her the drum and trumpet. It ends with murder, madness and drunken tragedy.

Critics say it's about the futility of existence and the dichotomy between heart and mind, but for anybody in love with showbiz – particularly if they are recovering from a nasty flop as Lionel was when he first adapted it – the enduring image is that of the strong man and the idiot girl and their dogged compulsion to make a show: if all you have is a broken drum and a stupid hat, you stand in the dust, gather a small audience and you make a show. Maybe you do it because of the futility of human existence and the dichotomy between heart and mind, maybe you do it as a pathetic bid for the love and attention that you were so cruelly denied etc, etc, or maybe some people are just born shameless show-offs, it doesn't matter. The need, in those who feel it, is irresistible. It's exactly what Lionel had been doing since he first made up dirty lyrics in the playground at Dempsey Street.

For his adaptation of *La Strada*, Lionel came up with a robust, theatrical score, with songs like 'Be A Performer', 'Something Special' and 'Belonging' at least as good as anything in *Oliver!* But *La Strada* was always going to be a difficult sell. Despite the success of *Sweet Charity*, very loosely based on Fellini's *Nights In Cabiria*, the Italian director was still better known for angsty explorations of the human condition than for boy-meets-girl romcoms with an Act 2 dream sequence and a wedding at the end.

While in America, Lionel had sold the *La Strada* rights to Charles K. Peck, a producer and writer, most notably of *Seminole,* a 1953 Rock Hudson western. In the autumn of 1969, Peck took *La Strada* on the road prior to a Broadway opening. The cast included the hugely talented, multi-award-winning Bernadette Peters, then just starting out on her Broadway career. The director was Alan Schneider, who had brought Pinter to Broadway and became a leading interpreter of Beckett's work – an ideal choice, in an imaginative world, to bring life to this Bart/Fellini hybrid.

The show never gelled. Presumably, like most of Lionel's work, the initial script was intended as no more than a jumping off point. "I usually leave holes in my songs," as he put it, "because if they're going onstage I like to be amazed by what the actors do."[96] But Lionel was not there at the rehearsals to be "amazed". He was in England, "packed off in disgrace" by Hollywood. He didn't like himself. Alma was dead, Eppy was dead, Judy was dead, musical theatre was probably dead, Anthony Haydon had conned him and stolen from him, *Twang!!* had flopped, his concept album had barely been noticed. He had sold his Palace because the Fun had gone out of it and retreated to his bolthole and a bottle.

By the time *La Strada* got to Broadway, only a couple of Lionel's songs were still standing. Charles K. Peck had full credit for the libretto. There were 'additional music and lyrics' credits for Elliot Lawrence and Martin Charnin. Lionel's name was still up there as principal composer and lyricist, but these were not his songs and this was not his show.

La Strada opened at the Lunt-Fontanne Theatre, West 46th Street on December 14, 1969. It closed on December 15, 1969.

And thus the Sixties, Lionel Bart's magic decade, came to an end.

Eighteen

WHEN it was a slow week in Celebrityland and the showbiz editors were stuck for a story, a reliable fallback throughout the Seventies, Eighties and Nineties was always an update on the story the *Daily Mirror* had run back in 1967: "Whatever Happened To Lionel Bart?" A junior would be sent to the cuttings files where he or she would read that the failure of *Twang!!* drove him to the bottle and he spent the next 15 years – they don't necessarily say this, but the assumption is there – a pauper, sitting in his vest, sucking vodka.

Nothing is that easy. The disintegration of a human being is a messy thing, not neat. It takes a great seething gruel of events and delusions, ideas and emotions, assumptions and misunderstandings, and dollops, probably, of Freud, Adler, Jung, Holland, Dozier, Holland, Wilson, Keppel and Betty to demolish a person. Only when the collapse leads to addiction – to booze or dope – does everything suddenly become simple again: because then every waking instinct is about where the next bottle, snort or squirt's coming from.

Two weeks into the new decade, Lionel was arrested for drunk driving the wrong way around Piccadilly Circus in his Bentley. Sean Kenny was with him in the car. They had been to a restaurant in Knightsbridge, then on to a club in Mayfair where they met up with some friends. Lionel offered to give them all a lift home.

He told the court that his passengers were all "tipsy" and arguing over the best route to take. It was when he turned around to ask them to be quiet that he made his crucial navigational error. In mitigation, he mentioned that his judgment might have been impaired by some strong decongestant tablets and by a methamphetamine injection his doctor had given him because he'd been feeling tired.[97]

He was acquitted.

"Do you know the truth of what they actually found in the car that day?" says Jon Gorman, Lionel's pal. "A black doctor's bag. And on the side in gold lettering it says Bart's Hospital. It was full of drugs – thousands of pills, half ounce of coke, whole variety. And they got that when they arrested him for driving the wrong way round Piccadilly, but they conveniently lost the bag 'cos he was Lionel Bart and a friend of Princess Margaret's and all that. But I know that bag ended up in Scotland Yard's Black Museum."

Though he still had the power to charm the judiciary, friends had spotted that there was something deeply amiss about Lionel. He wasn't very well.

In the summer, he took himself off to America again where he was briefly sighted by the writer/critic/producer/manager/encyclopedia Steven Suskin. "I was a teenaged usher at the Off-Broadway Orpheum Theatre; one night I found a gnome-like man, absolutely blubbering on the stairs to the balcony during the second act of *The Me Nobody Knows*. 'I'll go back in, but I just can't help it,' he said in all sincerity. 'It's just that the singing, it's so *beautiful*.' He told me about his new project, a version of *Gulliver's Travels* that never seems to have been finished."

The Me Nobody Knows is a tough show for the emotionally delicate. It's about poor kids from hellish backgrounds. They sing heroically about their terrible lives. Most audience members had to clutch a Kleenex or two. Even so, instances of people having to leave the theatre and blub on the stairs were rare.

But Lionel wasn't very well.

The litany of wretchedness reached some sort of nadir when, in the autumn, Yetta died.

John Gorman and his wife Pam were by then living in Aimes Green, a rural spot near Waltham Abbey in the north-east of London. Harvey Jacobs, Lionel's accountant, had spoken with John, expressing concern for Lionel's state of mind. Accordingly, John wrote to Lionel suggesting he come and stay for three months or so.

On New Year's Eve, 1970, Lionel replied, typing the letter himself, spacing all over the place, key words underlined. After a long and jokey, if confused, introduction about some dinner both had been invited to, Lionel writes:

> *Enough of all that. (If I haven't made you smile by now, I just might as well get down to the serious stuff of this epic before I reach the very bottom.)*
>
> *The very bottom – or close to it – is what old Harv, I venture, has probably intimated to yourself about my present state.*
>
> *Well, John. My present state is one of insanity/humanity – not all that different to the same bloke you first met in 1948. True, I have put myself through many changes & dangerous experiences. Please trust my*

motives are for love of Life & Truth. My body is still a very strangely constituted appendage to my sub-conscience. However, the first third of my life, was a mis-guided monster-ego pretence; used to achieve an immature ambition that was motivated by <u>more</u> than mere post-inception deprivation. All this has passed, with no regrets, because much good has occurred from it.

Look. I've gone on far too long without saying a proper <u>special</u> thank you for your last phone call.

('A-proper-special-thank-you-John-and-Pam.') Actually, it's not outside the realms of plausibility that the good, good life may . . . maybe, around the corner a voice is singing "<u>AIMES GREEN</u> – JE <u>T'AIME</u>" (<u>de Gaulle est morte! Vive de Gaulle</u>)

But, honestly John, can you really see us two spending three whole months together under the same roof unless we were jointly building a new empire, or making some kind of 'magi' like screen-print-manufacturing sheet-chocolate below the basement grating of a tiny sweet shop.

Well . . . the bottle of 'Airwick' at the foot-of-the-stairs has almost evaporated, and so I'd better stop "makingk laffingk-jokes!" [The man in the basement at G and B Arts' first premises was a Pole who used to complain about the smell of their printing ink. When John and Lionel humoured him he would say, 'You are makingk laughingk-jokes at me'.]

Sure we'll have a munch, a jar and a chat as soon as you want to see me. In the meanwhile, I'll continue to give the idea that you have put into my head a fair crack at being 'a new beginning' – But please John . . . and Pam . . . it is important that you should understand about me, (if you don't <u>already</u> realise), the following few basic principles; faults or virtues – which I irredeemably possess.

(a) Having persevered in learning how to acquire the grace to <u>accept</u> some of the 'gifts' – which I would by nature – much rather proffer; I <u>still</u> find it unbearably frustrating to be 'helped' by any-body whom I am not <u>simultaneously</u> 'helping' just as much, in return. (Like it takes <u>two</u> 'lovers' to create <u>one</u> 'love-child')

(b) I believe that the only way to truly identify with any experience – is to personally <u>experience</u> 'that' experience. This involves having absolutely no fear of <u>anything</u> known; un-known or abstract – fear like the fear of Death. One might as well be afraid of being born. Both are equally natural. And so I am not afraid.

Consequently:-

(c) I expect nor pre-anticipate an 'thing' – not even from my oldest *good friends. (You both qualify!) All I expect is that you should trust me as much; (at least), or as much, at most, like I trust my-own-self. This has to involve looking at 'problems' from the standpoint & values held not merely by your way – but also your friend's.*

(d) Finally, I am content to believe that the lives we all live in 'this life' ARE chosen by our own sub-conscious/soul in a prior state of 'being' to this present existence. And so therefore, I will certainly not 'die' until I arrive at my self-chosen moment. This will be more than 40 of our years away. I know that sounds demented to many; but I can't stop any one from thinking of me as a suicidal crank until they too are prepared to accept their own true-belonging to All past-present-future.

So that's it. Not evangelism, or any other 'ism'. Just the hope that I can present an example to your betterment as fair swap for the example of your bloody gracious and sincere gesture that has been towards our faith in Ourselves.

So now you know I'll always be, Lionel.

"Out of his head, I guess, but how nicely written," says Jon Gorman. "From 1970 Lionel again became a big part of our life. He would phone my father every morning to report what was going on. Most days he would report a new illness, real or imagined, Legionnaire's Disease one day, Galloping Cancer the next. The calls were more amusing than sad. It was just Lionel being Lionel."

Lionel poured out his woes to Don Short in the *Daily Mirror*'s Saturday Scene column, revealing that at his own estimate he was half a million pounds in the red, and selling assets – disastrously as it turned out – to pay off his debts. "I used to be a flash git who had everything, saw everything and got a kick out of being a celebrity. Now I've got nothing except for the one thing that counts – and that's a sense of reality," says Lionel, sounding strangely Lennonish. "From now on I want to be me. Just a working fella who's trying to earn a crust." He talks of his unfruitful time in Hollywood and the flop that *La Strada* turned out to be. "Maybe a less undaunted soul," says Short, "would not have survived. But Bart burned the midnight oil writing two more musicals, *Gulliver's Travels* and *The Hunchback Of Notre Dame*, and both still await Broadway openings."

"I'm 40 and just an ordinary cockney bloke who can whistle a song," said Lionel, with a sage understanding of the *Mirror* demographic.

Then comes an extraordinary, epoch defining statement. "'I suppose I'm a Communist homosexual junkie,' he declared skewering a piece of liver on his fork."

Four years after legalisation, 17 years before Sir Ian McKellen, 26 years before Jodie Foster, Lionel came out.

Remarkably, none of the other newspapers picked up the story, perhaps unwilling to credit the *Mirror* with a scoop, perhaps because Lionel's star had fallen so low they didn't think anybody would care, or most likely because they feared the words 'cockney', 'bloke', 'whistle' and 'homosexual' in such close proximity would upset treasured stereotypes, leading to confusion and anarchy.

The plods noticed, though. They were no longer allowed to arrest homosexuals – not just for being homosexuals anyway. Arresting Communists was still a grey area. Junkies, on the other hand . . .

The politics of law enforcement in the Seventies were complicated. There were still coppers prepared (if the story of the 'Bart's Hospital' bag is not another example of Lionel's prolific imagination) to make a stash disappear, and judges and juries content to fall for the old 'decongestant' defence if the accused was a world famous songwriter and friend of Princess Margaret. But there were others who believed they had a mission from God and the *Daily Express* to come down hard on entertainment industry dope-fiends. The drug squad had built its reputation on a series of rock star raids: Donovan, Keith Richards, Mick Jagger, John Lennon and George Harrison had all been done over.

Ten days after the publication of the *Mirror* piece (maybe the plods were slow readers), on February 16, 1971, the police arrived at Reece Mews, turned the place over and found "under 8 grams" of cannabis. Lionel was arrested, taken to Chelsea Police Station and charged under the Dangerous Drugs Act. At Marlborough Street Magistrates Court, on March 9, it was also revealed that traces of several other drugs had been found at the house, but the police were "satisfied that Mr Bart had no knowledge of these items" because "there had been gatherings of people, including strangers, at Mr Bart's flat in his absence."

"The songwriter," said *The Times*, "intends to change his style of life and restrict the hospitality he has shown to strangers who took advantage of his generosity. [. . .] Mr Bart wished to make it clear that he was in no way involved in the drug scene." Fifty pounds with ten pounds costs.

There were money problems too. From the start, Lionel had been a financial disaster waiting to happen. At G and B Arts, his instinct to burn pound notes had been kept in check by John Gorman's restraining influence, but once off the leash there was no stopping him.

"I need 20 quid," he used to say. And Tommy Steele[98] describes how this would lead to an expedition east to raid the cash box at G and B Arts.

"Lionel and his 20 quid stayed with us for years. When we took 'Rock With The Caveman' to a publisher, the publisher said, 'It's a very interesting song – how much do you want for it?' and Lionel said, '20 quid.' He wouldn't stop to talk about how much more you could get. Twenty quid was the operative price. Then, when we took the whole score of *The Tommy Steele Story* to the same publisher, the publisher said, 'What kind of advance would you like?' And before Mike and I could say anything about thousands or anything, Lionel came up with 'Oh, 20 quid'll do.' As long as he had 20 quid in his pocket so he could go round the corner, that's Lionel."

The arts have always been a happy playground for sharks and thieves. Writers, painters, sculptors, musicians – with some notable exceptions – are rubbish at maths and, particularly in their early years, care for nothing except the work. So when somebody comes along and offers to pay them hard cash for doing something they'd happily do for free, such is their excitement that it would seem impolite to question the amounts involved or the conditions attached. What do they matter anyway? When you can write a hit in 10 minutes and it makes a million pounds, the possibility that it could have made two million seems academic.

"Let's write a swimming pool," John Lennon used to say to Paul McCartney as they sat down to knock some tunes around. Did they care that their swimming pool made somebody else a water park? No, they were far too excited by the harmonic ambiguities of the minor seventh chord. And if they ran short of a few bob, writing another song was always going to be preferable to renegotiating a deal or any other sort of spirit-withering ordeal of offices, meetings and men.

Lionel was more incompetent than most, but then again he was more successful than most. At one point his royalties were making him what to others was a week's pay every minute – even the minutes when he was asleep. And the ideas kept coming – Go, Bart, Go.

He was the despair of his family. "My dad couldn't understand it," says brother Harry's son, Sammy. "Normally Jewish people are quite good with money, quite sensible, quite good with business. My dad couldn't understand how you can grow up in the East End where normally people are pretty canny and be like Lionel."

A work of musical theatre is protected by a web of copyright laws and restrictions to deal with theatrical rights, performing rights, mechanical rights, broadcast rights, print publishing rights, film rights and so on. Even the poster image and title font will be protected as trademarks. Many of these rights are administered by discreet bodies, like the Performing

Rights Society (PRS) and the Mechanical-Copyright Protection Society (MCPS), which collect and allocate royalties. And the tangle becomes yet more labyrinthine when the various rights, as often happens, are shared, leased, assigned or sold.

Many tried and many failed to untangle Lionel's mess: to figure out what he might be entitled to, who's getting it instead, and why they're getting it. Years after his death, surprises are still waiting to be unearthed. Friends and colleagues have variously blamed the mess on: Lionel's lack of belief in the long-term earning potential of his work that gave him greater faith in jam today than in jam tomorrow; a general partiality for cash in hand; a flamboyant delight in the luxury of being able to despise money; a wilful naivety; the belief that a few hundred thousand pounds was enough to last a lifetime and a million constituted a limitless amount; showing off; and refusal to take advice.

But advice, good advice, was usually available. As early as 1959, when Lionel was writing *Oliver!* in Spain, his then secretary wrote to him about some deal involving Larry Parnes. "You must not on any account give him those cheques," she says. "And don't whatever you do commit your-self in writing to *anyone*. Darling this is very important, so please be prudent."

He took no notice.

"Nobody got a gun and said 'sign here'," says Lionel's pal Eric Williams, "but they did take advantage. A lot of people did take advantage."

The notion of selling something that didn't exist – the future potential of a show – for hard cash in hand is one that seems to have intrigued Lionel.

"I could have had 25% of *Oliver!* for £2,000," says Eric Williams. Max Bygraves' company, Lakeview Music, did get a chunk of *Oliver!*'s publishing rights for £1,000. And so it was with his other shows. Various parties were allocated five per cent here, 10 per cent there.

Even so his earnings from five West End hits, one Broadway hit, one blockbuster movie, and a score or so of best selling records, many of which still continue to generate sales and airplay, must have been vast. Unloading such a fortune so that, by the end of the decade, the debts ran to the half a million he complained of to the *Mirror* would have taken frittering and financial mismanagement on a heroic scale. And his strategy for eradicating the debt was just as imprudent, if not more so.

"I was advised by the people who counted my money to go bankrupt and to sell my rights. I need not have done either. It was very bad financial advice," he told the *Daily Express* years later.[99]

The selling of the rights was particularly ill-advised. By the early Seventies, Lionel and his money had become so separate that their comings-and-goings were reported in different parts of the newspapers: the man in the showbiz and gossip columns; the money in the business section.

In April 1970, *The Times* business pages announced: "Shares of the show business group Hemdale, ended 1s 6d higher at 27s 3d yesterday after news of a major acquisition. The group has contracted to purchase Oliver Promotions which will include four subsidiaries, among which are Apollo Music and the Donald Langdon Agency. The consideration is £300,000 in 277,000 2s shares in Hemdale. Oliver Promotions owns an interest in the world film and stage rights of the musical *Oliver!* Apollo Music is a music publishing company with a catalogue of some 400 songs and has a joint publishing interest for the next six years in the musical work of Lionel Bart. Hemdale has reason to predict pre-tax profits of Oliver Promotions group for 1970 of at least £75,000."

Hemdale had been founded in 1967 by the actor David Hemmings and his manager, John Daly. Hemmings left the partnership in the early Seventies. It was originally a film company and talent agency which over time diversified into TV, the music industry (for a time they had an interest in Black Sabbath and Yes), and betting shops. As a film production company, it had a piece of *The Terminator, Tommy, Platoon* and 50 or so other titles. It also for a time owned the stage rights to *Grease*. And from 1970, for just £300,000, it owned a big chunk of Lionel Bart.

Lionel himself reckoned he had a pretty good deal. "He thought *Oliver!* had run its course," says nephew Sammy. "He said the film's been made and he didn't think it was going to carry on like it has done."

A few years later, when Lionel tried to buy the rights back from Hemdale, the price had risen to £2,000,000.[100]

On February 29, 1972, straight after a Jamaican holiday, Lionel filed for bankruptcy. To celebrate, he drove his drophead Bentley to Gerry's, an actor's drinking club.

"He came down the stairs, his pockets stuffed full of fivers," says Dudley Sutton, who was there at the time, "looked at the assembled actors and alkies and said, 'This place is for losers.'"

Then he turned on his heel and left, presumably, for somewhere more salubrious. Or maybe, having made his point, he just went home.

The creditors meetings and various hearings dragged on into the following year. At the first, it was established that his assets, in cash and personal belongings, amounted to £624. His debts ran to £158,457. He owed an estimated £41,364 in income tax. Lionel left the meeting in a chauffeur driven car.

At the next meeting, Larry Parnes popped up, claiming that Lionel owed him £11,600. Asked whether he had any hidden assets, "a spokesman for Mr Bart said, 'Lionel Bart does not have any hidden assets except his talent.'"

Outside court, Lionel played for the sympathy vote. "We were a very poor East End family," he told the *Sunday Express*. "My mother was 49 when I was born by which time she had very little strength left to give me the love and affection I craved. When I hit the big time with *Oliver!* the novelty of being wealthy was more than I could cope with. Trouble is money doesn't automatically bring love, does it? So I thought I could buy it. Money was no object. I used to think that giving an expensive gift was a foolproof way of buying their admiration. Today of course, by some irony, the whole thing is reversed. I'm so broke that it is they who are giving me the gifts."

Cab drivers, with whom Lionel had always had an affinity, refused to take the fare off him. "As long as he needs me," they thought to themselves, and switched off the meter.

The next meeting, on November 28, was concerned with winding up Lionel's company, Lionel Bart Ltd, established in 1957 with an issued capital of £1,000. Its income peaked at £91,000, but now its only assets were a piano, a stool and some bits of carpet. "You cannot get sentimental about objects," Lionel declared, and then went on to do so. "I bought that piano in the glorious Fifties on the never-never. I must have written a dozen shows and a thousand songs on it. Even The Beatles and Rolling Stones have written some of their hits on it."

At the public examination on January 25, 1973, Lionel blamed his dire financial straits on *Twang!!*, "losses from other works which had not been produced", bad advice, the hit he'd taken on the Seymour Walk sale, and generally "living beyond his income".[101] But he was keen to point out, "What I have been spending, I have been spending on my work. I have spent very little on myself."

Mr Royston Howard, the Official Receiver, pointed out that only three days before the bankruptcy petition, Lionel had run up a hotel bill of £2,369 in Jamaica.

"Mr Bart said he had presumed that the hotel would not charge him for the two weeks he stayed there.

"'I went there to work,' he said. 'I had stayed there in the past without paying and I did not make the arrangements myself this time.'"

Howard then asked: "Am I right that throughout your career you never really appreciated the state of your financial affairs?"

"I was told that I was earning a great deal of money and I let people get on with taking care of it."

By 1975, there seemed at last to be light at the end of the tunnel. The principal creditors had been paid back at 40p in the pound and it was anticipated that the balance would be paid off from future royalties accruing from *Oliver!* within seven years. "Fings are back to wot they used to be," he allegedly told the *Daily Express*, while raising a glass of champagne. "I'm no welcher. My creditors will get the lot back. I'm a street kid and I don't believe in welching."

Sometimes, as the old joke says, what seems to be the light at the end of a tunnel is in fact the lamp on the front of an approaching train.

The book, *Alcoholics Anonymous*, first edition published in 1939, is the nearest thing that the AA has to a bible. It provides a clear explanation of how AA works, together with 40 or so case studies.

"An illness of this sort – and we have come to believe it is an illness – involves those about us in a way no other human sickness can," it says. "If a person has cancer, all are sorry for him and no one is angry or hurt. But not so with the alcoholic illness, for with it there goes annihilation of all the things worthwhile in life. It engulfs all those whose lives touch the sufferer's. It brings misunderstanding, fierce resentment, financial insecurity, disgusted friends and employers, warped lives of blameless children, sad wives and parents."

Lionel called the Seventies his "Rip Van Winkle" period, when he "went to sleep, socially and professionally".

A study produced by the National Academy of Sciences in America, suggests that one or more of the following "personality factors" can contribute to addiction: "Impulsive behavior; difficulty in delaying gratification; an antisocial personality; a disposition toward sensation seeking; a high value on nonconformity combined with a weak commitment to the goals for achievement valued by the society; a sense of social alienation and a general tolerance for deviance; a sense of heightened stress."

Lionel never really stood a chance.

He barely drank at all in the RAF or at Unity. Throughout the Fifties his principal stimulant was frothy coffy. At Stratford there had been more of a drinker's culture. Frank Norman certainly liked a few, Richard Harris liked a lot, Brendan Behan didn't stop till he was fighting somebody, and back then Dudley Sutton was well on his way to the "alcoholic illness", but there's no evidence of Lionel bingeing. His nephew, Sammy, says that back then "he probably was a drinker but not a big drinker. He didn't really like the taste of drink."

Eric Williams knew Lionel longer even than Sammy. "He never liked booze," he says. "I'll tell you how I know he never liked booze because anybody who puts Coca-Cola in brandy does not like the taste of brandy. He hated the taste. He liked getting drunk. The high." It was the same with smoking. "He never actually smoked. He just lit them. He never actually inhaled. He didn't have a drink or a cigarette until he was 31. Nothing. Totally pure. Hardly any sex. Terrified of that. Just worked. Always working. And then he had a bit of success and he went all over the top and he had his cigarettes made for him, but he never ever inhaled. He just kept lighting more." His habit of lighting several cigarettes at the same time and abandoning them resulted in burnt sheets, tables and window-sills everywhere he went. Sometimes he'd put them out in his food.

John Gorman, Lionel's RAF friend and business partner, being a devout Communist/atheist, did not attend his son Jon's christening. Lionel did. He was to have many godchildren in his lifetime, but, in 1951, Jon Gorman became the first.

"My first real memory of Lionel was at my fourth birthday party. He bought me a crane and some magic flowers you put in water and they expanded."

A few years later, in school uniform, he remembers going to visit his godfather at the Fun Palace. Lionel was busy. Jon had to wait. Mick Jagger and Keith Richards were also waiting. They made nervous conversation. The next day at school his friends called him a liar.

Jon went to work for G and B Arts, but by then it was the Sixties. He developed a predilection for the kind of party where afterwards nobody could remember having been to a party at all and some of the partygoers woke up in an unfamiliar part of a different country.

When he was 21, he was organising publicity for a new discotheque opening in Southend. The country's favourite DJ at the time was Kenny Everett. Jon decided that it would be a fine thing if Kenny Everett could open the disco, and so contacted his godfather who, he seemed to remember, knew Kenny. Lionel did indeed know Kenny, and, as requested, delivered him for the grand opening. Lionel and Jon had lunch. They got on.

A few weeks later, "I was working for the print company and I was doing some posters and so on for Gerry Raffles and Joan Littlewood at

Theatre Royal and Lionel was there, too, and he said, 'I'll see you in the bar there at eleven' [am]. And I got there and he said, 'What you drinking?' and I said, 'I'll have the same as you.' And he said, 'Are you sure? It's quadruple brandy.'"

Just as John and Lionel had found an affinity when they first ran into each other in 1948, nearly 25 years later, Jon and Lionel did the same. "I never stopped seeing him. Every month, six weeks, we'd have lunch no matter what. I have to say at that time he wasn't particularly alcoholic. He drank a lot. The true alcoholism came later on."

In 1973, Lionel was hit by a string of misfortunes that must have done a lot to highlight the advantages of being pissed all the time. The slide into apparent hopelessness grew steeper and the drinks grew stiffer.

He began the year with a holiday to Marbella, only to have his knuckles rapped on his return by the Official Receiver for leaving the country without permission. It was becoming apparent that bankruptcy, apparently such a clever wheeze for writing off debts, came with strings attached.

On March 26, Noël Coward died of heart failure at Firefly, his place in Jamaica. For more than 20 years he had been a mentor to Lionel and, if not a damper on his excesses, at least a touchstone in a wayward world.

A month later, a van Lionel was travelling in somewhere near Reading was involved in a smash. He broke his collarbone and was taken to Battle Hospital.

He recuperated with some 'English pals' at Cap d'Antibes in the south of France where, just as he had done almost 20 years earlier, he ran into Andrew Loog Oldham.

"His 'English pals' were treating him like the village invalid, the Jew of Pooh Corner," says Oldham.[102] "They were enjoying the game of 'giving a helping hand to poor ol' needy Li' far too much."

There is a possibility that what Oldham means by this is that they were keeping an eye on Lionel's drink and drug intake, something Oldham would have found iniquitous. At the time, Gered Mankowitz described Andrew as "drinking a lot and taking an awful lot of prescription pills. It was now a recognised type of lifestyle; nobody knew it had its origin in severe depression."

Oldham whisked Li off to Hotel Martinez in Cannes and, as they sat on the balcony sipping their drinks, Lionel, ever so politely, asked Andrew – "Ang" – to go and chat up some nice-looking German boys he'd noticed in the street below. "Go on, Ang – if Terry Stamp was here he'd do it for me."

On June 11, Sean Kenny went to a meeting at the Mermaid Theatre to discuss a production of Sean O'Casey's *Juno And The Paycock* he was slated to design and direct. Halfway through the meeting, he suffered a stroke, keeled over and died. He was 43, just a year older than Lionel. His *Times* obituary said: "The unexpected death of Sean Kenny at such a young age robs us of one of the outstanding talents which had helped to usher the theatre into a period in which the conventional barriers were being broken down." And it robbed Lionel of an admired friend and sympathetic collaborator he'd known since *Lock Up Your Daughters*.

Then in October, his dad died. "He talked about his parents, about how he'd let them down; how he didn't bother to see them a lot," says Eric Williams. "In the end his father went into a home and so on and so forth."

The 'so on and so forth' is said with a dismissive wave of the hand. Eric knew Lionel well enough to recognise when feelings like grief and guilt were real and when they were bullshit. Alcoholics, when the grip has taken hold, only do bullshit. Everything is about the addiction. Even the death of a parent can become a self-justification, a useful excuse for habitual bad behaviour, a bid for attention and sympathy from friends who've lost patience, a chance – if money's short – to score a free one.

"I spent one Christmas with him at the Zetland, a big Victorian pub just at the end of Reece Mews," says Jon. "My first marriage had broken up and I was lonely and it was Christmas and we both ended up staying at the Zetland over the entire Christmas. We went there sort of about two days before Christmas and came home about two days after. It was only round the corner from where he lived but we were there four days and nights."

A garden gnome entrepreneur by the name of Colin Stone had acquired a baronial pile named Clyro Court, near Hay-On-Wye, and turned it into "the ultimate pleasure dome for jaded pop stars and dispossessed peers."[103]

". . . and this chap had sent a helicopter down for me and Lionel – picked us up from London and flew us down to Clyro Court. And while we're there, this girls' school at Hay-on-Wye are doing *Oliver!* and they want Lionel to go. So he takes the helicopter. I think he missed the performance of *Oliver!* but he turned up and he addressed the school. And when he came back he said, 'Jon, I've just been to Way-on-High and I can't remember a fucking thing but I gave them all a holiday and I got back in the helicopter and I came back.' He loved being a star. It was a wind-up. Good fun. He used to say, 'Jon, if you've got enough money you can wee on the furniture, they won't mind. As long as you pay 'em a few thousand, they won't mind.' He'd obviously done it."

"A pelt like a yak." Lionel works a singlet and cap. (POPPERFOTO/GETTY IMAGES)

In the garden at Seymour Walk with dad, Morris, 1960s. (COURTESY THE LIONEL BART FOUNDATION)

On holiday in Venice, with Alma and Annie and Tommy Steele. (COURTESY THE LIONEL BART FOUNDATION)

Mum, Yetta, in the garden at Seymour Walk, with one of the many nephews. (COURTESY THE LIONEL BART FOUNDATION)

On the sofa with Joan Collins while Joan's husband, Tony Newley, changes the record. (COURTESY THE LIONEL BART FOUNDATION)

The ladies' man (4). The only man in England to look Barbara Windsor in the face, 1965. RON CASE/KEYSTONE/HULTON ARCHIVE/GETTY IMAGES

The Shaftesbury Theatre gearing up for the most notorious flop in its history, January 1965. (TERRY DISNEY/EXPRESS/GETTY IMAGES)

"They're lovely girls, but dense." Barbara and a laid-back Lionel with a forest of showgirls, rehearsing *Twang!!*, 1965. (TERRY DISNEY/EXPRESS/GETTY IMAGES)

"He was a giant." With Sean Kenny and a passing cloud. (COURTESY THE LIONEL BART FOUNDATION)

On a field trip to the Cavern with Brian Epstein and Alun Owen. (MIRRORPIX)

King of Shaftesbury Avenue *and* Wardour Street. (PICTORIAL PRESS)

Inconsiderate parking in Reece Mews. (STEVE BRODIE/ASSOCIATED NEWSPAPERS/REX FEATURES)

"Mr Bart wished to make it clear that he was in no way involved with the drug scene." Outside court, empty handed, February 17, 1971 (POPPERFOTO/GETTY IMAGES)

The Fun Palace, showcasing Lionel's vinyl. (COURTESY THE LIONEL BART FOUNDATION)

The Fun Palace, with limed-oak panelling, ample sconces and what looks suspiciously like a satin sofa. (COURTESY THE LIONEL BART FOUNDATION)

Oliver! the movie with Harry Secombe, Shani Wallis, Ron Moody and Jack Wild, 1968. (CENTRAL PRESS/GETTY IMAGES)

A mutual admiration society. Lionel and Sir Cameron Mackintosh. (DAVID CRUMP/DAILY MAIL/REX FEATURES)

East Ender, back to his roots. (SNOWDON/CAMERAPRESS)

"All my friends then were pretty crazy," Lionel said[104] in an *Independent On Sunday* piece about his friendship with Richard O'Brien, the writer, composer, librettist and star of *The Rocky Horror Show*. "Richard often used to come over when I was really bankrupt. I didn't have a penny but we used to get up to madness. A lot of my friends couldn't cope with me putting myself through that aggravation and they just stayed away. Richard didn't scare easily. I wasn't easy to handle. Richard didn't lecture me, he nurtured me. He has done his fair share of everything, as I have. The difference is he is not an addictive personality; he can handle the occasional recreational drug. In between his marriages we went potty in the clubs."

"Tramp was one of his favourites," says Jon, ". . . the Revolution, Monkberry's. He'd got some special deal with the Medina restaurant in Kensington. We used to eat there regularly and I never saw him pay a bill. I don't know whether he'd written them something or given them something. We used to start the day with a bottle of brandy wherever we were going, I remember that very clearly."

David Charkham had known Lionel since the mid–Sixties, when as a young hopeful actor he found himself hitch–hiking with a friend on the Finchley Road. They were offered a lift in a Chevrolet Impala, owned by Andrew Loog Oldham and driven by Reg King, a semi–psychopathic chauffeur passed on to Andrew by Lionel. David can't quite remember how this eventually led to a meeting with Lionel, although good–looking young men were always welcome at the Fun Palace. By the Seventies, he too was suffering from the "alcoholic illness" and became another drinking companion.

"We used to have an act," he says, the memories recalled as if they were vanishing shreds of dreams. "We'd get to a certain point of being drunk and we'd become Glaswegians. We'd have whole conversations in Glaswegian."

David once had a promising acting career. He'd done a spell in the TV soap *Crossroads,* bits in sitcoms and played an ape in *2001 A Space Odyssey*. But by the late Seventies all that had gone. He was pissed and was working for his dad's garment firm in Soho. Like Jon Gorman, he's "clean and dry" these days, works as a life skills therapist at an addiction centre and helped set up Outside Edge, a company that makes theatre about addiction.

"I went on this wacky trip. This guy had a boat," he says, gathering the shreds of another dream, "and he couldn't bloody sail it. It was a flash sailing boat with a motor. He had it somewhere. Maybe it was Southampton. And we went on this trip to the Isle of Wight. There was me, Judy Geeson [actress and one-time girlfriend of Sean Kenny], this guy, his wife, and a hairdresser, and Lionel. And I remember taking quite a lot of Mandrax – not a good thing at the best of times. You're meant to take it and go to sleep, but I'm taking it and I'm on this boat. And something's happened. And Lionel's gone into a huff and sulked and he went into the cabin. And we didn't see Lionel. But even in my stonedness, I realised that this guy that was sailing this boat didn't know what the hell he was doing. It was very scary."

There was a moment, perhaps in 1974, when the addiction stepped up a gear: when there was transition from going out and getting pissed to the slow dance of death.

Back when they were working together on the Tommy Steele songs, Lionel had condemned Mike Pratt's drinking habits. Now they didn't seem nearly so bad. The 26 episodes playing Randall in the TV series *Randall And Hopkirk (Deceased)* had made Mike Pratt a star. He'd been up to his neck in work ever since, doing posh plays at the Aldwych and Royal Shakespeare Company, as well as tellies and the occasional movie.

"He could take some acid, that man," says Jon Gorman. "I've never seen anybody down acid like Mike Pratt. He didn't make old bones, but you can't really expect him to."

"I met Keith Moon round Lionel's place once," says Sammy. "I was about 16. And Keith Moon said, 'Who's that?' And Lionel said, 'That's my nephew.' And Keith Moon was amazed. He goes, 'What? You still in touch with your family? My family don't talk to me. They ain't spoke to me for years.' He was really amazed."

Some days were Ostrich Days for Lionel, when he would put his head beneath the bedclothes and leave it there, emerging only to suck more vodka until the pain and the madness seemed to subside.

"When Lionel was doing an Ostrich in Reece Mews," Sammy says, "Keith Moon'd climb up the drainpipe and knock on the window and get him up."

"We were driving round town like a couple of crazies," Lionel told Tony Fletcher, author of Keith Moon's biography *Dear Boy*.[105] "It was a matter of who was crazier, we were putting everything in every orifice."

At Marylebone Magistrates Court in July 1975, Lionel pleaded guilty to drunk driving, was fined £40 and banned for a year.

Anybody who was hanging out with Keith Moon was nearing the end of the road. Indeed, there was only one more step to take.

"Lionel told me a story about him, Keith Moon," says Sammy, "and Oliver Reed." The story, once again, has a dream-like quality. It begins with Bart, Moon and Reed on a lake, riding around on a personal hovercraft. It doesn't have a middle. And it ends with them all going to a pub.

Mike Pratt died in 1976, Keith Moon two years later. When Mike was dying of cancer in a hospital near Guildford, Dudley Sutton drove Lionel down to see him. Lionel had had some sort of argument with Mike – possibly an ancient dispute about songwriting credits and PRS payments. He was sure for some reason that Mike would be pissed off with him, wouldn't want to see him. "When Lionel walked into the room," says Dudley, "Mike's face lit up with absolute joy."

Nineteen

LIONEL was feeling rough when he spoke to Lynda Lee Potter for the *Daily Mail* at the start of 1978.[106] Wearing "a dotty beige shirt, a red cardigan, and a wristlet inscribed 'Lionel'," he nurses his hangover with a "morning coke laced with something stronger."

"When people tell me how well I look," he says, "I wonder if they really mean, 'My god, you're still alive'. [. . .] We're all getting older, of course. I started a song the other day, 'Took a look through my book / all the folks I want to see / are listed ex directory or crossed off RIP.'

"I'm not in great shape physically at the moment. I wish I had the old energy. I'm strong, otherwise I'd be dead over the abuse I've given to my body. I'm meant to be on the wagon but since Christmas I've been taking a drink. My doctor got his nine-year-old son to write out for me 'Alcohol is not good for Lionel.' I rarely cry, but when I do I cry for days. Fame was so easy to handle when I was very rich, when me mum and dad and Alma Cogan were alive. Alma I loved a lot, I wanted to marry her, we almost did.

"I'm just going now from day to day. We manage, but I'll not do another *Oliver!*"

Not for the want of trying. Throughout the Seventies, Lionel's name was attached to a string of shows. Some of them made it into production. Some of them were even quite good. But, as he told Lynda Lee-Potter, "the old energy" was gone, and with it the "drive and initiative".

He started well. Tigon British Films, the company responsible for *Curse Of The Crimson Altar* and *Witchfinder General*, tried a brief diversion into family films at the beginning of the decade with an adaptation of Anna Sewell's *Black Beauty*. John Cameron, who had arranged *Isn't This Where We Came In?*, scored the film, but Lionel provided the main title theme – not to be confused with the much better known *Black Beauty* theme that Denis King wrote for the TV series. Mark Lester starred. A record of Lionel's tune was released in Japan, with Mark Lester singing on the B-side and proving – as he himself has admitted – that Kathe Green's services to *Oliver!* were indispensible.

Stratford, London E15, had in the meantime been levelled. The Theatre

Royal, protected by a preservation order and thus cast uncomfortably as a guardian of tradition and solidity, stood amid a sea of rubble. Having been gallivanting around Africa, Europe and Newham Borough Council stirring up trouble and putting noses out of joint, Joan Littlewood was clearly in a mood to forgive and forget the vexations of *Twang!!* and opened her arms once again to Lionel. For better or worse, for richer or for poorer, in sickness and health, he was one of her 'nuts'.

"He was somebody you automatically cared about," says Victor Spinetti. "Like a kid. Joan tried to stop him drinking, tried to stop him taking drugs, played mummy but there were a lot of people hanging on . . ."

She invited Lionel to Stratford to work on her next project. It would be *Fings* all over again, kick-starting life back into the career, reinvigorating the "drive and initiative" by going back to basics. It would be a blast from the past: a revival of the 1960 Stephen Lewis play and 1963 film, *Sparrers Can't Sing*, reinvented as a full-blown musical and rechristened *The Londoners*.

This slice of cockney life set among the bulldozers and tower blocks put Lionel smack dab in the middle of his comfort zone, writing "rowdy knees-ups and comedy character songs". One song, 'Sparrers Can't Sing', was already done, dusted and proven as a winner – at least when Barbara Windsor sang it in the movie.

The pressure was further relieved by Bob Kerr's Whoopee Band, a trad jazz/kazoo/swanee whistle & musical saw outfit, who were hired as the pit band. Two notes from them were enough to tell anybody not to expect *West Side Story*.

The cast included the wonderful Rita Webb, a spherical woman with bright red hair and a voice that could shake forests. She was joined by Stephen Lewis, the original writer of *Sparrers*, by now revered as Blakey from *On The Buses*; Bob Grant, equally revered as Jack from *On The Buses*; and Lionel Bart himself, playing Rita Webb's "tearaway son whose release from prison has hitherto kept the cast in fear and trembling."[107] Lionel's spit and a cough earned him £25 a week.

Later Stephen Lewis left the production and Lionel got his part, playing a tramp who sold crap from a battered pram. A publicity photo of him, in tramp's gear, pushing the pram around Stratford market with a sign attached reading 'Wife & Small FAMILEE To SUPPORT' seemed an appropriate enough image for a bankrupt former millionaire to justify half a page in the *Sun*. The part also required him to sing a song called 'Mirror Man', of which Lionel was particularly fond. It was eight years since he'd made an impromptu appearance as the milkman in *Maggie May*, 13 years since he'd gurned two verses of 'Meatface' in *Fings Ain't Wot They Used*

T'Be. Much had changed since then to affect his self-confidence. A lot of drink had been taken.

Dudley Sutton and Gaye Brown were also in the show. Dudley, an ex-drinker by this time, was a keen student of human psychology. "For weeks," he says, "Lionel had been singing this song 'Mirror Man' at parties, but I was convinced he wouldn't be able to do it onstage. He'd find an excuse. He'd bottle out. I put a bet on with Gaye Brown. We stood in the wings. Lionel came on. His first night, his debut performance in the show. He has to make his entrance up some stairs. When he gets to the top of the stairs, he falls. He falls and twists his ankle. Deliberate? Who's to say? But I won my bet."

The picture of Lionel being stretchered into an ambulance with a base-ball cap pulled over his eyes and a lit fag in his hand was worth another half page in the *Sun*.

The critics, on the whole, were charitable towards *The Londoners*. Audiences liked it too. But there was never a chance of a West End trans-fer. Warm-hearted cockneys talking cockney onstage and singing rowdy knees-ups and comedy character songs might have been radical in 1959, but times had changed.

The Londoners stayed in people's memories, though: in some people's anyway. When Rita Webb died in 1981, at her funeral they sang 'Glory, Glory Hallelujah' and the reading was from Dylan Thomas's *Death Shall Have No Dominion*. Then Al "Mr Banjo" Jeffery, her partner of 43 years, took up his instrument and played a medley of her favourites. It included the song she sang in *The Londoners,* the song Lionel had originally written for Barbara Windsor, 'Sparrers Can't Sing'.

Joan persisted in her rehabilitation efforts. Her next show was even closer to the full *Fings* experience.

Frank Norman had been keeping himself busy with journalism, novels and autobiographical memoirs. Now he tempted Joan with an idea about the package tour industry called *Costa Packet*. Perhaps hoping a little com-petition might put lead in Lionel's pencil, Joan hired a second songwriter for this one, a man called Alan Klein.

Klein – no relation to the American accountant who was brought in to manage the financial affairs of The Beatles and The Rolling Stones – had written, composed and performed in *What A Crazy World*, a Theatre Royal show about a layabout and his family that spawned a hit single, 'What A Crazy World We're Living In' by Joe Brown, and a hit film star-ring Brown, Susan Maughan and Marty Wilde. The *Crazy World* songs and the *Fings* songs are out of the same mould: hard-boiled, knockabout lyrics coupled with singalong, music-hall tunes. Alan went on to work, billed as 'Tristram – Seventh Earl of Cricklewood' with the New Vaudeville Band, a Twenties revival comedy outfit that had a hit in 1966 with 'Winchester Cathedral'.

The creative, co-operative explosion that made *Fings* happen failed to ignite. Frank Norman got pissed off with the liberties Joan was taking with his script and, while Alan Klein turned up for work each morning with sheaves of new songs to replace the sheaves Joan had cut the previous day, Lionel's contribution came in fits and starts.

"Lionel Bart looked so sensitively involved with his musical tasks during rehearsal," said Charles Hamblett in *The Guardian*,[108] "that it would have been brutal to importune him for comment, but Alan Klein, an altogether tougher talent, has knocked around the States a great deal and is revelling in the challenge involved.

"'Lionel goes off and writes his songs,' he explains. 'We both know the story, the situations, but we work separately. Sometimes we don't see each other for days at a time. Joan takes our songs and tries them out. She'll maybe keep them in for a week or so and then chuck 'em out. I go off and write several more songs. At present Lionel's got four songs in, I've got five. But Lionel is writing one specially for me to sing in the show.'"

Costa Packet – A Holiday Musical opened on October 5, 1972. The programme came with a balloon and a stick of rock, which audience members sucked mirthlessly as the fun unfolded. Avis Bunnage played a snooty sun-worshipper from Edgbaston, Griffith Davies a comedy German who makes laffingk-jokes with unintended *entendres* and Maxwell Shaw a sexy Spanish con-man.

"The numbers, mainly by Alan Klein have the beat and lilt that the occasion demands," said Irving Wardle in *The Times,* trying to be charitable but unable to keep the patronising tone at bay. "It is an occasion worlds removed from the West End, but it is well worth the trip when you get there." Four of the most dismaying words in theatre criticism – "well worth the trip". The review makes no mention at all of Lionel.

The show limped on at Stratford until mid-December without a glimmer of hope for a transfer.

Lionel's and Joan's next collaboration was even more ignominious. *So You Want To Be In Pictures* "lifted the lid" on the film industry. It was, if the critics are to believed, sloppy and badly plotted; the characters were stereotypes, the situations hackneyed and the revelations banal. There were songs for which Lionel is credited as 'supervisor'.

Joan had looked after Lionel. She had goaded him, teased him, told him off, infuriated and, in Victor Spinetti's words, "given him permission to be a genius". *So You Want To Be In Pictures* was the last withered flowering of their relationship. In 1975, Gerry Raffles died. Joan, devastated, resigned from Theatre Workshop and moved to France where she lived, apart from the odd trip back to see old friends, for the rest of her life.

It's hard to tell who wrote what, but it's possible that Lionel may have taken no more that a 'supervisory' role on *The Optimists Of Nine Elms,* either. This was a 1973 film directed, and adapted from his own novel, by Anthony Simmons. Peter Sellers starred as a down-at-heel music-hall performer turned busker, haunted by the soul of Dan Leno. He has a dog. He meets children. George Martin, producer of The Beatles, has the main music credit. Lionel is credited with 'additional music', and Don Crown (a singer/songwriter who also trains performing budgerigars) as composer of the film's most notable song.

There wasn't much point in writing new stuff. "One publisher said, 'Anything you write, even if you just think it, we own it before you do.' There wasn't really much incentive to have an idea. I just went out and got drunk."[109] And anyway there was no need to write new stuff. He had a trunk full of quality merchandise – songs, ideas, complete scores – waiting for the right outlet.

The veteran Broadway producer Kermit Bloomgarden for a time championed Lionel's *Gulliver* and began to raise funds. When he died, in 1976, so did all hope that it was ever going to happen. Meanwhile Keith Moon had grown passionate about *Hunchback*.

Lionel's sticky out ears and nose-job hooter made his identification with Quasimodo a given. "It's about being someone that other people find ugly and repulsive and what that does to your confidence and emotions," he told *The Independent*. "It's about how difficult it is to know someone else's soul. Despite his physical ugliness Quasimodo has a child's heart and mind. We're all Quasimodos in a way – people judge us by the way we look, not how we are inside."

"Brilliant, dear boy, but were you on drugs when you wrote it?" was Noel's reaction when he saw the script. "It seems a little bit abstract here and there."

He had made a good demo of the songs with his pals helping out – Madeline Bell and Chris Farlowe taking the leads. Keith Moon heard it and loved it. "He played it to his mother," said Lionel.[110] "At one point Keith wanted to get it together as a proper album/film/show and he wanted to be involved. We went to see David Bowie, and he wanted to produce it, but we were all a bit mad then."

Another symptom of the madness was *Golda*, a musical based on the life of Golda Meir, Prime Minister of Israel from 1969 to 1974. This was a proposed collaboration with Roger Cook, former singer with Blue Mink and a songwriter with a CV that included The New Seekers' hit 'I'd Like To Teach The World To Sing'.

Dates are hard to pin down. Roger Cook remembers it all happening in the autumn of 1974. In one account Lionel reckons it was 1976, in another 1978. There's also uncertainty about who initiated the idea in the first place – did it come from Lionel, Roger or Golda herself? In 1975, Golda had published an autobiography, *My Life*, the showbiz potential of which may not have been immediately apparent but which was nonetheless there. Substitute farmers for kibbutzniks and cowboys for Palestinians, remove all political understanding or taste and the similarities between the foundation of the State of Israel and the plot of *Oklahoma!* are uncanny. A year later, Andrew Lloyd Webber and Tim Rice released *Evita,* a concept album about Argentinean politics which subsequently became a smash hit musical and blockbuster movie. And the year after that, *Golda,* a straight play by William Gibson with Anne Bancroft in the title role, was nominated for a Tony Award.

Roger and Lionel flew to Tel Aviv for a meeting with the former Prime Minister. There seems to have been general agreement that Barbra Streisand should be approached with a view to playing the lead. Golda had been born in Kiev, but emigrated to Milwaukee, Wisconsin. Her husband, Morris, was from Denver, Colorado. But any ideas along the lines of "When a corker from Milwaukee / travels far to Colorado / and she meets a mensch called Morris / on a bench in City Park" were dashed when Golda told them, "You got the job – just lay off the romance."

Musical theatre, meanwhile, had moved on. *A Chorus Line* had practically no set or plot. It explored the fears and ambitions of a group of dancers auditioning for a show. *Chicago*, based on a 1920s play, monkeyed about with narrative and theatrical conventions in a way that some have described as 'Brechtian'. *Jesus Christ Superstar* and *Evita* established that although it was traditionally forbidden to mention religion, politics or a lady's name at a polite dinner table, it was okay to sing about them onstage. *Follies, A Little Night Music* and *Pacific Overtures* proved that musical theatre did not have to restrict its subject matter to cheap sentimental tosh. *Annie* proved that it did.

Side By Side By Sondheim, originally devised by David Kernan and Ned

Sherrin for the Stables Theatre at Wavendon, was not musical theatre in any accepted sense but a retrospective of the works of Stephen Sondheim. Thirty or so of his songs were linked by a narrator, who put them vaguely into context. The show was brought into town by Cameron Mackintosh and became his first major success, running for two years in the West End, a year on Broadway, and taking home armfuls of awards.

As was subsequently proved by *Buddy, Mamma Mia, The Jersey Boys, We Will Rock You* and a clutch of others, this 'retrospective' idea of building a show around existing hits has obvious advantages. In effect half the work is already done. The audience that yelps with recognition as each new number begins is a contented audience. They sing along. They come again. They bring their friends. They buy the merchandise.

Lionel was a 1977 Bart retrospective put together by Allan Warren, an actor/photographer, and John Wells, one of the Oxbridge satire crowd. Disregarding the no-frills presentation that gave *Side By Side* a modest charm, they went big. An unruly set was constructed to contain an even more unruly plot which Ned Chaillet bravely tried to summarise for *The Times*: "[It's] about a songwriting child prodigy from the East End called Lionel. Lionel the prodigy is taken on as an investment by a group of East End characters who proceed to make him famous by performing his songs. They also make themselves rich, but when Lionel's talent dries up he is left to pay the bills."

Lionel was played by a 13-year-old Todd Carty, later to become, as a result of *Grange Hill, The Bill* and *EastEnders*, one of a small group of actors people think of as a long treasured friend. It was his first stage appearance. The London *Evening News* described him as "a star now, a comet to come".

Clarke Peters, Marian Montgomery, Adrienne Posta and Avis Bunnage were also in the cast, but – though top drawer every one of them – struggled to make sense of the book or compete with the set. The show cost £250,000, opened at the New London Theatre on May 16, 1977, closed five weeks later and lost every penny.

"Without Mr Wells' book," said Ned Chaillet, "it might have been a celebration of Bart's talent, a reminder of some of the best songs ever written for British musicals. With the book it manages to be biographically suggestive and yet flounder in fantasy."

At an early stage, Lionel was banned from rehearsals.

Roy Hudd, actor, comedian and national treasure, was at the Young Vic, playing Birdboot in Tom Stoppard's *The Real Inspector Hound*, when fate came to call. He was having a bite to eat before the show. Two men approached.

"One bore a remarkable resemblance to Rasputin," he wrote in his autobiography *A Fart In A Colander*[111], "and the other looked like a 14-year-old head prefect. They were a team I got to know very well: Robin Midgley (who ran the Haymarket Theatre, Leicester) and Cameron Mackintosh (before his knighthood – just out of short trousers). The show they were about to mount was the classic, and for my money the very best British musical ever, *Oliver!* And they wanted me to play Fagin! I'd never done a musical and I practically gave them both a big French kiss. I just couldn't believe it. The Butlins variety turn, concert party comedian being offered the plum role in a fail-safe winner."

It opened at the Haymarket, Leicester and then went on tour, playing a week in each town – or rather five days. They were playing on the original Sean Kenny set with the revolves and the flying London Bridge. The get-in took at least a day, so, for the cast, Monday was always a night off.

Wherever they played, an empty seat was a rarity and the curtain calls often went on until the last bus had left the depot.

Lionel was on the payroll as 'advisor' and turned up now and then to boost morale and have a laugh. Even though Roy Hudd is six years his junior, Lionel called him 'Dad'. Sometimes they travelled together. "We'd sing music-hall songs on the journeys and he would ad lib brilliant new lyrics. He was inventive, enthusiastic and a joy to be with."

After Wolverhampton they were supposed to move on to Cardiff for a two week run over Christmas. At the last minute, Cardiff was cancelled. Cameron had negotiated four weeks at the Albery Theatre – previously called the New Theatre, site of *Oliver!*'s original triumph. When the stage-hands began to assemble the Sean Kenny set on the stage it was designed for, they discovered that the original backdrop on the wall of the theatre itself had never been painted over. *Oliver!* was coming home.

"I watched the spotlight smite Lionel Bart," *The Times* Diary reported[112], "as he stood up in the stalls to acknowledge the roars of the first-night audience. It was a demonstration of warmth that stopped just short of hysteria."

After the show there was a backstage feast of hot sausage and mustard, cold jelly and custard, pease pudding and saveloys. "Mr Bart," said *The Times* diarist, "is now solvent again and looks it."

No thanks to *Oliver!* His royalties had, by now, all been signed away.

The four-week run at the Albery was eventually extended to two-and-a-half years. Once again Lionel had a show, his greatest hit, running in the West End. Audiences adored it and felt towards its creator "warmth falling just short of hysteria". But it wasn't making him a penny.

By this time only the very brave and the very drunk dared try to coax new work out of Lionel. Sammy, his nephew, a songwriter himself, was one of the brave.

"We did this thing for a children's TV show. I got roped in to co-write it with Lionel. He was quite hard to work with. There was this tune and it needed a middle eight writing. So I had a go at it and I played it to him and he said, 'No, that's not right.' So I said, 'Well, over to you maestro,' you know, being funny. And he came up with this really brilliant tune. If he'd just been left he wouldn't have done it but because I said I'll have a go at it, he said, 'All right then.'"

There were always new collaborations in the pipeline. Johnny Speight, another Unity veteran, was the creator of *Till Death Us Do Part,* the pioneering TV sitcom which launched Alf Garnett, a comedy bigot, into the world. Taking the piss out of bigots always comes with the problem that real bigots are rarely smart enough to spot that the piss is being taken and instead prefer to find comforting reassurance in having their prejudices so eloquently expressed. Speight followed up *Till Death Us Do Part* with *Curry And Chips,* which featured Spike Milligan in blackface playing an Irish/Pakistani. Though he defended the show as an attack on racism, the resulting semiotic confusion brought widespread dismay to the structuralist community and straightforward outrage from normal people.

Perhaps hoping to spread the dismay further, with Lionel he worked on a show called *If There Weren't Any Blacks They'd Have To Invent Them.* Sammy was roped in to help with that, too. "We didn't finish it but there were some good tunes in it," he says. "Lionel wrote this song for it about a gravedigger called 'Once More Round The Cemetery'. It's a fantastic song."

"When he was drunk he did let people down a few times. When he was doing that thing with Johnny Speight he wouldn't turn up and I'd have to tell him Lionel was in bed. He couldn't do the work. It's only so far people are going to go no matter how good you are. If you're going to let them down they're not going to work with you, are they?"

Roy Hudd kept up his friendship with Lionel. "He told me about two unproduced shows he'd written. One was a musical adaptation of *La Strada.* [. . .] Lionel had some stunning demo tapes with full orchestra, and a set designed by Sean Kenny." Knowing a hit when he saw one, Roy fixed up a meeting between Lionel and Patrick Garland, artistic director of the Chichester Festival Theatre. "I laid on a car to take the pair of us down to Chichester and called for Lionel." The door was answered by a house-keeper, who explained that Lionel wasn't well and wouldn't be coming.

"I was furious. I pushed past her into the Bart boudoir. He was sitting up in bed with a ladies' leather flying helmet on.

"'I'm not well, Dad,' he moaned.

"'You won't be if you don't get out of that pit right now!'

"I couldn't believe what I was saying but it did the trick. He was in the back of the car with scripts, demo tapes, the lot."

Lionel did his pitch. Patrick Garland was impressed. The glitch came some weeks later with "the discovery that Lionel had sold the rights to all sorts of people all over the world – anyone who would give him a few bob for a drink or the dreaded drugs. Even now, people are turning up with bits of paper, fag packets and bus tickets on which Lionel's signature guarantees them a piece of the action. Who actually did own the shows no one ever found out, but I doubt whether we'll ever see *The Hunchback* or *La Strada* on a stage. God, he was a clever bloke, if only someone could have harnessed that talent."

Though Lionel was never quite reduced to the depths of penury he some-times complained of, as the Seventies wore on the great swamp into which his royalties disappeared grew murkier and stickier. David Charkham remembers being hired for a week now and then to try to make some sense of the accumulated mess: "I would open these big envelopes. There were these old-fashioned computer printouts that fold up like a con-certina, and these things would list every single play of every single song. They'd go on for yards. But there was never any cheque. The cheque would go into anybody's account but Lionel's."

With no new work forthcoming, and the old work signed away, Lionel was dependent on £300 or so a month he'd parlayed in exchange for a huge slice of his royalties. Apart from that there were occasional sums, sometimes substantial amounts, but mostly dribs and drabs, that managed to find their way through the mess all the way to his own pocket without being diverted somewhere. And fame, even faded fame, always has some sort of market value.

"I think I hit rock bottom in my mews house one day when a friend was visiting," Lionel told the *News Of The World*.[113] "We were so desperate we eventually found enough pennies down the side of the sofa to buy a minia-ture of vodka, so my friend went out. The next minute he came rushing back and said, 'Do you know, Lionel, they're auctioning pictures of you and John Lennon for lots of money over the road?' I was living right opposite Christie's auction house at the time and I couldn't believe it. I quickly found some photos of myself and signed them. Although I looked like a tramp with three days' growth and crumpled clothes, we went over and sold them just so we could get some more booze."

On November 13, 1979, Patricia McCarthy, an O-level student from Liverpool, wrote to Lionel on Kermit-the-Frog notepaper asking for information "on your hit musical *Oliver!* To be used for my O-level project in music." Dotting her I's with little circles, she goes on to ask 10 questions and ends with, "Hope you can answer these questions for me. Thanking you in anticipation, Yours sincerely, Miss Patricia McCarthy."
   On November 22, Lionel replied.

> *"Dear Patricia McCarthy,*
>   *"I am very bad at writing letters. But here I am at 4.30 a.m. on a November Thursday morning – awake and writing some kind of reply to your green Kermit questionnaire about my musical Oliver! So put up with an insomniac."*

The letter, typed and single-spaced, goes on for three pages, and starts with a brief summary of his pre-*Oliver!* career. He ends with, "Finally I want to thank you for the care and love you have put into your questions and I hope these words can be of some help. Fond regards, Lionel Bart."
   In the Hollywood version of the Lionel Bart Story, that letter would come 80 or 95 minutes into the film, at the end of Act 2. Lionel, at rock bottom, writes the summary of his pre-*Oliver!* career and, as he writes it, we see it in flashback: Lionel and John Gorman laughing in the RAF, Lionel and Jack chewing pencils in a backroom at Unity, Lionel and Tommy at the 2Is, Lionel and Joan improvising at Stratford East, Lionel looking up at his mum in the dress circle of the New Theatre on the opening night of *Oliver!* Back at his desk, he looks at the Kermit notepaper. There's a little girl in Liverpool who believes that the guy who did all those things still might be worth a hill of beans: who puts care and love into her questions. Who needs his help. And, in this movie version, he stands with an evangelic fire in his eye and runs into the wintry streets, just like Jimmy Stewart in *It's A Wonderful Life*, shouting, "I want to live, Clarence. I want to live."
   And of course one can never know for certain whether that is not exactly what happened.

Twenty

LIONEL kicked off the Eighties with cirrhosis of the liver, a growing weight problem and a permanent hangover. Jon Gorman noticed. "He started to swell out and bruised really easily. He could start bleeding if you just knocked him. He was dying." Lionel's oldest friends, Eric Williams and John Gorman Senior, were alerted and rode to the rescue.

This time there were no arguments, no long letters, no "all I expect is that you should trust me as much; (at least), or as much, at most, like I trust my-own-self." Lionel submitted to his friends' ministrations. He went to stay with John and Pam for a bit and acknowledged he was no longer in a fit state, mentally or physically, to cope with anything.

"My father must have been some kind of saint," says Jon. "He had spent years coping with my addictions which were ongoing and then he took on Lionel's problems as well."

John Gorman's socialism was driven by a fanatical sense of justice. As soon as G and B Arts grew big enough to take on staff he, the boss, insisted on it being a fully unionised closed shop. In the early days, paying union rates often meant taking a wage cut, or no wages at all, himself, but he did it. And, in proud defiance of fat cat capitalist practice, he grew the company into a multi-million pound business.

Having nursed Lionel back to an approximate medical stability, he glanced through the shambles of his finances and knew he had a mission in life.

"Dad just wanted to stop the rot. If there was anything he could do to stop Lionel's money going to people who shouldn't be getting it, he got involved. It was a hell of a job dad took on. Dad was running a business and writing books himself. It was an immense task he took on there – you're fighting people who don't want to give you the information – so a lot of it was hostile. We had to take the right that Lionel had to sign anything away for a while. We had to stop him signing cheques. He'd sign cheques for anything."

In some respects Lionel remained gallingly headstrong. In May 1980, for instance, while John was on the verge of concluding delicate negotiations with one of the many businesses that had the royalties sewn up,

Lionel decided he'd rather sue. John Gorman wrote a pleading letter.

"You may well have a good case, Lionel, but as I have said before, it will take two years to come to High Court, your income will be frozen in the meantime and the cost of litigation will be very high. If you lost, I fear you would be bankrupt again.

"You may very well win but I doubt if I could support you for two years and advance the costs lawyers would demand before the hearing."

Lionel was 'difficult' in other ways, too.

"I've seen Lionel reduce meetings to anarchy," says Jon Gorman. "We'd have bankers, we'd have accountants, we'd have lawyers and we'd have 'em all round the table and within five minutes of Lionel arriving he'd have one out fetching him cigarettes, someone out getting something special to drink, someone out getting some flowers, someone opening a window to let a bit of air in and he would reduce these meetings to chaos. I've never seen anybody do it in a more accomplished way. It might have been a subtle way of showing his power over them but I don't think he gave a shit actually. He just wanted a packet of cigarettes and some flowers and he liked to destroy meetings."

Most of those who had a stake in Lionel were amenable to negotiation. In some cases stiff letters from men in wigs were issued. And a few were very tricky indeed.

"There was this one chap," says Jon, "who had Lionel stitched into this thing where he was taking all Lionel's money and he gave Lionel like a little wage every week. We made an appointment to go and see him and he wasn't there. He wasn't there on purpose, so we tacked a little note to his door with a five-inch nail, on his yellow Chelsea front door, saying we would be back and please would he have the decency to be in next time. We went back with a big Alsatian dog and a couple of blokes from the factory and we said, 'We're Lionel's mates and there's no way we're allowing this contract to continue. Will you release him from it?' And we got him released. We paid the bloke some money and released Lionel from that contract. But you gotta be a bit careful 'cos they can come up with even heavier people than you can."

For 20 years Lionel had been renting his little house in Reece Mews at £3 a week; a paltry sum held low by rent control regulations in operation at the time. He had kept it on all the time he was at the Fun Palace and in America, sub-letting it for a while as the London base for the Swedish record company, Sonet. At the end of the Seventies, his lease came to an end and he put the new lease in his company's name rather than his own. The result was that he was, quite legally, evicted.

He moved into the less classy surroundings of Redan Street, near Kensington Olympia, east of Hammersmith, south of Shepherd's Bush. His was a pretty cottage-style house lacking, perhaps reassuringly, secret saunas behind the wardrobe or cranes on the roof. The pub at the end of the road was a regular haunt of Billy Connolly's – then still deep into the drink – so Lionel made a new friend who could play David Charkham's 'Glaswegians' with a breathtaking authority.

Thanks to John and Eric's help, Lionel now had a few quid in the bank: enough for him to think about buying somewhere again; not a Fun Palace or a castle in Morocco, but maybe a modest house or flat. Property inflation had put his old stomping grounds of Kensington and Chelsea beyond his pocket. There was some idle talk of returning to his roots in the East End, but that was never going to happen. In the end he picked Acton.

There's nothing wrong with Acton. The press, reporting Lionel's doings in their "Where Are They Now?" columns, mentioned Acton a lot. Lionel didn't live in a flat, he lived in a flat in Acton. It was as if the very word suggested odious degradation: mould up the walls, sacking at the windows, aertex as daywear and empties on the mantelpiece. In fact, even though in the game of Postcode Top Trumps, W3 can be seen as something of a liability, Acton has a lot going for it. Phil Collins – a fine Artful Dodger – was brought up there. The first ever Waitrose super-market was established there. Some parts of *Only Fools And Horses* were shot there. Acton is a good, sturdy sort of a place. Not quite Chiswick, but very nearly Ealing.

"What happened," says Toni Palmer, "was he wanted somewhere to live and I knew a chap called Bogdan Kominowski [an actor and singer who, under the name Mr Lee Grant, had been New Zealand's King Of The Mods] who's now a builder. He converts houses into flats and does all that.

"And Lionel was saying, 'Oh, I want a house. I want a house in Acton.'

"I said, 'Bogdan lives in Acton. He's always converting houses. He'll probably be able to find you a nice house if that's what you want.'

"So Bogdan went to a huge amount of trouble finding places he thought Lionel would like but, not knowing Lionel terribly well, he didn't realise that he was doing quite the wrong thing. And he found him a couple of houses and said to me 'Toni, one of these houses was so beautiful – it was all panelled and it was really lovely.'

"And Lionel walked in and said, 'I couldn't live here. It's all dark. There's trees outside.'

"Bogdan said, 'It's lovely. It's a quiet road.'

"But Lionel said, 'No, no. You don't understand. I like to look out of the window and see people walking up and down, shops and cafes and things.'"

In the end he bought a flat from Adam Faith. Leo Sayer, the curly headed hyperactive singer, managed by Adam, had been its previous occupant. It consisted of the two upper floors of a sizeable Victorian building on a busy shopping street. Downstairs there was an accountant's office and a butcher's shop. Next door was an off-licence. Later, he admitted in an interview, "I was never attracted to Acton. To be perfectly honest I was very drunk when I saw this flat. I didn't know what I'd bought. I didn't unpack for three years."

James McConnel, not long out of the Royal College of Music, was trying to find his feet as a composer when he met a chap who knew Lionel and got himself invited round.

"I turned up one day and there he was, and he took one look at me and I thought, 'Uh-oh'. He tried it on with me quite a few times, which is fine. He used to say, 'Come on, just once,' and I'd say, 'I really like you but my wife wouldn't like it,' and he used to say, 'All I have to do to give you the best blow job in the world is take my teeth out.'

"I played him some of the stuff I'd written and he was very nice about it. He said, 'Look, mate, shall we write a show together?' And we started working on this thing. We even got Cameron Mackintosh vaguely interested in it at one point."

The show, an adaptation of Oscar Wilde's *The Canterville Ghost*, barely got off the ground.

"Lionel wasn't really up to it. He was knocking back the sauce. We'd go through about three or four numbers and he just came up with these brilliant one-liners but he never really knuckled down. He wrote a couple of lyrics. He wrote one lyric that was called 'The Fourth Dimension Of Space', which was a haunting refrain. I found it incredibly frustrating. I wanted to work. I wanted to get cracking. I found myself at the mercy of his alcoholism and – it wasn't even the alcoholism – it was sheer fear. He was terrified. Terrified that he couldn't do it anymore. And he could have done. He could turn out any number of songs, but he was frightened they wouldn't be good enough to be Lionel Bart songs. He was just very scared and it was just – 'let's have some lunch, can we do this tomorrow, let's do it a bit later, let's do it this afternoon.' So I'd come back in the afternoon and he'd be 'yeah, yeah, we won't do it now'."

One of Lionel's favourite displacement activities was to stick the video of *Oliver!* on "and he'd take me through the whole bloody thing and he'd press pause and say, 'See that guy there. I've shagged him.'"

All Lionel's attempts at collaboration – or work of any kind – tended to have a similar outcome. At the Berkeley Square ball, he ran into John Diamond, the journalist who later married Nigella Lawson. He had known John's mum, a designer, at St Martin's, and later worked with her at Unity. He and John had a drink. They had two drinks. They hatched a plan.

"At the time the West End was full of musicals," said John. "How would it be if he and I went to see all of them and then I wrote a piece in which our greatest living librettist gave a critique of the modern musical scene? Bart couldn't have been keener, and to celebrate took me to dinner in Kensington, where I just remember getting horribly drunk with Francis Bacon and nothing else happening.

"It engulfs all those whose lives touch the sufferers," it says in the AA book. "It brings misunderstanding, fierce resentment, financial insecurity, disgusted friends and employers, warped lives of blameless children, sad wives and parents."

Lionel was drunk when he went to see his brother, Bunny, Sammy's dad. Bunny was dying of cancer. They rowed, about Lionel's drinking and about the money. Bunny said he should have kept the money in the family, that he shouldn't have surrounded himself with so many hangers-on.

"At the time my dad died, Lionel was drunk almost all the time," says Sammy. "It made me really sad and I decided we had to help him. So we'd ask him round to our house and my mum would cook him breakfast. He even lived with us for a time. This was the first time that Lionel had ever turned to his family for help."

In September 1982 he was arrested for driving with twice the permitted level of alcohol in his blood. He claimed that he'd drunk several glasses of beer at a "country fair". He was later banned from driving for three years.

It is said that the alcoholic has to reach some sort of rock bottom state before fully acknowledging the extent of their problem. Lionel seems to have reached rock bottom several times before the moment of revelation.

Victor Spinetti remembers him talking about one of the many times the drink brought unconsciousness. "And I woke up," Lionel told him, "and I felt something falling on my face. I realised I was lying in the passage behind the front door. The postman had come. The letters were falling on my face. It was then I realised that I had to stop."

"I realised that I had become my own audience," he told Herbert Kretzmer. "Nobody else was looking."

For the next few years he became "a regular clinic-hopper", slowly struggling back to health with the help of a close network of friends.

Dudley Sutton was among the first of the Joan Littlewood/Soho crowd to seek a cure from the 'alcoholic illness' and was a sought-after source of advice. He arranged for Lionel to be admitted to Clouds House, a rehab clinic in Wiltshire, and went with him to sign in. It took a while for Lionel to get the hang of rehab.

"First thing he does is demand a helicopter," says Dudley. "Then he talks about letting the *Sunday Times* come and interview him there and take a few photographs." Dudley forbade it, pointing out that Step Eleven of AA's Twelve Step Plan categorically states: "Our public relations policy is based on attraction rather than promotion; we need always to maintain personal anonymity at the level of press, radio, and films." Not only did Lionel have to accept that "nobody was looking", he had to do everything he could to prevent them looking. It was a novelty.

Lionel also joined AA and remained committed for the rest of his life, going to three meetings a week, sometimes more. Wherever he travelled in the world, on arriving in a new town the first thing he'd do was find out where the meetings were held.

"He saw it as cool to be clean and sober," says Jon Gorman, who became clean and sober himself at around the same time as Lionel. "He said when he was drinking he thought it was really cool. Then he realised he was suffering from 'terminal coolness'. Being cool was killing him. So then he decided it was cooler to be straight. Some other people he knew had got straight and once he met up with them in AA, he was away. He'd found another little niche in life."

Jon is convinced that Lionel stayed clean and sober from the mid-Eighties until the day he died. Others reckon that, like many recovering alcoholics, Lionel was prone to the occasional lapse.

Toni Palmer was having lunch with him one day. He ordered champagne and a glass for himself. Nothing dramatic happened, although it's not unlikely the result was several Ostrich Days.

Champagne was produced in 1998 when Sammy's daughter was born, too, and Lionel helped himself to a glass. "You couldn't actually stop him, could you?"

It's understandable that Lionel, fearing he was setting a bad example, would have kept these lapses from Jon Gorman. And besides, Jon might tell his dad, and then there'd be trouble.

But for the most part he stayed clean and sober, and, in keeping with the AA ethos, helped others to do so, too.

"In 1985, I'd lost it all," says David Charkham. "I was kind of broken and sad and pathetic. I was in full-blown addiction and all that goes with it; not just the chemicals but the shame and the sense of loss. I ended up working for my dad who was the only man who would employ me. I was a packer in his factory. And eventually, when I hit what I describe as my rock bottom, I broke down in my dad's factory one day; desperate just desperate, but not knowing that I was an addict or an alcoholic because for me I couldn't be a drug addict 'cos I didn't have a needle hanging out my arm and I couldn't be an alcoholic 'cos I wasn't on a park bench. I still had a car. I still had a flat.

"When I broke down, my parents were away and I was in a terrible state, shaking, doubt ridden. I'd just become this blubbing mess. And this quite nice young man in the factory didn't know what to do. And at that moment Lionel came into my head. I picked up the phone, 8:30 on a Monday morning, I said, 'Lionel, I don't know what's happening.' But he knew. Of course he knew. As I know now in my position. When it's someone that's dear to you, you're waiting for that call.

"And he said, 'What you've got to do is get them to put you in a taxi and get over here to me.

"By the time I'd got there, he'd made an appointment with his doctor. By 12:30, I was in the doctor's surgery and by that afternoon I was in rehab. And Lionel rang my dad and explained. Lionel took care of me.

"I smoked my first joint with Lionel in 1967 or whatever. He was the man that opened the door to recovery for me, and that is a major part of saving my life. God knows what would have happened. I was 38–39 and I went to a clinic in Chelsea where they held me until there was a bed for me at Clouds House.

"So that's what happened to me. And Lionel was there for me."

It was clear to all his friends that the key to Lionel's continuing health and wealth would be a more settled lifestyle: healthy food, the occasional night's sleep, routine, organisation. The call went out. Could anybody come for maybe a few hours a week to help Lionel at least with his filing and typing?

The butcher whose shop was next door to the accountants downstairs from Lionel had a cousin who had a friend called Brenda Evans. Brenda was working as a doctors' receptionist but possibly had a couple of days a week free. She possessed the full range of office skills and the first record she ever bought was 'Rock With The Caveman', so her qualifications were impeccable.

"I went and rang on the bell and I said, 'I've come here 'cos I understand I've got to have an interview,'" says Brenda.

"'Oh.' he said, 'You can't come in. I'm not having a good day.'

"I said, 'Sorry, I've come a long way. You've got to let me in.'

"He said, 'Well, walk round the block then and I'll get my clothes on.'

"So we had this chat and he said, 'I think you'll do for me.'

"I went to him in '83, just to help out. From that it just blossomed into a massive great job. He said could I just go there and perhaps do a bit on the books. He'd just come out of clinic so he was getting himself well."

Brenda did not stand for nonsense.

"I'm basic, you know. I come from near Kilburn, Kensal Rise. My dad always said to me, 'Things To Get You Through Life. You're as good as anyone else. Don't let anybody tell you any different from that. They're only doing a different job to you.' And I actually said that to Lionel.

"I said, 'You're only doing a different job to me. You're my boss and you write music; and I do what I do. You're no better than me because of that.'

"He said, 'Who told you that?'

"I said, 'My dad.'

"We only had one row. I can't even think what it was about, but I know I said to him something like, 'Oh, don't speak to me like that. I'm going down to the office and when you can speak to me properly you can come and knock on the door and we'll start the day again.'

"And his friend phoned me. Eric. And he said, 'Lionel a bit upset. He thinks he's upset you.'

"I said, 'He's not upset me, but you know I can't have people speak to me like that.' And from that day on we gelled really."

Brenda made order out of chaos.

"He found it quite difficult. I said, 'In the morning can you sit down and prioritise what you want me to do, so if at the end of the day there's something not done that's your fault not mine?' I don't think he'd ever had anybody talk to him like that before."

Brenda kept him on the straight and narrow.

"The times I've chucked stuff down the sink. If people came round and had a meal with him they'd have a bottle of wine – he'd always say, 'No, feel free to have a bottle of wine.' But if it was there the next morning, I just used to tip it because he might think, 'Ooh, I'll just have one.'"

Brenda provided comfort and continuity.

"He said to me, 'Oh, d'you know what I really fancy? You can't get it anywhere. You can't even get it at The Ivy.'

"I said, 'What's that?'

"So he said, 'Sausage toad.'

"I said, 'Well, I'll knock you up a sausage toad. You carry on with what you're doing, I'll knock you up a sausage toad.'

"I said, 'The trouble is you can't knock up little sausage toads so I'll have to do a big one.'

"'Ooh,' he says, 'that's great. I'll eat it cold tomorrow. Can you do stews?'

"He liked an ordinary home life. He liked to sit in the kitchen to do his work. We had a lovely office, but no, we'd sit in the kitchen."

"Brenda was everything," says Jon Gorman. "She was mother, nurse, secretary, PA, you name it, Brenda did it. Everything bar lover. They did love each other really. They were good mates."

Lionel lived in Acton longer than he lived anywhere and became part of the local community.

"There's a greasy spoon across the way, where I eat on Brenda's day off," he told *The Daily Telegraph*.[114] "Then there's the barber's where I can go to have a shave and a hot towel. It's so close I can stroll across in my bathrobe. The local kids look after my car. What they do to other people's is another matter. Everybody round here knows me . . . though some of them think I'm Bob Hoskins."

The car was not a Facel Vega but a Honda Legend. The greasy spoon across the road, even when it wasn't Brenda's day off, became an important part of his routine. Somewhere to go for a cup of tea and a chat. And a bun. And a cake. And a pie.

Food replaced drink as his addiction of choice. He became Oliver, his plate permanently extended, "D'you think I could have just a little bit more of that?"

He was a regular at the table of the critic and columnist A.A. Gill, a close friend and an excellent cook; also at the restaurant of the Landmark Hotel in Marylebone where subdued live music was played; also at Toni Palmer's house down by the Thames at Shepperton; and such a proliferation of other venues that the conclusion that on some Sundays he was able to fit in two if not three roast dinners becomes inescapable.

"He got fatter and fatter," says Toni Palmer, who, with her late husband, the writer Ken Hill, regularly treated Lionel to haunches of beast and troughs of vegetables. "And he just ate all day. Huge meals."

The "thin, cadaverous" 26-year-old had grown a 43-inch waist along with an impressive set of quirks, mostly food related.

He was, for instance, fiercely sensitive to ambience.

"You'd go to a restaurant and he would say, 'I can't sit in here, it's doing my head in,'" says Victor Spinetti. "And then we'd go to another restaurant. 'Oh I don't like this one, it's doing my head in.'"

And when a restaurant met his exacting, indeterminate standards, there would be a fuss about the seating arrangements. It tried Eric Williams' patience to the point of homicide.

"He'd say, 'Right, I want to sit there. No, no, you sit over there. No, I've changed my mind. I've got to sit there.' And, 'I haven't taken my pills.' And then he'd go to the lavatory and everyone's got to wait. And then he'd come back and move everybody around again and put you there. It drove everybody insane. I used to say, 'Either sit down or I'm leaving. Lionel, sit down.' He was just impossible."

This obsessive need to control may have been a symptom of some form of Aspergers syndrome, or may have been another example of Lionel pushing the envelope of human tolerance, like pissing on the furniture: bossing people to see how much they'll take, testing their love to destruction. Or it may have been Lionel treating the world, just as he had when he was a kid, as his private theatre. What would happen if I said this, did this, pissed on this, told her to move over there, made him incredibly angry?

Once, on the phone, he told Eric Williams' mum that her son was scheduled to meet the Queen Mother.

"How did you get on on Sunday?" the mother asked when Eric went home that weekend.

"I said, 'What?'"

"She said, 'With the Queen Mother. Lionel said you were seeing the Queen Mother.'"

Rather than unravel the entire pointless lie, Eric told his mum that the Queen Mother had had a headache and had to cancel.

"I tackled him about it. Of course he denied it. I said, 'Lionel, I can't go on lying to my own mother and I can't tell her you're a lying bastard. I can't do it.'"

Lionel was strange about luggage, too. He was a chronic overpacker.

"He used to come down to Brighton for the weekend and bring three suitcases full of changes of clothes," says Victor Spinetti. "Three or four towels for lying on the beach, different changes of swimming trunks, and we'd be there for ten minutes. Three suitcases. He'd come down on the Saturday and leave on the Sunday. And when he first saw the guest room he said, 'I can't sleep on that. It'll do me head in. It's a patterned pillow. It has to be a plain pillow.'

"I remember once he came down to the house and I said, 'I'll fix breakfast for you.' So he sat there in the kitchen and I was cooking breakfast – he was having the lot.

"He said [Tommy Cooper whisper], 'It's a difficult meal to cook, innit? Timing it all together, like, the bacon and the eggs and the sausage and the beans. Bit difficult to fix, isn't it?'

"So, I fixed it. I put his plate down, I put my plate down and I sat down.

"He said, 'Oh, I can't eat with anybody.'

"'What?'

"'I can't have breakfast with anybody. I've got to have it on my own.'

"So I had to go in another room and leave him in the kitchen."

From time to time there would be outbursts of savage anger, too.

In the late Sixties Toni Palmer, appearing on some TV talk show, had made a couple of slighting references to *Twang!!* The next time she saw Lionel he was livid. He blamed her for the state of his career. "You're the reason I'm poor." It was years before they made it up.

Despite Lionel's dedication to AA and frequent attendance at meetings, many doubt whether he ever fully committed himself to the programme.

"If treatment totally works," says David Charkham, "you look at all your stuff – the good, the bad and the ugly – and you're given an opportunity in the safest surroundings to process it or come to terms with it; to see your part in it and move on. And if that's not done then you'll be dragging some baggage for the rest of your life."

"He did as much as was needed to keep him sober," says James McConnel. "But I don't think he'd really grasped the programme with both hands and just changed."

Dudley Sutton reckons he was a "dry drunk, full of suppressed rage. Unresolved recovery can be very dangerous." Dudley had once crossed Lionel – predictably by ignoring, or opposing, his arrangements for a morning excursion and lunch. Lionel's reaction was to grow "white with anger". Later, he did his best to humiliate Dudley as cruelly and as publicly as he could manage.

Which leaves the obvious question – why did anybody put up with such terrible rudeness?

"There was something lovable about him," says Victor. "Even though he didn't give out anything lovable, he just sat there smiling."

"He could be so kind," says Eric Williams. "There was this dichotomy, this extraordinary Jekyll and Hyde, this awful thing – and yet this wonderful human being, full of warmth and humour. And then at other times he was an evil motherfucker. His sisters wouldn't put up with it. There is somewhere a recording where he was drunk, talking to his sister Debbie. And she keeps saying, 'I don't want to know about bleeding Judy Garland. She ain't paying my bleeding rent, is she?'"

"He was very generous and very secretive at the same time," says James McConnel. "He was the most phenomenal egotist, it was 'me me me me me', which is fine. But occasionally you got little flashes that there was a little part of him – as if he'd locked something away like a little child. You had to know him quite well to even know it was there, because he was in other ways so open. I think there was some damage there somewhere. He was guarding something with his life. I'm not even sure he knew it was there. He didn't exactly not talk about his childhood, but he wasn't effusive about it."

What was Lionel locking away? There is a lot to choose from. He had a bullying father. People who were killing Jews by the million came back night after night to drop bombs on his family, his friends, his school and his neighbourhood. From the age of nine he was frequently sent away from home. He was buried alive for a while in a cupboard under the stairs. He knew from at least his teenage years that he had homosexual feelings at a time when they were illegal. His brother, whom he hero-worshipped, died when he was 11. Many other people close to him had died pitifully young. And so on.

"Lionel loved water," says Toni Palmer. "He just loved water. At my house I've got a terrace and there's a little white seat where you can put your feet in the river. You can put your feet in the water. And he would just sit there for hours, just sit down there and gaze at the water. He absolutely loved water. He'd go swimming in the river. He loved water. That's why he loved that terrible beach hut."

The beach hit was an acquisition he'd made: a "holiday home" – perhaps the closest he ever came to his Moroccan castle – at Whitstable in Kent. He called it 'South Fork' or 'Tara'. He would invite people down to his "place by the sea" and then delight in their subsequent disappointment.

"We'd get to that hut," says Toni, "and before we'd hardly got to the door he'd got his clothes off and he was in the sea. And he'd stay in the sea for hours. Like a great whale. We used to watch him swimming up and down. He'd come out and wave and he'd go back in again. He loved the water."

For his 65th birthday, Lionel decided to throw a party at his Acton flat, his first since the Fun Palace. Toni and Brenda were recruited to take care of the arrangements. Nothing they did was right. He wanted gilt chairs. He wanted snow-white tablecloths.

"I said, 'Lionel, it's just a little party for a few mates.'"

There was a good turn out: Barbara Windsor, Gaye Brown, Richard O'Brien, Sonia Swaby, Toni Palmer, Johnny Speight, Peter Straker, David Charkham and a bunch of others. It turned into a knees-up. Somebody got on the piano. They sang music hall songs and selections from *Oliver!* The neighbours, who under other circumstances might have paid between £40 and £60 to hear such a distinguished cast sing such distinguished songs, complained. Nobody took any notice.

"Now this is what's come into my mind," says David Charkham. "God knows, I don't think I'm embellishing. What happened eventually, everybody left, we all went home. And there was Lionel in his flat alone. And I think that might have been one of the times when he opened the fridge and had a drink. But I think also there must have been a real deep loneliness. People loved him but they all went home to their wives or their partners or their job and there was a sadness. And my later memories of Lionel are of him just sitting in front of the telly watching the History Channel."

Twenty-one

UNTREATED, the alcoholic illness would have brought this biography to an end about here. Lionel's obituaries would have been kept off the front pages by the Falklands War and the Miners' Strike. As it was, he lived long enough to see Elton John sing at Diana's funeral and – just – to party like it's 1999.

Those bonus years brought a gradual rehabilitation of his reputation, his fortune and his dignity, mirrored, the damage already done, by a less gradual decline in his health, punctuated by occasional life or death crises.

Cirrhosis had reduced his liver function by about two-thirds, leaving him prone to fatigue, allergies, infections, mental confusion and a dozen or so even less palatable symptoms. He was also diabetic.

When Lionel was permanently pissed, as James McConnel had observed, sustained work was all but impossible. Sobriety didn't bring much improvement. Fear of failure, of being unable to write a song worthy of the great Lionel Bart, still made it more comfortable to procrastinate.

"Everybody loved him dearly, but he needed looking after constantly," says Victor Spinetti. "It was like having a kid with you. I remember Joan Littlewood saying, 'Poor old Lionel, he's in a terrible state, we should help him out. He's stuck with this script.'"

The script was the one that had been obsessing him now for 20 years: *The Hunchback Of Notre Dame.*

"I spent about 18 months on and off with him working on that script," says Victor. "Never once did I see him put pen to paper. Every time it was, 'I've got to take a walk first. Or I've got to have something to eat first. Or I've got to have something else first.' I kept coming up with ideas for new songs, new openings, new everything and Lionel would go along with them for a while, but after 18 months Lionel said, 'Nah, I'm going to go back to what I wrote originally.' And it suddenly ended like that.

"I think what it was was that he needed somewhere to go. He'd come and visit me on tour. He'd say, 'I'm going to see Vic. We're working on a script so I'm going up to Manchester where the play is' – a few days in Manchester or a few days in Southsea. He had nowhere to go except AA meetings. Now I realise he was desperately lonely and wanted to be – not a part of showbiz – but 'I'm working on a project.' And I happened to be the one who said, 'All right, come on', and I got excited about all this and got into it."

There was a brief flurry of interest in *Hunchback* from Mark Bramble, the author/director/producer of *Barnum* and *42nd Street* who also got excited for a while about the *Golda* project, considering it as a vehicle for Georgia Brown – then appearing in the London production of *42nd Street*. Bramble put a lot of work in on the *Golda* script, replotting, restructuring and making sense of it, but Lionel had lost interest, claiming he "couldn't get behind the politics any more".

It was the old stuff that put his name back in lights. The 1977 revival of *Oliver!* had barely closed when Cameron Mackintosh laid plans to bring it back again, this time for a limited five-week run at the Aldwych over the Christmas of 1983. The production would stay true to the original, with the Sean Kenny set, Peter Coe directing, same costume designs, blocking, choreography and Ron Moody reprising his Fagin. Bullseye, Bill Sikes' dog, was played by Hector. "Consider yourself lucky to see it again," said the *Daily Mirror*.

In April 1984, the same production, with essentially the same cast, transferred to the Mark Hellinger Theatre on West 51st Street. It was Lionel's first Broadway presence since the humiliating closure of *La Strada*: just a limited two-week run, but enough to get Ron Moody nominated for a Tony Award.

More exciting still, a couple of years later, Lionel was back at number one in the charts.

The Young Ones, named after Cliff Richard's fifth number one hit, was the title of an early Eighties TV comedy show. Most of the performers in the show had been imported from the Comedy Store, birthplace of what came to be known as alternative comedy. It was variously described as "anarchic", "revolutionary", "violent", "infantile" and "stupid", but was very popular among the students, punks and ageing hippies it took the piss out of.

A running joke in the series was the insistence of Rick, the most avowedly radical character, that the music of Cliff Richard was inherently revolutionary.

At Christmas 1985, inspired by Live Aid – the biggest rock concert in the world which raised £150 million for famine relief – Richard Curtis, Lenny Henry, Rowan Atkinson and others set up Comic Relief. It was a similar idea but with comedy instead of music – and it instituted Red Nose Day, the annual feast-of-fools and fundraiser.

Live Aid had achieved a massive hit, 'Do They Know It's Christmas', which made a few extra squillions. It seemed only right that Comic Relief should do the same.

Cliff would be paired with the cast of *The Young Ones*. Together they would record a spoof of Lionel's 'Living Doll'. Hank B. Marvin, The Shadows' guitarist would play the solo, just as he had that first time. All proceeds – give or take a sizeable percentage allegedly siphoned off by the record company – including Lionel's, went to the charity.

The recording itself, at Master Rock Studios in Kilburn, was something of an occasion. Cliff was there, being filmed, fooling around with four principals from the show. Lionel wasn't. They never invite the writer to these things. Indeed, Nigel Planer, who played Neil the hippie in *The Young Ones*, doubts whether anyone present at the session, with the possible exception of Cliff, knew that Lionel had written the song.

'Living Doll', by Cliff Richard And The Young Ones, was released on March 22, 1986. A week later, nearly 26 years to the day since Lionel had hit the top spot with 'Do You Mind?', it was at number one. It stayed there for three weeks.

That year, at the Novellos, Lionel was awarded the Jimmy Kennedy Award "in recognition of his special contribution to songwriting".

"How does it feel to be number one again?" Gerald Mahlowe asked him.[115]

"Well. It was nice! We did it for about three weeks this time. It was very nice in as much as I'd given up the game, more or less. I've got four shows in the can, but for the last ten years I haven't really been writing."

"It's been an encouragement?

"Oh yes I'm starting work again."

The return to productive work was probably a cause of regret when *Winnie* happened. Details of the genesis and development of *Winnie* are sketchy and can only be of tangential interest because Lionel's involvement was slight.

A musical biography of Winston Churchill, starring Robert Hardy as Winnie himself and Virginia McKenna as his wife Clementine, it was directed by Robin Hardy, best known for his work on the cult classic *The Wicker Man*, and is reputed to have cost a million pounds. It also seems to have enjoyed the full backing of the Winston Churchill Memorial Trust.

Why? "For the money," said one anonymous court official. "Money, money, money. Vulgar, vulgar, vulgar."

Those involved were to learn that vulgarity is an art that takes a specialist talent and years of experience: it can indeed make vulgar amounts of money, but those who don't know exactly what they're doing are better advised to stick to refinement for which grants are sometimes available.

The plot took the form of a play-within-a-play: a displaced group of Shakespearean thesps and a concert party called Doris And The Daisies join forces to put on a show about Mr Churchill in a bombed-out Potsdam theatre at the end of the war.

Winnie tried out in Manchester (one can imagine Lionel's acid-flashbacks: "*Twang!!* the horror") where, though the press had made much of Lionel's involvement, he walked out along with the choreographer and three cast members, complaining that the show was "total and absolute chaos".

In the West End it lasted an implausible six weeks before closing. Lionel's name appeared on some of the early posters, but his contribution, if there ever was a contribution, had disappeared.

According to defective thinking, the rules of cosmic balance demand that for every bad thing a good thing must happen and *vice versa*. Thus the joy of 'Living Doll' reaching number one was balanced by the awfulness of *Winnie*, which, in turn, was balanced by the Abbey National Building Society.

Tim Mellors, an ad man whose previous work with the Saatchis had done so much to inform the British public of the advantages of flying with British Airways and voting for the Conservative Party, and who had combined the music of Leon Redbone with a chess-playing rabbi to advertise trains, was now working for the Publicis agency on the Abbey National account. Aware that, as *Oliver!* had proved by now on several occasions, Kids + Lionel Bart = Money, he dreamed a dream.

He approached Lionel and commissioned him to write a song, eventually called 'Abbey Endings', the composition of which drove everybody barmy.

Lionel bounced ideas off anybody who came near. Every idea, every suggestion, every line of inquiry was wrong, misconceived, inappropriate, not good enough. The deadline loomed. Brenda Evans grew concerned.

"I said, 'Have you done that yet?'

"'No, not yet.'

"I said, 'It's got to be in tomorrow.'

255

"'I know.'"

"So anyway a bit later on he came down and he said, 'How about this?' and he just sang a few bars and I said, 'Well, it's really catchy because now I'll be singing that all day.'"

The advert, directed by Tony Kaye and shot in black and white, features Lionel, looking avuncular not to say rabbinical in round glasses and pork pie hat, dark suit, buttoned up white shirt, no tie, pretending to play the piano while all around him mixed infants raid a dressing up box, sing along and show off.

"They flew this child over from America," says Brenda, "all curls and wonderful. They brought in some of the kids for the background and one of them was right off the street. And Lionel just took to her. She came to the front and the director kept saying, 'She still doesn't know the words.' But Lionel didn't care. She was the star."

The song, rechristened 'Happy Endings (Give Yourself A Pinch)', was released as a single. That Christmas, Tina Turner's 'I Don't Want To Lose You' was at number eight. Jive Bunny & The Mastermixers' 'Let's Party' was at number two. And at number one – the remake of 'Do They Know It's Christmas' by Band Aid II. 'Happy Endings' was at number 71, having peaked at 68. It was a chart entry, though. With a new song. Written and performed by Lionel Bart. An achievement for which most 59-year-old recovering alcoholic former chart heroes would happily swap a mouthful of cosmetic dentistry, a trophy wife, a guest slot on *The Late Show With David Letterman* and a vineyard. Two vineyards.

One good thing: one bad thing. Lionel's neighbour at the flat in Acton was Pete Briquette, the former bass player with The Boomtown Rats. On New Year's Eve 1989, Pete found Lionel with blood gushing from his mouth. He bundled him into his car and drove him to the Central Middlesex Hospital a couple of miles away in Park Royal.

"Park Royal phoned me," says Brenda Evans, "and said, 'Are you Lionel Bart's next of kin?'

"I said, 'Pardon?'

"They said, 'We've got you down on the paper as next of kin?'"

Brenda travelled to the hospital, fearing the worst. Lionel had lost a great deal of blood, but he was alive.

Esophageal varices – the equivalent of varicose veins in the esophagus – are a common side effect of cirrhosis. The veins had burst. In such cases somewhere between 40% and 70% of patients don't make it. If Peter Briquette had not acted so speedily, if he had called an ambulance or waited for a doctor, there's little chance that Lionel would have survived.

The various treatments are all unpleasant. During the initial part of the healing process, which can take several days, the patient is nil by mouth.

Lionel had lost a lot of weight by the time he came out. For a bit. He also gave up smoking. The fire brigades of the world relaxed.

Oliver! had by now seen revivals in the West End and on Broadway and most other places. A 1986 production at the Queen's Theatre at Hornchurch with Victor Spinetti as Fagin subsequently went on tour, filling theatres all over the country for two years.

During the course of a 1971 amateur production at Ridgecrest, California, "Wayne Carpenter, a 37-year-old amateur actor, was fatally wounded by a supposedly blank cartridge. [. . .] Carpenter, playing the role of villain Bill Sikes [. . .], fell to the floor as expected when a fellow actor fired a .38 calibre pistol at him in the dramatic finale. But he had suffered a real lethal wound in the chest. Sheriff's Sergeant Don Glennon said, 'One of the cartridges in the pistol apparently had part of a slug still left in it. These were blanks made by pulling the bullet from the cartridge with pliers, only one portion of the lead was pinched off and remained inside.'"

In 1982 there was a production at Eton College. Boris Johnson, later Mayor of London, was Captain of School at the time. David Cameron, subsequently Prime Minister of the United Kingdom, would have been a couple of years below him. As far as can be established, Johnson and Cameron were not given the parts of Bumble and Dodger.

Oliver! has the power, in a frozen school hall smelling of sick and Dettol, to generate an unnerving camaraderie. When a cast of uncoordinated year nines and tens come out for their curtain call and tunelessly mumble 'Consider Yourself' one more time, the most churlish, the most curmudgeonly audience members find themselves mysteriously compelled to rise to their feet, clap in time, smile and sing along. And the miracle is probably repeated somewhere in the world every day of the year.

Lionel, of course, enjoyed the acclaim, but there was that one bit of grit in the ointment. "The thing that does disturb me," he said, "is that the people who do own *Oliver!* now charge schools a lot of money to put on the show and I get all these angry letters from head teachers demanding to know how I could ask for so much. I do get the blame, but it's nothing to do with me now. I feel like writing back to say, 'I know just how you feel, darling.'"[116]

Meanwhile, Lionel's other shows languished. Nobody in Ridgemont,

California was shot during an amateur production of *Maggie May*. Boris Johnson was never dragged up to play a brass in *Fings*. In theatrical circles, the religious crossed themselves before even mentioning *Twang!!*

Blitz! too seemed to have joined *Pardon My English* and *Bring Back Birdie* as a "once produced forever forgotten" musical, until, in the mid-Eighties, Andrew Jarrett, a 19-year-old Australian musician, began painstakingly to reassemble a script and score from the scraps and fragments available. With help from friends he recreated lost orchestrations and eventually was able to mount a production. The Australian premiere of *Blitz!*, its first revival anywhere in the world, opened at the appropriately named Phoenix Theatre, Burwood, Melbourne at the beginning of 1987. Lionel was there to see it.

"The man who put music in the mouth of Oliver Twist is in Melbourne, courtesy of a local theatre group," said the Melbourne *Herald*.[117] "Members of the company pooled their money to buy his airfare to Melbourne for the opening night of their production of *Blitz!*

"'I received a letter from the people doing the show, and thought it was a very enterprising thing to do,' Bart said. 'I had been wanting to come to Australia for a long time, so this was my chance at last.' Bart plans to stay in Australia for the next six weeks."

While he was there he caught up with the Australian actress Diane Cilento "at her retreat in far north Queensland" and Barry Humphries, who had just finished filming *Sir Les Patterson Saves The World*.

Back in England, the Royal Shakespeare Company started sniffing around *Blitz!*, too. Cash-strapped by cutbacks and eager for a hit or two, they made plans to commemorate the 50th anniversary of the real thing with an all-new *Blitz!* at the Barbican Centre. Two East End lads would make it happen: Barry Kyle, one of the RSC's top men, would direct; Tony Marchant, now a distinguished TV writer, then little more than a boy, would come up with a new book. Lionel would write five new songs. There was even talk of flying in Bette Midler, 'The Divine Miss M', to play Mrs Blitzstein.

But it was not to be. The cuts bit deeper. On March 19, *The Times* reported that the RSC would "cancel its production of Lionel Bart's *Blitz!* this autumn if no commercial producer matches the £100,000 it plans to pay towards the show's production." If Lionel had been tempted for a moment to put his hand in his pocket, the finger-wagging ghost of Noel Coward would immediately have appeared and whispered, "*Twang!!*"

The show was cancelled along with all the RSC's other plans for the Barbican.

"We made the dialogue more dangerous and less dated and there were some good bits to what we were doing, but for me it was getting a bit pretentious," said Lionel.

Hard on the heels of this setback came a momentous encounter. Stephen Sondheim, the "greatest artist working in musical theatre", a man with more Tony awards to his name than any other songwriter ever, shelves groaning with Grammies and a Pulitzer Prize, arrived, as visiting tutor in musical theatre – a post funded by Cameron Mackintosh – at Oxford University. James McConnel signed up for the masterclasses.

"I was going through a Stephen Sondheim phase at that time," he says, "and I actually went to study with him which was fantastic. And I thought it would be interesting to get the two of them together, so I asked Lionel to come up to Oxford and meet Stephen Sondheim. Steve is just like a little boy, but he's also, you know, he's comfortable with being the most brilliant force in musical theatre in the twentieth century. And, of course, *Sweeney Todd* is the antithesis of *Oliver!*, but there's a lot of *Oliver!* in *Sweeney Todd*.

"Lionel didn't really know who Sondheim was. He said, 'Listen, mate, Sondheim is a useful lyricist – all right, he's a good lyricist.'

"I said, 'No, he's much, much more than that.' I was a complete hero worshipper of Stephen Sondheim. So I played [Lionel] *Sweeney Todd* on the record player and after the first bit I said, 'Shall I turn it off?'

"'No, no, no, bit more, bit more, bit more,' he said, 'This is really really good.'

"So he sat there for two-and-a-half hours listening to the whole of *Sweeney Todd* and he was really, really impressed.

"So I got these two together in the hallowed halls of Oxford and I said, 'Steve, I want you to meet Lionel Bart,' and he said, 'Hi, hello.' Then they sort of hovered at one end of the room, not speaking to each other. It was very funny, the image of the two alpha male gorillas, standing in the corner, not really communicating."

When the RSC finally dropped *Blitz!*, Ed Wilson, director of the National Youth Theatre, jumped on it. He wanted to do not the new 'pretentious' RSC version but the 1962 Lionel Bart/Joan Maitland original. Lionel was bucked.

The National Youth Theatre was founded in 1956 as an amateur company for teenagers. From the start it had always selected members on the basis of spirit as much as conventional acting skills with the result that its productions fizzed with energy and provided, more often than not, a better evening's entertainment, with higher standards of performance and direction, than anything the professional theatre could muster. It kick-started the careers of at least two theatrical knights, a Dame, two Bonds, two Doctor Whos, Sophie Ellis-Bextor and Kate Adie OBE.

When the RSC, still entertaining hopes that either a fairy godmother or Margaret Thatcher would shower them with the millions needed to make everything happen, warned him that an amateur NYT production in the West End would stymie any chance of a professional revival, Lionel told them to bugger off.

"I'm involved with a company here that's something else. The RSC hasn't got it or the National. The National Youth Theatre is a great ensemble."

Simon Nelson, now a producer at the BBC, was one of the young actors in that production. He remembers Lionel coming to rehearsal. They broke for lunch. Simon and his pals went over the road to a greasy spoon. After a while, Lionel popped his head around the door and asked if he could join them. The kids were understandably tongue-tied. After a while, Simon asked the naffest question anybody could have asked.

"So, how do you go about writing a song?"

Lionel smiled, picked up the menu and improvised an entire song based on the dishes on offer, complete with complex internal rhymes and a twist at the end. He then told them how he'd done it and encouraged them to have a try. He was funny, engaged, entertaining. And then he paid for everybody's lunch.

The NYT's *Blitz!* opened at the Playhouse on Northumberland Avenue on September 10, 1990, just over a month after Lionel's 50th birthday. It was not well reviewed.

"The show is so keen to evoke the warmth of working-class life that it gives the impression that we fought the war in order to make the world safe for jellied eels," said *The Daily Express*.

The Times previewed it with "Bart is back where he belongs", and reviewed it with "Oh, what an average war," condemning its "trite lyrics", "weak story" and "woeful predictability".

Michael Billington, for *The Guardian,* had nothing against the production or the cast but complained that "it remains an appalling piece of sentimental nostalgia about the jolly capacity of 1940 East Enders to survive nightly aerial bombardment."

Oddly, this beef about Lionel trivialising the tragic did not arise when a couple of months later the NYT's sister (or brother, or non-gender specific) group, the National Youth Music Theatre, presented yet another *Oliver!* revival at Sadler's Wells.

"A boy sold for £5, a woman bludgeoned to death, a workhouse swollen with starving children, and an incredibly nasty dog," said Alison Pearson in *The Independent*. "Few musical comedies have taken on such grim material and survived, never mind thrived as *Oliver!*"

The Times spoke of "rumbustious euphoria", of "sheer hummable vitality" and of "unmistakable knees-up quality".

Bullseye, "the incredibly nasty dog", was played by Dempsey.

Lionel's health continued to lurch from crisis to crisis. At the start of 1991 a pericardial effusion – fluid around the heart – was treated with a thoracotomy, an incision into the chest cavity. Post-operatively this can result, depending on how it's done, in extreme pain. It can also – and in Lionel's case did – lead to pneumonia.

"He was on all sorts of drips and drains," says Brenda. "And people were going to see him and saying, 'He's not going to last, is he?' And then first of all he went thin, then he bloated out, and then he was so ill. He was in for a couple of months, but they put him in a side ward so I could go and see him 'cos he just used to disturb everybody.

"'I need the nurse,' he used to say.

"I said, 'Please don't bother the nurses because they're so busy.'

"'Get the nurse.'

"'Don't even think about it.'

"'I need some food. I'm a diabetic. I can't sit up.'

"'Look, I'll put a rope from the bottom of the bed and you can pull yourself up.'"

In the outside world the roll he was on kept on rolling. The NYT, undismayed by the critical pasting given to *Blitz!*, mounted a production of *Maggie May* at the Royalty Theatre. It was by now Lionel's least known work and thus still had the power to surprise and delight. The *Daily Mail*[118] described it as "the work of his maturity. A fully paid-up, adult work with a tough, gritty and witty book by Alun Owen, which was in fact way ahead of its time. I don't believe Bart ever wrote a more interesting score or crafted cleverer lyrics. The themes it tackles are even now ambitious and ominously prophetic. Set on the docklands of Liverpool, it deals with issues as pertinent today as they ever were; probably more so. The questionable morality behind profit at any price is permanently centre stage."

Tony Patrick in *The Times*, was impressed, too, and speaks of Lionel not

in the accustomed way – as a wide-boy who got lucky a couple of times –
but as a craftsman who had a profound effect on musical theatre, recognis-
ing Willy Russell's *Blood Brothers* as "only one of several shows whose
indebtedness to Bart is ever more obvious".

After 20 years in the shadows, Lionel was edging back into the spotlight
– and this time the cruel arc-light he'd known in the Sixties had been
superseded by a quartz-halogen backlight, electronically dimmed and soft-
ened with an amber gel. He had stood grunting on equal terms with
Stephen Sondheim. *The Times* had called him influential.

It was time to launch something new – or at least something that hadn't
been produced yet, *Hunchback* or *Gulliver* or *Golda*.

"Cameron always says, 'When you're ready, Lionel, I'll be there,'" he
told Mark Steyn for *The Independent*.[119] "'Well I am and he's not.'
Cameron said, 'Oh we've got to have a script on the table.' I said, 'But
with that formula you'd have turned down *Oliver!*' We had six songs
when we went into rehearsal. I love spontaneity and I don't think things
should take five years."

The Mark Steyn interview in itself was an indicator of Lionel's new
status. Rather than a rehash of the traditional 'where are they now, Lionel
Bart, dirty old drunk' story, it was a lengthy profile in which Li was invited
to discuss the technicalities of songwriting and look back critically over his
body of work.

"It could be argued," he said, "that instead of being the doyen of flower
power I'd have been a lot cleverer to have stayed in my metier, writing for
the theatre and doing the odd movie score. But I was trying to be all things
to all children."

There was telly, too, talk shows, bits. He was a relaxed, benign presence, a
man who gave every indication of being at peace with himself.

Georgia Brown had been spending a lot of time in America, but was over
in London at the end of June 1992 to appear in a charity tribute for Sammy
Davis Jnr who had died a couple of years previously. She was admitted to
hospital with an 'intestinal obstruction' – no big deal. Brenda and Lionel
went to see her.

"She insisted on being on the main ward," Brenda says, "and she was
singing with all the old girls. 'Tell us what song you want to sing and we'll
sing 'em.' And they were all singing. Then the very next day they told us
she'd gone.

"'No,' he said. 'That's not right. We saw her yesterday. She was great.'

"It was septicaemia. I told him, in an emergency operation on the bowel they don't have a chance to really clean it out.

" 'No. It's negligence.'

"He wanted to sue somebody. I talked him out of it in the end. He didn't mean it. He was just upset. He was so upset."

By 1993, *Oliver!* was as ubiquitous as McDonald's. America alone saw professional productions in Oklahoma City, Chicago, St Louis, Buffalo and Washington. Canada was awash with them. It opened at the Vanemuine Theatre in Tartu, Estonia, with Roos Rosalu as Oliver. At an AIDS charity benefit at Las Palmas Theatre, Hollywood, it was performed, with Lionel's full authorisation, as a parody version in which Oliver is a 21-year-old gay monk. But Cameron Mackintosh was planning the biggest and best yet.

Sam Mendes was a terrifyingly self-confident whizz-kid who − a point of interest to astrologers but nobody else − shared a birthday with Lionel. He was 24, an age when many young men still find shoelaces a challenge, when he directed Chekhov's *The Cherry Orchard* at the Aldwych, starring Dame Judi Dench and Bernard Hill. The production was generally regarded by critics as a reason for getting up in the morning.

"Do you mind if I try something?" Dame Judi had asked one day in rehearsals.

"You can try it, but it won't work," replied the 24-year-old.

He could do musicals, too. He had directed the UK premiere of Sondheim's *Assassins* ("Sam Mendes directs with lucid animation" − *The Independent*) at the Donmar, the old banana warehouse where the original *Oliver!* had rehearsed.

And now Sam would direct this all-new *Oliver!*, with new sets and costumes by Anthony Ward, new choreography by Matthew Bourne, new orchestrations by William David Brohn, Jonathan Pryce as Fagin, Sally Dexter as Nancy, Miles Anderson as Bill Sikes, James Villiers as Mr Brownlow and a young Tamzin Outhwaite flitting around in the chorus. The venue would be the London Palladium. The budget was set at three-and-a-half million. Furthermore, Lionel would be involved in every stage of production, would be commissioned to write new material and − perhaps most significant − Cameron devised a scheme whereby, in recognition and gratitude, Lionel would be given back a portion of the rights.

"I thought it was the right thing to do," said Cameron. "Just because Lionel was silly doesn't mean he wasn't talented. It was the right thing to do."

Lionel – events may not have happened quite this connectedly or in quite this order – had a heart attack and was temporarily pronounced dead.

"I don't know about an afterlife but I've had a couple of near death experiences," he said when he was up and about again. "Once when my heart stopped, I remember looking out of the window in St Mary's hospital over the London skyline to Highgate. I realised someone else was in charge of the whole scenario, not me." Now he knew. That someone was probably Cameron Mackintosh.

Lionel was back on fine form when in March 1994, Deborah Ross interviewed him for the *Daily Express*.[120]

"He is tubby – 'not fat, *please*' – with sticky-out dumbo style ears and a sweet cherubically-round little face. He smells heavenly, too – of Guerlain's *L'Heure Bleue*. 'I used to nick it from my older sister, Renee, at 12 and have been using it ever since.'

"Is he vain? 'Yes. Very,' he chuckles boastfully. 'I take great care over my appearance, even now, although my ears seem to be getting bigger and bigger, I'm afraid. Do you know why I never committed suicide?' No, why? 'Because I would simply hate to be found in any condition other than utter splendour.'"

Speaking of the new *Oliver!* he says, "'I am very involved in the production. I am not just being wheeled in for the first night. I am rescoring bits of it. I am adding to it, extending it.' He adds with one of his happy gonk smiles, 'I am having a field day.'"

The first day of rehearsal did not go well. Lionel arrived peckish and summoned a young man he assumed was a runner to fetch him a sandwich. The young man was Sam Mendes.

A London Weekend Television film crew was on hand at one of the early read-throughs to record the proceedings for a *South Bank Show*. It's another contender for Pinnacle Moment In The Life Of Lionel Bart.

With piano accompaniment, the cast and crew sing through the entire score. Some of them are glancing at scripts. Most of them know it by heart. Lionel and Cameron sit next to each other bawling every song at the top of their voices. From time to time they exchange smiles. Lionel's got his songs back. He loves them. Cameron loves them. Everybody loves them.

The changes brought the stage show closer to the movie version. The orchestrations were ritzier; 'Consider Yourself', 'It's A Fine Life' and 'Who Will Buy?' were reworked to accommodate new dance routines; there were new scenes, new lyrics, new music and new dialogue provided by Lionel, Sam Mendes and, from time to time, Charles Dickens.

Somewhere between seven and 10 million pounds were taken in advance sales. In one single day, the Monday before the opening, more than a quarter of a million pounds worth of tickets were bought – a West End record for a single day.

The first night audience included Victoria Wood, Patsy Kensit, Sir Tim Rice, Britt Ekland, Robert Stigwood, Anna Ford, Barry Humphries, Julia McKenzie and Tommy Steele. The ovations were standing. Lionel got the biggest cheer. Afterwards, 300 guests were taken by specially commissioned tube trains to the gothic glories of Gilbert Scott's St Pancras Hotel, then undergoing restoration. The band of the Coldstream Guards played selections from the show.

Most of the reviews concentrated on the "Can We Have Some More" angle. Even the few that tried to buck the gushing trend by finding fault had to acknowledge that the thing had 'HIT' written all over it in thick, indelible, dayglo felt-tip.

The production finally closed in 1998, having gone through several cast changes. George Layton, Russ Abbot, Jim Dale and Robert Lindsay all had a turn at Fagin, with Robert Lindsay scooping an Olivier award for his. Sonia Swaby, Claire Moore and Ruthie Henshall gave their Nancies. Steven Hartley and Joe McGann stomped around as Bill Sikes.

Earlier in the year there had been another moment of time travel when *The Flintstones* movie was released. The soundtrack included a Big Audio Dynamite version of 'Rock With The Caveman'. Lionel subsequently recorded with the band, singing 'Mirror Man', the song that an accidental (or was it?) fall had prevented him from performing in *The Londoners*. It was released on the now hard-to-find Big Audio Dynamite EP *Looking For A Song*.

When *Joan's Book,* Joan Littlewood's autobiography, came out, Lionel, having lunch with Dudley Sutton, boasted that he was "on the list for the first copy". Shyly, from his bag, Dudley produced the copy Joan had already given him. Lionel grabbed it and turned to the index. Lionel had seven mentions, Dudley five. All square, then.

And that's how he was: an irascible, egotistical, infuriating, competitive, jealous, lying "evil motherfucker" who made you change restaurant five times, made you sit in another room while he ate his breakfast and lied to your mother; and whom everybody loved because he was generous, funny, clever, talented, damaged, lonely and so clearly on the side of the angels. Makes no sense at all.

In 1996 John Gorman died. He was the man who had saved Lionel's life at least twice, who had looked out for him since 1948. Lionel wrote a eulogy: "To John, my very best friend for all time. Always there. Always true. A man of his word, like his father before him – an artisan, a poet and a wise adviser.

"Every joke of his was followed by that maniacal laugh, which I often found irritating – but I wish I could hear it now. And of course I can – if I listen with my heart."

"He was also at my side just a few hours after dad died," says Jon Gorman, "when his support was most needed. Unbelievable it was Lionel who was a stabilising influence on me when I was at my own worst in the Seventies. I guess we were always there for each other."

There was yet another planned production of *Hunchback*, now definitely called *Quasimodo*. This one actually went into rehearsal for a brief space of time. There was talk of a revival of *Lock Up Your Daughters*. Lionel was in negotiation with a Hollywood studio about a *Wind In The Willows* adaptation. He was 'in dialogue' with Disney.

"I hate saying this, but I didn't believe him when he said he had cancer," says Eric Williams. "He'd do anything for attention. I said, 'Oh, what a pity' or something like that. But I didn't believe him because he always had to have everything. It was almost laughable in a way because he even had an excess of illness. His excesses even went that far."

At the end of 1998 Lionel went on holiday to Florida. He knew he had liver cancer. When he came back he looked fit and well and began work with Bob Carlton, director of the Queen's Theatre, Hornchurch, on plans for a revival of *Fings*.

He died at the Hammersmith Hospital in London on April 3, 1999.

He was worth about a million when he died. He divided the money and rights between friends and relatives. The Acton flat went to his nephew, Sammy. The beach hut in Whitstable went to Gary Strange, a pop star pal who'd had some good times there. He was cremated. Brenda Evans has his ashes. She keeps them beautifully.

And that is the life of Lionel Bart.

Endnotes

1 *Time Stood Still*, Paul Cohen-Portheim, Duckworth, 1931
2 *East End My Cradle*, Willy Goldman, Faber and Faber, 1940
3 *Time Out*, 15th August 1990
4 *Then And Now: The Jewish East End*, edited by Aumie Shapiro and Michael Shapiro, Springboard Education Trust, 1992
5 *London: A Nostalgic Look At The Capital Since 1945* Will and Tricia Adams; foreword by Lionel Bart, Wadenhoe: Past and Present, 1997.
6 From a personal memoir in the Lionel Bart archive
7 Sholem Aleichem, pen name of Solomon Naumovich Rabinovich, a leading Yiddish author and playwright. The musical *Fiddler On The Roof* was based on his stories.
8 BBC interview with Brian Matthew 20th August 1995
9 From a personal memoir in the Lionel Bart archive
10 BBC interview with Brian Matthew 20th August 1995
11 Ibid
12 Ibid
13 Ibid
14 *London: A Nostalgic Look At The Capital Since 1945*, Will and Tricia Adams; foreword by Lionel Bart, Wadenhoe: Past and Present, 1997
15 From a personal memoir in the Lionel Bart archive
16 *Daily Mail*, 22nd March 1994
17 *Knocking Down Ginger*, John Gorman, Caliban Books, 1994
18 *The Story Of Unity Theatre*, Colin Chambers, Lawrence and Wishart, 1989
19 BBC interview with Brian Matthew 20th August 1995
20 Owen Adams, http://www.myspace.com/owenadams/blog/252985613
21 *The Restless Generation*, Pete Frame, Rogan House, 2007
22 *Bermondsey Boy*, Tommy Steele, Michael Joseph, 2006
23 BBC interview with Brian Matthew 20th August 1995
24 Quoted in the excellent and scholarly *Enlightenment!* website, found at http://www.box.net/shared/a926k5q5tk
25 *Daily Mail*, 5th January 1957
26 BBC interview with Brian Matthew 20th August 1995

27 *The Story Of Unity Theatre*, Colin Chambers, Lawrence and Wishart, 1989
28 BBC radio interview 1992
29 At this time she was still Joan Clarke. She became Joan Maitland after marriage, but, for clarity's sake, it's easier to stick to the same name throughout.
30 *Kicking Against The Pricks*, Oscar Lewenstein, Nick Hern Books, 1994
31 The finest Christmas record ever made
32 *Joan's Book,* Joan Littlewood, Methuen, 1994
33 *Why Fings Went West*, Frank Norman, Lemon Tree Press, 1975
34 Probably a gross overestimate. At the time Equity minimum for a much more lucrative ITV contract was a meagre £10.50.
35 *The South Bank Show*, London Weekend Television, 1995
36 BBC Radio interview 1992
37 *Shake A Pagoda Tree*, Mike and Bernie Winters, W.H. Allen, 1976
38 *Barbara*, Barbara Windsor, Century, 1990
39 In *Joan's Book*, Joan Littlewood tells the same story, except the protagonist in her version is not Barbara Windsor but Barbara Ferris. The main thing is it almost certainly happened to somebody.
40 Michael Arditti, *Independent Magazine*, 26th March 1994
41 *The Songwriters*, BBC TV, 1978
42 *All Of Me*, Barbara Windsor, Headline Book Publishing, 2000
43 *Noises In The Head*, Laurie Johnson, Bank House Books, 2005
44 *The Restless Generation*, Pete Frame, Rogan House, 2007
45 Interview with Deborah Ross, *Daily Express,* 22nd March 1994
46 *A Still Untitled (Not Quite) Autobiography*, Ron Moody, JR Books, 2010
47 Private memoir in the Lionel Bart archive
48 *Funny, It Doesn't Sound Jewish*, Jack Gottlieb State University of New York in association with The Library of Congress, 2004
49 Private memoir in the Lionel Bart archive
50 *The Noël Coward Diaries*, ed. Graham Payn and Sheridan Morley, Weidenfeld & Nicolson, 2000
51 *Stoned,* Andrew Loog Oldham, Secker and Warburg, 2000
52 Née Muriel Dobkin, then Muriel Matteoda, now Muriel Walker. Again, for clarity's sake, it's easier to stick to the same name throughout.
53 *The Noël Coward Diaries*, ed. Graham Payn and Sheridan Morley, Weidenfeld & Nicolson, 2000
54 *Daily Express*, 11 November 1994
55 *Alma Cogan – A Memoir*, Sandra Caron, Bloomsbury Publishing Ltd, 1991

56 *Daily Mail*, 16th March 1961
57 *Sunday Dispatch*, 3rd August 1960
58 *The South Bank Show*, London Weekend Television, 1995
59 *The Noël Coward Diaries*, ed. Graham Payn and Sheridan Morley, Weidenfeld & Nicolson, 2000
60 *The South Bank Show*, London Weekend Television, 1995
61 *Daily Mail*, 16th March 1961
62 *Daily Mirror*, 14th September 1962
63 http://living.scotsman.com/features/Sixties-Icon-As-Carnaby-Street.6531464.jp
64 Interview for BBC radio 1992
65 *The South Bank Show*, London Weekend Television, 1995
66 In an extraordinary family tree connection, the art direction for the sleeve of the 1991 re-release of these recordings was by Tommy Steele.
67 BBC interview with Brian Matthew 20th August 1995
68 *Loving Peter*, Judy Cook, Piatkus, 2009
69 Liner notes, *Maggie May* original cast recording, Decca, 1964
70 *Stoned*, Andrew Loog Oldham, Secker and Warburg, 2000
71 *The Beatles – The Biography*, Bob Spitz, Little Brown and Company (Inc.), New York, 2005
72 http://www.sixtiescity.com/Mbeat/mbfilms75.htm
73 BBC Brian Matthew interview, 20th August 1995
74 *Stoned*, Andrew Loog Oldham, Secker and Warburg, 2000
75 *The Noël Coward Diaries*, ed. Graham Payn and Sheridan Morley, Weidenfeld & Nicolson, 2000
76 *No Bells On Sunday*, edited by Alexander Walker, Pavilion, 1984
77 *A Handful Of Songs*, BBC Radio 2, 2005
78 Quoted in Bob Spitz, *The Beatles – The Biography*, Little Brown and Company (Inc.), New York, 2005
79 Other estimates put the number of rooms at 25. David Roper in *Bart!* says there were 12. Possibly there were 12 'major' bedrooms and receptions, but add in bathrooms, servants' quarters, saunas and lavatories and Sammy's 27 begins to seem conservative.
80 *Paul McCartney – Many Years From Now*, Barry Miles, Secker and Warburg, 1998
81 This account of the making of *Twang!!* is assembled from several, often contradictory sources. They are *Joan's Book – The Autobiography of Joan Littlewood*, Joan Littlewood, Methuen, 2003; *All Of Me*, Barbara Windsor, Headline Book Publishing, 2000; *Barbara*, Barbara Windsor, Century, 1990; 'Down In The Forest Something Stirred', *Queen* magazine, April 1966; *A Personal Theatrical Odyssey*, Richard Mills, http://www.richardmmills.com/; and an anonymous

typescript found in Lionel's archives, authorship unknown, but almost certainly not by Lionel himself

82   BBC interview 1992

83   *Alma Cogan – A Memoir,* Sandra Caron, Bloomsbury Publishing Ltd, 1991

84   http://www.dailymail.co.uk/femail/article-389630/Footballers-wives-1966-relive-memories.html

85   *The Kenneth Williams Diaries*, ed. Russell Davies, Harper Collins, 1993

86   *The Beatles – The Biography*, Bob Spitz, Little Brown and Company (Inc.), New York, 2005

87   Hunter S. Thompson *New York Times Magazine*, 14 May 1967, republished in *The Faber Book Of Pop*, ed. Hanif Kureishi and Jon Savage, Faber and Faber, 1995

88   *The People*, 9th March 1969

89   *The Times*, 7th February, 1970

90   BBC interview 1992

91   *Mail On Sunday*, 19th December 2004

92   *Billboard*, 28 December 1968

93   *Billboard*, 15th March 1969

94   *Daily Mail*, 3rd August 1989

95   London *Evening Standard*, 16th May 1969

96   *The Songwriters*, BBC TV, 1978

97   David Roper

98   BBC interview 1992

99   *Daily Express*, 18th September 1994

100   London *Evening News,* July 1977

101   *Daily Express*, 26th January 1973

102   *2Stoned,* Andrew Loog Oldham, Secker & Warburg, 2002

103   *April Ashley's Odyssey* www.antijen.org/Aprilv1/

104   *Independent on Sunday,* 31st January 1999

105   *Dear Boy – The Life Of Keith Moon*, Tony Fletcher, Omnibus Press, 2005

106   *Daily Mail*, 13th January 1978

107   Irving Wardle, *The Times,* 29th March 1972

108   *The Guardian*, 30th September 1972

109   *Time Out*, 15th August 1990

110   *Dear Boy – The Life Of Keith Moon*, Tony Fletcher, Omnibus Press, 1998

111   *A Fart In A Colander,* Roy Hudd, Michael O'Mara Books, 2009

112   *The Times*, 30th December 1977

113   *News Of The World*, 26th November 1989

114   *The Daily Telegraph*, 9th December 1994

115 *Songwriter* magazine, quoted on
    http://www.songwriter.co.uk/page62.html
116 *News Of The World*, 26th November 1989
117 Melbourne *Herald*, 3rd February 1987
118 *Daily Mail*, 4th September 1992
119 *The Independent*, 29th December 1990
120 *Daily Express*, 22nd March 1994

Acknowledgements

Our thanks go first and foremost to Brenda Evans, formerly Lionel's personal assistant, now keeper of the Lionel Bart Archive, whose help, superhuman filing skills, general expertise, memory, patience and friendliness have made both an invaluable contribution to this project and provided a reassuring source of comfort and joy.

Many others gave us far more of their time than we had any right to expect, and/or generous permission to quote from their work. They include, in alphabetical order: Laura Beaumont, Marc Beeby, Sam Bergliter, Don Black, Bulls Head Bob, Susannah Buxton, Clem Cattini, David Charkham, John Cohen, Mick Conefrey, Michael Coveney, Terry Dene, Kathleen Dickson (BFI National Library), Vince Eager, Sheila Fitzgerald, Jon Gorman, Roberta Green, Jack Grossman, Len Harrow, Roy Hawkesford, Paulina Hepola, Nick Hicks-Beach, Harry Jackson, Cheryl Kennedy, Harry Landis, James McConnel, Richard Mills, Scott Mitchell, Richard O'Brien, Bill Oddie, Derek Paget, Toni Palmer, Harry Parker (BBC), Nigel Planer, David Prest (Whistledown Productions), Richard Sales (Camden Libraries), Alexei Sayle, Linda Sayle, Gilly Schuster, Warren Sherman, Jacqueline Smith, Victor Spinetti, Kate Stables, Steven Suskin, Dudley Sutton, Richard Tay, Jeff Walden (BBC Written Archives), Muriel Walker, Bruce Welch, Marty Wilde, Eric Williams, Barbara Windsor, Jane Wynn-Owen, John Wyver (BBC), Sylvia Young, and of course David Barraclough and Chris Charlesworth at Omnibus Press.

Apologies in advance to anyone we've missed.

Partial Discography

A comprehensive discography of Bart's work is beyond the scope of this biography. Merely tracking down all the recordings of *Oliver!* would be a major research project. Album tracks crop up in the most unlikely places and, thanks to Lionel's checkered financial history, the paperwork doesn't always make sense. It's a work in progress. In the meantime here's a truncated list of the recordings referred to in the text.

ARTIST	TITLE	LABEL	DATE
Tommy Steele	Rock With The Caveman / (*Rock Around The Town*)	Decca	1956
Tommy Steele	Doomsday Rock / (*Elevator Rock*)	Decca	1956
Tommy Steele	(*Knee Deep In The Blues*) / Teenage Party	Decca	1957
Tommy Steele	Butterfingers / Cannibal Pot	Decca	1957
Tommy Steele	(*Shiralee*) / Grandad's Rock	Decca	1957
Tommy Steele	**The Tommy Steele Story** (Soundtrack LP)	Decca	1957
Tommy Steele	Water, Water / A Handful Of Songs	Decca	1957
Tommy Steele	Hey You! / Plant A Kiss	Decca	1957
Tommy Steele	**The Duke Wore Jeans** (Soundtrack LP)	Decca	1958
Tommy Steele	Happy Guitar / Princess	Decca	1958
Tommy Steele	(*Nairobi*) / Neon Sign	Decca	1958
Tommy Steele	(*Only Man On The Island*) / I Put The Lightie On	Decca	1958

Tommy Steele	It's All Happening / What Do You Do?	Decca	1958
Tommy Steele	Come On, Let's Go / Put A Ring On Her Finger	Decca	1958
Marty Wilde	**Presenting Marty Wilde** (EP featuring Wild Cat)	Philips	1958
Tommy Steele	**Tommy The Toreador** (EP)	Decca	1959
Frankie Vaughan	**The Heart Of A Man** (EP featuring 'Sometime, Somewhere' and 'Walkin' Tall')	Philips	1959
Cliff Richard And The Drifters	**Serious Charge** (EP)	Columbia	1959
Cliff Richard And The Drifters	Living Doll / (*Apron Strings*)	Columbia	1959
Lionel Bart	**Bart For Bart's Sake** (LP)	Decca	1959
Tommy Steele	Little White Bull / Singing Time	Decca	1959
Original London Cast	**Lock Up Your Daughters** (Album)	Decca	1959
Alma Cogan (and Ocher Nebbish)	(*Train Of Love*) / The 'I Love You' Bit	His Master's Voice	1960
Joe Brown And His Bruvvers	Jellied Eels / (*Dinah*)	Decca	1960
Original London Cast	**Fings Ain't Wot They Used T'Be** (LP)	Decca	1960
Max Bygraves	Fings Aint' Wot They Used T'Be / When The Thrill Has Gone	Decca	1960
Russ Conway	Medley Of Tunes From Fings Ain't Wot They Used T'Be	Columbia	1960
Anthony Newley	Do You Mind / (*Girls Were Made To Love And Kiss*)	Decca	1960
Mark Wynter	Kickin' Up The Leaves / (*That's What I Thought*)	Decca	1960

Adam Faith	(*Someone Else's Baby*) / Big Time	Parlophone	1960
Original London Cast	**Oliver!** (LP)	Decca	1960
Shirley Bassey	As Long As He Needs Me / (*So In Love*)	Columbia	1960
Max Bygraves	Consider Yourself / (*Tra-La I'm In Love*)	Decca	1960
Marty Wilde	Hide And Seek / (*Crazy Dream*)	Philips	1961
Dave Sampson And The Hunters	Why The Chicken? / 1999	Columbia	1961
Adam Faith	Easy Going Me / (*Wonderin'*)	Parlophone	1961
Lionel Bart	Give Us A Kiss For Christmas / How Now Brown Cow	Decca	1961
Original London Cast	**Blitz!** (LP)	His Master's Voice	1962
Russ Conway	Oliver Medley / Blitz Medley	Columbia	1962
Shirley Bassey	Far Away / (*My Faith*)	Columbia	1962
Max Bygraves	Down The Lane / (*Every Street's A Coronation Street*)	Decca	1962
Shane Fenton	Too Young For Sad Memories / (*You're Telling Me*)	Parlophone	1962
Original Broadway Cast	**Oliver!** (LP)	RCA Victor	1962
Matt Monro	From Russia With Love / (*Here And Now*)	Parlophone	1963
Barbra Streisand	**Who Will Buy?** (EP featuring 'Who Will Buy?')	CBS	1963
Barbara Windsor	Sparrers Can't Sing / (*On Mother Kelly's Doorstep*)	His Master's Voice	1963
Matt Monro	**A Song For Europe** (EP featuring 'Choose')	Parlophone	1964
Original London Cast	**Maggie May** (LP)	Decca	1964

The Andrew Oldham Orchestra	**The Andrew Oldham Orchestra Plays Lionel Bart's Maggie May** (LP)	Decca	1964
Judy Garland	**Judy Garland Sings Lionel Bart's Maggie May** (EP)	Capitol	1964
Tsai Chin	*Tokyo Melody* (*Good Morning Tokyo*) / I Love A Man	Decca	1964
Shirley Bassey	It's Yourself / (*Secrets*)	Columbia	1965
Original London Cast	**Twang!!** (LP)	TER	1966
Original Soundtrack Recording	**Oliver!** (LP)	Colgems/ RCA Victor	1968
Lionel Bart	**Isn't This Where We Came In?** (LP)	Deram	1968
Cliff Richard And The Young Ones Featuring Hank Marvin	Living Doll / *All The Little Flowers Are Happy*	WEA	1986
Lionel Bart	Happy Endings / (Give Yourself A Pinch)	EMI Records	1989

Shows: Major Productions and Revivals

Again, a comprehensive list would fill the book. These are the milestones.

Wages Of Eve Unity Theatre 1953
Turn It Up Unity Theatre 1953
Cinderella Unity Theatre 1953
Wally Pone, King Of The Underworld Unity Theatre 1958
Fings Ain't Wot They Used T'Be Theatre Royal, Stratford East 1959
Lock Up Your Daughters Mermaid Theatre 1959
Fings Ain't Wot They Used T'Be Garrick Theatre 1960
Lock Up Your Daughters Her Majesty's 1960
Oliver! New (Albery) Theatre 1960
Blitz! Adelphi Theatre 1962
Oliver! The Imperial Theatre, Broadway 1963
Maggie May Adelphi Theatre 1964

Oliver! The Martin Beck Theatre, Broadway 1965
Twang!! Shaftesbury Theatre 1965
La Strada Lunt-Fontanne Theatre 1969
The Londoners Theatre Royal, Stratford East 1972
Costa Packet Theatre Royal, Stratford East 1972
Oliver! Albery Theatre 1977
Lionel New London Theatre 1977
Oliver! Aldwych Theatre 1983
Oliver! The Mark Hellinger Theatre, Broadway 1984
Winnie Victoria Palace Theatre 1988
Blitz! (National Youth Theatre) Playhouse Theatre 1990
Consider Yourself! Brighton Cares AIDS Benefit 1992
Oliver! The London Palladium 1994
It's a Fine Life Queens Theatre, Hornchurch 2006
Oliver! Theatre Royal 2009

Filmography
Again, just the milestones.

The Tommy Steele Story 1957
The Duke Wore Jeans 1958
Serious Charge 1959
In The Nick 1959
Heart Of A Man 1959
Tommy The Toreador 1959
Let's Get Married 1960
Light Up The Sky 1960
When Johnny Comes Marching Home 1960
From Russia With Love 1963
Sparrers Can't Sing 1963
Man In The Middle 1964
Oliver! 1968
The Touchables 1968
Lock Up Your Daughters 1969
Black Beauty 1971
Scalawag 1973
The Optimists Of Nine Elms 1973
The Alternative Miss World 1980
The Flintstones 1994

Sources

BOOKS & WEBSITES

AA Services, *Alcoholics Anonymous – Big Book,* (Hazelden Information & Educational Services, fourth revised edition, 2002)

Adams, Will & Tricia; foreword by Lionel Bart, *London: A Nostalgic Look At The Capital Since 1945* (Wadenhoe: Past and Present, 1997)

Ashley, April, *April Ashley's Odyssey* (www.antijen.org/April 1)

Bardsley, Garth, *Stop The World* (Oberon, 2003)

Black, Don, *Wrestling With Elephants* (Sanctuary Publishing, 2003)

Bulls Head Bob, *Bulls Head Bob* (http://bullsheadbob.blogspot.com/)

Caron, Sandra, *Alma Cogan – A Memoir* (Bloomsbury, 1991)

Chambers, Colin, *The Story Of Unity Theatre* (Lawrence & Wishart, 1989)

Clarke, Gerald, *Get Happy – The Life Of Judy Garland* (Random House, 2000)

Cohen-Portheim, Paul, *Time Stood Still* (Duckworth, 1931)

Cook, Judy, *Loving Peter* (Piatkus, 2009)

Coward, Noël (ed. Graham Payn and Sheriden Morley), *The Noël Coward Diaries* (Da Capo, 1982)

Coward, Noël (ed. Barry Day), *The Letters Of Noël Coward* (A&C Black, 2007)

Davies, Hunter, *The Beatles – The Authorised Biography* (Heinemann, 1968)

Dors, Diana, *For Adults Only* (W.H. Allen, 1978)

Fletcher, Tony, *Dear Boy – The Life Of Keith Moon* (Omnibus Press, 2001)

Frame, Pete, *The Restless Generation* (Rogan House, 2007)

Geller, Debbie, *The Brian Epstein Story* (Faber and Faber, 2000)

Goldman, Willy, *East End Is My Cradle* (Faber and Faber, 1940)

Gorman, John, *Knocking Down Ginger* (Caliban, 1995)

Gottleib, Jack, *Funny, It Doesn't Sound Jewish* (State University of New York in Association with The Library of Congress, 2004)

Hoare, Philip, *Noël Coward, A Biography* (Sinclair Stevenson, 1995)

Hudd, Roy, *A Fart In A Colander* (Michael O'Mara, 2009)

Inverne, James, *The Impresarios* (Oberon Books, 2000)

Johnson, Laurie, *Noises In The Head* (Bank House Books, 2005)

Kops, Bernard, *East End* (5 Leaves, 2006)

Kureishi, Hanif & Jon Savage (ed.), *The Faber Book Of Pop* (Faber and Faber, 1995)

Lewenstein, Oscar, *Kicking Against The Pricks* (Nick Hern Books, 1994)

Littlewood, Joan, *Joan's Book* (Methuen, 1994)

Mezzrow, Milton "Mezz", *Really The Blues* (Random House, 1946)

Miles, Barry, *Paul McCartney – Many Years From Now* (Secker & Warburg, 1998)

Miller, Andrew, *The Earl Of Petticoat Lane* (William Heinemann, 2006)

Mills, Richard, *A Personal Theatrical Odyssey* (http://www.richardmmills.com/)

Moody, Ron, *A Still Untitled (Not Quite) Autogiography* (JR Books Ltd., 2010)

Norman, Frank, *Much Ado About Nuffink* (Hodder & Stoughton, 1974)

Norman, Frank, *Why Fings Went West* (Lemon Tree Press, 1975)

Norman, Philip, *John Lennon, The Life* (Harper Collins, 2008)

Oldham, Andrew Loog, *Stoned* (Vintage, 2001)

Oldham, Andrew Loog, *2Stoned* (Vintage, 2003)

Paget, Derek, *British Library: Theatre Archive Project* (http://www.bl.uk/projects/theatrearchive/paget.html)

Richards, Keith, *Life* (Weidenfed & Nicolson, 2010)

Roper, David, *Bart!* (Pavilion, 1994)

Shapiro, Aumie & Shapiro, Michael, *Then And Now: The Jewish East End* (Springboard Education Trust, 1992)

Spinetti, Victor, *Up Front* (Robson Books, 2006)

Spitz, Bob, *The Beatles – The Biography* (Little Brown & Company [Inc.], New York, 2005)

Steele, Tommy, *Bermondsey Boy* (Michael Joseph, 2006)

Stevens, Christopher, *Born Brilliant, The Life Of Kenneth Williams* (John Murray, 2010)

Turner, Steve, *Cliff Richard, The Biography* (Lion Books, 1993)

Walker, Alexander, *No Bells On Sunday* (Pavilion, 1984)

Walker, Alexander, *Fatal Charm, The Life Of Rex Harrison* (Weidenfeld & Nicolson, 1992)

Whitcomb, Ian, *Irving Berlin & Ragtime America* (Limelight, 1998)

Williams, Kenneth (ed. Davies Russell), *The Kenneth Williams Diaries* (Harper Collins, 1993)

Wilson, Colin, *Adrift In Soho* (Victor Gollancz, 1961)

Windsor, Barbara, *Barbara* (Century, 1990)

Windsor, Barbara, *All Of Me* (Headline, 2000)

Winters, Mike & Bernie, *Shake A Pagoda Tree* (W. H. Allen, 1976)

LIBRARIES AND ARCHIVES

The BBC Written Archives Centre, Caversham
The British Film Institute National Library
The British Library
The British Newspaper Library
Heath Library, Keats Grove, London
Idea Store, Whitechapel
The National Archives, Kew
Swiss Cottage Library
Theatre and Performance Archive, V&A

Index

Abbey Endings, 225
Albery, Donald, 90, 91, 92, 94, 102, 104, 106, 125, 126, 130, 132, 200
Armstrong-Jones, Anthony, 74, 115, 131

Bacon, Francis, 99, 243
Barry, John, 85, 133, 161
Bart, Lionel,
    Alcoholism and Drugs, 27, 85, 172, 173, 181, 197–198, 212, 216, 221–229, 241–245, 251–252
    Childhood, 11–21, 97–98, 123, 234, 250
    Clothes, 26, 30–31, 136–139, 158–159, 248–249, 256
    Education, 19–20, 22–24
    Food, 247–248, 248–249, 261
    Health, 215, 239, 244, 245, 252, 256, 261, 264, 266
    Houses, 15, 57, 99, 162–168, 176, 193–196, 199, 203, 208–210, 240–242, 247, 251
    Love, Sex and Romance, 23, 64, 98, 110–116, 119–121, 145, 159, 193, 195, 197–198, 215–216, 222, 228
    Money and Bankruptcy, 14–15, 170, 188, 192, 216–221, 224, 238, 239, 240, 243
    Voice, 36, 135–136
Bass, Alfie, 34, 35, 176
Bassey, Shirley, 100, 163, 203
Bayntun, Amelia, 128, 131
Beatles, The, 8, 49, 137, 145, 148, 151, 164, 168, 181, 193, 196, 197, 198, 206, 220, 230

Begleiter, Bunny, 110, 243
Begleiter, Morris, 11, 12, 13, 14, 17, 18, 19, 21. 28, 30, 100, 121, 153, 188, 224, 228, 250
Begleiter, Renee, 11, 19, 29, 32, 264
Beglieter, Shear, 7, 21
Begleiter, Yetta, 11, 12, 13, 14, 15, 18, 19, 24, 30, 100, 102, 121, 123, 135, 136, 153, 213, 220, 228, 238
Behan, Brendan, 61, 62, 147, 221
Bell, Tom, 152,
Bergliter, Sammy, 14,18, 110, 137, 165, 217, 219, 222, 226, 236, 243, 244, 266
Berlin, Irving, 18
Big Audio Dynamite, 265
Blair, Lionel, 100, 120
Blitz!, 15, 49, 107, 117, 123, 124, 125, 127, 128, 129, 130, 131, 132, 135, 138, 146, 148, 151, 153, 154, 156, 157, 158, 159, 177, 178, 258, 259, 260, 261
Bloomgarden, Kermit, 232
Booth, James, 62, 64, 65, 68, 87, 160, 173, 176, 180, 184, 189
Bowie, David, 92, 233
Brahms, Caryl, 70
Bramble, Mark, 253
Brandon-Jones, Una, 34
Bresslaw, Bernard, 173, 176, 189, 196
Bricusse, Leslie, 88, 120, 161
Briquette, Pete, 256
Broccoli, Cubby, 86, 160, 201
Brookfield Productions, 171, 175, 200

Brown, Georgia, 92, 95, 96, 100, 103, 104, 109, 126, 128, 141, 143, 144, 145, 146, 152, 156, 159, 160, 172, 203, 253, 262
Bryan, John, 173, 175, 182, 183, 184, 187, 200
Bunnage, Avis, 160, 231, 234
Burrill, Tim, 175, 177, 183, 184
Bygraves, Max, 75, 87, 93, 100, 218

Cable Street, 17
Caine, Michael, 94, 126, 164
Calder, Tony, 169, 170
Caron, Sandra, 120, 183
Carty, Todd, 234
Chamberlain, the Lord, 33, 73, 74, 110, 183
Charkham, David, 138, 139, 225, 237, 241, 245, 249, 251
Churchill, Winston, 24, 127, 254, 255
Cinderella, 35, 94, 106
Coe, Peter, 81, 91, 92, 93, 94, 107, 125, 126, 141, 142, 253
Cogan, Alma, 92, 100, 119, 120, 145, 157, 164, 168, 183, 228
Collins, Joan, 120, 194
Collins, Phil, 203, 241
Connery, Sean, 84, 120, 137, 190, 200
Conrad, Jess, 100
Conway, Russ, 39, 87
Cook, Peter, 124, 126, 143
Cook, Roger, 233
Corbett, Harry H., 147
Corbett, Ronnie, 67, 176, 184, 189
Costa Packet, 230, 231
Cotton, Billy, 39, 41–44, 51, 58
Coward, Noël, 19, 72, 80, 88, 103, 109, 110, 115, 116, 117, 118, 120, 124, 125, 131, 135, 144, 145, 149, 157, 158, 164, 168, 169, 188, 194, 208, 223, 258
Crisp, Quentin, 23, 24, 112

Curtis, Richard, 253
Cyrano De Bergerac, 207, 208

Delaney, Shelagh, 61
Delfont, Bernard (Lord), 153, 155, 159, 175, 176, 182, 183, 184, 185, 186, 188
Dietrich, Marlene, 118
Donegan, Lonnie, 20, 41, 42, 46
Donmar Productions, 132
Donovan, 216
Driscoll, Julie, 193, 206

Eager, Vince, 55, 67, 80, 112, 113, 114
Epstein, Brian, 148, 153, 168, 169, 190, 197, 209
Evans, Brenda, 119, 195, 246, 247, 251, 255, 256, 261, 262, 266
Evans, Fred, 157

Faith, Adam, 39, 88, 133, 224
Fazan, Eleanor, 126, 127
Fings Ain't Wot They Used T'be, 57, 60, 62, 63, 66, 69, 72, 73, 75, 76, 87, 93
Finney, Albert, 120, 152
Frost, David, 190

Garland, Judy, 19, 75, 120, 143, 144, 145, 148, 149, 155, 156, 158, 209
Gershwin, George, 18, 19, 99, 147, 148
Gilbert, Lewis, 200, 201, 205
Gilbert, W.S., 35, 83, 98, 107, 118
Golda, 233, 253, 262
Gorman, John, 25, 26, 28, 29, 32, 35, 36, 89, 36, 138, 164, 207, 213, 216, 222, 238, 239, 240, 245, 266
Gorman, Jon, 100, 119, 172, 207, 212, 215, 222, 226, 239, 244, 247
Grossman, Jack, 34, 35, 36, 106, 111
Guinness, Alec, 93, 204
Gulliver's Travels, 206, 213, 215

Haigh, Kenneth, 44, 141, 152, 157, 158
Haley, Bill, 41, 52, 135
Hammerstein, Oscar, 149, 150
Hamshere, Keith, 94, 103
Hardy, Oliver, 22
Hardy, Robert, 254
Harris, Richard, 64, 65, 221
Harrison, George, 181, 216
Harrison, Rex, 92, 100, 109, 152, 154, 157, 159, 196, 202
Hart, Lorenz, 18, 44, 118, 149
Haydon, Anthony, 193, 209, 210, 211
Hayward, Justin, 193, 206
Hazell, Hy, 83
Hemdale, 219
Hudd, Roy, 234–235
Humphries, Barry, 94, 141, 143, 153, 258, 265
Hunchback Of Notre Dame, The (*Quasimodo*), 150, 151, 171, 197, 206, 208, 215, 232, 237, 252, 253, 262, 266
Huxtable, Judy, 92, 148, 164

Jagger, Mick, 9, 164, 170, 216, 222
James, Sid, 84, 87, 92,176
Jarrett, Andrew, 258
Johnson, Laurie, 82, 83, 84, 88
Jones, Davy, 142, 145, 202
Junkin, John, 96, 153, 154, 155, 157, 186

Karlin, Miriam, 68, 72, 74, 144, 172
Kennedy, John, 46, 52, 55, 66, 85
Kenny, Sean, 81, 82, 91, 92, 95, 101, 107, 124, 126, 130, 131, 132, 148, 151, 155, 158, 164, 174, 196, 206, 212, 224, 236
Klein, Alan, 230. 231
Kotcheff, Ted, 154, 158, 159
Kretzmer, Herbert, 101, 103, 122, 244

La Rue, Danny, 67
La Strada, 206, 210, 211, 215, 236, 237, 253
Lakeview Music, 218
Landis, Harry, 11, 34, 106, 111, 128, 135
Lane, Jackie, 101
Lennon, John, 50, 105, 151, 155, 168, 216, 217, 238
Leslie, Cole, 72, 116, 117, 118, 131
Lester, Mark, 202, 204, 205, 228
Levin, Bernard, 70
Lewenstein, Oscar, 59
Lewis, Stephen, 160, 220
Lionel, 234
Littlewood, Joan, 59, 60, 62, 63, 66, 67, 70, 72, 90, 91, 93, 128, 152, 160, 171–190, 222, 229, 230, 231, 232, 244, 252, 265
Lloyd Webber, Andrew (Lord), 233
Lock Up Your Daughters, 82, 83, 91, 97, 122, 142, 224, 266
Londoners, The, 229, 230, 265
Lynn, Vera (Dame), 127

Mackintosh, Cameron (Sir), 234, 235, 242, 253, 259, 263, 264
Maggie May, 19, 20, 49, 96, 146, 147, 150, 151, 153, 155– 160, 170, 171, 175, 178, 195, 196, 202, 258, 261
Maitland, Joan, 59, 90, 106, 107, 119, 123, 124, 172, 259
Margaret, Princess (HRH), 54, 74, 115, 131, 164, 166, 167, 174, 205, 213, 216
Marriott, Steve, 202
McCartney, Paul, 105, 168, 190, 217
McConnel, James, 20, 79, 105, 242, 249, 250, 252, 259
McGrath, John, 126, 127
Meir, Golda, 233
Mendes, Sam, 263, 264
Merrick, David, 141, 143

Messel, Oliver, 174, 175, 177–179, 181, 182, 189
Miles, Bernard, 80–82, 91
Mills, Beaudouin, 163
Mills, Richard, 155, 175–177, 183, 184, 186, 187, 192
Moody, Ron, 93–96, 99, 102, 103, 104, 109, 126, 142, 143, 144, 204, 253
Moon, Keith, 7, 226, 227, 232
Murray, Alex, 132

National Youth Theatre, 259, 260
Nelson, Simon, 260
Newley, Anthony, 9, 86, 87, 120, 143, 159, 160, 161, 174
Nocturnes, The, 153, 170
Norman, Frank, 60, 62, 63, 64, 68, 71, 147, 221, 230, 231
Novello, Awards, 53, 57, 78, 84, 254

O'Brien, Richard, 225, 251
Oldham, Andrew Loog, 109, 157, 164, 168, 169, 223, 225
Oliver!, 8, 23, 49, 59, 60, 65, 88–95, 97, 99, 100, 103–107, 109, 114, 122, 123, 125, 126, 129, 130, 132, 137, 141–45, 148, 149, 152, 157, 159, 160, 162, 185, 170, 171, 178, 184, 186, 188, 196, 200, 201–203, 205, 206, 211, 218–221, 228, 235, 255, 257, 259, 261–264
Orkin, Harvey, 173, 178, 181, 182, 189
O'Toole, Peter, 120, 152, 200, 204, 207
Owen, Alun, 146, 147, 148, 151, 153, 154, 159, 261
Owen, Bill, 34, 36

Palmer, Toni, 126, 130, 131, 135, 136, 165, 176, 241, 244, 247, 248, 249, 250, 251
Parnes, Larry, 46, 52, 54–56, 111–113, 218, 220
Peacemeal, 36

Pember, George, 138
Peters, Bernadette, 211
Picasso, Pablo, 109, 139, 145
Pippin, Donald, 145
Planer, Nigel, 254
Porter, Cole, 18, 43, 44 , 99, 105, 118
Pratt, Mike, 44, 46, 50, 84 – 86, 226, 227
Pryce, Jonathan, 263

Quasimodo (see *Hunchback Of Notre Dame*)

Raffles, Gerry, 59–61, 91, 93, 178, 22, 232
Ray, Andrew, 78, 80
Reed, Carol [Sir], 201, 202, 203, 205
Reed, Oliver, 226, 227
Richard, Cliff, 9, 77, 126, 127, 253, 254
Richards, Keith, 9, 105, 164, 168, 216, 222
Roberts, Rachel, 152, 157–159, 195, 202
Robeson, Paul, 33
Rodgers, Richard, 69, 99, 103, 149, 150
Russell, Betrand, 199

Secombe, Harry, 45, 125, 203
Sellers, Peter, 45, 47, 92, 157, 160, 171, 173, 175, 200, 204, 232
Sewell, Danny, 65, 94, 141, 160
Sewell, George, 65
Sharples, Bob, 129, 132
Sherrin, Ned, 233
Shevelove, Burt, 186, 187, 189, 190
Sondheim, Stephen, 7, 18, 72, 150, 186, 233, 234, 259, 262, 263
Speight, Johnny, 34, 236, 251
Spinetti, Victor, 62, 139, 141, 160, 208, 229, 232, 243, 243, 248, 249, 252, 257
St Martins School of Art, 24, 100, 243

Stamp, Terence, 126, 164, 223

Starr, Ringo, 139, 153

Steele, Tommy, 9, 22, 36, 40, 44–47, 49–57, 59, 66, 77, 80, 84–86, 90, 104, 11, 113, 120, 135, 136, 152, 167, 194, 206, 216, 217, 226, 238, 265

Stone, Paddy, 158, 175, 177, 179, 181, 182, 185, 186

Stratford E15 (see Theatre Workshop)

Sutton, Dudley, 40, 62, 65, 97, 219, 221, 227, 230, 244, 249, 265

Swaby, Sonia, 251, 265

Taylor, Elizabeth, 203

Theatre Royal, Stratford E15 (see Theatre Royal)

Theatre Workshop, Theatre Royal, Stratford, London E15, 60–67, 221–222, 228–232, 232

Twang!!, 8, 173–178, 186, 188–192, 197, 200, 205, 206, 211, 212, 220, 229, 249, 255, 258

Unity Theatre, 11, 32, 33, 34, 36, 37, 43, 45, 57, 58, 59, 88, 91, 106, 111, 112, 128, 136, 166, 171, 176, 221, 236, 238, 243

Wages Of Eve, The, 34

Walker, Muriel, 111, 112, 119, 120, 138, 162, 163, 164, 165, 166. 171, 172, 180, 187, 191, 195

Wallis, Shani, 203

Wally Pone, 57–59, 61, 69, 71, 97

Webb, Rita, 229, 230

Welch, Bruce, 78

Wells, John, 234

Why The Chicken?, 126, 127

Wild, Jack, 202

Wilde, Marty, 7, 55, 90, 107, 110, 114, 132, 149, 230, 242

Williams, Eric, 29, 111, 114, 136, 164, 192, 196, 218, 222, 224, 239, 241, 246, 248, 250, 266

Wilson, Ed, 259

Windsor, Barbara, 64, 67, 68, 70, 71, 72, 74, 102, 160, 173, 176, 179, 180, 181, 182, 183, 184, 188, 189, 190, 196, 229, 230, 251

Winnie, 254, 255

Winters, Mike and Bernie, 66, 87, 94, 120

Young Ones, The, 253, 254

Zec, Philip, 24, 25